D1047083

MATTHEW ARNOLD: THE POETRY
THE CRITICAL HERITAGE

THE CRITICAL HERITAGE SERIES

GENERAL EDITOR: B. C. SOUTHAM, M.A., B.LITT. (OXON.)
Formerly Department of English, Westfield College, University of London

For a list of books in the series see the back end-paper

MATTHEW ARNOLD
the Poetry

THE CRITICAL HERITAGE

Edited by
CARL DAWSON

Department of English
University of New Hampshire

ROUTLEDGE & KEGAN PAUL: LONDON AND BOSTON

First published in 1973
by Routledge & Kegan Paul Ltd
Broadway House, 68–74 Carter Lane,
London EC4V 5EL and
9 Park Street,
Boston, Mass. 02108, U.S.A.
Copyright Carl Dawson 1973
No part of this book may be reproduced in
any form without permission from the
publisher, except for the quotation of brief
passages in criticism

ISBN 0 7100 7565 0

821.8
A7572d

Printed in Great Britain
by W & J Mackay Limited, Chatham

For Cecil and Lorna Dawson

METHODIST COLLEGE LIBRARY
Fayetteville, N. C.

082503

General Editor's Preface

The reception given to a writer by his contemporaries and near-contemporaries is evidence of considerable value to the student of literature. On one side we learn a great deal about the state of criticism at large and in particular about the development of critical attitudes towards a single writer; at the same time, through private comments in letters, journals or marginalia, we gain an insight upon the tastes and literary thought of individual readers of the period. Evidence of this kind helps us to understand the writer's historical situation, the nature of his immediate reading-public, and his response to these pressures.

The separate volumes in the *Critical Heritage Series* present a record of this early criticism. Clearly, for many of the highly productive and lengthily reviewed nineteenth- and twentieth-century writers, there exists an enormous body of material; and in these cases the volume editors have made a selection of the most important views, significant for their intrinsic critical worth or for their representative quality—perhaps even registering incomprehension!

For earlier writers, notably pre-eighteenth century, the materials are much scarcer and the historical period has been extended, sometimes far beyond the writer's lifetime, in order to show the inception and growth of critical views which were initially slow to appear.

In each volume the documents are headed by an Introduction, discussing the material assembled and relating the early stages of the author's reception to what we have come to identify as the critical tradition. The volumes will make available much material which would otherwise be difficult of access and it is hoped that the modern reader will be thereby helped towards an informed understanding of the ways in which literature has been read and judged.

B.C.S.

Contents

Merope (1857, dated 1858)

New Poems (1867) and Poems (1869)

The 1870s

The 1880s

Preface

> Nothing seems odder about that age than the respect which
> its eminent people felt for each other.
>
> T. S. Eliot on *In Memoriam*

'The future,' Coventry Patmore wrote to William Allingham in 1856,
'belongs to you and me and Matthew Arnold.'* Allingham's inheritance
remains meagre at best, and even Patmore's share is dubious. But what
of Matthew Arnold? And which Arnold? Patmore could only know
the poet, author of *The Strayed Reveller, Empedocles on Etna,* and *Poems*
(1853). The other Arnold, the powerful and influential writer of prose,
had published only prefaces to his own poems. Many of Arnold's later
critics thought that his prose had ensured an audience, or a substantial
audience, for the poems, as though, like Wordsworth, he had created the
taste by which he could be enjoyed. But they thought in terms of two
Arnolds, the poet and the writer of prose, the private and the public
man. This volume follows their precedent. Although it includes
references to and a few discussions of Arnold the critic and advocate, it
is about Arnold the poet.

A more desirable arrangement, and what I originally had in mind,
was a two-part division concerned with both poetry and prose. The
difficulty lay in doing justice to the range and quality—as well as bulk—
of the available writings, for Arnold's poems were themselves the
object of many commentaries, and Arnold's prose stirred almost continual debate. The choice to devote this first volume to the poems was
arbitrary, but it happens to fit the course of Arnold's life. Disregarding
the privately issued school poems, 'Alaric at Rome' and 'Cromwell', I
have attempted to offer a full, representative collection of essays,
chapters, and miscellaneous remarks about the poetry, so that the one
side of Arnold's career would be illustrated. The commentaries run
from 1849, the year *The Strayed Reveller* appeared, to 1900, an arbitrary
date though a useful one, in that it allows a decade of criticism following

---

* *Memoirs and Correspondence of Coventry Patmore,* ed. Basil Champneys (1900), ii, 184.

Arnold's death and indicates the major tendencies of discussions for the next thirty or forty years.

I have selected criticism, for the most part, by identifiable and often well-known writers, though a few anonymous pieces seemed too central to be omitted. Identification of authors has begun with the invaluable *Wellesley Index to Victorian Periodicals,* but has included ascriptions of authorship in letters, biographies, memoirs, and other apparently reliable sources. Some of the ascriptions are tentative, and I have indicated my own doubt by a question mark. But I have not tried to account for the variety of sources or the reasons for ascription, since space was not available.

For help at various times in the compiling of this book, I am grateful to R. Gardiner Potts, W. H. Owen, John Pfordresher, Edmund Miller, Gordon Stimmell, Mary Mihelic, John Rouman, and U. C. Knoepflmacher. A grant from the Graduate School of the University of New Hampshire made part of the work possible. Professor Walter Houghton generously offered information from the forthcoming volumes of the *Wellesley Index.* I wish also to thank Professor Kenneth Allott for permission to quote from the Longmans' *The Poems of Matthew Arnold,* and the Clarendon Press, Oxford, for permission to quote from *The Letters of Matthew Arnold to Arthur Hugh Clough,* edited by H. F. Lowry. Throughout the work on this volume I have received courteous help from many libraries, especially the Huntington Library, the British Museum, and the libraries of Cambridge, Dartmouth, Harvard, and the University of California at Berkeley. Finally, I would like to thank Hannelore Dawson for her usual patience.

Introduction

I

Whereas Robert Browning 'lived to realize the myth of the Inexhaustible Bottle,' W. E. Henley wrote, 'Matthew Arnold says only what is worth saying' (No. 28). There were many of Arnold's contemporaries who would have vigorously disagreed with Henley, either because they had come to think of Browning as their poet-prophet, or because they found Arnold a poet of mere gloom. But many readers shared Henley's estimate; for them, too, Arnold said exactly what was worth saying, so much so that he had given a voice to the doubts and perplexities of the age. Alfred Austin contrasted his trenchant and powerful expression with Tennyson's 'golden mediocrity' (No. 19). Arnold was, said Henry James, the poet 'of our modernity' (No. 27).

But how are we to construe such comments? What do they mean to us? And what do they mean for our understanding of Arnold's nineteenth-century reputation? In the first place, all three comments occur in periodical essays. Henley was writing for the *Athenaeum,* an influential weekly; James was writing, as an American, for the *English Illustrated Magazine;* Austin was writing for *Temple Bar.* Henley's assessment marked a new direction for the *Athenaeum,* which had remained cool to Arnold's poems throughout most of his lifetime, but which reflected a dramatic and partly nostalgic reassessment of his work in the eighties. Similarly James, who called his essay something of a puff, offered the English magazine he wrote for an apology: a defence of a writer whom he found inadequately appreciated both at home and abroad. He finds faults, as Henley and Austin do, but he writes with a purpose and with a particular audience in mind.

Throughout the nineteenth century we can find dozens of references to Arnold's poems in letters, journals, or commentaries on other poets. Tennyson, for example, asks his son to bid Arnold put aside his prose 'and give us more poems like The Scholar Gipsy';[1] Oscar Wilde urges a young lady to read the quintessential Oxford poet, who is perhaps our best composer of elegy (No. 25g). But to talk about Arnold's nineteenth-century reputation is to account primarily for the responses of the periodicals. Arnold himself was aware of this, as his discussion of English criticism in 'The Function of Criticism' makes clear. The difference between French and English criticism, he says, is the difference between the disinterested *Revue des deux mondes* and the politicized *Edinburgh Review*. (In fact, he disliked the one review of his poems in the *Revue des deux mondes*.) With the exception of the *Home and Foreign Review*, which had just discontinued publication, British periodicals were, he said, organs of bias, their criticism 'directly polemical and controversial'. Arnold was hardly alone in his censure. In earlier years, Goethe had pitied Byron for having to contend with the awful power of the reviews, and their power had vastly increased. The press carried an authority which could give inferior writers, such as Alexander Smith, impressive if temporary reputations, but which could also inhibit good writers—the young Browning would be an obvious example—and to a great extent control sales. John Henry Newman explained the power of the reviews in terms of a general intellectual or spiritual disorder. 'Most men in this country', he wrote, 'like opinions to be brought to them . . . Hence the extreme influence of periodical publications . . . quarterly, monthly, or daily, these teach the multitude of men what to think and what to say.'[2] Although the reviews were organs of opinion, they also reflected opinion, that is, they catered to particular groups of readers. Walter Graham gives an indication of the range and the editorial policies of the main periodicals; he also clarifies what Arnold had asserted, that the responses of a magazine usually reflected religious or political ideology. Often, however, this was not the case. *Blackwood's* could be conservative politically and—using the term loosely—liberal in its reception of new books. And after the *Fortnightly* introduced the policy of signed articles, periodical reviewing became increasingly more personal, more independent of predictable positions. But the dominance of the 'review essay and the essay-like review'—in Walter Bagehot's phrase—remained for most of the century unchallenged. A given essay might be published several times, if it was picked up by the *Eclectic Magazine*, say, or *Living Age*, to be reprinted in the United States, then collected later—like those of Henley, and Austin—into a book. (Full-length critical books, at least of contemporary authors, were rare before the late years of the century, when, for example, George Saintsbury wrote his pioneer study of Arnold.)

Obviously the limitations of the periodicals argued by Newman and Arnold could be extended. Some publications, like the feminine *Victoria Magazine,* are simply amusing in their obtuseness, in their crude insistence that the poet must first of all teach. Even the better periodicals, as Arnold knew, purveyed implicit as well as overt judgment, and the recurrent words *great, genius, sincere, honest, duty,* indicate a series of unarticulated presuppositions about the nature of the poet and the functions of art, some of which Arnold himself shared. For most of Arnold's contemporaries, poetry is 'the crown of literature', and therefore of all the arts; literature has an immediate social and religious purpose; the great poet is the healer of the age; the dilettante is of no consequence; sincerity is a touchstone of excellence—and so on. The question here is not the rightness of any or all these assumptions but rather their currency in the criticism of the time, which tended to take too much for granted. Once we accept these limitations, the strengths of the criticism may seem more striking than the pervasive faults.

Arthur Quiller-Couch said of the early reviews of Arnold's poems that they came at a time when English criticism was at its lowest point, and when the few good critics were occupied with Browning and Tennyson.[3] Many of the early notices are slight, at times merely a paragraph in length. Long, careful essays on Arnold's verse appeared sporadically in the early years, though most followed the establishment of his reputation—as poet and critic—in the 1860s. But already by mid-century criticism reflected the incredible diversity of the periodical press, which was clearly the outlet for some of the best energies of the time. Arnold himself, after all, was to write extensively for periodicals. If Quiller-Couch had in mind theoretical criticism such as Coleridge's, or even the quality of essay that Arnold wrote, perhaps the level of reviewing was, and remained, unsatisfactory. Yet the reviews seldom were ungenerous, and they were usually informed. From the outset critics were intent on ascertaining just where Arnold stood (to use his own phrase), not only in relation to his contemporaries, like Tennyson, who served as a general standard, but also to great figures of the past, like Wordsworth, Goethe, or the Greek writers whom Arnold so esteemed. Indeed, after publication of the 1853 volume of *Poems*, critics tended increasingly to scrutinize Arnold according to his own critical precepts, and if the judgments were not always commendatory, they were often no less so than Arnold's own severe critiques of his work. Scarcely any reviewer or essayist would have said, as Arnold himself did say, that his poetry was 'fragments', or was 'nothing'.

Of course with Arnold as with Keats before him, self-criticism was as much a means of self-defence, an anticipation of criticism, as it was simple dissatisfaction with his own work. Arnold provided his critics with terms of discourse as well as the means of judging his poetry, but he also provided himself with the justification that he had anticipated criticism. Although Arnold usually denigrated contemporary critics (he was hardly more generous to the poets) and discounted specific criticism of his poems, his reaction is much more complex than he admits. His letters show a consistent and close attention to what his critics say.

Arnold resolved in 1853 (in a letter to 'K', his favourite sister) not to be 'occupied' by the reviews of his poems, but his letter is otherwise a recounting of what people are writing and saying.[4] Even in later letters (and prefaces) there is no indication that his 'resolution' helped him to dismiss the criticism, in spite of his expressed contempt. 'Empedocles' is illustrative here. It seems likely, for example, that his rejection of the poem resulted from impatience with the judgments of his readers. Arnold accounted for his republishing of the poem in 1867, not because he found it improved, he said, but because Browning had persuaded him to restore it. (Ironically, for most reviewers of New Poems 'Empedocles' was the pre-eminent work.) Arnold withdrew both The Strayed Reveller and Empedocles from circulation soon after they were published (no doubt to the dismay of Fellowes, who did not publish the 1893 volume) probably because he was displeased with them. But his displeasure must have been increased by the public's reception. Not to have published the volume in the first place would have indicated doubt about their quality; to withdraw them after publication suggested concern about reputation.

In a perceptive remark about Arnold's literary criticism, R. H. Hutton, one of Arnold's most persuasive nineteenth-century apologists, suggested that in spite of his theories Arnold rarely offered intense scrutiny—Hutton intended more than what was then termed 'minute criticism'—of the poets he discussed (No. 21). Arnold in reply might have pointed to his essays on Wordsworth and Byron; but even in these essays Hutton would have had his evidence. 'How then will Byron stand?' Arnold asks. And his answer to the rhetorical question is that Byron, with Wordsworth, will stand high indeed. What Hutton has in mind is just this tendency to rank poets, this preoccupation with relative stature. His observation reflects on Arnold's response to readers of his verse. Given the desire to establish the reputation of other poets, it would seem obvious that he was concerned with his own reputation and with the reactions of intelligent critics to his work.

Many of his critics were as distinguished and influential as they were intelligent. Lionel Trilling speaks in his study of Arnold about 'the rough and ready' reviewers of *The Strayed Reveller*.[5] Luckily, we can now identify most of the critics and need no longer dismiss the anonymous voices of *Blackwood's* or *Fraser's*. The reviewer for *Fraser's*, for example, was Charles Kingsley, no inspired reader, but no mere hack (No. 1). Indeed he was new to reviewing. Other early critics included William Aytoun (No. 2), Arthur Clough (No. 5), William Michael Rossetti (No. 3), J. D. Coleridge (No. 7), and George Lewes (No. 6). These men suspected Arnold's theories; most were adamant about his limitations; but they listened without rancour and read with some care. It is true that the response to the early volumes was often patronizing, and it was usually less than ecstatic. Still it is not fair to say, as Herbert Paul and others have, that Arnold's early critics were shockingly few and negative,[6] though the disheartened poet himself might have thought so. Arnold met with sympathetic attention from the outset.

If we could draw a line to show the development of Arnold's reputation as a poet, it would be a slowly rising curve, broken at the publication of *Merope* (even *Merope* was received without hostility), rising again in the later 1860s, and then rising sharply until at least the turn of the century. The growing number of periodical articles about the poetry and the number of editions make this point clear. Arnold always had defenders. Early in his career Lord John Russell spoke of him as the rising young poet;[7] Benjamin Disraeli later complimented him as a living classic.[8] Swinburne, though he afterwards recanted, wrote a long apology for him, placing him high on the Victorian Parnassus (No. 16).

Swinburne was alone neither in his praise nor in his opinion that Arnold's verse was superior to his prose. Throughout his career Arnold was urged to write more verse, to stop teasing the readers with reworked older poems. For all the importance of his prose, Arnold's critics often called it self-defeating and temporal. H. W. Garrod has written that Arnold was considered mainly a writer of prose in his own century, mainly a poet in ours.[9] Almost any of the later critiques in this volume will indicate how widespread was the desire to have Arnold devote himself to poetry and how deep the conviction, among a large number of his readers, that it was for his poetry he would be remembered.

From the beginning Arnold seems to have expressed something of vital importance, including for the Victorians who appreciated him the loneliness and incertitude of the time. Sensitive to what he did as a poet and what he demanded of poetry, his contemporaries sought to account for him as a puzzling poet in an admittedly 'transitional' age. What so many of them tried to understand is the still unanswered riddle: that of an imperfect poet with a clearly limited appeal who continues to win an almost astonishing share of critical scrutiny. Readers of Arnold still find his poetry limited in passion, flawed in technique, even slender in appeal. But few would agree with Edith Sitwell's observation, that those who like Arnold's poetry are precisely the people who do not like poetry.[10] The more common attitude has come to be that of Gerard Hopkins, who wrote at one point that he had read Arnold's poems with more interest than pleasure, but who later defended the poems, to Robert Bridges, with a mixture of doubt, gratitude, and admiration.[11]

II

The Strayed Reveller

Among the most interesting responses to *The Strayed Reveller* were Arnold's own. At one moment he could write: 'My last volume I have got absolutely to dislike.'[12] At another—and he was writing in both letters to K (Mrs Forster)—he was clearly pleased with the poems.[13]

I will say a little about [the volume]. I hear from Fellowes [the publisher] that it is selling very well; and from a good many quarters I hear interest expressed about it, though every one likes something different (except that everyone likes the Merman) and most people would have this and would have that which they do not find. At Oxford particularly many complain that the subjects treated do not interest them. But as I feel rather as a reformer in poetical matters, I am glad of this opposition.

It was not only at Oxford that readers complained about the subjects, and Arnold could hardly, at the time of his letter (sometime in 1849), have anticipated the variety of responses that his reviewers were to provide. In later years Arnold was to be censured for making his subjects and his manner too Oxford, and Mrs Oliphant, among others, was to accuse him of being strictly an academic poet (No. 38). When he published *The Strayed Reveller,* Arnold had a much different view of himself. 'Rather as a reformer' involves the characteristic disclaimer, but it reveals Arnold's high notion of his role. 'More and more', he writes to K, 'I feel bent against the modern English habit (too much encouraged by Wordsworth) of using poetry as a channel for thinking aloud, instead of making anything.'[14] The Preface to the 1853 poems was to make this sentiment explicit, and after 1853 many critics were to praise Arnold for offering an alternative to the excesses of 'Romanticism', especially as they were manifest in Alexander Smith and other 'Spasmo-

6

dic Poets'. But the early reviewers apparently did not satisfy Arnold. Whether he was disappointed with a lack of enthusiasm in his critics, or whether the critics corroborated his earlier 'dislike', his temporary judgment on the poems was the act of withdrawal. Good sales and the initial desire for 'opposition' notwithstanding, he took the volume out of circulation. As usual, he was a harsher critic than the men who reviewed him.

One of the first of Arnold's reviewers was a man whom the poet, had he known the author, might have found unfit for the job; he later called him 'too coarse a workman for poetry.'[15] In an unsigned review for *Fraser's Magazine*, Charles Kingsley praised 'the care and thought, delicate finish and almost faultless severity of language' in the shorter poems (No. 1). But Kingsley sounded a note that was to recur in later reviews, for he found the poems inadequately responsive to the needs of the age. 'A' is patently 'a scholar, a gentleman, and a true poet', but 'To what purpose all the self culture . . .?' 'When we have read all he has to say, what has he taught us?' For Kingsley, 'A' is a man of 'rare faculties' who as yet has not fulfilled them. He even invokes Arnold's father—perhaps aware of the poet's identity?—to urge that the young man put his abilities to better use.

Obviously Kingsley thinks of the poet as a special kind of public servant who must adjust his material and his manner to the abilities of the 'general reader'. The question of Arnold's relation and responsibility to his readers appears in almost every nineteenth-century commentary on his work. In its more general form, of course, it remains fundamental. 'For whom can the poet write?'

Much of the response to the first volume paralleled Kingsley's, and judgments on the quality of the verse often reflected an essentially, if not specifically, political assumption. In the opinion of the critic for the *English Review,* Arnold was too doubting, too full of melancholy (No. 12a). Despair was an untenable emotional or philosophical position, and 'Mycerinus' was 'the apotheosis of despair'. William Aytoun similarly disapproved of the melancholy, finding it a debilitating characteristic of the times, at best a bad fashion (No. 2). But after a facetious beginning that is reminiscent of Lockhart on Keats (the tone was still common in the Scottish quarterlies), and after two points that must have hurt—a criticism of Arnold's Greek material and a negative comparison with Elizabeth Barrett Browning—Aytoun acknowledges that 'A' *may* become a successful poet. (Mrs Browning's own, brief remark on *The Strayed Reveller* was that it contained two good poems, 'The

Sick King in Bokhara' and 'The Forsaken Merman'.[16] She too thought that Arnold was not yet an artist.)

The most astute of the early reviews was that by William Michael Rossetti in the second number of the Pre-Raphaelite *Germ* (No. 3). Rossetti's was the first truly sensitive appreciation. It was long enough to allow both close scrutiny and broad remarks about contemporary poetry. Rossetti's approach is more exclusively aesthetic than Kingsley's and Aytoun's, and much less biased. He finds Arnold unfortunately lacking in 'passion' (he assumes 'A' to be an older poet), but he isolates the poet's 'reflective' powers and his technical facility (Arnold has little to 'unlearn'), which he illustrates in the title poem and 'The Sick King'.

Rossetti begins his essay with an apt remark about 'self-consciousness', a characteristic which, like Carlyle, he finds 'common to all living poets'. In short, he discovers what Arnold himself objected to in modern poetry, but he finds it no less a characteristic of Arnold's own poems. 'Self-consciousness' is a legacy, 'the only permanent' legacy of Byronism. Its obvious negative consequence for Rossetti is that it engenders 'opinions' and assertions in poetry. Yet it also makes possible a closer bond between poet and reader. Rossetti's shrewd observation remains brief, but he evidently sees some of the consequences of the breakdown of poetic genres and the triumph of lyric modes, and he toys with the paradox of poetry that can become at the same time more private or revelatory and more engaging for its readers. (His concern partially anticipates that of Robert Langbaum's in *The Poetry of Experience*.) More pertinently, Rossetti is offering in a sophisticated way what Kingsley, Aytoun, and other reviewers are merely hinting at. He sees Arnold both as a representative poet and a possibly great poet, and he introduces the issues that lingered in Arnold criticism for over a century: the problem of a gifted poet who, so to speak, expresses his time, but whose audience is assumed to be small and exclusive.

How small Arnold's audience was at this time would be impossible to say; certainly there could not be many readers of *The Strayed Reveller*. Even later in the century, Arnold had a small audience compared with Tennyson's (in our own century he has overtaken Tennyson). But the ever growing number of reviews, references, chapters in books, and occasional essays about Arnold suggests that, while many people were reading and buying his poetry, the illusion of exclusiveness persisted, reflecting an obsolete notion about the audience for poetry.

Arnold himself always maintained that his audience was small, though he thought it would grow, and in a sense he fostered the idea of exclusiveness throughout most of his career. In 1853, four years later than his claim to be a reformer, but in the same year as his influential preface, Arnold wrote to K: 'You—Froude—Shairp—I believe the list of those whose reading of me I anticipate with any pleasure stops there or thereabouts.'[17] This is not a matter that Arnold is consistent about, but the letter indicates something about his conception of his audience, and it helps to clarify the discrepancy between his manner and his poetry that people familiar with him pointed out early. Edward Quillinan in a brief remark to Henry Crabb Robinson (who still had an ear for literary news) admitted that he liked some of Arnold's poems 'very much'. But the public he was sure would not. He says: 'To tell the truth . . . I never suspected that there was any *poetry* in the family'.[18] Even someone as sensitive and intelligent as Arnold's sister Mary could be surprised by the poems. 'His poems seemed to make me know Matt so much better than I had ever done before. Indeed it was almost like a new introduction to him. I do not think those Poems could be read . . . without leading one to expect a great deal from Matt.'[19] Mary accounted for her surprise by explaining that the reading of the poems 'was *strangely like experience*'. It was perhaps the combination of a sense of intimacy and a sense of surprise, the sharing of a man's thoughts, that at once excluded and drew readers to Arnold, so that the illusion of privacy outlived the private audience.

III

Empedocles on Etna

The age, George David Boyle wrote in a review of Arnold's *Empedocles,* 'seems unfavourable' for poetry. 'Poetry is scarce' (No. 4). Very good poetry is usually scarce, but what Boyle was saying about his own times was what Arnold himself had to say, that they were especially unpropitious for poets, while the need for poetry seemed paramount. To twist Arnold's own remarks, this, the nineteenth century, was the age of prose. Boyle's question about the *Empedocles* volume was therefore fundamental: Did it meet the need by providing poetry of substantial merit? He defined merit in terms of imaginative independence, intellectual stature, and achievement in relation to that of Tennyson, whose influence he found pervasive.

Boyle admits to having liked *The Strayed Reveller,* which he says was favourably reviewed, but the volume under review 'constantly disappoints us'. The little poem—and his response is fairly typical—'is an utter mistake'. Boyle does not, as some critics did, object to Arnold's classical predilections, but he finds the imitation of Tennyson (conspicuously in 'The Forsaken Merman') a weakness endemic to young poets, and Arnold's attitudes offend him, especially what he calls an 'indolent, selfish quietism' and a sense of 'refined indolence'.

Boyle's response to the volume differs little from that of the other reviewers, with the exception of Arnold's friend J. A. Froude; yet Francis Palgrave was only partly right when he wrote, to Arthur Clough, '"Empedocles" has fallen . . . on evil days—having been scarcely reviewed at all—but when reviewed, generally favourably.'[20] 'Partly favourably and with respect' would be a better description. Even Boyle, while questioning the achievement recognizes the promise, and it is no mere play on words to say that to show promise is in itself a kind of achievement.

Arnold soon withdrew *Empedocles*, as he had withdrawn *The Strayed Reveller*, from circulation. Again, only five hundred copies had been printed, and the sales had amounted to less than fifty by the time he acted. Arnold evidently had reservations about the poems, and his censure of the title poem may have equalled that of Boyle, for he attacked *Empedocles* in the 1853 preface and did not reprint it until 1867. But his original ambitions for the poem must have been high. Was it then disappointment, embarrassment, sudden realization of the poem's failings, or merely whim, that caused him to withdraw the volume? One guess is that Arnold's doubts about the nature of his poems coincided in a peculiar way with the criticisms of his friends and reviewers, which at once convinced him of his talents and reinforced his sense of limitation, his lack of the 'natural magic'.

Arnold's correspondence with Arthur Clough suggests that conversations with his friend helped him to sharpen his judgment—which was preternaturally keen—and to identify his ideals. Knowing, for example, that Clough was writing a review of *Empedocles* in the summer of 1852 (for the *North American Review*; No. 5), and knowing, too, that Clough disliked some of his work, he could speak about his poems almost as though a stranger had written them. 'As for my poems they have weight, I think, but little or no charm . . . I feel now where my poems (this set) are all wrong, which I did not a year ago.' Then, characteristically, he moves on to consider their public reception, saying finally—as if to check the vanity—'But woe was upon me if I analysed not my situation: and Werter[,] Réné[,] and such like[,] none of them analyse the modern situation in its true *blankness* and *barrenness,* and *unpoetry-lessness.*'[21]

'Empedocles' presumably analysed and expressed 'the modern situation' by means of the ancient setting and the fate of the Greek philosopher, who was not, for Arnold, the embodiment of 'indolent, selfish quietism', but a prophet unheard in his land. 'Empedocles' was, despite Arnold's protestations, unmistakably a projection of the poet himself—few of Arnold's contemporaries thought otherwise—and the critics considered Empedocles' leap to be an intolerable gesture. They judged the poem on its subject, and their judgment was close to Arnold's own.

An odd response to the *Empedocles* volume as well as the title poem is suggested by Arnold's phrase about the poems having 'weight . . . but little or no charm'. Here, too, he seems to have been making his own a judgment that was common to his friends and to his public critics (they were often, in fact, the same men). Only the rare critic, like Kingsley, asserted that Arnold's culture amounted to nothing. Most saw potential excellence in the poems while, like Boyle, expressing 'disappointment' in the achievement. But the lack of *charm* was another matter. Arnold's critics tended to agree with him on this point, and though the word *charm* is vague, it points to effect, to the capacity of the poems to delight by 'a fine excess', but also to appeal to the temperaments of large numbers of readers. When J. C. Shairp, later 'Principal Shairp', wrote to Arthur Clough in early 1853, he expressed an almost standard doubt both about Arnold's 'view of life' and his lack of *charm*:

I fear Mat's last book has made no impression on the public mind. . . . It does not much astonish me, for though I think there's great power in it, one regrets to see so much power thrown away upon so false and uninteresting (too) a view of life. . . . Anything that so takes the life from out things must be false. . . . Mat, as I told him, disowns man's natural feelings, and they will disown his poetry. (No. 12b)

Arnold's 1853 preface grew out of criticisms like this and out of the poet's own dissatisfaction. If Arnold thought before the publication of *Empedocles* that he had been meeting the demands of Kingsley and Boyle for poetry that 'analysed' 'the modern situation', he came to agree that he had not. 'My poems . . . are all wrong' is no doubt overstatement, but it points to an ideal for poetry that Arnold held from the outset and that his critics, speaking of promise and potential, reminded him that he had not achieved.

There is a question here about Arnold's relation with his reviewers which might be expressed in this way: Did Arnold share his critics' views of *Empedocles* to such an extent that he, first, enunciated a position inimical to his own talents and, second, increasingly either wrote verse that was not his natural mode of expression or wrote no verse at all? Perhaps his critics were too deferential, too close to the poet's own feelings about the inadequacies of the poems. So much of the 1853 preface is specific response to critics of *Empedocles*. Instead of representing the 'modern' temper, Arnold would strive for a classical significance (he had already advocated a 'classical' simplicity of language in letters to Clough), action supplanting meditation.[22] 'Natural feelings' and their consequence, charm, or reader impact, would find their expression in a new medium. Arnold would prove modernity by radical new means. But how new the 1853 *Poems* were is ironically clear in the fact that most of them were reprints of the first two volumes, 'Empedocles' itself conspicuously missing.

Robert Buchanan was to write, shortly after the poet's death, that Arnold committed 'poetical suicide' by making demands on himself that no poet could fulfil.[23] Like many readers he recognized a change after the *Empedocles* volume, and he did not like it. One peculiar development in Arnold's reputation was that the early poems, though criticized and liked with reservations, soon became sentimental favourites. Swinburne writes to a friend in 1878, asking his intercession in retrieving copies of Arnold's early poems. 'I have hardly any I should be so sorry to have lost.'[24] George Eliot, writing in 1869, finds the early poems—she does not say why—'very superior to the later ones'.[25] Browning's request that Arnold republish 'Empedocles' is well known, since Arnold acknowledged it, but Browning's affection for the poem was common. Bulwer-Lytton wrote: 'I have read [it] not once but many times . . . There is great thought in the poem.'[26] Finally, Walter Bagehot, whose essays unfortunately do not include a piece on Arnold's verse, admitted defects in 'Empedocles', but praised 'great' passages, saying that only a 'freak of criticism' could have caused the poem's banishment.[27] Whether, as T. Sturge Moore asserted, 'Empedocles' was the most important poem of its length by a Victorian,[28] many of Arnold's contemporaries came to think so.

IV

Poems (1853)

George Saintsbury (No. 39) has not been alone in considering Arnold's 1853 *Poems* his best collection, partly because of its preface, partly because it contains 'Sohrab and Rustum', 'The Scholar Gipsy', and 'Requiescat', as well as 'The Forsaken Merman' and other poems from the two earlier volumes. It is in any case, with the *New Poems* (1867), the most important volume. And its importance was recognized from the outset. Many periodicals noticed it, and Froude (No. 6), Patmore (No. 9), J. D. Coleridge (No. 7), Kingsley (No. 12f), Goldwin Smith, and William Roscoe (No. 12e) all wrote review essays.

Arnold might have responded to the reviews of *Poems* as Wordsworth responded to readers of *Lyrical Ballads*, for everyone seemed to like different poems, a failure for one reader standing as a 'gem' to another. Yet there was, as Arthur Clough recognized at the time, a rough pattern to the opinions: 'The critics here have been divided into two sets— one praising Sohrab highly and speaking gently of the preface; the other disparaging the preface and the general tone, and praising Tristram.'[29] The preface and the two poems, especially 'Sohrab and Rustum,' became focal points, and the preface itself served as a springboard for discussion as well as a means of evaluation in so many of the discussions of Arnold's poetry that were to follow. Clough was also right in pointing to an odd response to the preface even on the part of those who apparently appreciated Arnold's classical tendencies. From others, those who did not, the preface drew much of the negative criticism or became a means of directing it.

Few critics agreed with Arnold's announced theories, and fewer still appreciated critical apparatus introducing a book of poems. In the later essay in which he commented on the literary 'freak' that rejected 'Empedocles', Walter Bagehot expressed succinctly the feeling of a number of Arnold's reviewers. 'No other critic could speak so,' he said, 'and not be laughed at.'[30] To Bagehot it was less the absolute truth of Arnold's theories that mattered, though he rejected the theories, than their dubious application to Arnold's poems. As William Aytoun wrote (reviewing Arnold again after four years), the poet, if he wants to be a poet, 'should give theories to the winds.' Nevertheless, if the preface failed to help Arnold's reputation, at least immediately, it placed the poet in a recognizable camp, and it raised powerfully and unavoidably issues of imitation, diction, subject matter, and the relation of a poet to his times.

One reason for the unpopularity of the preface seldom became explicit, for Arnold had confronted cherished assumptions as to the function and hence, too, the mode of poetry. Whatever he was doing in practice, Arnold was pronouncing dead a popular kind of poetic expression—the lyric, personal, in Schiller's term, the 'sentimental' manner.

'Shairp urges me to speak more for myself', he had written to Clough as early as 1849. 'I less and less have the inclination to do [so]: or even the power.' But because Arnold's classicism was rather a tendency than a complete achievement, and because—unlike Browning's, for example—his poems were not aggressively novel, his readers were forced either to appreciate the theories without being able to apply them to the poems (except that 'Empedocles' was *not* there), or to dismiss the theories as so much academicism ('the faults of the scholar'), while appreciating poems that partly fulfilled their expectations.

Some critics did appreciate the preface. William Roscoe, for example, wrote that Arnold held 'the uncommon and valuable conviction that poetic art has its nature and rules'. Roscoe was later to republish his review (from the *Prospective Review*) with the title 'the classical school of poetry' (No. 12e). But his notion of classicism seems different from Arnold's; he has in mind a type of neoclassicism wherein the 'absence of deep feelings' can be a virtue (his comparison is with Wordsworth, whom he also finds to lack 'deep feelings'). More typical was George Lewes, from whom 'the past is past' (No. 6); or 'Anthony Poplar' (Stuart Stanford?) who says that 'poetry, as the reflex of the age, must, to be popular, exhibit the inner life of man'.[31] Implying that a poet ought to be popular and that Arnold's theories precluded his meeting the needs of the age, Stanford denies his 'modernity' and therefore his essential stature. A poem like 'Sohrab and Rustum' involves a seduction into the past, a denial of present realities.

Again, 'Sohrab' proved to be something of a test poem. Was it classical? How was it classical? Did it compare with the great epics? And could what was essentially a fragment based on Persian myth actually be considered in epic terms?

For William Aytoun, 'Sohrab' contained 'the elements of power', but it was too imitative: it did not come out of the poet's own 'smithy' and lacked vital originality.[32] Similarly for the *New Quarterly* reviewer something was radically wrong. Anticipating criticism of *Merope*, this critic said that Arnold's 'original strain resembles the bald, bad translation of a Greek chorus'.[33]

Arnold himself had reservations about the poem, though he was also, and rightly, proud of it. He tells Clough in August 1853:[34]

I have written my Sohrab and Rustum and like it less [than he did at first? or than the idea he had had of the poem?].—Composition, in the painter's sense— that is the devil. And, when one thinks of it, our painters cannot *compose* though they can show great genius—so too in poetry is it not to be expected that in the same article of *composition* the awkward incorrect Northern nature should shew itself? though we may have feeling—fire—eloquence—as much as our betters.

He writes in a later letter (November 1853), 'I am glad you like the Gipsy Scholar—but what does it *do* for you? Homer *animates*—Shakespeare *animates*—in its poor way I think Sohrab and Rustum *animates*—the Gipsy Scholar at best awakens a pleasing melancholy. But this is not what we want.' What men want 'is something to *animate* and *ennoble* them—not merely to add zest to their melancholy or grace to their dreams.—I believe a feeling of this kind is the basis of my nature—and of my poetics' (No. 12c).

Arnold's ambivalence in these letters, which express contrary notions both about the quality of the poem and its functions, paralleled the reactions of his critics, who were clearly baffled about the context in which to read his work. James Froude, the historian, who was a friend of Arnold, called 'Sohrab' 'a poem which alone would have settled the position which Mr. Arnold has a right to claim as a poet' (No. 6). Indeed Froude's only reservation—an odd one in view of Sohrab's subject but appropriate from a disciple of Carlyle—was this: 'Why dwell with such apparent exclusiveness on classical antiquity . . .?' Otherwise, Froude's praise of the poem is absurdly high, as though he has to champion Arnold. He calls the poem as good as anything in *The Aeneid*, arguing that Arnold touches 'deeper chords of feeling . . . than Vergil ever touched'.

In private, Froude wrote to Clough that 'Sohrab and Rustum' was *all but* 'perfect') and that Arnold had been careless about repetition, insufficiently concerned with 'sound', and excessive in his 'plainness of expression'.[35] One wonders about the public/private voices and their implicit disingenuity. This was a real problem for John Coleridge, another of Arnold's friends who reviewed *Poems* for the *Christian Remembrancer* (No. 7). Like Clough, Coleridge was honest in his criticisms: he accused Arnold of being derivative, overly imitative, and, as a theorist, 'fallacious and inadequate'. The tone, as A. P. Stanley told Coleridge, may have been inappropriate from a friend, especially since Coleridge used information provided by the poet himself.[36] But the issue went beyond good manners and concerned the task of the reviewer. Public commentators on Arnold's poems evidently felt with William Aytoun that 'We are not writing for [the poet] alone; we are attending to the poetical reputation of the age.'[37]

Arnold himself, of course, had a similar mission at heart, not only in writing poetry that would 'animate' his contemporaries, but equally in providing a theoretical statement that would clarify his position and provide a standard of judgment for all modern poems; and the poet who, in the same year as the 1853 preface, told K that she and one or two others provided his audience, soon became one of the best-known and most persuasive public critics.

Most of the reviewers of *Poems* expected Arnold to write a good deal more poetry, and whether they liked what they had read, they felt that Arnold was a poet of stature. It was partly the recognition of Arnold's importance that was to make the response to *Merope*, still five years away, one almost of sadness. The tragedy was not to be *Merope*, but the apparently unfulfilled poet himself.

V

Merope

To Arnold's contemporaries *Merope* came as a disappointment. The reviews were not hostile. On the contrary, from the weeklies to the big quarterlies, the sentiment was regret, the criticisms almost reluctant. Every reviewer applauded Arnold's commitment to literature, his desire to improve the climate for poetry, and his dedication to a new medium of expression. What reviewers failed to credit him with was a successful example and an adequate theory. 'In Merope,' wrote the reviewer for the *Dublin University Magazine*, '[Arnold] has striven, with . . . questionable success, to carve beautiful forms out of the white marble in . . . Greek poetry.'[38] Both Arnold's poems and its preface elicited comments like those provoked by the edition of 1853, and again the poetry was read in terms of the pronouncements. In fact, the major reviews in *Fraser's* (No. 13) and the *National Review* (No. 14c) began with the elaborate commentary on the preface, and both were written by men with classical predilections, inclined to approve of Arnold's poetic direction. But the *Athenaeum*, usually reserved in its response to Arnold, was typical in calling the poet theory-bound, and finally tedious, at the same time acknowledging Arnold's scholarship and the obvious importance of his experiment.[39]

The response to *Merope* was in fact essentially the judgment of time, and Arnold's contemporaries differed from critics later in the century or from those in our own time in only two important ways. They were somewhat less negative than late-nineteenth-century critics, who spoke of the play as clothes without body, form without life; and they

differed from modern critics largely by seeing the play as a determined
and necessary alternative to prevailing modes of poetry. William
Roscoe, a young critic who had himself written classically-based plays,
had reviewed Arnold's 1853 volume, and reviewed *Merope* both for the
National and for the *New Quarterly Review* (No. 14c). Roscoe was sensitive to Arnold's strengths but honest about his weaknesses. 'We have
said that the limitations of Mr. Arnold's genius drew him towards the
Greek art,' he writes, 'and so it is [with *Merope*]. We have given him full
credit for his love of finish and proportion; but his powers have everywhere shown that he is deficient in the higher power of conception.
. . . He is pure in language and clear in verse; but instead of a tragedy,
he writes a melodrama with a separate tragical end to it.' Like John
Conington, whom I assume to be the 'J.C.' who reviewed *Merope*
for *Fraser's* (No. 13), Roscoe carefully compares the movement, the
choice of subject, the type of language, and the nature of the play's
appeal with certain Greek tragedies, and he accuses Arnold of mis-
apprehending his own talents. For the faults of *Merope* 'are such as were
to be looked for from our former experience of the author's writings'.
In short, Arnold has unfortunately brought to their inevitable conclusion what Roscoe, like many other critics, had recognized as endemic
weaknesses in the early volumes. Arthur Dudley, the reviewer in the
Revue des deux mondes, had intimated that Arnold's real gifts were for
prose, and had anticipated his shift to essays and prose works.[40] Roscoe
is pointing to temperamental and technical flaws that necessitated a
limited poetic career. Of course he had no way of knowing about, nor
would he have expected, the *New Poems* of the next decade.

Roscoe's review appeared in April. Already in January, and after
looking at the reviews in the *Spectator*, *Athenaeum*, and *Saturday Review*,
Arnold was writing to his mother, 'I have no intention of producing,
like Euripides, seventy dramas in this style, but shall now turn to something wholly different.' Always sensitive to criticism and eager for
praise, Arnold both defended and played down his work, and his
critics rightly sensed an equivocal attitude on his part. He could argue
with William Forster, his brother-in-law, saying that 'Merope does
excite.' He could also assert what remains a singular judgment, that the
play would prove 'a vigorous tragedy upon the stage,'[41] while apologiz-
ing in a way to Fanny du Quaire because the play—'that you are not in
the least bound to like'—'is calculated to inaugurate my Professorship
with dignity [rather] than to move deeply the present race of *humans*'.[42]
Here was surely a damning self-judgment.

Arnold told Fanny Arnold, that he was 'dead sick of criticism' and therefore would not forward all the review clippings. Ironically, he has just mentioned with gratification George Lewes's review in the *Leader* (No. 14b) and was to offer immediately afterward one of his many defences of the poem, followed by remarks about 'the British public', an 'obstinate multitude', and a comment on a pleased response of a friend.[43] A few days later he asks Fanny du Quaire to solicit Browning's opinion of the play.[44] (Browning evidently had nothing to say.) He seems to have recognized the relationship of his critics' responses to his own doubts about the play, which were, of course, linked intimately to doubts about his poetic career. Thus, in spite of his earlier remarks to his mother about pushing on to new things, *Merope* safely behind him, he writes in August 1858 to K, in a profounder and evidently more honest way.[45] (Perhaps to his mother he always maintained the ideal and the inevitability of success as a kind of filial obligation.)

People do not understand what a temptation there is, if you cannot bear anything not *very good*, to transfer your operations to a region where form is everything. Perfection of a certain kind may there be attained, or at least approached, without knocking yourself to pieces, but to attain or approach perfection in the region of thought and feeling, and to unite this with perfection of form, demands not merely an effort and a labour, but an actual tearing of oneself to pieces.

He then mentions what many critics used as an explanation of Arnold's slow abandonment of poetry: the need to devote oneself to it totally. Given the time one *might* tear oneself to pieces for the muse. But clearly the crucial admission is that of escape. It was not that prose better expressed Arnold's mind, or that prose better suits the older man; possibly not that Arnold was too aware of his limitations as a poet (and indeed the publication of so many flawed lines would indicate limited ability for this kind of self-criticism); the problem seems rather to have been the excruciatingly painful nature of the creative process. *Merope* represented a flight more than it represented an experiment, as the critics tended to imply. For Arnold knew that the play was flawed, that it was pure 'form'—'petrified feeling', as he said of *Madame Bovary*—if it was anything at all. Yet apparently he hoped that it might be taken for something more. The *Christian Remembrancer*, discussing the play ten years after its publication, along with Swinburne's *Atalanta* and a number of totally forgotten pieces, summed up the play's limitations and anticipated the judgment of history: they praised its intellectual aspiration, its conceivable value as a model, while regretting that, after all, it wants 'life'. 'Must we confess it?—indeed has not the literary world anticipated our confession? "Merope" is a failure.'[46]

In 'The Modern Element of Literature' Arnold was to write: 'The human race has the strongest, the most invincible tendency to *live*, to develop itself. It retains, it clings to what fosters its life . . . to the literature which exhibits it in its vigour; it rejects . . . what does not foster its development, the literature which exhibits it arrested and decayed.' Possibly this was Arnold's own censure of *Merope*; in any case it has been evident to most readers of the play that it wants the 'vigour' and 'life' that Arnold demanded of literature.

VI

New Poems (1867)

Between publication of *Merope* in 1858 and *New Poems* (1867) most of what was written about Arnold—and it was plentiful—concerned his prose rather than his poetry. The famous debate that culminated in *Culture and Anarchy* (1869) partly coincided with Arnold's publication of *New Poems* and *Poems* (1869) and perhaps influenced the reception of the poetry; but in the earlier years the prose dominated. Henry Sidgwick's shrewd analysis of 'The Prophet of Culture' (1867) typified what was during this period of first importance to Arnold's contemporaries. Indeed, from 1858 to 1867, apart from a reprint of Roscoe's essays and two brief American notices, the only essay on the poems seems to have been one by Mortimer Collins (in the *British Quarterly*, October 1865), and even that concerned the 'Poet and essayist'. It is true that Arnold's poems meant a great deal to a number of writers privately, as Swinburne's later comments (No. 16) and Herman Melville's notes on Arnold's earlier volumes testify,[47] but the public estimate of the poet was probably as low at this time as it has ever been. *Merope* had done little for Arnold's reputation, and except for 'Thyrsis' (published in *Macmillan's Magazine*, 1866), 'Saint Brandan', 'Men of Genius', and 'A Southern Night', Arnold published no verse in the near-decade between *Merope* and *New Poems*.

The 1867 volume came as a welcome surprise. There were criticisms and objections, and the poems drew some hostility because of Arnold's polemical role as a prose writer; still there were almost a dozen reviews, nearly all, on balance, favourable. As usual, the three big weeklies noticed the volume quickly, while following their usual pattern—the

Athenaeum less approving than either the *Saturday* (No. 15) or the *Spectator* (No. 20a). Since these weeklies had combined sales of maybe twenty-five thousand, and since their standards were fairly high, their judgments must have counted, even for Arnold himself. (He spoke in *Culture and Anarchy* with a certain respect for 'my old adversary, the *Saturday Review* [which] may, on matters of literature and taste, be fairly enough regarded . . . as a kind of organ of reason.'[48])

The *Spectator* reviewer, like most of the reviewers of *New Poems*, discussed Arnold as if—and of course this was substantially the case—no more poetry was to be forthcoming. With a tone that must have sounded odd to the poet, the critic for the *Athenaeum* lamented: 'The poet is dead.' Returning to the precepts of Kingsley in the late forties, he wrote: 'To a sensitive . . . mind there is something very painful in the writings of Mr. Matthew Arnold. They are clever, yet so dissatisfying, —so full of culture, yet so narrow . . . so deficient in vitality.' Arnold has 'aged before his time'. For this reviewer, the later poems are generally less pleasing than the earlier ones; they are cold and lacking in passion, the remnants of a poetic temperament rather than poetry itself. The reviewer is almost elegiac in tone: 'We have lost a poet.' And the extremity of his censure—though, again, the *Athenaeum* tended to be reserved in its praise of Arnold—is also a measure of his disappointment, or even of his affection for the early poems. It was to take several years for poems such as 'Dover Beach' to be seen as representative or at least excellent in their own right. The *Athenaeum* reviewer typically differentiated between early and late poems, not in kind but in quality. 'Empedocles' for this reviewer, as for many, was the favourite, the most powerful of the poems.[49]

The *Athenaeum* review caught in another way a common response to the poems. That sense of finality, of dealing with a past or established rather than a living and active poet can be found in so many of the commentaries on Arnold's poems that were to follow, regardless of the discrepancies in judgment or assumptions. This is true of the best critiques of the 1867 volume: a short essay in the *Saturday Review* by Leslie Stephen (No. 15), and a long, almost lyric piece by A. C. Swinburne in the *Fortnightly* (No. 16).

Swinburne's was, like other articles in the *Fortnightly*, signed. The review, edited at this time by George Lewes, was only two years old, and though its circulation was less than three thousand, it was already an important new voice. Swinburne's essay was characteristically personal and polemical (the *Fortnightly* invited outspoken commentaries);

he offered, not simply a review of the 1867 volume or even a survey of Arnold's poems, but an apology and testimonial to the poet. Swinburne begins by expressing a position dear to the *Fortnightly*: that a critic must 'explain clearly what he wants' and say who he is. In his opinion, Arnold is a great poet, misunderstood if judged by his prose. Many later writers disagreed with Swinburne's relative estimate of the poetry, in fact used Swinburne's essay as a point of departure, but the consensus towards the end of the century was inclined to his judgment.

In later years Swinburne was to speak of Arnold in negative, even harsh, terms. At this time he considered Arnold to be, if not the best, very close to being the best English poet of the generation. Dante Rossetti, who has left only the briefest references to Arnold, records Swinburne's telling a group of friends that Arnold was superior to Tennyson, which is tantamount to saying that he was inferior to none of his contemporaries. For, as Swinburne writes in the *Fortnightly* essay, 'No poet has ever come so near the perfect Greek.' 'No one has in like measure that tender and final touch.' If there is too much dejection in Arnold's verse, the elegaic power of 'Thyrsis' makes a close third with that of 'Lycidas' and 'Adonais', and Arnold's feeling for nature ranks with that of Wordsworth, who served for more than Swinburne as a standard of modern poetic excellence.

Swinburne's essay is full of polemics and asides, but his diffuseness is also partially a strength, in that the unity of the piece is personal, Swinburne's response to Arnold's poems—from the time of his boyhood—affording a loose survey. He is above all grateful to the older poet, and he has always been conscious of him *as* an older poet, who has taught him about poetry and provided keys to his own emotions. In spite of the praise, the implication is that Arnold's days as a poet are gone.

Leslie Stephen's brief remarks in the *Saturday Review*—by this time the most powerful of the intellectual weeklies—express at once pleasure and irritation. 'Alas,' he writes, 'why should his muse now wear a mien so little young, so little radiant?' Stephen was and remained fond of Arnold, whose poems as an older man he enjoyed quoting for his daughters, but he sensed the finality, which he ascribed to a weakness implicit even in the best poems, 'Thyrsis' and 'Stanzas from the Grande Chartreuse'. Why then the sense of loss? Stephen suggests, in a distinction that was already hackneyed, that Arnold was a 'made' rather than a 'born' poet. (Compare John Stuart Mill's 'poets of culture' and 'poets of nature'.) Partly, Stephen says, the fault was that of the age (as the distinction certainly was). There is too much of the unspontaneous in Arnold, too much of the ratiocinative, because these are the overwhelming characteristics of the age. The implication is that what the age deserves, and therefore demands, is what it gets. Stephen is close here to Arnold's proclamations about the cultural climate necessary for poetry; he also anticipates and provides a comment on one of Arnold's own statements about his poetry.

Writing to his mother in the late sixties, Arnold says:[50]

My poems represent, on the whole, the main movement of mind of the last quarter of a century, and thus they will probably have their day as people become conscious to themselves of what that movement of mind is, and interested in the literary productions which reflect it. It might be fairly urged that I have less poetical sentiment than Tennyson, and less intellectual vigour and abundance than Browning; yet, because I have perhaps more of a fusion of the two . . . I am likely enough to have my turn, as they have had theirs.

Arnold was shrewd enough about his future reputation, if overly modest about the reasons for it, but the tone of his remarks is odd. In the first place, it is not so far from 'the movement of mind' to 'the march of mind' and the utilitarian assertion that poetry must come to include (as one of Arnold's reviewers wanted) the power of the blast furnaces and the hegemony of British commerce. But even to speak of poets as representing their times was a cliché that Arnold had himself lambasted. True poets, he says in the 1853 preface, 'do not talk of their mission, nor of interpreting their age, nor of the coming poet; all this, they know, is the mere delirium of vanity'.[51] Arnold had accepted a criterion of excellence he had once scorned, partly no doubt because it had been used so often in praise of his poems, partly because he had come to share with his critics the sense of his poetry being finished, his reputation alone remaining to be fixed.

VII

Poems (1869) AND THE 1870S

In 1881, a little more than a decade after publishing *New Poems*, Arnold received a fine but peculiar compliment from Benjamin Disraeli, who called him 'the only living Englishman who had become a classic in his lifetime'.[52] Evidently Disraeli meant to praise Arnold's poems, which he preferred to those of Browning. But he was not offering unadulterated praise in this ambiguous remark, and if he intended Browning as a poet who was decidedly not a classic, Browning himself might have been flattered. No doubt Disraeli wanted to imply his conviction of Arnold's lasting value and to praise the poet in terms that Arnold must appreciate. Yet what poet wants to be a classic in his lifetime? Possibly Arnold did. His notion of his emerging fame, his escape into the formalism of *Merope*, his increasing commitment to the public voice—all bespeak a desire for premature finality. Perhaps, too, Arnold had come to share Newman's feeling that the poet, like any artist, stops upon reaching 'his point of failure'.

By the 1870s, long before the meeting with Disraeli, Arnold was an established public spokesman, his essays, introductions, and speeches in great demand. He was controversial but courted. In fact he was what he remained until T. S. Eliot took his place: the foremost man of English letters. But as a poet he seemed no more alive than Wordsworth or Goethe or the man with whom he often came to compare himself, Thomas Gray. Writing in the year after Disraeli's compliment, Arnold was to say of his relations with 'the great reading public': 'I always feel that the public is not disposed to take me cordially; it receives my things, as Gray says it received all his except the Elegy, with more astonishment than pleasure . . . however, that the things should wear well, and be found to give pleasure as they come to be better known, is the great matter.'[53] His reference is to a comparable figure, yet to a past poet, to a classic. And however much respected and revered, Arnold was right in seeing himself as his critics saw him, a poet of an earlier generation. Ironically, by the time of Disraeli's remark, Arnold's poems had begun to be praised by poets and critics alike, not for their classicality or established excellence, but for their modernity. A dramatic change was in store. But in the seventies, the sense of the finished poetic career was dominant.

Many critics were already nostalgic. As a reflection of his own feeling of completion, Arnold was scrupulously careful about the arrangement of his poems in the many editions beginning with 1867. Moreover, his critics were just as concerned. Nearly all the periodical commentators on his poems were aware exactly of what had been included and excluded, as well as in which form. The degree of familiarity with such textual details suggests, as John Jump has made clear, the high level of competence characteristic even of the weekly reviewers. By the seventies it was the weeklies, the *Saturday Review,* the *Athenaeum,* and the *Spectator,* which accounted for much of the impact of a book and the number of its sales. The great quarterlies were becoming less influential and less powerful, as a glance at relative circulation figures will indicate.[54] In a letter to his mother (in 1869), Arnold mentions a *Spectator* review, then says he will have to 'change back "the gipsy Child" to its old form as no one seems to like the new one'. The 'no one' is a specific reference to the *Spectator*. Arnold also adds: 'The Spectator's review [of the 1869 volume] was a very satisfactory one, and will do the book good.'[55]

So Arnold proved responsive to specific criticisms and showed his readiness to alter his texts in future editions, which he took for granted. They were in fact plentiful, both in his own lifetime and throughout the remainder of the century. *New Poems* was followed in 1868 with a second edition. *Poems* (1869) went without an early second edition (though Macmillan editions were fairly large; the 1867 *Poems* had sold over a thousand copies by autumn of that year), but there were *Poems* (1877), *Selected Poems* (1878), *Poems* (1885, with a new edition after three years), *Poetical Works* (1890), and even a *Birthday Book* (1883). In addition, G. C. Macaulay, William Sharp, and Richard Garnett all edited selections of his poems, and he was anthologized by the 1860s. He was undoubtedly being read.

If the number of periodical reviews and essays is a good indication, it was with the 1869 edition of *Poems* that Arnold's readership and reputation became substantial. Essays by Alfred Austin (No. 19), John Skelton (No. 20b), R. H. Hutton (No. 21), Henry Hewlett (No. 22), and Buxton Forman (No. 18) appeared within a few years. Suddenly, too, Arnold's reputation as a poet—his reputation as a critic had gone before—extended, if not to Europe, at least to Canada and the United States.

Arnold never was to have much of a readership in France, perhaps, as E. K. Brown has pointed out, because a foreign reader is apt to want an author to be substantially different from his native poets.[56] Brown comments on the ironic acceptance of Carlyle in France and the neglect of Arnold, though the one had nothing but contempt for France, the other so much sympathy. On the other hand, there was also little attention paid to Arnold in Germany, at least before the dissertations began to be written in the 1890s. Also, whatever Arnold's sympathies, his poetry is scarcely French in character, and to a Frenchman his verse would be as alien as Carlyle's prose. In any case, he made no reputation in France, either as a poet or critic. There had been an early review of his poems in the *Revue des deux mondes*, but 'Arthur Dudley', its author, was an Englishman. And though the influential Sainte-Beuve had private praise for Arnold, corresponded with him, and translated

'Obermann', his mention of Arnold in *Chateaubriand et son groupe litteraire* could have no substantial impact.[57] Much like Wordsworth's, though with the paradox of Arnold's self-asserted, and real, cosmopolitanism, Arnold's reputation was to reside almost exclusively within the English-speaking world.

In America, Arnold had his apologists. First among them was Clough, whose review of *Empedocles* and *The Strayed Reveller* had been tepid, but who sponsored Arnold's poems among influential men such as Lowell and Charles Eliot Norton (both reserved in their response) and who arranged for publication of the poems with Ticknor and Fields. Then, too, writers including Henry James and Herman Melville testified to the powerful impact of the poems on them as young men. Melville's impressions became public knowledge only recently, and though James's essay was reprinted in America, it was written for an English magazine (No. 27).

James's essay on Arnold includes the remark that 'Superior criticism, in the United States, is at present not written.' Certainly good periodicals were rare. With the exception of the *North American Review*, where Clough's article had appeared, American periodicals remained obviously inferior to their English counterparts, and the few of them that turned to Arnold's poems offered little of interest. Despite the growing frequency of essays on Arnold later in the century, in the *Dial*, *Harper's*, *Scribner's*, the *Nation*, the *Dark Blue*, and others, the level of discussion remained low, or at least derivative, either reflecting comments in earlier English magazines, or reprinting English essays in their entirety. William LeSueur, a Canadian (No. 25a), and E. S. Nadal wrote strong endorsements of Arnold in the 1870s (Arnold knew and respected Nadal), but in asserting the superiority of Arnold's poems to his essays, they were echoing earlier arguments of the sort in England.

In England, Arnold's reputation was reflected but also helped by the able writings of a man who turned into one of his best critics. From the early 1870s until close to the turn of the century, Richard Holt Hutton reviewed Arnold's poems for the *Spectator*. He also wrote, in 1872, an essay for the *British Quarterly* (No. 21). Of Arnold's many critics, Hutton was one of the most acute and most persuasive, despite his own admission that he fundamentally disagreed with Arnold's philosophical and religious positions.

In Hutton's long essay for the *British Quarterly*, his essential interest lay in Arnold the careful student of Goethe and Wordsworth, in the poetic thinker whose 'poems are one long variation on a single theme, the divorce between the soul and the intellect'. While limited in the range both of his intellect and his poetic gifts, Arnold is still, for Hutton, a major poet writing in a major tradition, at the same time an exquisite interpreter 'of the spiritual pangs and restlessness of this age'. Hutton differs from so many of his contemporaries, not in the basically humanistic approach to the poet, but in the technical facility with which he can illustrate his points. For example, he conceives of Arnold primarily as a meditative poet, but he also points to an 'oratorical' and therefore 'persuasive' quality to the verse, and he defines that quality technically as a kind of poetic 'recitative'.

What Hutton assumes, and what became common to assume, was the permanence of Arnold's reputation as a poet. The comparison with Wordsworth and Goethe is in itself flattering, and Hutton asserts the originality and self-sufficiency of his contemporary. Because of this respect, Hutton's tone is quite different from that of earlier critics, such, for example, as Kingsley; but more importantly, the respect changes the terms as much as the tone of criticism. Instead of advice to the poet, Hutton attempts an objective 'placing' of the poet. He accepts Arnold as a representative poet and tries, while acknowledging the guesswork, to sort things out for posterity. Here is our great poet, he is saying, but will he, or in which ways, remain great to later readers?

Hutton's questions were to grow common, as critics spoke about Arnold more as an institution than as a living poet. 'Any excuse for re-reading his poems', as one *Spectator* reviewer said, 'is an excuse for one of the purest enjoyments of life.' A critic for the *Saturday Review* (No. 23) said: 'Every year widens the circle of those who recognize in [Arnold] that "lucidity of soul", that Greek clearness of touch, which nearly thirty years ago a small band of readers discovered in the author of the "Poems by A".' And the inevitable question: why should a man 'who employs no popular arts, and who neither paints nor plays upon any passion . . . so steadily advance in favour?' Perhaps 'his *Essays in Criticism* have taught us to judge'.

But if, in the seventies, the general assessment of Arnold was increasingly high—high in praise as well as high, like Hutton's, in quality—there were of course critics who considered his work to be of a distinctly low order. These, too, may have been taught to judge, but they were inclined to judge harshly. Conspicuous among Arnold's detractors was Henry Buxton Forman, for whom endemic flaws in the verse spelled an overall artistic deficiency (No. 18). 'There is the same want of life and fervour about the great bulk of the author's volumes of verse;

[and] the chief cause of this is doubtless want of real poetic power.'
Forman's account of Arnold's weaknesses was to provide the dominant
criticisms in years to come, as Arthur Quiller-Couch's representative
remarks in 1918 would indicate.[58] Forman's question, a central question—though with him an angry one—was to be summed up by T. S.
Eliot: 'Why was the critic so incapable of self-criticism?' Forman
accuses Arnold of technical inadequacy, arguing that the 'elegant
Jeremiah' tends to 'the redundancy of personal pronouns', 'ineffective
and irrelevant' comparisons, and a 'pseudo-epigrammatic' manner. In
short, as Arnold himself wrote of Byron, the poet 'has no fine and exact
sense for word and structure and rhythm'.

Forman was typical of the kind of negative criticisms raised against
Arnold, but he was not typical in his estimate of the poet's worth; indeed, the extremity of his censure is itself a kind of rhetorical pose,
based on the awareness that many people did admire Arnold, the faults
acknowledged notwithstanding. And Forman himself later judged
mildly. He was to edit a selection of Arnold's poems for the 'Temple
Classics'.

VIII

THE 1880s

The most dramatic and most puzzling shift in the assessment of Arnold
occurred sometime in the 1880s, and it was a shift not unlike that in our
own time, when, after long years of relatively unfruitful criticism, good
critics once again turned their attention to Arnold and found him to be
a different kind of poet. In the 1880s it was not so much that better
critics wrote better or more sympathetic works, it was rather that the
whole assumption behind their essays seemed to have changed. Whereas, Swinburne, Stephen, and to some extent even Hutton, had spoken
of Arnold as a fine classic, later writers began, even more than Arnold's
early contemporaries, to describe him as a modern poet. Henry James
spoke for many critics in the late decades of the century when he called
Arnold 'the poet of our modernity' (No. 27). Again, there is a rough
parallel with T. S. Eliot, whose 'classical' poems seemed at first the very
voice of their time, but whose critical precepts so long eclipsed the
poetry.

Disraeli's comment that Arnold was a classic came in the 1880s, and
it was perfectly possible, as James illustrates, to think of Arnold both as
classic *and* as 'the poet of our modernity'. But the shift is evident. By

the 1880s the general assessment of Arnold concentrated on what in modern parlance would be his 'relevance': his power to articulate the spiritual aridity, the sense of isolation, nostalgia, despair, in a rapidly changing age. Arnold catches 'the profound isolation of the individual man'; 'he expresses the unrest, the bewilderment . . . the perplexity of a doubting age'; he is 'the poet and critic of an age of transition'. Arnold's own analysis (in 1869) of his role, his sense of his poems catching 'the movement of mind', points to the importance this notion had, even for the poet himself.

But again, to call Arnold 'modern' was to praise him for qualities that he had once shunned or tried in his work to suppress. One notices that by the 1880s Arnold's most sympathetic readers are talking about him less in terms of the severe and formidable standards in the 1853 preface than in terms of standards implicit in the poems themselves or applied, loosely, from later essays. Arnold's phrase-making had an early effect in critical vocabularies. Thus, Edward Dowden asserts in an essay for the *Fortnightly* (in 1887) that he will 'strike at once for the centre' of Arnold's poems by asking how they serve as a 'criticism of life'.

The question raised by the *Spectator* reviewer about Arnold having 'taught us how to judge' is pertinent here. No one can say with authority how much Arnold's criticism reminded Victorian readers of his poems or won for them a larger audience; and his critics divided themselves on the point. It is on the other hand easy to show, both how frequently Arnold's critical precepts occur in criticism of the time and how much his thought had permeated criticism generally. E. K. Brown has written that 'It was because of the taste he scourged that [Arnold's] own poetry was enjoyed.'[59] In the first place, of course, 'the greatest critic of his age' was himself sensitive and responsive to men who did not write according to his ideals, Wordsworth notably among them. Furthermore, Arnold's ideals were not fixed. Henry Hewlett's discussion (in 1874) of Arnold's gradual swing from Hellenism to Hebraism was too pat, but it indicated the complexity of Arnold's ideals and his increasing catholicity of taste (No. 22). If he himself found it hard to tolerate the kind of poetry that, temperamentally, he had to write, he did not school his readers to one taste. He did school them to look at poetry with a certain disinterestedness (or show of it), even to pay close attention to matters of form and detail. Moreover, Arnold's reputation as a poet flourished, not when the assumptions of Carlyle but when his own assumptions, or at least his own precepts, dominated periodical criticism; so that instead of being enjoyed 'because of the taste he scourged', he may have created the taste by which he could be enjoyed.

Still it was not the rigid formalism, the theory of the 1853 preface that appealed to Arnold's readers. They liked instead the kind of remark that Arnold made in 'Pagan and Medieval Religious Sentiment', where he says: 'The poetry of later paganism lived by the senses and understanding; the poetry of medieval Christianity live by the heart and imagination. But the main element of the spirit's life is neither the senses and understanding, nor the heart and imagination; it's the imaginative reason.' Arnold's late contemporaries would have understood Dwight Culler's recognition of the centrality of that last phrase, 'the imaginative reason', because it was how they came to read Arnold's poetry. William Adams's 'The Poetry of Criticism' (1875) is a typical attempt to understand poetry that is a kind of poetic reason (No. 25b). The standards are nonetheless Arnold's, and the taste is to a large extent a reflected version of his own.

'Imaginative reason' may have been Arnold's phrase for a kind of poetry that would include Tennyson's and Browning's as well as his own. It may also have been an attempt to justify what became a common charge against his poetry: that it was too prosaic, altogether too close in its rhythms and diction to prose. Early critics made the charge, too, especially when they commented on Arnold's faulty ear, but the later criticism was an apparent result of a quality in some of Arnold's 1867 poems, especially 'Growing Old', 'The Progress of Poetry', 'The Last Word', and 'Pis Aller'. Lionel Trilling has written about these poems that they 'do not question but reply, do not hint but declare'.[60] They speak in an idiom close at times in its spareness to prose: direct, unambiguous (or apparently so), and stark. R. H. Hutton had perhaps intended his term 'recitative' to describe their texture, and Frederic Harrison definitely intended them when (in the 1890s) he discussed Arnold's 'Gnomic' quality (No. 41). For many critics the characteristic of these poems, or the characteristic of Arnold's poetry most dominant in these poems, illustrated, not—as H. D. Traill wrote—that Arnold was 'cold', but that he wrote 'without genuine poetic impulse' (No. 32). His poetry was too explicitly 'a criticism of life'.

The common conclusion drawn from Arnold's prosaic or critical quality was that his audience had to be limited. But even as they called Arnold a 'made' poet, critics could assert that he wrote with a distinct 'voice'. E. K. Brown has said that 'Everyone knows that [Arnold] lacks a distinctive manner of his own, differing in this from Tennyson and

Browning, Swinburne and Rossetti.'[61] This was a charge brought against Arnold by the early reviewers which later readers tended to deny. C. E. Tyrer, for example, in an essay for the *Manchester Quarterly* (1888) found Arnold's 'style and language . . . emphatically his own' (No. 36a). Possibly because they concentrated on the vehicle rather than the tenor of poetry, Arnold's contemporaries could forgive blemishes, and they seldom confused inconsistency of quality with an indeterminate poetic voice. This is true of Henry James's letter to the English about their inadequately realized poet (No. 27). James calls Arnold's verse 'singular' without being quite 'inevitable'. (That Arnold was not 'inevitable' was a standard complaint.) For James it is obvious, yet surprisingly not damning, that 'we find in [Arnold] no great abundance' of 'splendour, music, passion, breadth of movement and rhythm'. 'What we do find is high distinction of feeling . . . and a remarkable faculty for touching the chords which connect our feelings with the things that others have done and spoken.' Arnold is, then, the true voice of Victorian feeling: not the voice of sentimental fiction, not the ranting voice of politics, but rather the discriminating voice of those emotions that truly matter.

Arnold's death in 1888 elicited the predictable eulogies and obituary notices, but it was also the occasion for a number of fine, long scrutinies of Arnold's career by men who felt that he had been an important and singular voice. Rowland Prothero wrote a discerning essay for the *Edinburgh* on Arnold's aesthetic temperament, suggesting that the 'real' Arnold was the poet, thwarted in his development, who began by expressing the unrest of a doubting age, and who moved, beyond paganism, to a kind of aesthetic and moral stoicism—hence the quality of 'Growing Old' and similar poems (No. 34). Frederic W. H. Myers wrote an essay for the *Fortnightly* with fine insights, especially about Arnold's 'poems of cosmic meditation' (No. 31). Edmund Gosse, Mowbray Morris, R. H. Hutton, and Andrew Lang, all wrote essays. H. D. Traill's essay for the *Contemporary Review* is an astute attempt at summing up and an attack on what he saw as a common assumption: that Arnold would be remembered largely for his poems (No. 32). The large number of obituary essays (and poems—for example by Lionel Johnson and Richard Gallienne, No. 36d) suggest Arnold's prominence at the time of his death, as a poet as much as a writer of prose. By 1888 it was no longer uncommon to see Arnold as a less gifted technician than Tennyson, a less 'robust' poet than Browning, but otherwise at the least their equal.

'When a poet is dead,' wrote Augustine Birrell in an obituary of Arnold, 'we turn to his verse with quickened feelings.' Birrell was explaining his own nostalgia for a poet who had long represented for him, as for many readers, what he called a 'retreat' and a 'consolation' (No. 36f). Birrell's praise of Arnold was, in terms of almost any modern critical position, gratuitous, and for us the recurrent question 'Is Matthew Arnold's poetry consoling?' seems at best misguided. But Birrell shared Newman's assumption that poetry must console; and though he himself did not quote Novalis's famous slogan, several of Arnold's critics did: 'Poetry heals the wounds', Novalis wrote, 'which the understanding makes.' Similarly dated is Birrell's remark that Arnold proved 'the most useful poet of his day'—a type of assertion that has seemed the more distorting the more the years have passed. Yet for Birrell and many of his contemporaries a poet had a potential power that is no longer even imaginable, and a poet's social function was assumed to be definable. Therefore Birrell wants to identify the nature of the poet's appeal, to ask what Arnold's poetry does for us. Even the word 'useful' reflects a century-long search for an adequate rebuttal to the utilitarian threat to poetry, the threat which Shelley and Keats, Mill and Carlyle, had tried in various ways to meet. For poetry, as another of Arnold's critics wrote, had lived throughout the century 'in uneasy antagonism with the spirit of the age'.

Birrell's public testimony to the power of Arnold's verse was, as an obituary, understandably nostalgic, and it was typical of a large number of readers. In *The Republic of Letters*, W. M. Dixon stated what many felt: 'We have been the recipients', he writes, 'of a truly rich gift; and to him our gratitude will be as lasting as it is pure—to him who was the chief poet of the autumnal season of this century' (No. 42). 'Autumnal season' suggests a longer career than Arnold enjoyed as a poet, but it illustrates the kind of appeal Arnold was making at the end of the century. Edmund Gosse, who lectured privately on Arnold to a ladies' club, spoke in his *Literature of the Victorian Era* about Arnold's poems having 'come to seem to younger readers, in their pure and strenuous passion, not the greatest, but perhaps the most characteristic rendering in poetry of what has been best in the spirit of the Victorian Age'.

But Arnold's fame, in spite of his power to win new readers, was always somehow mitigated. In the essay on Gray he had written about both Gray and Collins that their 'reputation was established and stood extremely high [at the end of the previous century] even if they were not popularly read'. The observation applies to himself at the close of the nineteenth century. Again, however, 'popular' is a confusing term. R. H. Hutton could point out that while most critics nodded to the 'fact' of Arnold's select audience, there had been, between 1878 and 1893, some thirteen reprints of *Selected Poems* alone. It may have been true, as Frederic Harrison said, or as Hugh Walker wrote in *The Greater Victorian Poets*, that Arnold was 'the one poet farthest from the place he deserves' (No. 40) and that time alone would prove his significance. Yet Walker's comparisons were obviously with men like Tennyson, and with statistics of publication that seem to us unreal. If 'popular' meant selling, as Tennyson's poems had sold, up to forty thousand copies of a work within a few weeks, then Arnold was certainly never popular. By this criterion, only Scott, Byron, and Tennyson have been popular poets. But the 'select few' that so many of Arnold's apologists pointed to was not as limited as they implied, and Hutton was right in observing the steady call for new editions, a call which increased after the poet's death.

To some extent, Arnold's reputation in the 1890s was as an already institutionalized 'Victorian poet'. Walker, for example, was a university professor, one of many writers of nineteenth-century literary histories that appeared in these years and that began to make Arnold into something of the stiff man of letters which he soon became. In the United States during the nineties there flourished textbook editions of Arnold's poems—usually with 'Sohrab and Rustum' as the main title poem—which told how to read the poet and what salient facts to remember. The drab Arnold was being created. Also in the nineties, Arnold was being translated; Edmund Gosse praised the efforts of Norwegian friends to render 'Balder Dead' into Danish; and Arnold's reputation began to spread to European universities: he was being written about in Basel and Florence.

In spite of this predictable shift, Arnold did, as Edmund Gosse suggested, continue to appeal to younger readers (No. 42c); and what these men said in private was often as fulsome as what Birrell or Gosse said in print. Andrew Lang expressed the sense of allegiance of many young writers when he said of Arnold that 'he was to me what Wordsworth was to him'—in short his master.[62] Arnold's impact on the younger generation was not uniform. Yeats speaks of him often, but only as a critic; and Hardy and Housman (who clearly learned from him) seem to have had nothing to say.[63] Others, like Ernest Dowson, were less than flattering. Dowson, complained 'how passionately serious all these Arnolds are even to the third & fourth generation'.[64] Francis Thompson, perhaps a more gifted critic than he was a poet, responded to a review of his poems that included comparison with Arnold (already a kind of standard himself)in this way:[65]

I only deprecate in it the implied comparison to Dante, and the to-me-bewildering comparison to Matthew Arnold. 'Tis not merely that I should have studied no poet less; it is that I thought we were in the sharpest contrast. His characteristic fineness lies in that very form and restraint to which I so seldom attain: his characteristic drawback in the lack of that full stream which I am seldom without. The one needs and becomes strict banks—for he could not fill wider ones; the other too readily overflows all banks.

Thompson is probably accurate, though unwittingly more critical of himself than of Arnold, who knew Goethe's precept about genius having to recognize its limits.

But while Hardy and Thompson were either negative or silent, other poets offered warm tributes. Hopkins's response to Bridges, for example, illustrates a complex but basically positive estimate of Arnold. Hopkins says: 'I have more reason than you for disagreeing with him [Bridges had called Arnold 'Mr. Kidglove Cocksure'] and thinking him very wrong, but nevertheless I am sure he is a rare genius and a great critic.' W. E. Henley, whose criticism tended to short appreciations, also wrote about Arnold, whom he found uncertain and hobbled as a poet: 'But, then, how many of the rarer qualities of art and inspiration are represented here, and here alone, in modern work!' (No. 28). I have already quoted some of Oscar Wilde's praise of Arnold, especially of 'Thyrsis'. Wilde included a collection of Arnold's poems among the books he requested while in Reading Gaol. Among other 'aesthetes and decadents', Arnold's position was mixed, although his poems were probably preferred to his criticism. Thanks to the fawning of Arthur Galton, he was praised (immoderately) in the Century Guild *Hobby Horse*, and Arthur Waugh applauded his literary 'reticence' in the pages of the *Yellow Book*. The strongest, most intelligent commentary by one of Yeats's 'tragic generation' was that by Lionel Johnson, whose elegiac poem 'Laleham' (No. 42a) had already placed Arnold, with Gray, among a select group of immortals.

Johnson wrote his short review of the Popular Edition (1891) for the *Academy*, the distinguished journal that Arnold had helped to sponsor

(No. 37). A discerning critic, who wrote a fine early study of Hardy, and a poet himself, Johnson began his review with a discussion of Arnold's 'few and venial faults'. They include an 'imperfect ear', occasional failings in 'conception', and a baffling inability to 'polish'. 'These things are worth a few words, because admirers of Arnold are in danger of being held his worshippers also, unless they show themselves aware of his faults. Arnold, great and admirable as he is, is no more perfect than Gray, Milton, or Sophocles; but he stands above the first, and the others were his most successful masters.' Although but a page or two in length, Johnson's review is extremely suggestive. He has comments on Arnold's English temperament, but also on his relation to various cultures, the Celtic included, and he indicates that while Arnold may be associated with Oxford in one narrow sense and the nineteenth-century *Zeitgeist* in another, his fine meditative strain is neither for one time nor one place. (He was answering the explicit objections of writers like Mrs Oliphant, No. 38, who damned Arnold as an Oxford snob.) 'Surely', he writes, 'these poems are more than the records of a transitory emotion, the phase and habits of an age. Such a description would apply to Clough; his mournful, homesick, desultory poems are indeed touched with decay, because they are composed without care . . . but Arnold's thoughts and emotions are profoundly human.' He ends his review with an apt and rare comparison of Arnold and Verlaine, implying the centrality of both to a poet of the *fin de siècle*.

In a recent discussion of Arnold's popularity, Geoffrey Tillotson wrote: 'During the last decade no other English poet of the nineteenth century, or earlier, can show so many reprintings—except the poet who died the year after Arnold, Gerard Manley Hopkins . . . On bibliographical evidence, then, Arnold is something of a popular poet.'[66] 'Something of a popular poet' is about as accurate as one can be about Arnold's stature—now, as well as at the turn of the century. Just as in our own day Lionel Stevenson has argued that Arnold is no longer read much,[67] and Harold Bloom has said that Arnold vies with Hopkins for the most overrated poet of his time,[68] so in the nineties apologists for the critics of Arnold disagreed as to his stature and popularity. Then as now, the extremity of opinion suggested a high degree of concern: whether liked or not, Arnold was—and is—being read. In the nineties, Thomas Smart did a bibliography; George Saintsbury wrote the first book-length study (1899); men like Walker drew Arnold into the academy (No. 40). At the same time, while Arnold had appealed to some of the Pre-Raphaelites forty years before, he could still appeal to a new 'counter-culture', that of the aesthetes, and to an increasingly large part of the 'great reading public', whose taste, Arnold had long ago complained, was not for his type of verse, but whom he had thought his poems would finally reach. 'I have had very little success with the general public', he had written to Bulwer-Lytton in 1867, 'and I sincerely think that it is a fault in an author not to succeed with his general public, and that the greatest authors are those who do succeed with it.'[69] But his later comment, in 1869, is more accurate: 'I am likely enough to have my turn.'

X

A NOTE ON THE LATER REPUTATION

A glance at any bibliography of writings about Arnold will indicate that the flow of criticism continued unabated after the turn of the century. Herbert Paul's volume for the English Men of Letters Series appeared in 1902, to be followed by several full-length studies in the next few years, studies of the man, the thinker, or the poet. Few of these books, or essays of the time, offer much to a modern reader, although Herbert Grierson's, Stuart Sherman's, W. P. Ker's, Quiller-Couch's, and Oliver Elton's are partial exceptions. But what is true of lesser critics is to a great extent true of these who are better and better known: essentially they have little to say that is not to be found in nineteenth-century studies. Quiller-Couch's censure of Arnold's faults can be seen in Buxton Forman and a number of earlier writers, although his tone would suggest that he was making dramatic discoveries. *Discoveries* (1924) was the title for a collection of Middleton Murry's essays; but on Arnold, at least, Murry's remarks are well-phrased reiteration of previous judgments. Murry may have been unaware of essays by H. D. Traill, George Saintsbury, Lionel Johnson, or Frederic Harrison—his readers were doubtlessly unaware of them—but the point is that, like most critics, Murry was asking few new questions and saying what had long been said.

Among the reasons for the longevity of nineteenth-century critical positions was the paradoxical one that attitudes had become fixed, so that Arnold, like most Victorians, suffered from narrow and lingering assumptions which dated back to the Victorians' assessment of themselves. It was not really before E. K. Brown and Lionel Trilling, in the

mid- and late thirties, that new approaches to Arnold's work appeared
again, although readers will still turn to studies by Hugh Kingsmill
(1928), H. W. Garrod (1931), and Edmund Blunden (1932). H. F.
Lowry's important work also dates back to the early thirties. In view
of the excellent bibliographical studies available, there would be no
point here in trying to account for recent criticism of Arnold's poetry.
Frederic E. Faverty's fine discussion in *The Victorian Poets: a Guide to
Research* (1956; 1968) is invaluable; and R. H. Super's 'Matthew Arnold'
in the revised *Cambridge Bibliography* (1969) offers a basic checklist. A
short but brilliant review of several important critiques of Arnold's
poetry is David J. De Laura's 'What, Then, Does Matthew Arnold
Mean?' (*Modern Philology,* May 1969).

What may be appropriate here is a final word about the centrality of
so many nineteenth-century essays to recent Arnold criticism. For however disparate their own aesthetic standards and however far they may
seem from us in their predominant interests, the best critics of the late
nineteenth century were asking important questions about Arnold's
poetry. To mention an extreme example, Norman Holland's scrutiny
of 'Dover Beach' in *The Dynamics of Literary Response* is directed as
much at the reader as it is at the poem, and Holland does not omit the
poet himself. Many nineteenty-century critics—granting they would
have been appalled at the sexual nature of Holland's inquiry—would
have shared his interest in the affective, formal, and expressive capacities
of literature. They were also interested in reader response and in an
understanding of art which subsumed the technical in more general
inquiry. They failed in any number of ways, but they were far more
acute, far more informed and concerned than we usually assume.

It is intriguing to see R. H. Hutton, William Michael Rossetti,
Leslie Stephen, George Eliot, or Henry James wrestling with problems
that have provided the focus of critical articles and entire books in the
last decades. I am thinking of E. D. H. Johnson's study of the divided
Victorian mind, which he—like the Victorians—found so well illustrated in Arnold; or Dwight Culler's analysis of Arnold's new verse
medium, including patterns of imagery; or Paull Baum's exegesis of
Arnold's main poems; or William Madden's understanding of Arnold,
first and last, as a man of 'aesthetic temperament'; or Leon Gottfried's
concern with Arnold and the Romantics, Robert Stange's discussion of
the humanist poet, Alan Roper's scrutiny of Arnold's poetic landscape,
or W. Stacy Johnson's description of the poetic voices. These are fine
studies, and it is no ill reflection on them to say that many of their pri-

mary interests were the interests of Arnold's Victorian critics. They, too, considered Arnold to be—in Walter Houghton's phrase—'the poet of Victorian loneliness'; like Kenneth Allott and Henry Duffin, they could argue his modernity. They were divided about his quality as a poet—and no less about his quality as a critic. Some considered him 'popular', some thought him bleak, academic, and too learned for all but a small audience. They wondered whether his career as a poet led naturally to that of the critic, or whether Arnold's sceptical temperament crippled his poems. They began the dialogues about Arnold, and they would have responded to the continuing dialogues in our time. If they were manifestly limited, their sense of themselves as 'public' critics, as men with a real audience, speaking about things that mattered, are qualities we may need reminder of. One of the biggest differences between Victorian and modern criticism is precisely the question of implied audience and the restriction of audience consequent on increasingly refined or specialized study. No doubt concentration is inevitable, and it is not necessarily undesirable, but it makes refreshing the immediacy and the sense of importance common to so many of the essays that follow.

NOTES

1 *Alfred Lord Tennyson, A Memoir by His Son* (1898), ii, p. 225.
2 'Christ Upon the Waters' (1850), quoted in Walter Houghton, *The Victorian Frame of Mind* (1957), p. 104.
3 Sir Arthur Quiller-Couch, *Studies in Literature, First Series* (1918), p. 234.
4 *Unpublished Letters of Matthew Arnold*, ed. Arnold Whitridge (1923), p. 22. Cited hereafter as *U.L.*
5 *Matthew Arnold* (1939), p. 142.
6 Herbert Paul, *Matthew Arnold* (English Men of Letters, 1902), pp. 20–4.
7 *Letters of Matthew Arnold*, ed. G. W. E. Russell (1895), i, p. 30.
8 Quoted in Russell, ii, pp. 188–9.
9 'The Poetry of Matthew Arnold', *Poetry and the Criticism of Life* (1931), p. 24.
10 Quoted by Jerome H. Buckley, in *The Victorian Poets* (1956 ed.), p. 3.
11 Jean-Georges Ritz, *Robert Bridges and Gerard Hopkins, 1863–1889, A Literary Friendship* (1960), p. 135.
12 *U.L.*, p. 14.
13 *U.L.*, p. 15.
14 *U.L.*, p. 17.
15 *The Letters of Matthew Arnold to Arthur Hugh Clough*, ed. Howard Foster Lowry (Oxford, 1932), p. 139.

16 *The Letters of Elizabeth Barrett Browning,* ed. Frederic G. Kenyon (1898), i, p. 429.

17 *U.L.,* pp. 20–1.

18 *The Correspondence of Henry Crabb Robinson with the Wordsworth Circle 1808–1866,* ed. Edith Morley (Oxford, 1927), ii, p. 695.

19 Mrs Humphry Ward, *A Writer's Recollections* (1918), i, p. 59.

20 *The Correspondence of Arthur Hugh Clough,* ed. Frederick L. Mulhauser (1957), ii, p. 363.

21 Lowry, p. 126.

22 See e.g. Lowry, p. 124, letter of 28 October 1852.

23 'The Modern Young Man as Critic', *Universal Review* (March 1889), p. 353.

24 *The Swinburne Letters,* ed. Cecil Y. Lang (1960), iv, p. 37.

25 *The George Eliot Letters,* ed. Gordon Haight (1955), v, p. 11.

26 *Personal and Literary Letters of Robert First Earl of Lytton,* ed. Lady Betty Balfour (1906), ii, pp. 50–1.

27 *Literary Studies,* ed. R. H. Hutton (1898), ii, pp. 338–9.

28 Quoted in Frederic E. Faverty, 'Matthew Arnold', *The Victorian Poets: a Guide to Research,* 2nd ed. (1968), p. 197.

29 Mulhauser, ii, p. 477.

30 *Literary Studies,* ii, p. 338.

31 'Midsummer with the Muses', *Dublin University Magazine* (June 1854), p. 739.

32 'The Two Arnolds', *Blackwood's Edinburgh Magazine* (March 1854), p. 307.

33 'A Raid Among Poets' (January, 1854), p. 40.

34 Lowry, p. 139.

35 Mulhauser, ii, p. 467.

36 Ernest Hartley Coleridge, *Life and Correspondence of John Duke Coleridge* (1904), i, pp. 123–5.

37 'The Two Arnolds', *Blackwood's Edinburgh Magazine* (March 1854), p. 312.

38 William Alexander, 'Matthew Arnold and MacCarthy' (April 1858), p. 260.

39 'Merope, A Tragedy' (2 January 1858), p. 13.

40 'Arthur Dudley', 'Matthew Arnold et Alexandre Smith', *Revue des deux mondes* (15 September 1854), p. 1136.

41 *U.L.,* pp. 35–8.

42 Russell, i, p. 60.

43 Russell, i, p. 59.

44 Russell, i, p. 61.

45 *U.L.,* pp. 62–3.

46 'The Neo-Classical Drama', *Christian Remembrancer* (January 1868), p. 45.

47 See Walter Bezanson, 'Melville's Reading of Arnold's Poetry', *PMLA* (1954), pp. 365–91.

48 *Complete Prose Works,* ed. R. H. Super (1965), v, p. 147.

49 'Matthew Arnold's New Poems', *Athenaeum* (31 August 1867), pp. 265–6.

50 Russell, ii, p. 9.
51 *Poems*, ed. Kenneth Allott (1965), pp. 604–5.
52 W. F. Monypenny and G. E. Buckle, *The Life of Benjamin Disraeli* (London, 1929), ii, p. 1474.
53 Russell, ii, p. 197.
54 See Allvar Ellegård, *The Readership of the Periodical Press in Mid-Victorian Britain* (Goteborg, 1957).
55 Russell, ii, p. 15.
56 'The French Reputation of Matthew Arnold', *Studies in English by Members of University College, Toronto* (1931), p. 225.
57 See Sainte-Beuve's letter to Arnold, dated 6 September 1854, in which he expresses pleasure in 'Obermann', *U.L.*, pp. 68–70. See also Arnold Whitridge, 'Arnold and Sainte-Beuve', *PMLA* (1938).
58 'Matthew Arnold', *Studies in Literature*, pp. 231–45.
59 *Matthew Arnold, A Study in Conflict* (1948), p. 5.
60 *Matthew Arnold*, p. 293.
61 *A Study in Conflict*, p. 5.
62 'At the Sign of the Ship', *Longman's Magazine* (June 1888), pp. 230–1.
63 See T. S. Dorsch and E. H. S. Walde, 'A. E. Housman and Matthew Arnold', *Boston University Studies in English* (1960).
64 *The Letters of Ernest Dowson,* ed. D. Flower and H. Maas (1967), p. 52.
65 Everard Meynell, *The Life of Francis Thompson* (1913), p. 170.
66 'Matthew Arnold in Our Time', *Mid-Victorian Studies* (1965), p. 152.
67 'Matthew Arnold's Poetry; A Modern Appraisal', *Tennessee Studies in Literature* (1959).
68 'Recent Studies in the Nineteenth Century', *Studies in English Literature* (Autumn 1970), p. 823.
69 *The Life of Edward Bulwer, First Lord Lytton* (1913), ii, p. 444.

Note on the Text

The materials included in this volume are taken from the first printed texts and, occasionally, from revised nineteenth-century reprints. Some of the brief sections of miscellaneous remarks are perhaps arbitrarily chosen, but the main body of reviews offers a full picture of the contemporary response to Arnold's poetry. Because of limited space, I have omitted a number of passages that seem tangential, and I have excluded all loosely illustrative quotations from Arnold's verse. But except for silent corrections of spelling and punctuation, and the deletion of a few footnotes, I have explained my tamperings, indicating what has been omitted in the way of commentary and giving line numbers and the first phrases of deleted verse. Numbered footnotes are my addition.

THE STRAYED REVELLER,
AND OTHER POEMS

---

1. Charles Kingsley, unsigned review,
Fraser's Magazine

May 1849, xxix, 575–80

Kingsley (1819–75) was a socially concerned clergyman as well
as a writer of polemical fiction. At the time of this review, Kingsley
was deeply involved with reform movements; he had published
his first novel, *Yeast*, the preceding year in *Fraser's*. His review of
'Recent Poetry and Recent Verse' reflects his social conscience.
He says, after discussing several contemporary poets, that writers
ought always to aim for 'something higher and more earnest;
something which shall bear directly on the cravings and ideas of
the age'. Arnold expected Kingsley to review a later edition of his
poems, apparently unaware that Kingsley had written this
assessment of *The Strayed Reveller*.

We are sorry to have to reiterate all these complaints in speaking of a
volume of poetry of a far higher class than any that we have yet noticed,
—*The Strayed Reveller and other Poems, by A*. It is evidently the work of a
scholar, a gentleman, and a true poet. The short pieces which it contains shew care and thought, delicate finish, and an almost faultness
severity of language and metre. 'Mycerinus' is a fragment worthy of
Tennyson.

There is a sonnet to Shakespeare, among other, well worth giving as
an extract:—

[Quotes 'Shakespeare' in its entirety]

But the gem of the book is 'The Forsaken Merman,' one of the most painfully affecting pieces of true poetry which we have fallen on for a long time past. It is too long, we regret to say, to quote at length; but some extracts will, perhaps, suffice to tell the story, and give a fair notion of the whole, which, though it reminds us in subject of poor Hood's exquisite poem of 'Hero and Leander,' and also of Tennyson's 'Merman and Mermaid,' surpasses them, we think, in simple natural-ness, and a certain barbaric wildness of metre and fancy, thoroughly appropriate to the subject:—

[Quotes 'The Forsaken Merman', ll. 1–107, 124–43]

We are not ashamed to confess that this poem 'upset' us. We have seldom read deeper or healthier pathos in the English language. The half-human, simple affection of the husband, the wonderful church-yard scene, the confusion of feeling and arrangement in the former part of the poem, and the return to the simple and measured melody of re-signation in the close, are all perfect. And consciously or unconsciously, probably the latter, there is in it 'godly doctrine, and profitable for these days,' when the great heresy of 'Religion *versus* God' is creeping on more subtilly than ever: by which we mean the setting up forms of worship and systems of soul-saving in opposition to the common instincts and affections of humanity, divine, because truly human; in opposition to common honesty and justice, mercy and righteousness; in short, in opposition to God. Any one who opens just now the leading religious periodicals on any side of the question, and has human eyes to see and a human heart to feel, will not be at a loss to understand our drift. The poet may have had no such intentional meaning; but no man can write true poetry, that is true nature, without striking on some eternal key in harmony with the deepest laws of the universe.

But having praised thus far, we must begin to complain. To what purpose all the self-culture through which the author must have passed ere this volume could be written? To what purpose all the pure and brilliant imagination with which God has gifted him? What is the fruit thereof? When we have read all he has to say, what has he taught us? What new light has he thrown on man or nature, the past awful ages or this most awful present one, when the world is heaving and moaning in the agonies, either of a death-struggle, or a new birth-hour more glorious than that which the sixteenth century beheld? Is he, too, like our friends the fashionable novelists, content to sit and fiddle while Rome is burning? Can he tell us no more about the French Revolution than—

Yet, when I muse on what life is, I seem
Rather to patience prompted, than that proud
Prospect of hope which France proclaims so loud;
France, famed in all great arts, in none supreme.
Seeing this vale, this earth, whereon we dream,
Is on all sides o'ershadow'd by the high
Uno'erleap'd mountains of Necessity,
Sparing us narrower margin than we deem.
Nor will that day dawn at a human nod.
&c. &c.?

Who ever expected that it would? What does the age want with fragments of an Antigone? or with certain 'New Sirens?'—little certainly
with these last, seeing that the purport of them is utterly undiscoverable
(as is, alas! a great deal more of the volume)—or with sleepy, melancholy meditations, not really on a 'Gipsy Child,' but on his own feelings
about the said child? or with *fainéant* grumblings at the 'credulous zeal'
of one Critias, who reasonably enough complains:—

Why in these mournful rhymes,
Learn'd in more languid climes,
Blame our activity,
Who with such passionate will
Are what we are meant to be?

What, indeed, do we want with the 'Strayed Reveller' itself, beautiful as it is, a long line of gorgeous and graceful classic sketches, with a
moral, if any, not more hopeful than that of Tennyson's 'Lotos-Eaters'?
We say if any, for, in too many of these poems, it is very difficult to get
at any clear conception of the poet's idea. The young poets, now-a-days,
are grown so wondrous wise, that our weak brains have to flee for the
intelligible to Shakspeare and Milton, Bacon and Kant. Would that
the rising generation would bear in mind that dictum of Coleridge's
(which he did not, alas! always bear in mind himself in his prose), that
perplexed words are the sure index of perplexed thoughts, and that the
only reason why a man cannot express a thing plainly, is, that he does
not see it plainly.

What, again, on earth do we want with a piece of obscure trans-
cendentalism headed, *In utrumque paratus;*[1] the moral, or we should
rather say immorality, of which seems to be, that if there is a God, the
author knows how to get on, and knows equally well how to get on if
there is none? We should like to see his secret, for he has not very clearly

1 'prepared for either eventuality'.

revealed it: merely, of course, as a matter of curiosity—we have not quite sufficient faith in it to steal it for our own use; for though such an alternative is 'a' one to him,' it is by no means a' one to his humble reviewer, or, as we opine, to various poor, hardworked bodies who take a somewhat deeper interest in heaven and earth than this new Phœbus Apragmon seems to do.

Lastly, what in the name of all grim earnest do we want with 'Resignation, to Fausta,' a yawn thirteen pages long, with which the volume finally falls fast asleep, and vanishes in a snore? Resignation! to what? To doing nothing? To discovering that a poet's business is swinging 'on a gate,' though not, indeed, to eat fat bacon, as the country-boy intended to do when he was made king; the food of A.'s poets seems to be that more ethereal ambrosia called by some 'flapdoodle;' for the materials of which delectable viand we must refer our readers to O'Brien, in Marryat's *Peter Simple*. But let us hear the poet himself:—

> Lean'd on his gate, he gazes: tears
> Are in his eyes, and in his ears
> The murmur of a thousand years:
> Before him he sees life unroll,
> A placid and continuous whole;
> That general Life which does not cease,
> Whose secret is not joy, but peace;
> That Life, whose dumb wish is not miss'd
> If birth proceeds, if things subsist;
> The Life of plants, and stones, and rain;
> The Life he craves, if not in vain.
> Fate gave what Chance shall not control,
> His sad lucidity of soul.

'Life,' forsooth! what is this hungry abstraction called 'Life,' which with a dozen more, stolen from the dregs of German philosophy, have supplanted those impersonated virtues and vices with capital letters, who ousted the Joves and Minervas of the *ancien régime*, and reigning from Gray and Collins down to the gentleman who began his ode with,

> Inoculation, heavenly maid, descend!

linger still among the annuals and 'books of beauty?'—Just as good in their way as 'Life,' and such-like novel slang. Life unrolling *before* him! as if it could unroll to purpose any where but *in* him; as if the poet, or any one else, could know aught of life except *by living it,* and that in bitter, painful earnest, being tempted in all points like his kind, a man

44

of sorrows, even as The Highest was. But we forget. It is 'the Life of plants, and stones, and rain,' which 'he craves.' Noble ambition! Why not the life of beasts also? That might, indeed, be in most species too active for the poet, but he might at least find a congenial sphere of existence in the life—of the oyster.

But we will jest no more. In sober sadness, here is a man to whom God has given rare faculties and advantages. Let him be assured that he was meant to use them for God. Let him feast himself on all beautiful and graceful thoughts and images; let him educate himself by them, for his capacity for them indicates that in that direction lies his appointed work. Let him rejoice in his youth, as the great Arnold told his Rugby scholars to do, and walk in the sight of his own eyes; but let him remember that for all these things God will bring him into judgment. For every work done in the strength of that youthful genius he must give account, whether it be good or evil. And let him be sure, that if he chooses to fiddle while Rome is burning he will not escape unscorched. If he chooses to trifle with the public by versifying dreamy, transcendental excuses for laziness, for the want of an earnest purpose and a fixed creed, let him know that the day is at hand when he that will not work neither shall he eat. If he chooses, while he confesses the great ideas with which the coming age is pregnant, to justify himself, by the paltry quibbles of a philosophy which he only half believes, for taking no active part in God's work, instead of doing with all his might whatsoever his hand finds to do, we recommend for his next meditation the significant story of that nobleman of Samaria, who in the plenitude of his serene unbelief, chose to sneer and sniff at the prophet's promise of near deliverance:—

'If the Lord should make windows in heaven, might this thing be?'

'Behold,' was the answer, '*thou shalt see it with thine eyes, but thou shalt not eat thereof.*' On the morrow, for all his serene sniffing, the deliverance came. 'But it came to pass' (he acting on behalf of order and the constituted decencies) '*that the people trod him down in the gate, and he died.*' *Verbum sat sapienti.*[1]

We must raise a complaint, also, against the poet's attempt to graft Greek choric metres on our English language. How unsuccessful he has been a single quotation will shew: for instance, from the *Strayed Reveller*:—

[Quotes ll. 162–211]

---

[1] 'A word is enough for the wise.'

In this beautiful passage, which might be a fragment from a lost play of Æschylus, we are at once struck with a radical defect—utter want of rhythm and melody. It is nervous and picturesque prose cut up into scraps, and nothing more; for it is simply impossible, we believe, to adapt these Greek choric metres to our language.

But read the verses aloud, with any accents you will, fair or unfair, and what is the effect but prose, with just enough likeness to verse to become tantalising and disagreeable, from the way in which it seems perpetually to stumble into rhythm for a foot or two, and then stumble miserably out again? No doubt it may be said that the sin is in our coarse English ears, that there is a true rhythmic sequence if we could but hear it—just as there is in the most intricate fugue or variation in music, though impalpable to the ears of an unlearned vulgar. No doubt we are a very ill-educated people, we English—the worst educated in Europe; and we are beginning to find it out. But while we are babes in metre, we must plead for a milk diet—the milk of Moore, Southey, and Tennyson. When the whole British public have been well drilled for twenty years by Messrs. Hullah and Sterndale Bennett, as we sincerely wish that they may be, and not before, will it be worth while for those who wish to be deservedly popular poets to publish these delicate metrical fantasias. And even then the poet will be bound, for his own sake as well as for ours, to publish at the same time complete musical scores for them, and to get them sung at some theatre, with full chorus, before sending them forth in print.

2. W. E. Aytoun, unsigned review, *Blackwood's Magazine*

September 1849, lxvi, 340–6

William Edmonstone Aytoun (1813–65) was a poet, man of letters, and public servant. Best known for his contributions to the *Bon Gaultier Ballads* (1854), he also wrote, in the year of this review, *Lays of the Scottish Cavaliers*. Aytoun was to coin the satiric tag 'Spasmodic School' to satirize Alexander Smith and other contemporary poets. In his review of *The Strayed Reveller* he has praise for 'The Forsaken Merman', and he thinks that Arnold has promise, but he is characteristically sceptical, patronizing, and facetious.

The other evening, on returning home from the pleasant hospitalities of the Royal Mid-Lothian Yeomanry, our heart cheered with claret, and our intellect refreshed by the patriotic eloquence of M'Whirter, we found upon our table a volume of suspicious thinness, the title of which for a moment inspired us with a feeling of dismay. Fate has assigned to us a female relative of advanced years and a curious disposition, whose affection is constantly manifested by a regard for our private morals. Belonging to the Supra-lapsarian persuasion, she never loses an opportunity of inculcating her own peculiar tenets: many a tract has been put into our hands as an antidote against social backslidings; and no sooner did that ominous phrase, *The Strayed Reveller,* meet our eye than we conjectured that the old lady had somehow fathomed the nature of our previous engagement, and, in our absence, deposited the volume as a special warning against indulgence in military banquets. On opening it, however, we discovered that it was verse; and the first distich which met our eye was to the following effect:—

> O Vizier, thou art old, I young,
> Clear in these things I cannot see.
> My head is burning; and a heat
> Is in my skin, which angers me.

47

This frank confession altered the current of our thought, and we straightway set down the poet as some young roysterer, who had indulged rather too copiously in strong potations, and who was now celebrating in lyrics his various erratic adventures before reaching home. But a little more attention speedily convinced us that jollity was about the last imputation which could possibly be urged against our new acquaintance.

One of the most painful features of our recent poetical literature, is the marked absence of anything like heartiness, happiness, or hope. We do not want to see young gentlemen aping the liveliness of Anacreon, indulging in praises of the rosy god, or frisking with supernatural agility; but we should much prefer even such an unnecessary exuberance of spirits, to the dreary melancholy which is but too apparent in their songs. Read their lugubrious ditties, and you would think that life had utterly lost all charm for them before they have crossed its threshold. The cause of such overwhelming despondency it is in vain to discover; for none of them have the pluck, like Byron, to commit imaginary crimes, or to represent themselves as racked with remorse for murders which they never perpetrated. If one of them would broadly accuse himself of having run his man through the vitals—of having, in an experimental fit, plucked up a rail, and so caused a terrific accident on the South-Western—or of having done some other deed of reasonable turpitude and atrocity, we could understand what the fellow meant by his excessively unmirthful monologues. But we are not indulged with any full-flavoured fictions of the kind. On the contrary, our bards affect the purity and innocence of the dove. They shrink from naughty phrases with instinctive horror—have an idea that the mildest kind of flirtation involves a deviation from virtue; and, in their most savage moments of wrath, none of them would injure a fly. How, then, can we account for that unhappy mist which floats between them and the azure heaven, so heavily as to cloud the whole tenor of their existence? What makes them maunder so incessantly about gloom, and graves, and misery? Why confine themselves everlastingly to apple-blossoms, whereof the product in autumn will not amount to a single Ribston pippin? What has society done to them, or what can they possibly have done to society, that the future tenor of their span must be one of unmitigated woe? We rather suspect that most of the poets would be puzzled to give satisfactory answers to such queries. They might, indeed, reply, that misery is the heritage of genius; but that, we apprehend, would be arguing upon false premises; for we can discover very little genius to vindicate the existence of so vast a quantity of woe.

We hope, for the sake of human nature, that the whole thing is a humbug; nay, we have not the least doubt of it; for the experience of a good many years has convinced us, that a young poet in print is a very different person from the actual existing bard. The former has nerves of gossamer, and states that he is suckled with dew; the latter is generally a fellow of his inches, and has no insuperable objection to gin and water. In the one capacity, he feebly implores an early death; in the other, he shouts for broiled kidneys long after midnight, when he ought to be snoring on his truckle. Of a morning, the Strayed Reveller inspires you with ideas of dyspepsia—towards evening, your estimate of his character decidedly improves. Only fancy what sort of a companion the author of the following lines must be:—

[Quotes 'A Question: To Fausta', 'Joy comes and goes', etc. in its entirety]

It is impossible to account for tastes; but we fairly confess, that if we thought the above lines were an accurate reflex of the ordinary mood of the author, we should infinitely prefer supping in company with the nearest sexton. However, we have no suspicion of the kind. An early initimacy with the writings of Shelley, who in his own person was no impostor, is enough to account for the composition of these singularly dolorous verses, without supposing that they are any symptom whatever of the diseased idiosyncrasy of the author.

If we have selected this poet as the type of a class now unfortunately too common, it is rather for the purpose of remonstrating with him on the abuse of his natural gifts, than from any desire to hold him up to ridicule. We know not whether he may be a stripling or a grown-up man. If the latter, we fear that he is incorrigible, and that the modicum of talent which he certainly possesses is already so perverted, by excessive imitation, as to afford little ground for hope that he can ever purify himself from a bad style of writing, and a worse habit of thought. But if, as we rather incline to believe, he is still a young man, we by no means despair of his reformation, and it is with that view alone that we have selected his volume for criticism. For although there is hardly a page of it which is not studded with faults apparent to the most common censor, there are nevertheless, here and there, passages of some promise and beauty; and one poem, though it be tainted by imitation, is deserving of considerable praise. It is the glitter of the golden ore, though obscured by much that is worthless, which has attracted our notice; and we hope, that by subjecting his poems to a strict examination, we may do the author a real service.

It is not to be expected that the first essay of a young poet should be faultless. Most youths addicted to versification, are from an early age sedulous students of poetry. They select a model through certain affinities of sympathy, and, having done so, they become copyists for a time. We are far from objecting to such a practice; indeed, we consider it inevitable; for the tendency to imitate pervades every branch of art, and poetry is no exception. We distrust originality in a mere boy, because he is not yet capable of the strong impressions, or of the extended and subtile views, from which originality ought to spring. His power of creating music is still undeveloped, but the tendency to imitate music which he has heard, and can even appreciate, is strong. Most immature lyrics indicate pretty clearly the favourite study of their authors. Sometimes they read like a weak version of the choric songs of Euripides: sometimes the versification smacks of the school of Pope, and not unfrequently it betrays an undue intimacy with the writings of Barry Cornwall. Nor is the resemblance always confined to the form; for ever and anon we stumble upon a sentiment or expression, so very marked and idiosyncratic as to leave no doubt whatever of its paternity.

The same remarks apply to prose composition. Distinctions of style occupy but a small share of academical attention; and that most important rhetorical exercise, the analysis of the Period, has fallen into general disregard. Rules for composition certainly exist, but they are seldom made the subject of prelection; and consequently bad models find their way into the hands, and too often pervert the taste, of the rising generation. The cramped, ungrammatical style of Carlyle, and the vague pomposity of Emerson, are copied by numerous pupils; the value of words has risen immensely in the literary market, whilst that of ideas has declined; in order to arrive at the meaning of an author of the new school, we are forced to crack a sentence as hard and angular as a hickory-nut, and, after all our pains, we are usually rewarded with no better kernel than a maggot.

The *Strayed Reveller* is rather a curious compound of imitation. He claims to be a classical scholar of no mean acquirements, and a good deal of his inspiration is traceable to the Greek dramatists. In certain of his poems he tries to think like Sophocles, and has so far succeeded as to have constructed certain choric passages, which might be taken by an unlettered person for translations from the antique. The language, though hard, is rather stately; and many of the individual images are by no means destitute of grace. The epithets which he employs bear the stamp of the Greek coinage; but, upon the whole, we must pronounce these specimens failures. The images are not bound together or grouped artistically, and the rhythm which the author has selected is, to an English ear, utterly destitute of melody. It is strange that people cannot be brought to understand that the genius and capabilities of one language differ essentially from those of another: and that the measures of antiquity are altogether unsuitable for modern verse. It is no doubt possible, by a Procrustean operation, to force words into almost any kind of mould; a chorus may be constructed, which, so far as scanning goes, might satisfy the requirements of a pedagogue, but the result of the experiment will inevitably show that melody has been sacrificed in the attempt. Now melody is a charm without which poetry is of little worth; we are not quite sure whether it would not be more correct to say, that without melody poetry has no existence. Our author does not seem to have the slightest idea of this; and accordingly he treats us to such passages as the following:—

[Quotes 'Fragment of an *Antigone*', ll. 45–75, 'No, no old man', etc.]

We are sincerely sorry to find the lessons of a good classical education applied to so pitiable a use; for if, out of courtesy, the above should be denominated verses, they are nevertheless as far removed from poetry as the Indus is from the pole. It is one thing to know the classics, and another to write classically. Indeed, if this be classical writing, it would furnish the best argument ever yet advanced against the study of the works of antiquity. Mr Tennyson, to whom, as we shall presently have occasion to observe, this author is indebted for another phase of his inspiration, has handled classical subjects with fine taste and singular delicacy; and his 'Ulysses' and 'Œnone' show how beautifully the Hellenic idea may be wrought out in mellifluous English verse. But Tennyson knows his craft too well to adopt either the Greek phraseology or the Greek rhythm. Even in the choric hymns which he has once or twice attempted, he has spurned halt and ungainly metres, and given full freedom and scope to the cadance of his mother tongue. These antique scraps of the *Reveller* are further open to a still more serious objection, which indeed is applicable to most of his poetry. We read them, marking every here and there some image of considerable beauty; but, when we have laid down the book, we are unable for the life of us to tell what it is all about. The poem from which the volume takes its name is a confused kind of chaunt about Circe, Ulysses, and the

Gods, from which no exercise of ingenuity can extract the vestige of a meaning. It has pictures which, were they introduced for any conceivable purpose, might fairly deserve some admiration; but, thrust in as they are, without method or reason, they utterly lose their effect, and only serve to augment our dissatisfaction at the perversion of a taste which, with so much culture, should have been capable of better things.

The adoption of the Greek choric metres, in some of the poems, appears to us the more inexplicable, because in others, when he descends from his classic altitudes, our author shows that he is by no means insensible to the power of melody. True, he wants that peculiar characteristic of a good poet—a melody of his own; for no poet is master of his craft unless his music is self-inspired: but, in default of that gift, he not unfrequently borrows a few notes or a tune from some of his contemporaries, and exhibits a fair command and mastery of his instrument. Here, for example, are a few stanzas, the origin of which nobody can mistake. They are an exact echo of the lyrics of Elizabeth Barrett Browning:—

[Quotes 'The New Sirens', ll. 41–64, 'Are the accents of your luring', etc.]

High and commanding genius is able to win our attention even in its most eccentric moods. Such genius belongs to Mrs Browning in a very remarkable degree, and on that account we readily forgive her for some forced rhyming, intricate diction, and even occasional obscurity of thought. But what shall we say of the man who seeks to reproduce her marvellous effects by copying her blemishes? Read the above lines, and you will find that, in so far as sound and mannerism go, they are an exact transcript from Mrs Browning. Apply your intellect to the discovery of their meaning, and you will rise from the task thoroughly convinced of its hopelessness. The poem in which they occur is entitled 'The New Sirens', but it might with equal felicity and point, have been called 'The New Harpies', or 'The Lay of the Hurdy-Gurdy'. It seems to us a mere experiment, for the purpose of showing that words placed together in certain juxtaposition, without any regard to their significance or propriety, can be made to produce a peculiar phonetic effect. The phenomenon is by no means a new one—it occurs whenever the manufacture of nonsense-verses is attempted; and it needed not the staining of innocent wire-wove to convince us of its practicability. Read the following stanza—divorce the sound from the sense, and then tell us what you can make of it:—

With a sad majestic motion—
With a stately slow surprise—
From their earthward-bound devotion
Lifting up your languid eyes:
Would you freeze my louder boldness,
Humbly smiling as you go!
One faint frown of distant coldness
Flitting fast across each marble brow?

What say you, Parson Sir Hugh Evans? 'The tevil with his tam; what phrase is this—*freeze my louder boldness*? Why, it is affectatious.'

If any one, in possession of a good ear, and with a certain facility for composing verse, though destitute of the inventive faculty, will persevere in imitating the style of different poets, he is almost certain at last to discover some writer whose peculiar manner he can assume with far greater facility than that of others. The *Strayed Reveller* fails altogether with Mrs Browning; because it is beyond his power, whilst following her, to make any kind of agreement between sound and sense. He is indeed very far from being a metaphysician, for his perception is abundantly hazy; and if he be wise, he will abstain from any future attempts at profundity. But he has a fair share of the painter's gift; and were he to cultivate that on his own account, we believe that he might produce something far superior to any of his present efforts. As it is, we can merely accord him the praise of sketching an occasional landscape, very like one which we might expect from Alfred Tennyson. He has not only caught the trick of Tennyson's handling, but he can use his colours with considerable dexterity. He is like one of those second-rate artists, who, with Danby in their eye, crowd our exhibitions with fiery sunsets and oceans radiant in carmine; sometimes their pictures are a little overlaid, but, on the whole, they give a fair idea of the manner of their undoubted master.

The following extract will, we think, illustrate our meaning. It is from a poem entitled 'Mycerinus', which, though it does not possess the interest of any tale, is correctly and pleasingly written:—

[Quotes 'Mycerinus', ll. 79–99, 'So spake he, half in anger', etc.]

This really is a pretty picture; its worst, and perhaps its only fault, being that it constantly reminds us of the superior original artist. Throughout the book indeed, and incorporated in many of the poems, there occur images to which Mr Tennyson has a decided right by priority of invention, and which the *Strayed Reveller* has 'conveyed' with little attention to ceremony. For example, in a poem which we never much admired, 'The Vision of Sin', Mr Tennyson has the two following lines—

> And on the glimmering limit, far withdrawn,
> God made himself an awful rose of dawn.

This image is afterwards repeated in 'The Princess'. Thus—

> Till the sun
> Grew broader toward his death and fell, and all
> The rosy heights came out above the lawns.

Young Danby catches at the idea, and straightway favours us with a copy—

> When the first rose-flush was steeping
> All the frore peak's awful crown.

The image is a natural one, and of course open to all the world, but the diction has been clearly borrowed.

Not only in blank verse but in lyrics does the Tennysonian tendency of our author break out, and to that tendency we owe by far the best poem in the present volume. 'The Forsaken Merman,' though the subject is fantastic, and though it has further the disadvantage of directly reminding us of one of Alfred's early extravaganzas, is nevertheless indicative of considerable power, not only of imagery and versification, but of actual pathos. A maiden of the earth has been taken down to the depths of the sea, where for years she has resided with her merman lover, and has borne him children. We shall let the poet tell the rest of his story, the more readily because we are anxious that he should receive credit for what real poetical accomplishment he possesses, and that he may not suppose, from our censure of his faults, that we are at all indifferent to his merits.

[Quotes 'The Forsaken Merman', ll. 48–107, 'Children dear, was it yesteryear', etc.]

Had the author given us much poetry like this, our task would, indeed, have been a pleasant one; but as the case is otherwise, we can do no more than point to the solitary pearl. Yet it is something to know that, in spite of imitation, and a taste which has gone far astray, this writer has powers, which, if properly directed and developed, might insure him a sympathy, which, for the present, must be withheld. Sympathy, indeed, he cannot look for, so long as he appeals neither to the heart, the affections, nor the passions of mankind, but prefers appearing before them in the ridiculous guise of a misanthrope. He would fain persuade us that he is a sort of Timon, who, despairing of the tendency of the age, wishes to wrap himself up in the mantle of necessity, and to take no part whatever in the vulgar concerns of existence. It is absolutely ridiculous to find this young gentleman—after confiding 'to a Republican friend' the fact that he despises

> The barren, optimistic sophistries
> Of comfortable moles, whom what they do
> Teaches the limit of the just and true,
> And for such doing have no need of eyes,—

thus favouring the public in a sonnet with his views touching the on-ward progress of society:—

[Quotes 'To a Republican Friend: Continued', in its entirety]

What would our friend be at? If he is a Tory, can't he find work enough in denouncing and exposing the lies of the League, and in taking up the cudgels for native industry? If he is a Whig, can't he be great upon sewerage, and the scheme of planting colonies in Con-naught, to grow corn and rear pigs at prices which will not pay for the manure and the hogs'-wash? If he is a Chartist, can't he say so, and stand up manfully with Julian Harney for 'the points', whatever may be their latest number? But we think that, all things considered, he had better avoid politics. Let him do his duty to God and man, work six hours a-day, whether he requires to do so for a livelihood or not, marry and get children, and, in his moments of leisure, let him still study Sophocles and amend his verses. But we hope that, whatever he does, he will not inflict upon us any more such platitudes as 'Resignation,' addressed 'to Fausta,' or any sonnets similar to that which he has writ-ten in *Emerson's Essays*. We tender our counsel with a most sincere regard for his future welfare; for, in spite of his many faults, the *Strayed Reveller* is a clever fellow; and though it cannot be averred that, up to the present time, he has made the most of fair talents and a first-rate education, we are not without hope that, some day or other, we may be able to congratulate him on having fairly got rid of his affected misanthropy, his false philosophy, and his besetting sin of imitation, and that he may yet achieve something which may come home to the heart, and secure the admiration of the public.

3. W. M. Rossetti, review, *Germ*

February 1850, no. 2, 84–96

William Michael Rossetti (1829–1919), brother of D. G. Rossetti, was a member of the Pre-Raphaelite brotherhood and editor of the *Germ*, the short-lived organ of the Pre-Raphaelites, in which this review of Arnold appeared. A sensitive reader—he was also a respected art critic—Rossetti offered an early, balanced assessment of Arnold, commenting on his range, his methods, and his likely reputation. Arnold's major flaw, according to Rossetti, is his want of 'passion'; but as a poet he has little to 'unlearn'.

If any one quality may be considered common to all living poets, it is that which we have heard aptly described as *self-consciousness*. In this many appear to see the only permanent trace of the now old usurping deluge of Byronism; but it is truly a fact of the time,—less a characteristic than a portion of it. Every species of composition—the dramatic, the narrative, the lyric, the didactic, the descriptive—is imbued with this spirit; and the reader may calculate with almost equal certainty on becoming acquainted with the belief of a poet as of a theologian or a moralist. Of the evils resulting from the practice, the most annoying and the worst is that some of the lesser poets, and all mere pretenders, in their desire to emulate the really great, feel themselves under a kind of obligation to assume opinions, vague, incongruous, or exaggerated, often not only not their own, but the direct reverse of their own,— a kind of meanness that has replaced, and goes far to compensate for, the flatteries of our literary ancestors. On the other hand, this quality has created a new tie of interest between the author and his public, enhances the significance of great works, and confers value on even the slightest productions of a true poet.

That the systematic infusion of this spirit into the drama and epic compositions is incompatible with strict notions of art will scarcely be disputed: but such a general objection does not apply in the case of lyric poetry, where even the character of the subject is optional. It is an instance of this kind that we are now about to consider.

The Strayed Reveller and other Poems, constitutes, we believe, the first published poetical work of its author, although the following would rather lead to the inference that he is no longer young.

> But my youth reminds me: 'Thou
> Hast lived light as these live now;
> As there are thou too wert such.'

And in another poem:

> In vain, all, all, in vain,
> They beat upon mine ear again,
> Those melancholy tones so sweet and still:
> Those lute-like tones which, in long-distant years,
> Did steal into mine ears.

Accordingly, we find but little passion in the volume, only four pieces (for 'The Strayed Reveller' can scarcely be so considered) being essentially connected with it. Of these the 'Modern Sappho' appears to us not only inferior, but as evidencing less maturity both of thought and style; the second, 'Stagyrus,' is an urgent appeal to God; the third, 'The New Sirens,' though passionate in utterance, is, in purpose, a rejection of passion, as having been weighed in the balance and found wanting; and, in the last, where he tells of the voice which once

> Blew such a thrilling summons to his will,
>   Yet could not shake it;
> Drained all the life his full heart had to spill;
>   Yet could not break it:

He records the 'intolerable change of thought' with which it now comes to his 'long-sobered heart.' Perhaps 'The Forsaken Merman' should be added to these; but the grief here is more nearly approaching to gloomy submission and the sickness of hope deferred.

The lessons that the author would learn of nature are, as set forth in the sonnet that opens the volume,

> Of toil unsevered from tranquillity;
>   Of labor that in one short hour outgrows
>   Man's noisy schemes,—accomplished in repose,
> Too great for haste, too high for rivalry.

His conception of the poet is of one who

> Sees before him life unroll,
> A placid and continuous whole;
> That general life which does not cease;
> Whose secret is, not joy, but peace;
> That life, whose dumb wish is not missed
> If birth proceeds, if things subsist;
> The life of plants and stones and rain;
> The life he craves:—if not in vain
> Fate gave, what chance shall not control,
> His sad lucidity of soul.—'Resignation'

Such is the author's purpose in these poems. He recognises in each thing a part of the whole: and the poet must know even as he sees, or breathes, as by a spontaneous, half-passive exercise of a faculty: he must receive rather than seek.

> Action and suffering tho' he know,
> He hath not lived, if he lives so.

Connected with this view of life as 'a placid and continuous whole,' is the principle which will be found here manifested in different modes, and thro' different phases of event, of the permanence and changelessness of natural laws, and of the large necessity wherewith they compel life and man. This is the thought which animates the 'Fragment of an "Antigone:" ' 'The World and the Quietist' has no other scope than this:—

> Critias, long since, I know,
> (For fate decreed it so),
> Long since the world hath set its heart to live.
> Long since, with credulous zeal,
> It turns life's mighty wheel:
> Still doth for laborers send;
> Who still their labor give.
> And still expects an end.

This principle is brought a step further into the relations of life in 'The Sick King in Bokhara,' the following passage from which claims to be quoted, not less for its vividness as description, than in illustration of this thought:—

[Quotes ll. 189–208, 'In vain therefore', etc.]

The author applies this basis of fixity in nature generally to the rules of man's nature, and avows himself a Quietist. Yet he would not despond, but contents himself, and waits. In no poem of the volume is this character more clearly defined and developed than in the sonnets 'To a Republican Friend,' the first of which expresses concurrence in certain broad progressive principles of humanity: to the second we would call the reader's attention, as to an example of the author's more firm and serious writing:—

[Quotes 'To a Republican Friend; Continued', in its entirety]

In the adjuration entitled 'Stagyrus,' already mentioned, he prays to be set free

> From doubt, where all is double,
> Where Faiths are built on dust;

and there seems continually recurring to him a haunting presage of the unprofitableness of the life, after which men have not 'any more a portion for ever in anything that is done under the sun.' Where he speaks of resignation, after showing how the less impetuous and self-concentred natures can acquiesce in the order of this life, even were it to bring them back with an end unattained to the place whence they set forth; after showing how it is the poet's office to live rather than to act in and thro' the whole life round about him, he concludes thus:

[Quotes 'Resignation', ll. 215–78, 'The world in which we live', etc.]

'Shall we,' he asks, 'go hence and find that our vain dreams are not dead? Shall we follow our vague joys, and the old dead faces, and the dead hopes?'

He exhorts man to be *in utrumque paratus*. If the world be the materialized thought of one all-pure, let him, 'by lonely pureness,' seek his way through the colored dream of life up again to that all-pure fount:—

> But, if the wild unfathered mass no birth
>   In divine seats hath known;
> In the blank echoing solitude, if earth,
> Rocking her obscure body to and fro,
>   Ceases not from all time to heave and groan,
> Unfruitful oft, and, at her happiest throe,
>   Forms what she forms, alone:

then man, the only self-conscious being, 'seeming sole to awake,' must, recognizing his brotherhood with this world which stirs at his feet unknown, confess that he too but seems.

Thus far for the scheme and the creed of the author. Concerning these we leave the reader to draw his own conclusions.

Before proceeding to a more minute notice of the various poems, we would observe that a predilection is apparent throughout for antiquity and classical association; not that strong love which made Shelley, as it were, the heir of Plato; not that vital grasp of conception which enabled Keats without, and enables Landor with, the most intimate knowledge of form and detail, to return to and renew the old thoughts and beliefs of Greece; still less the mere superficial acquaintance with names and hackneyed attributes which was once poetry. Of this conventionalism, however, we have detected two instances; the first, an allusion to 'shy Dian's horn' in 'breathless glades' of the days we live, peculiarly inappropriate in a sonnet addressed 'To George Cruikshank on his Picture of "The Bottle;"' the second a grave call to Memory to bring her tablets, occurring in, and forming the burden of, a poem strictly personal, and written for a particular occasion. But the author's partiality is shown, exclusively of such poems as 'Mycerinus' and 'The Strayed Reveller,' where the subjects are taken from antiquity, rather in the framing than in the ground work, as in the titles 'A Modern Sappho,' 'The New Sirens,' 'Stagyrus,' and '*In utrumque paratus.*' It is Homer and Epictetus and Sophocles who 'prop his mind;' the immortal air which the poet breathes is

> Where Orpheus and where Homer are;

and he addresses 'Fausta' and 'Critias.'

There are four narrative poems in the volume:— 'Mycerinus,' 'The Strayed Reveller,' 'The Sick King in Bokhara,' and 'The Forsaken Merman.' The first of these, the only one altogether narrative in form, founded on a passage in the 2nd Book of Herodotus, is the story of the six years of life portioned to a King of Egypt succeeding a father 'who had loved injustice and lived long;' and tells how he who had 'loved the good' revels out his 'six drops of time.' He takes leave of his people with bitter words, and goes out

> To the cool regions of the groves he loved . .
> Here came the king holding high feast at morn,
> Rose-crowned; and ever, when the sun went down,
> A hundred lamps beamed in the tranquil gloom,
> From tree to tree, all thro' the twinkling grove,
> Revealing all the tumult of the feast,
> Flushed guests, and golden goblets foamed with wine;

> While the deep-burnished foliage overhead
> Splintered the silver arrows of the moon.

(a daring image, verging towards a conceit, though not absolutely such, and the only one of that character that has struck us in the volume.)

> So six long years he revelled, night and day:
> And, when the mirth waxed loudest, with dull sound
> Sometimes from the grove's centre echoes came,
> To tell his wondering people of their king;
> In the still night, across the steaming flats,
> Mixed with the murmur of the moving Nile.

Here a Tennysonian influence is very perceptible, more especially in the last quotation; and traces of the same will be found in 'The Forsaken Merman.'

In this poem the story is conveyed by allusions and reminiscences whilst the Merman makes his children call after her who had returned to her own earth, hearing the Easter bells over the bay, and who is not yet come back for all the voices calling 'Margaret! Margaret!' The piece is scarcely long enough or sufficiently distinct otherwise than as a whole to allow of extract; but we cannot but express regret that a poem far from common-place either in subject or treatment should conclude with such sing-song as

> There dwells a loved one,
> But cruel is she;
> She left lonely for ever
> The kings of the sea.

'The Strayed Reveller' is written without rhyme—(not being blank verse, however,)—and not unfrequently, it must be admitted, without rhythm. Witness the following lines:

> Down the dark valley—I saw.—
> Trembling, I entered; beheld—
> Thro' the islands some divine bard.

Nor are these by any means the only ones that might be cited in proof; and, indeed, even where there is nothing precisely contrary to rhythm, the verse might, generally speaking, almost be read as prose. Seldom indeed, as it appears to us, is the attempt to write without some fixed laws of metrical construction attended with success; never, perhaps, can it be considered as the most appropriate embodiment of thought. The

METHODIST COLLEGE LIBRARY
Fayetteville, N. C.

082503

fashion has obtained of late years; but it is a fashion, and will die out. But few persons will doubt the superiority of the established blank verse, after reading the following passage, or will hesitate in pronouncing that it ought to be the rule, instead of the exception, in this poem;

[Quotes 'The Strayed Reveller', ll. 244-53, 'They see the merchants', etc.]

The Reveller, going to join the train of Bacchus in his temple, has strayed into the house of Circe and has drunk of her cup; he believes that, while poets can see and know only through participation in endurance, he shares the power belonging to the gods of seeing 'without pain, without labor;' and has looked over the valley all day long at the Maenads and Fauns, and Bacchus, 'sometimes, for a moment, passing through the dark Stems.' Apart from the inherent defects of the metre, there is great beauty of pictorial description in some passages of the poem, from which the following (where he is speaking of the gods) may be taken as a specimen:—

[Quotes ll. 151-61, 'They see the Indian', etc.]

From 'The Sick King in Bokhara,' we have already quoted at some length. It is one of the most considerable, and perhaps, as being the most simple and life-like, the best of the narrative poems. A vizier is receiving the dues from the cloth merchants, when he is summoned to the presence of the king, who is ill at ease, by Hussein; 'a teller of sweet tales.' Arrived, Hussein is desired to relate the cause of the king's sickness; and he tells how, three days since, a certain Moollah came before the king's path, calling for justice on himself, whom, deemed a fool or a drunkard, the guards pricked off with their spears, while the king passed on into the mosque: and how the man came on the morrow with yesterday's blood-spots on him, and cried out for right. What follows is told with great singleness and truth:

[Quotes ll. 58-132, 'Thou know'st, how fierce', etc.]

The Vizier counsels the king, that each man's private grief suffices him, and that he should not seek increase of it in the griefs of other men. But he answers him, (this passage we have before quoted,) that the king's lot and the poor man's is the same, for that neither has his will; and he takes order that the dead man be buried in his own royal tomb.

We know few poems the style of which is more unaffectedly without labor, and to the purpose, than this. The metre, however, of the earlier part is not always quite so uniform and intelligible as might be desired; and we must protest against the use, for the sake of rhyme, of *broke* in lieu of *broken*, as also of *stole* for *stolen* in 'The New Sirens.' While on the subject of style, we may instance, from the 'Fragment of an Antigone,' the following uncouth stanza, which, at the first reading, hardly appears to be correctly put together:

> But hush! Hœmon, whom Antigone,
>   Robbing herself of life in burying,
>   Against Creon's laws, Polynices,
>   Robs of a loved bride, pale, imploring,
>   Waiting her passage,
>   Forth from the palace hitherward comes.

Perhaps the most perfect and elevated in tone of all these poems is 'The New Sirens.' The author addresses, in imagination, a company of fair women, one of whose train he had been at morning; but in the evening he has dreamed under the cedar shade, and seen the same forms 'on shores and sea-washed places,'

> With blown tresses, and with beckoning hands.

He thinks how at sunrise he had beheld those ladies playing between the vines; but now their warm locks have fallen down over their arms. He prays them to speak and shame away his sadness; but there comes only a broken gleaming from their windows, which

> Reels and shivers on the ruffled gloom.

He asks them whether they have seen the end of all this, the load of passion and the emptiness of reaction, whether they dare look at life's latter days,

> When a dreary light is wading
>   Thro' this waste of sunless greens,
> When the flashing lights are fading
>   On the peerless cheek of queens,
> When the mean shall no more sorrow,
>   And the proudest no more smile;
> While the dawning of the morrow
> Widens slowly westward all that while?

And he implores them to 'let fall one tear, and set him free.' The past was no mere pretence; it was true while it lasted; but it is gone now, and the East is white with day. Shall they meet again, only that he may ask whose blank face that is?

> Pluck, pluck cypress, oh pale maidens;
> Dusk the hall with yew.

This poem must be read as a whole; for not only would it be difficult to select particular passages for extraction, but such extracts, if made, would fail in producing any adequate impression.

We have already quoted so largely from the concluding piece, 'Resignation,' that it may here be necessary to say only that it is in the form of speech held with 'Fausta' in retracing, after a lapse of ten years, the same way they had once trod with a joyful company. The tone is calm and sustained, not without touches of familiar truth.

The minor poems comprise eleven sonnets, among which, those 'To the Duke of Wellington, on hearing him mispraised,' and on 'Religious Isolation,' deserve mention; and it is with pleasure we find one, in the tenor of strong appreciation, written on reading the Essays of the great American, Emerson. The sonnet for 'Butler's Sermons' is more indistinct, and, as such, less to be approved, in imagery than is usual with this poet. That 'To an Independent Preacher who preached that we should be in harmony with nature,' seems to call for some remark. The sonnet ends with these words:

> Man must begin, know this, where nature ends;
> Nature and man can never be fast friends;
> Fool, if thou canst not pass her, rest her slave.

Now, as far as this sonnet shows of the discourse which occasioned it, we cannot see anything so absurd in that discourse; and where the author confutes the Independent preacher by arguing that

> Nature is cruel; man is sick of blood:
> Nature is stubborn; man would fain adore:
> Nature is fickle; man hath need of rest:

we cannot but think that, by attributing to nature a certain human degree of qualities, which will not suffice for man, he loses sight of the point really raised: for is not man's nature only a part of nature? and, if a part, necessary to the completeness of the whole? and should not the individual, avoiding a factitious life, order himself in conformity with his own rule of being? And, indeed, the author himself would converse with the self-sufficing progress of nature, with its rest in action, as distinguished from the troublous vexation of man's toiling:—

Two lessons, Nature, let me learn of thee,
  Two lessons that in every wind are blown;
  Two blending duties harmonised in one,
  Tho' the loud world proclaim their enmity.

The short lyric poem, 'To Fausta' has a Shelleian spirit and grace in it. 'The Hayswater Boat' seems a little *got up*, and is scarcely positive enough. This remark applies also, and in a stronger degree, to the 'Stanzas on a Gipsy Child' and the 'Modern Sappho', previously mentioned, which are the pieces least to our taste in the volume. There is a something about them of drawing-room sentimentality; and they might almost, without losing much save in size, be compressed into poems of the class commonly set to music. It is rather the basis of thought than the writing of the 'Gipsy Child,' which affords cause for objection; nevertheless, there is a passage in which a comparison is started between this child and a 'Seraph in an alien planet born,'—an idea not new, and never, as we think, worth much; for it might require some subtlety to show how a planet capable of producing a Seraph should be alien from that Seraph.

We may here notice a few cases of looseness, either of thought or of expression, to be met with in these pages; a point of style to be particularly looked to when the occurrence or the absence of such forms one very sensible difference between the first-rate and the second-rate poets of the present times.

Thus, in the sonnet 'Shakspear,' the conclusion says,

All pains the immortal spirit must endure,
  All weakness that impairs, all griefs that bow,
  Find their sole *voice* in that victorious brow;

whereas a brow's voice remains to be uttered: nor, till the nature of the victory gained by the brow shall have been pointed out, are we able to hazard an opinion of the precise value of the epithet.

In the address to George Cruikshank, we find: 'Artist, whose hand with horror *winged;*' where a similar question arises; and, returning to the 'Gipsy Child,' we are struck with the unmeaningness of the line:

Who massed round that slight brow these clouds of doom?

Nor does the following, from the first of the sonnets, 'To a Republican Friend,' appear reconcileable with any ideas of appropriateness:

> While before me *flow*
> The *armies* of the homeless and unfed.

It is but right to state that the only instances of the kind we remember throughout the volume have now been mentioned.

To conclude. Our extracts will enable the reader to judge of this Poet's style: it is clear and comprehensive, and eschews flowery adornment. No particular model has been followed, though that general influence which Tennyson exercises over so many writers of this generation may be traced here as elsewhere. It may be said that the author has little, if anything, to unlearn. Care and consistent arrangement, and the necessary subordination of the parts to the whole, are evident throughout; the reflective, which appears the more essential form of his thought, does not absorb the due observation or presentment of the outward facts of nature; and a well-poised and serious mind shows itself in every page.

EMPEDOCLES ON ETNA

1852

---

4. G. D. Boyle, unsigned review, *North British Review*

May 1853, ix, 209–14

George David Boyle (1828–1901) was to become an influential cleric and served as Dean of Salisbury during the last twenty years of his life. For Boyle, 'Poetry is scarce', and indeed the age itself seems inimical to poetry. Boyle's dissatisfaction with the mannerisms of the Pre-Raphaelites, his desire for a more 'healthy' verse, and for the climate that would make it possible, reflect some of Arnold's own preoccupations. Ironically, Boyle prods the poet of 'Empedocles' to introduce more *action*, anticipating the dominant theme of the 1853 preface. His comment that '"A." constantly disappoints us' was to recur in Arnold criticism.

Poetry is scarce. Our age, famous as it is in many ways—abounding in great deeds, and far from being destitute of great men—seems unfavourable to the growth of the ever welcome flower. Many volumes of verses are published annually, evincing taste, feeling, and sometimes an artistic carefulness and finish. There is no indifference on the part of the public; on the contrary, we feel convinced that the '*Vates Sacer*,'[1] were he to come among us, could easily command an audience. The encouragement so freely afforded to anything which looks like promise, and the indulgence displayed to the poets of America, are the best proofs we could advance in favour of the existence of a genuine love of poetry.

[1] 'sacred prophet, or seer'.

It would be ungenerous to omit mention of an improvement which has taken place in the tone of many of our writers of verse. That there is often a delicacy and purity of feeling, a desire after noble objects of ambition, and what is better than either, an earnest and sometimes pathetic expression of sympathy for the wants of the poor, few of those who are in the habit of bestowing attention on the literature of the day will feel inclined to deny. For the higher attributes and mysterious qualities of song, we look in vain. But at least let us be grateful for the absence of misanthropical monodies, and voluptuous love songs. There is another peculiarity in many of the recently published volumes of verses, which can hardly fail to force itself on the notice of every reader. We mean the unmistakeable traces which they bear of the influence exercised on his age and contemporaries by Mr. Tennyson. When the earlier poems of Tennyson first made their appearance, the admirers and disciples of the sensational school claimed their author for themselves. In his more recent productions, however, the poet has shown himself in an entirely new light. The debateable land that lies between the regions of sensation and the regions of thought, Mr. Tennyson has fairly claimed to hold. Where a great genius walks securely, how few there be that can follow! In the efforts of the pupils there is a want of proportion, and an absence of harmony which render the varied ease and facile gracefulness of the master only more apparent. It is far from unnatural that the younger portion of the community should fix their admiration on the poet who is nearest them. Grave seniors may hint at the propriety of rigid adherence to classic models, and point to 'the pure well of English undefiled,'—but in spite of all that has been, or that can be said, the poet whose verse comes bounding over the soul, who is continually in the thoughts and language of youth, must be he who has felt the difficulties, and perhaps solved the problems of the present time. There is one, it is true, who is for all ages and for all times, but it is rare to discover that the first affections of male or female students of poetry centre in Shakspeare. 'Knowledge comes, but wisdom lingers.'

But it is time to turn from our somewhat desultory reflections and introduce our readers to 'A.'

The Strayed Reveller has been before the world for some time, and was, we believe, favourably noticed by more than one journal, on its first appearance. It is in all respects a pleasing and interesting collection. The writer, evidently a man of high culture, gave in this volume a promise of excellence which, we regret to say, his last production, *Empedocles on Etna*, has not fulfilled. The poems in the first volume, as regards smoothness of rhythm, and elaboration of style, are strikingly superior to those of the second. Nor is the philosophy and general tone of the *Reveller* improved in *Empedocles*. An indolent, selfish quietism pervades everything that 'A.' has written, mars the pleasure of the reader, and provokes him into thinking severe thoughts about the poet. But 'A.' is a poet. He has held deep communion with nature. He has studied in a way that we wish was more common than it is. From the works of Sophocles, and Homer, Goethe, and Wordsworth, he has gathered fruits, and he has garnished his gains with fresh blooming flowers of his own. The *Strayed Reveller* is an imitation of the antique. Though containing some fine imagery, there is little which we care to extract. A 'Fragment from an Antigone' is well executed, but hardly worth the trouble which must have been bestowed upon it. As a specimen of the graceful fashion in which 'A.' can write, we give the following poem, 'To my friends, who ridiculed a tender leave-taking.' It reminds us in many ways of Goethe:—

[Quotes 'A Memory Picture', ll. 1–24, 'Laugh, my friends', etc.]

There is grace and pathos in the poem of 'The Forsaken Merman,' but it recalls certain poems of Tennyson rather too vividly. 'The New Sirens' does more than recall Mrs. Browning, and that too by no means in her happiest mood. We advise our friends to avoid 'The Sick King in Bokhara,' and assure them that there is nothing to be gained from the mystical pieces addressed to Fausta.

'A.' constantly disappoints us. We are in hopes all throughout his volumes that we are about to be delighted with a flow of melody, or a noble train of sentiment. He is often on the verge of excellence. He has been astride Pegasus. We can hardly venture to assert that he has ridden him.

'Empedocles on Etna' is an utter mistake. If fills seventy pages, and though the author calls it a drama, it hardly possesses one attribute of dramatic poetry. Every thing about it is modern. But the thoughts and images which the author has accumulated in this poem are often original. Callicles, a young harp-player, has followed the sage up the mountain side, and endeavours by snatches of song to soothe the sorrows of Empedocles. Here is an exquisite description of the scene:—

[Quotes ll. 36–48, 'The track winds down', etc.]

Oh *si sic omnia*![1] But alas, 'A.' has indulged to excess in poems of a

[1] 'If only it were all like this!'

meditative cast, reflecting, indeed, the culture and refinement of their author's mind, but failing to touch the reader. 'Tristram and Iseult' display the author's characteristic power to great advantage. 'The Memorial Verses' on Wordsworth's death, originally published in *Fraser's Magazine*, are really very memorable. Our readers will thank us for

[Quotes 'Longing' in its entirety]

There are indications throughout these volumes that the glorious scenery which surrounds the English lakes has especial attraction for 'A.' When we next meet with him, we trust that his poetry will exhibit more than it does at present of the severe manliness and exalted tone which must ever be associated in the minds of lovers of poetry with the hills and dales of Westmoreland. Less of aversion to action in all its forms,—greater sympathy with the wants of the present generation, will endear him to many who would now turn away contemptuously from the self-complacent reverie, and refined indolence, which too often disfigure his pages. It is not merely as an artist that men love to regard a favourite poet. He must not only himself obey the dominion of moral and religious ideas, he must do more—he must teach others to go and do likewise. But, when all deductions have been made, and every critical objection has been stated, there still remains enough in the poetry of 'A.' to justify a warm eulogy, and to entitle us to hope that he may yet produce poems worthy of a higher praise.

5. A. H. Clough, 'Recent English Poetry', *North American Review*

July 1853, lxxvii, 12–24

Arthur Hugh Clough (1819–61), commemorated in Arnold's 'Thyrsis' (1867), was at once an intimate of Arnold's and a rival poet. Although a long way from home (in fact he was returning from America when the review appeared), Clough offered a cool assessment of his friend's poems. But the two men had disagreed almost consistently about poetry in general and about the respective merits of their own poems, so that Arnold was probably forewarned. He did write, after the review appeared: 'There is no one to whose aperçus I attach the value I do to yours—but I think you are sometimes—with regard to *me* especially—a little cross and wilful.'

Empedocles on Etna and other Poems, with its earlier companion volume, *The Strayed Reveller and other Poems,* are it would seem, the productions (as is, or was, the English phrase) of a scholar and a gentleman; a man who has received a refined education, seen refined 'society', and been more, we dare say, in the world, which is called the world, than in all likelihood has a Glasgow mechanic. More refined therefore, and more highly educated sensibilities,—too delicate, are they, for common service?—a calmer judgment also, a more poised and steady intellect, the *siccum lumen*[1] of the soul; a finer and rarer aim perhaps, and certainly a keener sense of difficulty, in life;—these are the characteristics of him whom we are to call 'A.' Empedocles, the sublime Sicilian philosopher, the fragments of whose moral and philosophic poems testify to his genius and character,—Empedocles, in the poem before us, weary of misdirected effort, weary of imperfect thought, impatient of a life which appears to him a miserable failure, and incapable, as he conceives, of doing any thing that shall be true to that proper interior self,

[1] 'dry light'.

> Being one with which we are one with the whole world,

wandering forth, with no determined purpose, into the mountain solitudes, followed for a while by Pausanias, the eager and laborious physician, and at a distance by Callicles, the boy-musician, flings himself at last, upon a sudden impulse and apparent inspiration of the intellect, into the boiling crater of Etna; rejoins there the elements. 'Slave of sense,' he was saying, pondering near the verge.

[Quotes 'Empedocles', ll. 390–417, 'Slave of sense', etc.]

The music of the boy Callicles, to which he chants his happy mythic stories, somewhat frigidly perhaps, relieves, as it sounds in the distance, the gloomy catastrophe.

Tristram and Iseult (these names form the title of the next and only other considerable poem) are, in the old romantic cycle of North-France and Germany, the hero and the heroine of a mournful tale. Tristram of Lyonness, the famed companion of King Arthur, received in youth a commission to bring from across the sea the Princess Iseult of Ireland, the destined bride of the King of Cornwall. The mother of the beautiful princess gave her, as a parting gift, a cup of a magic wine, which she and her royal husband should drink together on their marriage-day in their palace at Tyntagil; so they should love each other perfectly and forever.

[Paraphrases the story and quotes widely from Parts I and II]

When we open upon Part III.,

> A year had flown, and in the chapel old
> Lay Tristram and Queen Iseult dead and cold.

Beautiful, simple, old mediæval story! We have followed it, led on as much by its own intrinsic charm as by the form and coloring—beautiful too, but indistinct—which our modern poet has given it. He is obscure at times, and hesitates and falters in it; the knights and dames, we fear, of old North-France and Western Germany would have been grievously put to it to make him out. Only upon a fourth re-reading, and by the grace of a happy moment, did we satisfy our critical conscience that, when the two lovers have sunk together in death, the knight on his pillows, and Queen Iseult kneeling at his side, the poet, after passing to the Cornish court where she was yesternight, returns to address himself to a hunter with his dogs, worked in the tapestry of the chamber here, whom he conceives to be pausing in the pictured

chase, and staring, with eyes of wonder, on the real scene of the pale
knight on the pillows and the kneeling lady fair. But

> Cheer, cheer thy dogs into the brake,
> O hunter! and without a fear
> Thy golden-tasselled bugle blow,
> And through the glade thy pastime take!
> For thou wilt rouse no sleepers here,
> For these thou seest are unmoved;
> Cold, cold as those who lived and loved
> A thousand years ago.

Fortunately, indeed, with the commencement of Part III., the most
matter-of-fact quarterly conscience may feel itself pretty well set at
ease by the unusually explicit statements that

> A year had fled; and in the chapel old
> Lay Tristram and Queen Iseult dead and cold.
> The young surviving Iseult, one bright day
> Had wandered forth; her children were at play
> In a green circular hollow in the heath
> Which borders the sea shore; a country path
> Creeps over it from the tilled fields behind.

Yet anon, again and thicker now perhaps than ever, the mist of more
than poetic dubiousness closes over and around us. And as he sings to us
about the widowed lady Iseult, sitting upon the sea-banks of Brittany,
watching her bright-eyed children, talking with them and telling them
old Breton stories, while still, in all her talk and her story, her own
dreamy memories of the past, and perplexed thought of the present,
mournfully mingle, it is really all but impossible to ascertain her, or
rather his, real meanings. We listen, indeed, not quite unpleased, to a
sort of faint musical mumble, conveying at times a kind of subdued
half-sense, or intimating, perhaps, a three-quarters-implied question;
Is any thing real!—is love any thing?—what is any thing?—is there
substance enough even in sorrow to mark the lapse of time?—is not
passion a diseased unrest?—did not the fairy Vivian, when the wise
Merlin forgot his craft to fall in love with her, wave her wimple over
her sleeping adorer?

> Nine times she waved the fluttering wimple round,
> And made a little plot of magic ground;
> And in that daisied circle, as men say,
> Is Merlin prisoner to the judgment day,

73

> But she herself whither she will can rove,
> For she was passing weary of his love.

Why or wherefore, or with what purport, who will venture exactly to say?—but such, however, was the tale which, while Tristram and his first Iseult lay in their graves, the second Iseult, on the sea-banks of Brittany, told her little ones.

And yet, dim and faint as is the sound of it, we still prefer this dreamy patience, the soft submissive endurance of the Breton lady, and the human passions and sorrows of the Knight and the Queen, to the high, and shall we say, pseudo-Greek inflation of the philosopher musing above the crater and the boy Callicles, singing myths upon the mountain.

In the earlier volume, one of the most generally admired pieces was 'The Forsaken Merman.'

> Come, dear children, let us away
> Down, and away below,

says the Merman, standing upon the sea-shore, whither he and his children came up to call back the human Margaret, their mother, who had left them to go, for one day—for Easterday—to say her prayers with her kinsfolk in the little gray church on the shore:

> 'Twill be Easter-time in the world—ah me,
> And I lose my poor soul, Merman, here with thee.

And when she staid, and staid on, and it seemed a long while, and the little ones began to moan, at last, up went the Merman with the little ones to the shore, and so on into the town, and to the little gray church, and there looked in through the small leaded panes of the window. There she sits in the aisle; but she does not look up, her eyes are fixed upon the holy page; it is in vain we try to catch her attention.

> Come away, children, call no more,
> Come away, come down, call no more.

Down, down to the depths of the sea. She will live up there and be happy, among the things she had known before. Yet sometimes a thought will come across her; there will be times when she will

> Steal to the window and look at the sand;
> And over the sand at the sea;
> And anon there breaks a sigh,
> And anon there drops a tear,

From a sorrow-clouded eye,
And a heart sorrow-laden,
A long, long sigh,
For the cold strange eyes of a little mermaiden,
And the gleam of her golden hair.

Come away, children, come down. We will be happy in our bright
home under the sea—happy, though the cruel one leaves us lonely for
ever. Yet we too, sometimes at midnight, when winds blow softly,
and the moonlight falls clear,

[Quotes ll. 132–43]

It is a beautiful poem, certainly; and deserves to have been given at
full length. 'The Strayed Reveller' itself is more ambitious, perhaps a
little strained. It is a pleasing and significant imagination, however, to
present to us Circe and Ulysses in colloquy with a stray youth from
the train of Bacchus, who drinks eagerly the cup of the enchantress,
not as did the sailors of the Ithacan king, for gross pleasure, but for the
sake of the glorious and superhuman vision and knowledge it imparts.

Does the reader require morals and meanings to these stories? What
shall they be, then?—the deceitfulness of knowledge, and the illusiveness
of the affections, the hardness and roughness and contrariousness of the
world, the difficulty of living at all, the impossibility of doing any thing,
—*voilà tout!* A charitable and patient reader, we believe, (such as is the
present reviewer,) will find in the minor poems that accompany these
pieces, intimations—what more can reader or reviewer ask?—of some
better and further thing than these, some approximations to a kind of
confidence, some incipiences of a degree of hope, some roots, retaining
some vitality of conviction and moral purpose.

[Quotes 'A Farewell', ll. 49–60, 'And though we wear out life', etc.]

In the future, it seems, there is something for us; and for the present also,
which is more germane to our matter, we have discovered some precepts about 'hope, light, and *persistence*,' which we intend to make the
most of. Meantime, it is one promising point in our author of the initial,
that his second is certainly on the whole an improvement upon his
first volume. There is less obvious study of effect; upon the whole, a
plainer and simpler and less factitious manner and method of treatment.
This, he may be sure, is the only safe course. Not by turning and twisting
his eyes, in the hope of seeing things as Homer, Sophocles, Virgil, or
Milton saw them; but by seeing them, by accepting them as he sees

them, and faithfully depicting accordingly, will he attain the object he desires.

[Digresses on 'taste' and begins comparison with Alexander Smith]

Let us remark also in the minor Poems, which accompany Empedocles, a disposition, perhaps, to assign too high a place to what is called Nature. It may indeed be true, as the astronomers say, though after all it is no very great piece of knowledge, that the heavenly bodies describe ellipses; and go on, from and to all the ages, performing that self-repeating, unattaining curve. But does it, therefore, of necessity follow that human souls do something analogous in the spiritual spaces? Number is a wonderful thing, and the laws of nature sublime; nevertheless, have we not a sort of intuition of the existence, even in our own poor human selves, of something akin to a Power superior to, and transcending, all manifestations of Nature, all intelligible forms of Number and Law. We quote one set of verses, in which our author does appear to have escaped for once from the dismal cycle of his rehabilitated Hindoo-Greek theosophy—

[Quotes 'Morality' in its entirety]

It is wonderful what stores of really valuable thought may lie neglected in a book, simply because they are not put in that form which serves our present occasions. But if we have been inclined to yield to a preference for the picture of simple, strong, and certain, rather than of subtle, shifting, and dubious feelings, and in point of tone and matter to go along with the young mechanic, in point of diction and manner, we must certainly assign the palm to 'A,' in spite of a straining after the rounded Greek form, such as, to some extent, vitiates even the style of Milton.

[Continues his comparison of Arnold and Alexander Smith, whom in some ways he finds the better writer]

POEMS

1853, 1854, 1855

---

6. G. H. Lewes, 'Schools of Poetry, Arnold's Poems', *Leader*

26 November and 3 December 1853, iv, 1146–7, 1169–71

George Henry Lewes (1817–78) is now best known for his relationship with George Eliot, whom he met in 1851; but Lewes was also an energetic contributor to—and editor of—various periodicals, a scientific writer, and the author of a pioneer work on Goethe. Lewes had reviewed Arnold's first two volumes, rather coolly, earlier in 1853, and he was to review *Merope* a few years later. Although he liked *Merope* and its classicism, his main comments on the 1853 volume concern the preface, which he finds the work of 'a scholar' rather than the expression of a man 'of poetical genius'.

I

It is with individuals as with nations, the baffled turbulence of Youth subsides into the calm acquiescence of Age, but in both the ideal is placed beyond the Present. Jean Paul has said, 'Keiner ist mit der Zeit zufrieden: das heisst die Jünglinge halten die Künftige für idealer als die Gegenwärtige, die Alten die Vergangene,' (None are content with the age: the young believe the Future, the old the Past to be the ideal era.) And with this we may connect what Goethe says of all men being Radicals in their youth, and Conservatives in their old age. We see a Goethe and a Schiller escaping from the notoriety of the 'storm and stress period' which they had created, into Grecian classicality, just as we see the unrestrained and 'chartered libertinism' of the Elizabethan

77

period changing to the classicality of Charles and Anne, which in its turn was to be set aside by a 'new school;' and that new school, now old, will perhaps have to give place to another revival of the classical: indications whereof may be read in the vehement protests against Tennyson and Alexander Smith, as also in the artistic strivings of some poets, Arnold among the number. Scorn of the past we hold to be as unwise as scorn of 'our wondrous Mother-Age;' but with whatever reverence and retrospective longing the Past is regarded, it should always be regarded as *past:* it should have historical, not absolute significance: it is our Ancestry, and not our Life. And as the retention in our organism of the elements which *have lived* is in itself a fatal source of destruction, poisoning the very life these elements once served, so in the onward progression of Humanity the old elements must pass away, transmitting to successors the work they had to perform:

'Et quasi cursores vitae lampada tradunt!'[1]

Matthew Arnold, in the Preface to this new edition of his poems, defends himself against those critics who bid him 'leave the exhausted past, and fix his thoughts upon the present.' It seems to him that his critics know very little of what they are talking about. Whatever he may once have thought of 'Our Age,' it is clear he does not now regard it as so fruitful in poetry as the olden time; and all he says on this point is worthy of attention:—

What are the eternal objects of Poetry, among all nations, and at all times? They are actions; human actions; possessing an inherent interest in themselves, and which are to be communicated in an interesting manner by the art of the Poet. Vainly will the latter imagine that he has everything in his own power; that he can make an intrinsically inferior action equally delightful with a more excellent one by his treatment of it: he may indeed compel us to admire his skill, but his work will possess, within itself, an incurable defect.

The Poet, then, has in the first place to select an excellent action; and what actions are the most excellent? Those, certainly, which most powerfully appeal to the great primary human affections: to those elementary feelings which subsist permanently in the race, and which are independent of time. These feelings are permanent and the same; that which interests them is permanent and the same also. The modernness or antiquity of an action, therefore, has nothing to do with its fitness for poetical representation; this depends upon its inherent qualities. To the elementary part of our nature, to our passions, that which is great and passionate is eternally interesting; and interesting solely in proportion to its greatness and to its passion. A great human action of a thousand years ago is more

---

[1] 'And as if the runners hand over the lamp of life.'

interesting to it than a smaller human action of to-day, even though upon the representation of this last the most consummate skill may have been expended, and though it has the advantage of appealing by its modern language, familiar manners, and contemporary allusions, to all our transient feelings and interests. These, however, have no right to demand of a poetical work that it shall satisfy them; their claims are to be directed elsewhere. Poetical works belong to the domain of our permanent passions: let them interest these, and the voice of all subordinate claims upon them is at once silenced.

Achilles, Prometheus, Clytemnestra, Dido—what modern poem presents personages as interesting, even to us moderns, as these personages of an 'exhausted past?' We have the domestic epic dealing with the details of modern life which pass daily under our eyes; we have poems representing modern personages in contact with the problems of modern life, moral, intellectual, and social; these works have been produced by poets the most distinguished of their nation and time; yet I fearlessly assert that Hermann and Dorothea, Childe Harold, Jocelyn, The Excursion, leave the reader cold in comparison with the effect produced upon him by the latter books of the Iliad, by the Orestea, or by the episode of Dido. And why is this? Simply because in the three latter cases the action is greater, the personages nobler, the situations more intense; and this is the true basis of the interest in a poetical work, and this alone.

It may be urged, however, that past actions may be interesting in themselves, but that they are not to be adopted by the modern Poet, because it is impossible for him to have them clearly present to his own mind, and he cannot therefore feel them deeply, nor represent them forcibly. But this is not necessarily the case. The externals of a past action, indeed, he cannot know with the precision of a contemporary; but his business is with its essentials. The outward man of Œdipus or of Macbeth, the houses in which they lived, the ceremonies of their courts, he cannot accurately figure to himself; but neither do they essentially concern him. His business is with their inward man; with their feelings and behaviour in certain tragic situations, which engage their passions as men; these have in them nothing local and casual: they are as accessible to the modern Poet as to a contemporary.

The date of an action, then, signifies nothing: the action itself, its selection and construction, this is what is all-important. This the Greeks understood far more clearly than we do. The radical difference between their poetical theory and ours consists, as it appears to me, in this: that, with them, the poetical character of the action in itself, and the conduct of it, was the first consideration; with us, attention is fixed mainly on the value of the separate thoughts and images which occur in the treatment of an action. They regarded the whole; we regard the parts. With them, the action predominated over the expression of it; with us, the expression predominates over the action. Not that they failed in expression, or were inattentive to it; on the contrary, they are the highest models of expression, the unapproached masters of the *grand style*: but their expression is so excellent because it is so admirably kept in its right degree of prominence; because it is so simple and so well subordinated; because it draws its force directly from the pregnancy of the matter which it conveys.

There is excellent matter amid some that is questionable here. We remark, in passing, that he maintains opinions respecting the Greek and Latin poets, which are *traditional,* but which, to our experience, are very far removed from the truth. We will not, however, encumber the argument by questioning his illustrations; let us grant for a moment that the Greeks *are* what he describes, and quote his criticism on the contrasted defects of modern poets:—

We have poems which seem to exist merely for the sake of single lines and passages; not for the sake of producing any total-impression. We have critics who seem to direct their attention merely to detached expressions, to the language about the action, not to the action itself. I verily think that the majority of them do not in their hearts believe that there is such a thing as a total-impression to be derived from a poem at all, or to be demanded from a poet; they think the term a commonplace of metaphysical criticism. They will permit the Poet to select any action he pleases, and to suffer that action to go as it will, provided he gratifies them with occasional bursts of fine writing, and with a shower of isolated thoughts and images. That is, they permit him to leave their poetical sense ungratified, provided that he gratifies their rhetorical sense and their curiosity. Of his neglecting to gratify these, there is little danger; he needs rather to be warned against the danger of attempting to gratify these alone; he needs rather to be perpetually reminded to prefer his action to everything else; so to treat this, as to permit its inherent excellences to develope themselves, without interruption from the intrusion of his personal peculiarities: most fortunate, when he most entirely succeeds in effacing himself, and in enabling a noble action to subsist as it did in nature.

True, most true, and needful to be said. But when he lays it down as a canon that the 'highest problem of an art is to imitate actions,' he seems to us either to employ an abusive extension of the term 'action,' or else to misconceive the problem and the function of Art. Indeed, one may say that Art is only an imitation of actions in its earliest and rudest forms. He himself is forced to admit that according to this canon *Faust* is not a great work of Art:—

Wonderful passages as it contains, and in spite of the unsurpassed beauty of the scenes which relate to Margaret, Faust itself, judged as a whole, and judged strictly as a poetical work is defective: its illustrious author, the greatest poet of modern times, the greatest critic of all times, would have been the first to acknowledge it; he only defended his work, indeed, by asserting it to be 'something incommensurable.'

A canon which excludes *Faust*, must *ipso facto* be suspicious. But Mr. Arnold's friends, the Ancients, will also fare badly if this rule be applied to them; even among the dramatists, in spite of action being the *principium et fons*[1] of the drama, one meets with a *Philoctetes* for example, of which no one will say that the interest or beauty lies in the action; and if we turn to the *Divine Comedy* we shall find it as defective as *Faust* according to this rule. Actions are not ends in Art, but means to an end; they are not for their own sake, but for the sake of the thoughts and emotions they excite in us. Admirable as means, they are still only means. If the poet can reach his end through other means we do not tell him he has sinned against Art.

Turn to the other forms of Art, and the incorrectness of the canon will be obvious: it is not through action that Music reaches its effect; it is not through the representation of any story that Sculpture necessarily excites in us the emotions proper to it. Titian's portrait of a 'Young Man with a Glove' is a finer work of Art than Haydon's 'Judgment of Solomon;' although one has no story, no action, the other a noble story, and a situation of deep interest. It may be answered that Haydon has ill-executed his idea; but this draws the question from the 'choice of a subject,' to that of 'representation;' and while it is a truism to assert that execution being equal, rank will depend on the greatness of the thing represented, it is a falsism to assert the rank of a work of Art depends on its *idea*—its conception. Not that Mr. Arnold asserts this, but others do who start from the same point.

It is to the classics Mr. Arnold would have our poets turn for guidance. Dissatisfied with the Present, and having no vision of it as an ideal life, he is also dissatisfied with its utterances in Art:

> Ah! how unlike
> To that large utterance of the early gods!

Overlooking the fact that if a man has something of his age to say or sing, some expression by which he can make articulate what is inarticulate in the mass or class of which he is one, he will imperiously say or sing it without much regard to 'models' at all, Mr. Arnold tells us:

The confusion of the present times is great, the multitude of voices counselling different things bewildering, the number of existing works capable of attracting a young writer's attention and of becoming his models, immense: all he wants is a hand to guide him through the confusion, a voice to prescribe to

[1] 'source and fountain'.

him the aim which he should keep in view, and to explain to him that the value of the literary works which offer themselves to his attention is relative to their power of helping him forward on his road towards this aim. Such a guide the English writer at the present day will nowhere find.

Shakespeare he considers a dangerous model (but indeed all models are dangerous to minds that 'copy' them), and he prefers the Greeks. If his counsel be rightly interpreted, it will be useful to that large class of Amateurs who write verse but who are not 'born Singers;' but, if rigidly interpreted, it will lead the despairing classicists to exclaim with Charles Lamb, 'Hang the critics, *I'll write for antiquity!*'

Our own belief is, that schools of poetry are the changing fashions of one eternal spirit; and that good poetry is everywhere the same in its essential conditions, everywhere fluctuating with the fluctuating modes of thought and language. Further our belief is, that all conscious imitation is weakness, and that 'models' produce no real good, though little harm, because the servile mind is one which if emancipated would not be strong. To study models with a view to *emulate* them is not the same as to study them with a view to *imitate* them; the one is an invigorating —the other an enervating study.

We have tarried so long over Mr. Arnold's preface that we must defer till next week all attempt to characterise his poems.

II

Having in a previous article discussed the propositions of Mr. Arnold's preface, and tried to come to an understanding on the subject of his critical precepts, we have now to consider his practice, and to read his poems in the light of his precepts.

Study the Classics, and beware of the syren-charms which enervate the Moderns! that is the text from which he preaches. The logical consequence is Imitation.

Study the Classics, and the Moderns too, but beware of the rudeness and baldness of the one, no less than of the rhetoric and glitter of the other! That is our text. For we believe the Ancients to have had every virtue and every vice conspicuous in the Moderns, over and above the *remoteness* of their ideas and feelings, which to us moderns becomes a vice. When the Classics are good, they are so by virtue of qualities essential in all excellent works of Art; when they are bad, which is mostly the case, they are so by vice of qualities noticeable in every age—rudeness, incongruity, untruth, greater regard for manner than for matter, and for the mere fopperies of manner. Homer, with all his fine qualities, is as rude as hemp; Æschylus is often as fantastic, obscure, and incongruous, and Virgil as feeble, affected, and unpictorial as the very worst specimens which can be selected from eminent poets of Modern times. To deny this would be to deny evidence. It is the traditional belief, but it is a fact.

Such being our critical faith, instead of Imitation we counsel Emulation; instead of following the mere fashions of Greek Art, follow no fashions but those which bear the general verdict of your age, and while learning from the Greeks the lessons they and all great artists have to teach, beware, above all things, of imitating them.

Mr. Arnold, as a scholar, and one of poetical tendencies rather than of poetical genius, a man of culture, reflection, and sensibility, but not forming one of that small band of Singers who 'sing as the birds sing,' naturally looks towards Greece for inspiration. His poems will delight scholars, who will with curious pleasure follow him in his undisguised imitations of works which long have been their ideals; they will note his curiosities of verse, and his Græcism of imagery. Nor will the larger public read without delight. Poems such as these are not common. Some of the qualities most easily appreciable these poems possess, and they will secure an audience. But the fit audience is that of the cultured few. The longest poem in the volume, *Sohrab and Rustum,* will be the greatest favourite, for it tells an intelligible and interesting story, and the story moves through pictures and pathos such as we rarely meet in 'volumes of poetry.' It has its Græcisms, but they are little more than ornaments of questionable taste; the real attractiveness lies in the qualities just named. Let a brief analysis make this apparent.

Sohrab, who is Rustum's son, unknown to Rustum, is everywhere seeking his father; and the place most certain to find Rustum is a battle-field. In order that his fame may reach his father's ear, Sohrab entreats to be allowed to challenge, in single combat, a champion from the Persian ranks. The request is granted. In the following graphic description of the filing hosts, the reader will have no difficulty in tracing Homer and Milton:—

[Quotes 'Sohrab and Rustum', ll. 104–69, 'The sun, by this, had risen' etc.]

The imitation mars this for all except scholars. But, to continue. The Persians accept the challenge, and then go to Rustum's tent, as the Greeks did to that of Achilles, and implore his arm:

[Paraphrases and quotes extensively from the poem]

It will be confessed that this is far from ordinary writing. The poem, indeed, is not an ordinary production; but we should have an easy task to show that its excellencies are not derived from the Greek, although most of its defects are. More than this, its defects are often the mere defects of rude art, which are copied from Homer; such, for example, as the practice of conducting the narrative through lengthy similies, elaborately circumstantial, positively retarding and encumbering what they are meant to accelerate and lighten. If Homer lived in our days he would not write like Homer's imitators. In fact the mistake of all imitation is that it naturally fastens on the fleeting modes, and not on the eternal spirit.

Criticism might also have something to say in other directions, if this poem were to be closely scrutinised. We point, in passing, to such prosaisms as 'fate' treading something or other down, with an 'iron heel,' and to . . . mistaken familiarities of illustration. . . . But we need not dwell on them. Our purpose is gained if we have directed the reader's attention to an unequal but delightful volume of poems, and if we have, at the same time, indicated the real position which the poet is to hold, with respect to both Ancients and Moderns.

7. J. A. Froude, unsigned review, *Westminster Review*

1 January 1854, lxi, no. 119, 146–59

James Anthony Froude (1818–94) was in many respects a barometer of the times. He was influenced by Newman, became a friend of Kingsley, and, a few years before the writing of this review, turned disciple of Carlyle. Best known as a historian, he was also a periodical essayist and, for more than a decade, editor of *Fraser's*. His discussion of Arnold, whom he knew personally, centres on the poet's stature, which Froude thinks considerable, and on the relative merits of a number of poems, including the inadequacies of the title poems in the first two volumes. Froude also looks at Arnold's preface, drawing attention, like the student of Carlyle he was, to the substantial claims of German literature for the poet's attention.

Five years ago there appeared a small volume entitled *The Strayed Reveller, and other Poems, by A*. It was received we believe with general indifference. The public are seldom sanguine with new poets; the exceptions to the rule having been for the most part signal mistakes; while in the case of 'A.' the inequality of merit in his poems was so striking that even persons who were satisfied that qualities were displayed in them of the very highest kind, were yet unable to feel confidence in the future of an author so unusually incapable, as it appeared, of knowing when he was doing well and when he was failing.

Young men of talent experience often certain musical sensations, which are related to poetry as the fancy of a boy for a pretty face is related to love; and the counterfeit while it lasts is so like the reality as to deceive not only themselves but even experienced lookers-on who are not on their guard against the phenomenon. Time in either case is requisite to test the quality both of the substance and of the feeling, and we desired some further evidence of A.'s powers before we could grant him his rank as a poet; or even feel assured that he could ultimately obtain it. There was passion, as in a little poem called 'Stagyrus,' deep and searching; there was unaffected natural feeling, expressed sweetly and musically; in 'The Sick King of Bokhara,' in several of the Sonnets and other fragmentary pieces, there was genuine insight into life and whatever is best and noblest in it;—but along with this, there was often an elaborate obscurity, one of the worst faults which poetry can have; and indications that the intellectual struggles which, like all young men in our times, he was passing through, were likely to issue in an in-differentism neither pleasing nor promising.

The inequality in substance was not more remarkable than the inequality in the mechanical expression of it. 'The Forsaken Merman' is perhaps as beautifully finished as anything of the kind in the English language. The story is exquisitely told, and word and metre so carefully chosen that the harmony of sound and meaning is perfect. The legend itself we believe is Norwegian. It is of a King of the Sea who had married an earthly maiden; and was at last deserted by her from some scruples of conscience. The original features of it are strictly preserved, and it is told indirectly by the old Sea King to his children in a wild, irregular melody, of which the following extract will convey but an imperfect idea. It is Easter time, and the mother has left her sea palace for the church on the hillside, with a promise to return—

[Quotes 'The Forsaken Merman', ll. 62–107, 'She smiled, she went up through the surf', etc.]

Not less excellent, in a style wholly different, was A.'s treatment (and there was this high element of promise in A. that, with a given story to work upon, he was always successful) of the Ægyptian legend of Mycerinus, a legend not known unfortunately to general English readers, who are therefore unable to appreciate the skill displayed in dealing with it. We must make room for one extract, however, in explanation of which it is only necessary to say that Mycerinus, having learnt from the oracle that being too just a king for the purposes of the gods, who desired to afflict the Ægyptians, he was to die after six more years, made the six years into twelve by lighting his gardens all night with torches, and revelled out what remained to him of life. We can give no idea of the general conception of the poem, but as a mere piece of description this is very beautiful.

[Quotes 'Mycerinus', ll. 85–99, 'There by the river bank', etc.]

Containing as it did poems of merit so high as these, it may seem strange that this volume should not have received a more ready recognition; for there is no excellence which the writer of the passages which we have quoted could hereafter attain, the promise of which would not be at once perceived in them. But the public are apt to judge of books of poetry by the rule of mechanism, and try them not by their strongest parts but by their weakest; and in the present instance (to mention nothing else) the stress of weight in the title which was given to the collection was laid upon what was by no means adequate to bearing it. Whatever be the merits of the 'Strayed Reveller' as poetry, it is certainly not a poem in the sense which English people generally attach to the word, looking as they do not only for imaginative composition but for verse;—and as certainly if the following passage had been printed merely as prose, in a book which professed to be nothing else, no one would have suspected that it was composed of an agglutination of lines.

The gods are happy; they turn on all sides their shining eyes, and see below them earth and men. They see Tiresias sitting staff in hand on the warm grassy Asopus bank, his robe drawn over his old, sightless head, revolving inly the doom of Thebes. They see the Centaurs in the upper glens of Pelion, on the streams where the red-berried ashes fringe the clear brown shallow pools; with streaming flanks and heads reared proudly, snuffing the mountain wind. They see the Scythian on the wide steppe, unharnessing his wheeled house at noon; he tethers his beast down and makes his meal, mare's milk and bread baked on the embers; all around the boundless waving grass plains stretch, thick starred with saffron and the yellow hollyhock and flag-leaved isis flowers.

No one will deny that this is fine imaginative painting, and as such poetical,—but it is the poetry of well written, elegant prose. Instead of the recurring sounds, whether of rhyme or similarly weighted syllables, which constitute the outward form of what we call verse, we have the careless grace of uneven, undulating sentences, flowing on with a rhythmic cadence indeed, but free from all constraint of metre or exactitude of form. It may be difficult, perhaps it is impossible, to fix the measure of license which a poet may allow himself in such matters, but it is at least certain that the greatest poets are those who have allowed themselves the fewest of such liberties: in art as in morals, and as in everything which man undertakes, true greatness is the most ready to recognise and most willing to obey those simple outward laws which have been sanctioned by the experience of mankind, and we suspect the originality which cannot move except on novel paths.

This is but one of several reasons which explain the apathy of the public on A.'s first appearance. There was large promise, but the public require performance; and in poetry a single failure overweighs a hundred successes. It was possible that his mistakes were the mistakes of a man whose face was in the right direction—who was feeling his way, and who would ultimately find it; but only time could decide if this were so; and in the interval, the coldness of his reception would serve to test the nature of his faculty.

So far we have spoken with reserve, for we have simply stated the feelings with which we regarded this little volume on first reading it; but the reserve is no longer necessary, and the misgivings which we experienced have not been justified. At the close of last year another volume was published, again of miscellaneous poems, which went beyond the most sanguine hopes of A.'s warmest admirers. As before with 'The Strayed Reveller,' so again with 'Empedocles on Etna,' the *pièce de résistance* was not the happiest selection. But of the remaining pieces, and of all those which he has more recently added, it is difficult to speak in too warm praise. In the unknown A., we are now to recognise a son of the late Master of Rugby, Dr. Arnold. Like a good knight, we suppose he thought it better to win his spurs before appearing in public with so honoured a name; but the associations which belong to it will suffer no alloy from him who now wears it. Not only is the advance in art remarkable, in greater clearness of effect, and in the mechanical handling of words, but far more in simplicity and healthfulness of moral feeling. There is no more obscurity, and no mysticism; and we see everywhere the working of a mind bent earnestly on cultivating whatever is highest and worthiest in itself; of a person who is endeavouring, without affectation, to follow the best things, to see clearly what is good, and right, and true, and to fasten his heart upon these. There is usually a period in the growth of poets in which, like coarser people, they mistake the voluptuous for the beautiful; but in Mr. Arnold there is no trace of any such tendency; pure, without effort, he feels no enjoyment and sees no beauty in the atmosphere of the common passions; and in nobleness of purpose, in a certain loftiness of mind singularly tempered with modesty, he continually reminds us of his father. There is an absence, perhaps, of colour; it is natural that it should be so in the earlier poems of a writer who proposes aims such as these to himself; his poetry is addressed to the intellectual, and not to the animal emotions; and to persons of animal taste, the flavour will no doubt be over simple; but it is true poetry—a true representation of true human feeling. It may not be immediately popular, but it will win its way in the long run, and has elements of endurance in it which enable it to wait without anxiety for recognition.

Among the best of the new poems is 'Tristram and Iseult.' It is unlucky that so many of the subjects should be so unfamiliar to English readers, but it is their own fault if they do not know the 'Morte d'Arthur.' We must not calculate, however, on too much knowledge in such unpractical matters; and as the story is too long to tell in this place, we take an extract which will not require any. It is a picture of sleeping children as beautiful as Sir Francis Chantrey's.

[Quotes 'Tristram and Iseult', ll. 327–71, 'But they sleep in sheltered rest', etc.]

This is very beautiful; a beautiful description of one of the most beautiful objects in nature; but it is a description which could never have been composed except by a person whose mind was in tune with all innocent loveliness, and who found in the contemplation of such things not merely a passing emotion of pleasure but the deepest and most exquisite enjoyment.

Besides Tristram and Iseult, we select for especial mention out of this second volume, 'A Farewell,' 'Self-Dependence,' 'Morality;' two very highly-finished pieces called 'The Youth of Nature' and 'The Youth of Man,' expressing two opposite states of feeling, which we all of us recognise, and yet which, as far as we know, have never before found their way into language; and 'A Summer Night,' a small meditative poem, containing one passage, which, although not perfect—for, if the metre had been more exact, the effect would, in our opinion, have been very much enhanced—is, nevertheless, the finest that Mr. Arnold has yet written.

[Quotes 'A Summer Night', ll. 34–72, 'And I', etc.]

In these lines, in powerful and highly sustained metaphor, lies the full tragedy of modern life.

> Is there no life but these alone,
> Madman or slave, must man be one?

We disguise the alternative under more fairly-sounding names, but we cannot escape the reality; and we know not, after all, whether there is deeper sadness in a broken Mirabeau or Byron, or in the contented prosperity of a people who once knew something of noble aspirations, but have submitted to learn from a practical age that the business of life is to make money, and the enjoyments of it what money can buy. A few are ignobly successful; the many fail, and are miserable; and the subtle anarchy of selfishness finds its issue in madness and revolution. But we need not open this painful subject. Mr. Arnold is concerned with the effect of the system on individual persons; with the appearance which it wears to young highly sensitive men on their entry upon the world, with the choice of a life before them; and it is happy for the world that such men are comparatively rare, or the mad sort would be more abundant than they are.

We cannot but think it unfortunate that this poem, with several others of the highest merit, have been omitted in the last edition, while others find a place there, for which comparatively we care little. Uniformity of excellence has been sacrificed to uniformity of character, a subsidiary matter which in itself is of slight importance, and which the public would never quarrel for if they were treated with an ever pleasing variety. As it is, we have still to search three volumes for the best specimens of Mr. Arnold's powers, and opportunities are still left for ill-natured critics to make extracts of an apparently inferior kind. There is a remedy for this however in the future, and the necessary sifting will no doubt get itself duly accomplished at last. In the meantime, before noticing the late edition, we have a few words to say about Empedocles, the ground of objection to which we cannot think Mr. Arnold adequately understands, although he has omitted it in his present edition, and has given us his reasons for doing so. Empedocles, as we all know, was a Sicilian philosopher, who, out of discontent with life, or from other cause, flung himself into the crater of Mount Ætna. A discontent of this kind, Mr. Arnold tells us, unrelieved by incident, hope, or resistance, is not a fit subject for poetry. The object of poetry is to please, and the spectacle of a man too weak to bear his trials, and breaking under them, cannot be anything but painful. The correctness of the portrait he defends; and the fault, as he thinks, is not in the treatment, but in the subject itself. Now it is true that as a rule poetry is better employed in exhibiting the conquest over temptations than the fall under them, and some escape of this kind for the feelings must be provided in tragedies, by the introduction of some powerful cause, either of temptation acting on the will or of an external force controlling the action, in order to explain and reconcile us to the catastrophe. A mere picture of imbecility is revolting simply; we cannot conceive ourselves acting in the same way under the same circumstances, and we can therefore feel neither sympathy with the actor nor interest in his fate. But we must be careful how we narrow our theories in such matters. In Werther we have an instance of the same trial, with the same issue as Mr. Arnold has described in Empedocles, and to say that Werther was a mistake, is to circumscribe the sphere of art by a definition which the public taste will refuse to recognise. Nor is it true, in spite of Schiller's authority, that 'all art is dedicated, to enjoyment.' Tragedy has other objects, the κάθαρσις[1] or purifying of the emotions for instance, which, if we are to continue to use words in their ordinary sense, is something distinct from enjoyment, and not always reconcileable with it. Whatever will excite interest in a healthy, vigorous mind, that is a fair object of poetry, and there is a painful as well as a pleasant interest; it is an abuse of language to describe the sensations which we experience on reading 'Philoctetes' or 'Hamlet' as pleasant. They are not unmixedly painful, but surely not pleasant.

It is not therefore the actual fate of Empedocles which fails to interest us, but we are unable to feel that Mr. Arnold's account of him is the true account. In the absence of authentic material, the artist who hopes to interest us in his fate must at least make the story probable as he tells it; consistent in itself, with causes clearly drawn out proportioned to the effects resulting from them. And this it cannot be said that Mr. Arnold has done. Powerful as is much of the language which he places in the mouth of Empedocles, he has failed to represent him as in a condition in which suicide is the natural result. His trials, his disgusts, as far as he exhibits them, are not more than man may naturally be supposed able to bear, while of the impulses of a more definite character there is no trace at all. But a more grave deficiency still is, that among all the motives introduced, there is not one to make the climb of Ætna necessary or intelligible. Empedocles on Ætna might have been Empedocles in his room at Catana, and a dagger or a cup of hemlock would have answered all purposes equally well with a plunge in the burning crater. If the tradition of Empedocles is a real story of a thing which really happened, we may feel sure that some peculiar feeling connected with the mountain itself, some mystical theory or local tradition, led such a man as he was to such a means of self-immolation.

We turn from Empedocles which perhaps it is scarcely fair to have criticised, to the first poem in the latest edition. 'Sohrab and Rustum,' a poem which alone would have settled the position which Mr. Arnold

[1] 'catharsis'.

has a right to claim as a poet, and which is remarkable for its success in every point in which Empedocles appears deficient. The story comes down out of remote Persian antiquity; it is as old, perhaps it is older, than the tale of Troy; and, like all old stories which have survived the changes of so long a time, is in itself of singular interest. Rustum, the Hercules of the East, fell in with and loved a beautiful Tartar woman. He left her, and she saw him no more; but in time a child was born, who grew up with the princes of his mother's tribe, and became in early youth distinguished in all manly graces and noblenesses. Learning that he was the son of the great Rustum, his object is to find his father, and induce him, by some gallant action, to acknowledge and receive him. War breaks out between the Tartars and the Persians. The two armies come down upon the Oxus, the Sohrab having heard that Rustrum had remained behind in the mountains, and was not present, challenges the Persian chief. Rustum, unknown to Sohrab, had in the meantime joined the army, and against a warrior of Sohrab's reputation, no one could be trusted to maintain the Persian cause except the old hero. So by a sad perversity of fate, and led to it by their very greatness, the father and the son meet in battle, and only recognise each other when Sohrab is lying mortally wounded. It is one of those terrible situations which only the very highest power of poetry can dwell upon successfully. If the right chord be not touched to the exactest nicety, if the shock of the incident in itself be not melted into pathos, and the nobleness of soul in the two sufferers, be not made to rise above the cruel accident which crushes them, we cannot listen to the poet. The story overwhelms and absorbs us; we desire to be left alone with it and with our own feelings, and his words about it become officious and intrusive. Homer has furnished Mr. Arnold with his model, and has taught him the great lesson that the language on such occasions cannot be too simple and the style too little ornamented. Perhaps it may be thought that he has followed Homer's manner even too closely. No one who has read 'Mycerinus' and the 'Forsaken Merman' can doubt that Mr. Arnold can write richly if he pleases. It is a little startling, therefore, to find the opening of this poem simpler than one would make it, even if telling it in prose to a child. As in the *Iliad,* the same words are repeated over and over again for the same idea, without variation or attempt at it; and although it may easily be that our taste is spoiled by the high seasoning of the modern style, the result is that it strikes the attention to an extent which would have been better avoided. A perfect style does not strike at all, and it is a matter in which the reader ought to be considered even more than the abstract right. We have soon, however, ceased to think of that; the peculiarity which we have mentioned is confined to the beginning, and the success of the treatment is best proved by our forgetfulness, as we read on, of art and artist language and manner, in the overpowering interest of the story as it is drawn out before us. Extracts will convey a poor idea of a poem in which the parts are so wholly subordinate to the effect of the whole, and yet, in spite of this disadvantage, we can justify at least partially to our readers the opinions which we have generally expressed.

We will take the scene of the recognition, when Sohrab, lying wounded, and as yet ignorant of the name of his adversary, has declared himself Rustum's son. The father, at first incredulous and scornful, is led step by step, through the mention of old names and times, towards the ἀναγνώρισις,[1] and after the most delicately traced alternations of feeling, all doubt is ended by the mark of the seal on Sohrab's arm which Rustum had given to his mother.

> How say'st thou? [Sohrab says.] Is that sign the proper sign
> Of Rustum's son, or of some other man's?
> He spoke: but Rustum gazed, and gazed, and stood
> Speechless; and then he uttered one sharp cry,
> Oh, boy, thy father!

This is the first hint to Sohrab who has been his foe.

[Quotes 'Sohrab and Rustum', ll. 691–730, 'And his voice choked there', etc.]

As a picture of human life in Homer's manner, we cannot see why this passage, and indeed the whole poem, should not be thought as good as any one of the episodes in the *Æneid*. We are not comparing Mr. Arnold with Virgil: for it is one thing to have written an epic and another to have written a small fragment; but as a working up of a single incident it may rank by the side of Nisus and Euryalus, and deeper chords of feeling are touched in it than Virgil has ever touched.

And this leads us to Mr. Arnold's preface, and to the account which he gives us of the object which he proposes to himself in poetry: and our notice of this must be brief, as our space is running to its conclusion. He tells us, in a manner most feelingly instructive, something of the difficulties which lie round a young poet of the present day who desires to follow his art to some genuine purpose; and what he says will remind

---

[1] 'anagnorisis': recognition.

readers of Wordsworth of Professor Wilson's beautiful letter to him on a very similar subject. Unhappily the question is not one of poetry merely, but of far wider significance. Not the poet only, but every one of us who cannot be satisfied to tread with the crowd along the broad road which leads—we used to know whither, but desires 'to cultivate,' as Mr. Arnold says, 'what is best and noblest' in ourselves, are as sorely at a loss as he is with his art. To find the best models,—that indeed is the one thing for him and for us. But what are they and where? and the answer to the æsthetic difficulty lies as we believe in the solution of the moral one. To say this, however, is of infinitely little service for the practical direction of a living poet; and we are here advised (and for present purposes no doubt wisely) to fall back on the artists of classic antiquity. From them better than from the best of the moderns, the young poet will learn what art really is. He will learn that before beginning to sing it is necessary to have something to sing of, and that a poem is something else than a collection of sweet musical sentences strung together like beads or even jewels in a necklace. He will learn that the subject is greater than the manner; that the first is the one essential without a worthy choice of which nothing can prosper. Above all, he will learn that the restless craving after novelty, so characteristic of all modern writing, the craving after new plots, new stories, new ideas, is mere disease, and that the true original genius displays itself not in the fabrication of what has no existence, but in the strength and power with which facts of history, or stories existing so fixedly in the popular belief as to have acquired so to say the character of facts, shall be exhibited and delineated.

But while we allow with Mr. Arnold that the theory will best be learnt from the ancients, we cannot allow, as he seems to desire us to allow, that the practice of it was confined to them, or recommend as he does the disproportionate study, still less the disproportionate imitation of them. All great artists at all times have followed the same method, for greatness is impossible without it. The Italian painters are never weary of the Holy Family. The matter of Dante's poem lay before him in the creed of the whole of Europe. Shakespeare has not invented the substance of any one of his plays. And 'the weighty experience' and 'composure of judgment' with which the study of the ancients no doubt does furnish 'those who habitually practice it,' may be obtained we believe by the study of the thoughts of all great men of all ages; by the study of life in any age, so that our scope be broad enough.

It is indeed idle nonsense to speak, as some critics speak, of the 'present' as alone having claims upon the poet. Whatever is great, or good, or pathetic, or terrible, in any age, past or present, belongs to him, and is within his proper province; but most especially, if he is wise, he will select his subjects out of those which time has sealed as permanently significant. It is not easy in our own age to distinguish what has the elements in it of enduring importance; and time is wiser than we. But why dwell with such apparent exclusiveness on classic antiquity, as if there was no antiquity except the classic, and as if time were divided into the eras of Greece and Rome and the nineteenth century? The Hellenic poet sang of the Hellenes, why should not the Teutonic poet sing of the Teutons?

Vixere fortes *post* Agamemnona.[1]

And grand as are Achilles and Clytemnestra, they are not grander than their parallels in the German epic Criemhilda and Von Tronjè Hagen. We do not dream of prescribing to Mr. Arnold what subject he should choose. Let him choose what interests himself if he will interest his readers; and if he choose what is really human, let it come from what age it will, human hearts will answer to it. And yet it seems as if Teutonic tradition, Teutonic feeling, and Teutonic thought had the first claim on English and German poets. And those among them will deserve best of the modern world, and will receive the warmest welcome from it, who will follow Shakespeare in modelling into forms of beauty the inheritance which has come down to them of the actions of their own race. So most faithfully, if least directly, they will be treading in the steps of those great poets of Greece whom they desire to imitate. Homer and Sophocles did not look beyond their own traditions and their own beliefs; they found in these and these only their exclusive and abundant material. Have the Gothic annals suddenly become poor, and our own quarries become exhausted and worthless?

[1] 'There have been strong men who lived *after* Agamemnon.'

8. J. D. Coleridge, unsigned review,
Christian Remembrancer

April 1854, xxvii, 310–33

(Sir) John Duke Coleridge (1820–94) became first Baron Coleridge
and was to serve, after long public life, as Lord Chief Justice. He
was also a friend of Arnold, too much a friend, according to J. C.
Shairp, to indulge in the less than ecstatic remarks published in the
Christian Remembrancer. Arnold himself wrote: 'My love to
J. D. C., and tell him that the limited circulation of the *Christian
Remembrancer* makes the unquestionable viciousness of his article
of little importance.' Coleridge has high praise for some poems,
including 'Tristan and Iseult'; he defends the conclusion of 'Sohrab and Rustum.' But he finds Arnold uneven and imitative, and,
like many early reviewers, he sees the poetry as dangerously un-
Christian.

The appearance of the name of a son of Dr. Arnold on the title-page of a
volume of poems, cannot but excite a kindly interest in all those who admired, even when they could not agree with, his well-known father. Our
good-will, moreover, is conciliated towards Mr. Arnold himself, by the
filial consideration for his father's name which has led him to publish two
smaller volumes anonymously, and to reserve the avowal of his own
authorship, till success, important in its nature if moderate in amount, had
shown that he was not likely to discredit a name which any one might be
proud to bear. He is not without grounds for the confidence he appears to
have assumed. The volume indeed is open on many points to critical remark; but no one of any poetical feeling can peruse it without recognising
in the author the possession of remarkable powers, even where a mistaken
theory of poetry has thwarted their development and cramped their
exercise. All persons of taste would not agree that it was a volume
throughout of remarkable excellence. We should not ourselves be inclined to say so much. But we should think little of the poetical sensibility

of any one who could be blind to the loveliness, or deaf to the harmony, of many of the separate poems which it contains.

No young poet, even if his powers are the greatest, can ever shake himself free at first from the influence of his forerunners and contemporaries. Originality of style, at least where the style is good, comes late, and is the result of mature taste and experienced powers. And this is especially true of those greater and more cultivated authors, whose genius is the healthiest, and whose own style ultimately the most original. Penetrated with the beauties of their favourite masters, which none can so thoroughly appreciate as great disciples, the echoes of their predecessors' strains may be caught lingering in their own; and their manner takes the unconscious impress of the models they have so reverently studied and so profoundly admired. Take the early works of Shakspere himself, and see how much of Marlow and of the still older dramatic writers is to be found therein. It is, perhaps, profitless to add examples after an instance so great and so undeniable, yet Spenser, Milton, Wordsworth, Coleridge and Tennyson, in their early works, exhibited traces of the influence of their predecessors in the art. To go further back, the whole range of Latin poets, with (perhaps) scarcely an exception, in the great bulk of their productions, formed their styles distinctly upon Greek models, which to them were ancient, and occasionally descended to direct verbal imitation. It is not therefore in the way of blame that we note the influence of great masters upon Mr. Arnold's style; but as a mark of his powers being yet immature, and that it is at present impossible to predict with any confidence the position in the poetical commonwealth which he may be hereafter entitled to assume. For at present even the best of his compositions, with perhaps a single exception, are referable to some well-known original, which the cadence of his verses, or the general tone and spirit of his work, whether intentionally or not, at least indisputably, recall. The models are indeed various and good, but the imitation is obvious though successful. Taste, therefore, rather than power, is as yet the characteristic of Mr. Arnold's muse; and he succeeds less in creating a fresh impression upon his readers, than in reminding them of other great writers, and in reproducing the effects which those writers have already succeeded in creating.

Take for instance the following passage from one of his latest poems:—

[Quotes 'Sohrab and Rustum', ll. 116–25, 'As when some grey November morn', etc.]

This is a direct and very successful imitation of Milton's manner; not only the general air has been cleverly caught, but the very phrases and words are Miltonic. We have no objection to the passage in itself, but we feel that the thing has been done, and better done, before. Equally close and equally successful is the imitation of a different model in the passage we subjoin from an earlier poem on the striking story of Mycerinus, as given in Herodotus:—

[Quotes 'Mycerinus', ll. 31–48; 67–78, 'Seems it so light a thing', etc.]

Who does not recognise in this passage an imitation of the majestic music of Wordsworth's 'Laodamia' by one who has felt the beauty of that poem and has aimed at repeating its effects?

Once more, we find Mr. Arnold struck with the melody of another considerable writer, and accurately reproducing it. The passage we subjoin is from the conclusion of the same poem of 'Mycerinus,' in which, if the rhyme be 'after' Wordsworth, in the blank verse he does homage to Tennyson:—

[Quotes 'Mycerinus', ll. 85–99; 122–7, 'There by the river banks', etc.]

No reader of 'Œnone,' or 'Ulysses,' or the 'Morte d'Arthur,' can have any doubt as to the original which suggested these very picturesque and harmonious lines. It is the manner of Mr. Tennyson, caught and employed by a man of taste and ability.

We do not desire to pursue Mr. Arnold through the various poems of this volume merely for the purpose of showing the originals to whom he is indebted. But in a right estimate of his powers it ought not to be forgotten that he *is* thus indebted, and indebted even to a greater degree than a careless perusal might perhaps disclose. For not only in such passages as we have quoted is the style and manner of another writer unconsciously caught or directly imitated; but often where the manner is his own, and the treatment appears to be original, we may detect the recollection of some beautiful passage lurking in Mr. Arnold's mind, and forming the theme as it were for a graceful and melodious variation. The following little poem, for instance, is one of the sweetest in Mr. Arnold's whole volume:—

[Quotes 'To Marguerite—Continued' in its entirety]

Beautiful verses indeed. But would they have been written but for the famous passage in 'Christabel'?—

[Quotes 'Christabel', ll. 408–26, which Coleridge called 'the best and sweetest' he had written]

Here it is not the manner of 'Christabel' which is imitated, but the thought of Coleridge, which is suggested by Mr. Arnold's poem. We could not carry on this kind of examination in detail, without occupying a great deal more space than is now at our disposal, for where the likeness is not of style, but of thought, the parallel passages require to be set out at length, and the attention must be drawn to those parts which are intended to be compared. In general, however, we may say that there are but a few of Mr. Arnold's poems which do not inevitably remind us of the works of some former writer, either in their language, or in the thoughts of which their language is the expression. In this, however, Mr. Arnold does not differ from the multitude of young verse-writers, of whose productions 'the public little knows, the publisher too much,' and who, after a certain period of friendly praise and moderate social success, pass to the trunkmakers, and are forgotten. He does differ from them in the quantity of original matter which he blends with, or superadds to the stores of others, and in the fine taste and poetical feeling which all his productions display. He differs from them also in the possession of a wide learning and varied accomplishment, which furnish him with an abundance of allusion, and a fertility of unexpected yet appropriate illustration, no less interesting than delightful. Above all, he stands alone in his sedulous cultivation of the classical writers, as the best sources of poetical inspiration, and the highest teachers of the poetical art. He appears to be a finished scholar, intimately acquainted with the great works of Greece and Rome, and passionately fond of their characteristic beauties. Homer, and the Attic tragedians, especially Sophocles, are however those amongst the classics whom he regards with the deepest veneration; a veneration shown not only by an occasional verse or stanza, but in elaborate attempts to reproduce their style, in a selection of classical subjects for his own compositions, and a pretty frequent adoption of classical epithets, or epithets formed upon a classical analogy, into all his poems, whether of an antique or modern cast.

Mr. Arnold has not escaped the dangers inevitably attendant on such a course. It is true that he has occasionally transferred to his own poems some of the great qualities which he so admires in his Greek models. The clear descriptive epithets, the simple yet distinct pictures of Greek poetry, are not unfrequently to be found in Mr. Arnold. But his love of the ancients has led him into many a harshness and obscurity, many a bald passage intended to be austere, many a childish one intended to be simple; and has filled his poems with a multitude of affectations quite fatal to the perfect enjoyment of them. A Greek statue is a noble thing, and a portrait of a modern gentleman, by Sir Joshua Reynolds, is a noble thing, and both give pleasure to a cultivated mind; but it is an ignoble thing, and does not give pleasure, to see an Englishman straining after the postures, and attempting to wield the weapons of a Grecian hero, and imagining that he attains the faultless beauty of antique form, because he denudes himself of modern drapery. It is true, that a classical image, a heroic subject, a quaintly translated phrase from a Greek or Latin writer, (e.g. 'the ringing plains of windy Troy;' 'this way and that dividing the swift mind,') will, when met with in a modern poem, often from association and from an unexpected and pleasing strangeness give singular delight to a reader acquainted with the classics. But such arts must be used sparingly, and with the skill and taste of Mr. Tennyson, who perhaps of all great modern writers most frequently employs them, or they degenerate into grotesqueness and affectation, and ceasing to be agreeable, become ridiculous. Mr. Tennyson always takes care that his antique subjects shall be treated in a thoroughly modern fashion, that the mind of the present day shall be distinctly seen moulding ancient stories and associations to its own purposes; but never for a moment striving really to imitate classical authors, or to reproduce classical modes of thought. This blending of antiquity with modernism constitutes the peculiar and unrivalled charm of such pieces as 'The Lotos-Eaters,' and 'Œnone,' and above all, 'Ulysses.' Mr. Arnold has much of his art to learn, and a great deal of tact and experience to acquire, before he can safely indulge in so difficult and delicate a style of composition: a style in which even success is hazardous, and failure is fatal.

Mr. Arnold, however, has not been content to allow his practice to speak for itself, and the faults and beauties of his verses to stand upon their own merits, and to be found out by his readers in the ordinary course. He has been induced to write a Preface, in which he favours us with a theory of poetry, which we take leave to think entirely fallacious and inadequate, based upon untenable assumptions, and conducting us to conclusions which we utterly repudiate. As a general rule, it is a great mistake for a poet to commit himself to a theory of poetry. To theorise on poetry is not his vocation, and it is seldom that he has the intellectual qualities requisite for the work. It may be a fit and interesting subject for the critical faculty to discuss the principles of art, and to endeavour to elicit from great works the laws which guided their construction. But it is the critic, not the artist, who is properly thus employed. In all the highest qualities of his art, a great man seldom works consciously by laws at all. Technical rules of course there must be in all arts, such as the laws of metre, of grammar, or of perspective; and a great artist will know all these, and use them as familiarly as we do our alphabet. But these are not laws of construction or of treatment as applied to the whole work, and the effect of any great effort of genius taken as a whole, arises from no conscious application of definite laws on the part of the artist, but from something indefinable and inexpressible, which distinguishes a great artist, a ποιητής,[1] or creator in any kind, from his fellow-men. No artist worth a straw could tell us how his own great works had been produced. Sir Joshua Reynolds, the foremost artist-critic of modern times, analysed with acuteness, and described with eloquence, styles wholly different from his own. Inimitable and excellent as his own productions are, they are utterly unlike those which it was the chief object of his famous lectures to recommend. Wordsworth, again, wrote a celebrated essay on poetical diction, which contained *a* truth no doubt, but not the whole truth, and of the theory of which all his own finest poems were more or less violations. No compositions can be so flat as those which are made up like a grammatical exercise as definite examples of consciously-applied rules; while at the same time to put forth a poetical theory, especially if it is one which requires considerable power to fulfil it, is to challenge for your poems an unusual severity of critical examination, and to increase the disgrace of failure by having openly proclaimed your own standard of success. Few men's works fulfil the measure of their teaching: and the self-confidence implied in prefixing to a man's poems a kind of lecture on their characteristic excellences, and on the somewhat novel principles of taste, according to which they have been composed, and of which they are put forward as examples, is not with most readers the safest or best method of insuring for the poems themselves a genial and sympathetic perusal. We come to a poet to be moved or delighted with his strains, and we do not want to be told by him that we must admire his poems, because they are written according to certain true and ancient laws, which it seems have been forgotten by most great modern writers. These very writers, nevertheless, ignorant readers have persisted in admiring for those same qualities which a truer view of the principles of poetry would, we are assured, have shewn to be mere blemishes and mistakes.

[1] 'maker, poet, etc.'

Of course, if a poet really happens to be a great critic, and to hit upon a true theory of poetry, there can be no reason why he should not communicate it. But the chances are greatly against his doing so, and we cannot say that we think Mr. Arnold has been lucky enough to form any exception to the ordinary rule. It is not easy, as every one will admit, to lay down with precision the objects, the limits, the elements, or the laws of a thing so wide, so various, so profound as poetry. The attempt to do so has, in all ages, led to profitless discussions; such as, whether satire is poetry, whether this or that writer is a poet; which have ended in nothing but occasionally narrowing the sphere of natural and legitimate admiration and delight, by the imposition of unnatural and arbitrary rules. We are not about to follow examples which we condemn, and to add another instance of failure in the attempt to describe the indefinite, and to place bounds upon the illimitable. From the sublime strains of Hebrew prophets down to the latest and most artificial rhymers of these last ages, there is, amidst the infinite variety of gifts, and diversity of powers, something in common which separates the poet from the mass of his fellow-men, and enables him to impart delight to their minds and gratification to their taste. A great poet, like a great orator or a great philosopher, will undoubtedly do much more than this; a poet, however, differs from them not in the thoughts which he creates, but in the dress wherewith he clothes them. In their appeal to the sense of harmony and beauty which all men possess, in the imaginative and musical vehicle which they employ, Homer and Horace, Anacreon and Virgil, Shakspere and Burns, may be classed together. A theory which rejects Dryden and Pope, nay even the still more technical writers of French literature, such, for instance, as Racine, from the rank of poets, is as unsatisfactory, and as far from meeting all the facts of the case, as one which would throw doubts on Wordsworth, or question the claims of Shelley or of Keats. It is simply idle to say that poetry is this or that, when it really pervades the universe; or to lay down that this or that is its peculiar province, when there is scarcely a subject or an object which it cannot make its own. It is, as it were, the medium through which the poet sees, and by which he speaks, which colours everything he beholds, and robes in splendour or in beauty every creation of his mind.

We do not pretend to say that this is definite or technical, and we should very much doubt the truth of any statement of the nature and objects of poetry which pretended to be either. But beyond most such statements which we have seen, that of Mr. Arnold appears to be altogether inadequate, and to result in conclusions which the common feeling of mankind will agree to reject with something akin to indignation.

'What,' says Mr. Arnold, 'are the eternal objects of poetry among all nations and at all times? They are actions,—human actions,—possessing an inherent interest in themselves, and which are to be communicated in an interesting manner by the art of the poet. Vainly will the latter imagine that he has everything in his own power; that he can make an intrinsically inferior action equally delightful with a more excellent one by his treatment of it: he may, indeed, compel us to admire his skill, but his work will possess within itself an incurable defect.' He then proceeds to argue that time is unessential, and that a great action of a thousand years ago is more interesting and fitter for poetry than a small one of yesterday. From this he arrives, by a curious sort of logic, at the conclusion that ancient subjects are *in themselves* fitter for poetical handling; and that 'an action of the present day,' to use his words, 'is too near us, too much mixed up with what is accidental and passing, to form a sufficiently grand, detached, and self-subsistent object for a tragic poem.' Amongst ancient subjects he classes, as we understand him, such essentially different ones as Macbeth and Œdipus; and by the selection of such examples altogether baffles our best endeavours to comprehend the meaning of his rule. Ancient subjects, however, whatever those may be, are to be preferred, and, as we gather, almost exclusively preferred, to those of modern times. It follows from this, that as human action is the only object of poetry, human action, to admit of proper treatment, should be concerned with grand characters, and far removed from us in point of time; and as the classical writers of Greece and Rome selected antique subjects, and treated them in the grand style, a modern poet should go to them as models, and study them as the true originals of art, whose perfections it is hopeless to surpass, and difficult to rival. No modern writer, however great, no modern subject, however good, is to compare, in Mr. Arnold's view of the poetical art, with Sophocles and Homer, with Dido and Achilles.

Such is the theory, which we have endeavoured fairly to represent, although it suffers much by not being given to the reader in the remarkably choice and vigorous prose of Mr. Arnold himself; nor is there anything in what we may call the positive half of it to which we desire to object. So far forth as Mr. Arnold recommends the study of classical writers, and celebrates the intellectual and moral benefits derivable therefrom; so far as he does justice to their calmness and simplicity, their dignity and pathos, their refined and severe sense of art, we go along with him entirely. We do not doubt the truth of what he says, that 'commerce with the ancients appears to produce, in those who constantly practise it, a steadying and composing effect upon their judgment, not of literary works only, but of men and events in general. They are like persons who have had a very weighty and impressive experience: they are more truly than others under the empire of facts, and more independent of the language current among those with whom they live.' We subscribe to all this; but we fail to apprehend how it leads to the conclusion that an Englishman should write of Medea or of Empedocles in preference to Mary Queen of Scots or Cromwell; that an English poet's allusions should be to classical events, or to the heroes of the ancient world, his style be formed upon that of writers in a foreign language, and his thoughts moulded upon those of believers in a heathen creed.

We will not waste our space, nor our readers' time, with discussing at length the strictures which Mr. Arnold passes upon all modern writers, including Shakspere. However necessary to his theory, they are so little creditable to his taste, that we cannot help feeling they would hardly have been ventured upon except under the stimulus of thoroughly defending a thesis, which, from the time of Aristotle, has made men intellectually unscrupulous. Even in this portion of his Preface, however, there is much which is sensible and true. He contrasts the simplicity of classical writers with the fussiness of many moderns, who loudly 'talk of their mission, and of interpreting the age, and of the coming poet.' The comparison is fair enough, and doubtless greatly to the disadvantage of our contemporaries. But when Mr. Arnold comes to use it as an argument in support of his theory, the matter changes. Does he suppose that there was no cant in the days of Plato, or that because men now write nonsense in multitudes, therefore Burke and Wordsworth are not fit to rank with the greatest authors of any age or any country? He compares the small men of the present day with the great men of antiquity; and though the victory is easy, the terms of the conflict are manifestly unjust. In our day, as in theirs, the calling of a great poet is not to interpret an age, but to affect a people; and he would be a bold man who should deny to the great singers of our time an influence as wide and deep as ever was exerted at any period of the world's history by the great masters of their art. He would be a yet bolder, in our judgment, who would place such poems as Wordsworth's 'Triad,' or his famous 'Ode,' such compositions as 'The Cenci,' or 'King Lear,' in point of mere artistic skill, at all below any single composition of the Greek or Roman minds.

But the whole breaks down together as a theory of poetry. It is not by straining after one model or another, nor yet by definite and conscious effort, that great poems are produced. Homer, it has been finely said—

> *Beheld* the Iliad and the Odyssee
> Rise to the swelling of the voiceful sea;

and there is so much of gift and inspiration in every great poet, that his best works are written, his greatest efforts achieved, in a simple, half-unconscious fashion, by means often the most homely and ordinary, by appeals to those emotions of the heart which are, indeed, all-powerful, but all-pervading, which all men share in common, and in which one age does not differ from another. Subjects thoroughly known, illustrations universally understood, are perhaps essential to the construction of the greatest poems, certainly to the construction of those which acquire the most enduring fame. Disguised, therefore, in a robe of lofty pretensions and severe requirements, it is, in reality, a low and narrow view of poetic art that would make it serve for the delight and instruction of the rich and highly educated alone, and which would exclude altogether the generality of women from its highest enjoyments. Yet this must be the inevitable result of a theory which proposes to a poet as his best subject a story of classical times, to be treated in a classical style, and adorned with classical illustrations. If the best poetry is not to be understood without a profound acquaintance with, and relish for, the classics, the best poetry is to be written for a hundred or two of the male sex only out of the whole population of a great country. And if it be true that grandiose *human* action is the proper object of poetry, what becomes of Milton, and Spenser, and the Georgics, and Horace, and Lucretius, and Catullus, and Simonides, and Cowper, and Wordsworth, and a list of writers as long as Mr. Arnold's Preface, whom no one ever yet thought of banishing from the catalogue of great poets, and whose works all mankind have agreed to consider as poetry of the highest order?

Mr. Arnold's practice has not at all tended to reconcile us to his theory. Those are by far his best poems in which he has trusted most exclusively to himself, and those portions of his poems the most striking in which he has been contented to be original and modern. For this reason we cannot, on the whole, admire the long blank-verse poem of *Sohrab and Rustum*, a composition evidently put together upon the theory which we have just been discussing. The story of the Persian Hercules slaying his son in single combat, and the discovery of their relationship after the fatal blow has been given, is, indeed, a very solemn and pathetic subject, and much of Mr. Arnold's poem is written in a strain of deep yet subdued feeling worthy of the occasion. The imitation of Homer and Milton is, however, too palpable throughout; the numerous similes elaborately worked out into distinct pictures, and the minute descriptions, remind us of the former; the language is obviously and intentionally imitated from the latter, as we showed some pages back. If from the style we go to the treatment, we are under some embarrassment from not being sure how much of it is Mr. Arnold's own. The subject itself, it is well known, is from Firdousi. But in the first volume of the *Causeries du Lundi* by Sainte Beuve, there is a review of M. Mohl's translation of Firdousi; and some of the passages given by Sainte Beuve from M. Mohl's version, are simply translated, and very closely translated, by Mr. Arnold. We give one of them, that our readers may judge for themselves:—

> O thou young man, the air of heaven is soft,
> And warm, and pleasant; but the grave is cold.
> Heaven's air is better than the cold dead grave.
> Behold me! I am vast, and clad in iron,
> And tried; and I have stood on many a field
> Of blood, and I have fought with many a foe:
> Never was that field lost, or that foe saved.
> O Sohrab, wherefore wilt thou rush on death?
> Be govern'd: quit the Tartar host, and come
> To Iran, and be as my son to me,
> And fight beneath my banner till I die.
> There are no youths in Iran brave as thou.

The following is from M. Mohl's version of Firdousi:—

'O jeune homme, si tendre!' lui dit-il, 'la terre est sèche et froide, l'air est doux et chaud. Je suis vieux; j'ai vu maint champ de bataille, j'ai dêtruit mainte armée, et je n'ai jamais été battu. Mais j'ai pitié de toi et ne voudrais pas t'arracher la vie. Ne reste pas avec les Tures; je ne connais personne dans l'Iran qui est des épaules et des bras comme toi.'

Sometimes the translation is literal, as, *e.g.*—

> for like the lightning to this field.
> I came, and like the wind I go away:

which is a mere literal rendering of—'Je suis venu comme la foudre, et je m'en vais comme le vent.'

This is not the only passage furnished by the short paper we have referred to which has been similarly transferred, and it at once leaves us in uncertainty whether the whole work of M. Mohl, which we have never seen, may not have been used throughout, and the study of antiquity carried so far as simply to reproduce an ancient poem as well as an ancient subject. For Mr. Arnold has not thought fit to offer a single syllable of acknowledgment to an author to whom he has been manifestly very largely indebted.

We must not, however, leave *Rustum* without an extract, which, if the language is a little affected, is yet very beautiful:—

[Quotes ll. 556–72, 'As when some hunter', etc.]

This certainly is a very noble picture. Our readers will, we are sure, feel also the solemn beauty of this conclusion, reminded perhaps, as we have been throughout the poem, by its similarity to a beautiful composition on the story of Atys and Adrastus in Herodotus, published several years ago by Mr. Faber, under the title of *The Dream of King Crœsus*.

[Quotes ll. 838–92, 'He spoke; and Sohrab', etc.]

We have seen the river objected to as being out of place, and distracting the attention from the action and the persons. We do not think so. Independently of the remarkable power of the passage, as a piece of poetical geography, it seems to carry us out of the blood and sorrow of the terrible story into light and peace, and concludes the poem quietly and sweetly, without an attitude or a peroration. It is the way with many great lyric masters, and has for us an especial charm. Every one knows the quiet conclusion of Horace's noble Ode on the story of Regulus, which we have always thought singularly happy, in spite of much criticism to the contrary:—

[Quotes Horace, *Atqui sciebat*, etc.]

Thus far nothing can be objected on the score of style to Mr. Arnold's imitations of the classical authorities. Nor would it be possible to find a more graceful passage than the following, on a Greek legend from the poem of Empedocles, which poem Mr. Arnold has excluded (except this passage) from the volume before us:—

[Quotes 'Empedocles', ll. 427–60, 'Far, far from here', etc.]

The poem of 'The Forsaken Merman,' however, has much more a character of its own, and though reminding us of Mr. Tennyson, has a sharpness and rapidity which he never gives us. It is the song of a Sea King deserted, together with his children, by his human wife, whom he seeks to regain, but who will not leave earth and her Christian worship any more. Its singular vigour and sweetness are very striking. The wife has gone away, and the Merman wants her:—

[Quotes 'The Forsaken Merman', ll. 64–84, 'Children dear, were we long alone?' etc.]

The two concluding stanzas are very beautiful:—

[Quotes ll. 108–143, 'Come away, away children', etc.]

Reminding us perhaps a little of Schiller, yet with a character of its own too, is the poem of 'The Church of Brou,' in three parts. The first describes the Duke and Duchess, a happy bride and bridegroom, the death of the Duke out hunting, the building of the church and of monuments for herself and her husband by the Duchess, and her death. The second describes the church; the third, the tomb. The last two parts are lovely, their tender feeling and perfect finish alike admirable. We give the second part:—

[Quotes 'The Church of Brou', ll. 1–40, 'Upon the glistening leaden roof', etc.]

But of all Mr. Arnold's poems, our favourite by far is 'Tristram and Iseult,' the most original and picturesque of all his compositions, bearing more than any of them the marks of a distinct and individual style. The ordinary story of Tristram and Iseult of Ireland is well known. In this poem we are introduced to the less familiar Iseult of Brittany, whom he married, and by whom he had two children, loving all the while the elder Iseult. He is dying, and his gentle wife watches him; a messenger has been sent to the other Iseult, who arrives in time to die with him; the wife living on with her children a plaintive sort of life, which is beautifully told in the conclusion of the poem. The different metres, some of them difficult and peculiar, are exquisitely managed; and the feeling which we might be tempted to have, as to the morality of centering so much of interest upon lawless love, must, we are sorry to say, be excited by the original romances in which sins of this kind seem to be considered as taking but little from the standard of chivalrous or even religious perfection. It is curious to observe, in so religious a book as the

Morte D'Arthur, and still more in other books of the same class, how lax in this respect was the morality of knighthood, and how venial such offences were deemed by those who lived virtuously themselves. We must append a passage to justify our encomium; a passage of almost perfect beauty:—

[Quotes 'Tristram and Iseult', ll. 327–71, 'But they sleep in sheltered rest', etc.]

One final passage, to show Mr. Arnold's mastery over a common yet very difficult metre. It is the conclusion of the whole poem, the story which Iseult tells her children, walking with them along the heaths of the coast of Brittany:—

[Quotes ll. 163–224, 'In these lone sylvan glades', etc.]

It will be seen, that in all these passages there is but little of the ancients; that the beauty, great as it is, is of a thoroughly modern cast; and farther, that the man who composed them, is undoubtedly capable, if he does justice to his genius, and is not led astray by any false or affected theory of art, of taking a high rank among modern poets. We do not mean to say, that the whole volume can be judged of by the extracts we have given. There are a number of rhymeless lyrics which are mere prose, printed in varying-sized lines; and a whole poem called 'The Strayed Reveller,' written in imitation of the Greek, which is about as like an ode of Pindar, or a chorus of Æschylus or Sophocles, as the banquet after the manner of the ancients in *Peregrine Pickle,* was an adequate representation of Lucullus's supper in the Hall of Apollo. Mr. Arnold will drop these disagreeable eccentricities from succeeding editions of his poems, as he has already excluded several earlier compositions from this volume, to its great and decided benefit. It would be well if he carried the process of weeding still farther, and as he has dropped Empedocles, would drop sundry other moral and quasi-religious musings, which are very painful if they represent the author's real opinions, and hardly ought to be published if they do not.

Any student of Mr. Arnold's poems can hardly fail to be struck with the genuine love of nature, and the accurate and picturesque delineation of its beauties, which the best of them contain. All her aspects are familiar to him, and have been comprehended by him. But they seem to teach him nothing. The beauties which he sees begin and end in themselves. There is no reference to the hand that made them, no intimation of those lessons which they were appointed to convey. In the many melancholy and pathetic passages in which natural images are introduced, there is no suggestion of the comfort to be derived from them, no such use of them as Scripture and great Christian poets have abundantly sanctioned.

[Cites as example Pico de Mirandola and says that such Christian sentiments 'find no answering voice' in Arnold]

His descriptions of nature are like those of Keats and Shelley, full of loveliness, but devoid of soul. With another writer it might perhaps not be unreasonable to imagine that he had of set purpose restrained a natural impulse, from a manly repugnance to join in a practice which the mawkish imitations of Cowper and Wordsworth are fast rendering a merely sentimental and insincere fashion. In him, however, it is clearly part of a system of writing which deliberately rejects all such considerations, either as inartistic or as untrue. It is not from a dislike of pretended sentiment, but from a repugnance to the sentiment itself, that he never connects nature with her Creator and her God.

In Mr. Arnold's earlier volumes, the unsatisfactory and depressing tone of his writing was more conspicuous, and consequently more disagreeable, than in this. Many of the more gloomy and desponding poems are rejected from this collection; and we would fain hope that those which are preserved will in process of time disappear in like manner. But enough remains to render the volume a really painful one to those who do not think the destiny or the duty of man a doubtful question; and who feel, as we feel, the incalculable mischief of a sceptical and irreligious train of thought when presented to the mind in melodious verse, and clothed with the graces of a refined and scholarlike diction. Mr. Arnold, for instance, is asked, 'Who prop in these bad days his mind?' and he answers in a sonnet, that he finds consolation for his spiritual doubts and moral questionings in Homer, Sophocles, and Epictetus. In another sonnet he extravagantly eulogises Mr. Emerson, and appears to think highly of religious isolation. Elsewhere he speaks of our 'sick fatigue and languid doubt,' of our 'casual creeds,' and of how we pine,

> And wish the long unhappy dream would end,
> And wave all claim to bliss, and try to bear,
> With close-lipp'd Patience for our only friend,
> Sad Patience, too near neighbour to Despair.

And he has selected as a motto to his whole book, a beautiful fragment of Chœrilus of Samos, the utterance of a repining and weary soul, coming naturally enough from a Greek in the train of Lysander, at the close of the Peloponnesian war, but not the key-note we should have desired for the songs of a Christian Englishman at the present day.

The prevalence of a literature, the writers of which appear to think themselves justified in standing *ab extra*[1] to Christianity, is one of the most difficult and dangerous intellectual problems with which we have to deal. It is not easy to comprehend the state of mind in which a believer can feel secure in taking up such a position. So it is, however; and for the most part these writers adopt one of two modes of dealing with religion. Sometimes they patronise the Christian revelation, point out its philosophical coherence, translate its dogmas into popular phraseology, get rid of some of its stern precepts as a little out of date, and produce it to the world as really after all a very reasonable scheme, by no means objectionable, when rightly understood, and when modified by the intelligence of the nineteenth century. Sometimes they simply pass it by on the other side. They leave it out, observe a perfect silence on the subject, and discuss questions, which, if it be true, it has for ever settled, as if they were open questions, and admitted of discussion. It may be true, apparently, or it may not; but it would excite prejudice to discuss such a point as this, and meanwhile the sensible man will go on exactly as if it were not true. Then we have the influence of nature, the cultivation of art, a right understanding of the dignity of man, the arguments of philosophers upon the nature of the soul, put forward as the means by which poor human kind can be regenerated, and the life of man rounded to that complete and perfect whole of temperate and satisfactory enjoyment, which in this philosophy is the very highest object we can attain.

Any one, however slightly acquainted with the literature, especially the poetical literature, of the day, cannot fail to have been struck with the fact we have described. It is perhaps hard to say which of the two methods of handling religion is the more offensive; but it is not the offensiveness, so much as the practical mischief which results from them, which makes it necessary to notice them. We live in an age, not infidel indeed in profession, not without its strong religious feeling, and great religious works, yet penetrated, especially amongst the more highly educated classes, with an infidel and worldly spirit, which often employs those who are by no means infidels as allies in its assaults on the fortress of religion. The strongholds of Christianity are no longer beleaguered

[1] 'on the outside, apart from'.

by open enemies, and exposed to unconcealed attacks. The method now is to sap their foundations in time of peace, and gain entrance among the unsuspicious garrison, in the guise of friends. And many an unwary and careless person suffers himself to be betrayed by fashion into proceedings really hurtful to the truth, which he never would adopt if he clearly saw the full consequences of what he does. These are, indeed, days of doubt and pain, when the dangers of society and the temptations of individuals multiply day by day. 'The armies of the homeless and unfed,' of whom Mr. Arnold speaks, may any day be upon us, brutalized by the physical and social depravity in which they have been permitted to welter, trained on an openly profligate and infidel literature which circulates amongst them by millions of copies, and ready, in course of years, for any savage and fierce excesses which their excited and degraded natures may suggest. It is not for us to blame or to condemn them. To a great extent we have made them what they are. But if anything is to be done it must be done by Christianity alone, by Christian institutions, Christian charity, Christian self-devotion. A lazy philosophical literature, which looks at these things as curious social problems, and proposes to meet the world's wickedness with the precepts of Epictetus, must, if possible, be disdainfully swept away as an incumbrance and obstruction in the path of those who are going forth in God's name to fight the battles of Our Lord.

We must sincerely apologize to Mr. Arnold for seeming to include him personally in the scope of these remarks. We have no reason to believe, and we do not, in fact, believe that, except as a writer, he is obnoxious to them. Indeed, upon him, in his individual relations, it would be impertinence to observe; and we make this disclaimer in truth and sincerity, only lest our words should be taken by others in a sense they were never meant to bear. As an author, however, we conceive him to be open on this score to great and grave objection. It may be, it very likely is, that according to his theory of art, and along with his study of the antique, this is the attitude which he deems it fitting that a poet should assume towards the Gospel scheme; this the sort of counsel he should give to a baptized people. Poetry, perhaps, is to be high, distant, and apart from the turmoil of sinful life, and the everlasting conflict of Our Lord with Satan. We do not the least agree with him. To us this sort of feeling appears to be as bad in art as it is mischievous to religion and to truth. The art that has no relevancy to actual life, that passes by God's truth and the facts of man's nature as if they had no existence, the art that does not seek to ennoble and purify and help us in our life-long struggle with sin and evil, however beautiful, however outwardly serene and majestic, is false, and poor, and contemptible. It is not worth the serious attention of a man in earnest. All noble and true and manly art is concerned with God's glory and man's true benefit; and we do not believe that the grave and severe artists of Mr. Arnold's favourite Greece, if they had known of the Christian revelation, and if they had believed that in it God had spoken to mankind, would have passed it by in silence and neglect, and attempted to feed the yearning hearts of their countrymen upon the miserable dregs of some Egyptian superstition, or the more refined and intellectual mistakes of the Magian philosophy. If they had known where the problem of man's existence was solved for ever, and where the guide of man's conduct was infallibly to be found, they would have led their disciples to those glorious sources, and have raised their own loftiest strains to celebrate the virtues of the River of Life.

9. Coventry Patmore, unsigned review, *North British Review*

August 1854, xxi, 493–504

There is some doubt about the authorship of this article, the *Wellesley Index* ascribing it to J. C. Shairp. But Shairp himself refers to the review as by another, and the views expressed are closer to those of Patmore than to those of Shairp.

Patmore (1823–96) had published his own *Poems* in 1844, and, like Arnold, had withdrawn his first volume from circulation. His second volume, *Tamerton Church Tower*, appeared in the same year as this review of Arnold, whom he evidently recognized as a kindred spirit. Patmore speaks of Arnold as 'a man of undeniable power and high culture', whose discipline, independence, and seriousness are marred by 'dejection' and by misleading theory. Patmore divides the poems into the 'classic' and 'romantic', suggesting that Arnold's strength lies in the romantic.

It is not very long since two volumes of poetry, by 'A,' *The Strayed Reveller*, and *Empedocles on Ætna*, passed under our review. If we return so soon to this author it is because his present work comes to us enriched by new and interesting poems, together with an Essay, remarkable for its vigorous contrast between ancient and modern poetry, and endorsed on its title-page no longer by the abstraction 'A,' but by a well-known and honourable surname. The date of Fox How and the name of Arnold will awaken interest in many hearts, which remember the earnest voice that once spoke from that retirement. They will listen perhaps in hope of hearing the tones that once stirred them prolonged to a younger generation. But the resemblance hardly reaches beyond date and name. These poems so little recall, either in subject, form, or sentiment, the works of the late Dr. Arnold, that they will derive small favour from hereditary association, but must stand or fall by their intrinsic merit.

The most rapid glance at Mr. Arnold's poems must convince every reader that they are the work of a man of undeniable power and high culture; nor can any one fail to perceive the author's fine eye for beauty and the artistic mould in which all his poems are cast;—for his whole mind is of the cultivated and artistic order, and it is to a place among the learned and artistic poets that he aspires. Learned and artistic poets! some one may exclaim. Is it not the very essence of the poet that he is a child of nature, one who works without aid of learning or of art? True, the poetic soul is the first indispensable condition—that without which there can be no poet. But starting from this common basis, one order of poets sings straight from their own heart, in the native dialect, to a self-taught tune, in whatever form comes readiest to hand. This is the natural or unlearned race of poets, of which the great names are Homer, Æschylus, Shakespeare, Burns, Scott, and Wordsworth. The other order is not content with beauty deeply felt and naturally expressed, till they have found for their thought the most perfect expression, and set it to a more elaborate music. Such are Sophocles, Virgil, Dante, Milton, and, they say, Goethe in his latter days. These, of course, as the former, had an inspiration of their own, or they would not have been true poets, but it is an inspiration which, if it is enriched, is also tinged with all the hues of past cultivation. To the first, the subject so fills their eye, the feeling it awakens so absorbs them, that the form in which it is embodied is wholly subordinate. To the second, subject and form seem of equal, or nearly equal, importance. That this is a real distinction, a line which separates into two orders the whole poetic brotherhood, is no theory, but a fact which the history of literature compels us to recognise. We may,—no doubt most men will prefer the natural poets, while the artistic will be dear chiefly to the scholar, but this should not blind us to a style of excellence which some noble poets have chosen as their own.

Whatever may be the comparative merits of these two methods it is to the second that Mr. Arnold has given himself. In that school he has prepared himself with a thoroughness of discipline not often devoted to poetry in our age and country. His mind has turned back from modern times to brace and elevate itself by severe and independent contemplation of the Hellenic masters. His seriousness and respect for the work he has on hand, and the earnest vigour with which he addresses himself to execute it, are in themselves, we trust, an omen of ultimate success. For whatever errors may have misled, whatever mists may still encompass him, we cannot but hope that such strength of mind and fixedness of purpose will shake them all aside, and force their way victoriously through.

But let us open the work and look at its contents. These are of two kinds. One, and by far the larger part, consists of poems on external subjects, founded on classical legends or historical actions; the other part contains poems of personal sentiment and reflection. 'Sohrab and Rustum,' the longest of the pieces, is an epic fragment, taken from a story long famous in Persian tradition. The Persian and Tartar hosts are encamped in front of each other on the flat low sands of Oxus. Sohrab, a young warrior, who has wandered through all central Asia in search of his hitherto unseen father, and has nowhere met his peer, stands forth to challenge the best of the Persian chiefs to single combat. Rustum accepts the challenge. They fight; Sohrab falls, and in his fallen foe the father recognises his son. A noble story, full of the simplest and deepest elements of human feeling; and Mr. Arnold has told it not unworthily. Three things especially distinguish the poem. First, the vividness with which he has seized and expressed the whole environment of his picture, the vast spaces of central Asia, and the wild freedom of the Tartar life. Secondly, the more than usually free and untrammelled movement which he has given to much of his blank verse. Lastly, and chiefly, the expressiveness of many of the Homeric similes with which the poem is so thickly strewn. Here is one descriptive of Rustum, standing above the fallen Sohrab before he knows him for his son:—

[Quotes ll. 556–75, 'As when some hunter', etc.]

The action and personages of the poem have, we are aware, strongly interested many who know nothing of Homer. For ourselves, we confess that the poem fixes our attention rather as a vivid reproduction of Homer's manner and spirit, than as a new and independent creation. The shade of old Mæonides passes continually between our mind and the warrior forms, and intercepts our primary and genuine interest, allowing only a faint portion to reach the main figures. Indeed the old Greek is everywhere so prominent, that you cannot but doubt whether the subject was chosen for its own inherent attention, or as a block, out of which a fine epic fragment might be hewn. It is to be regretted that the author had not remembered the excellent rule which his own preface contains, and 'preferred his action to everything else;' that, 'having chosen a fitting action he had not penetrated himself with a feeling of its situations,' and not allowed recollections of the Homeric or any other style to intrude between him and his subject. Had he but kept his eye fixed steadily and singly on the scene and the characters, and portrayed them in the native words which his own feeling would have dictated, the result would have been not as now, a fine picture after the style of Homer, but a grand and stirring battle-piece of his own.

One quotation more from 'Sohrab and Rustum,' the description of the Oxus with which it closes.

[Quotes ll. 875–93, the conclusion]

Such a close is not Homeric, nor Greek, but modern, and none the worse for that. It is one of several passages that shew how much at home the author's imagination is among the steppes and nomad plains of Central Asia, and with what a fine hereditary eye he seizes the great lineaments which mark the earth's surface, the picturesque groupings of different races, and the movements of crowding hordes, on which the historian loved to dwell.

What 'Sohrab and Rustum' are to Homer, 'The Strayed Reveller,' 'Cadmus and Harmonia,' and some other pieces, are to Sophocles,—as vivid reproductions of the tragic style and spirit as the former is of the epic. If we were asked what new thing Mr. Arnold has accomplished, with what has he enriched his country's poetry, we should answer that he has added to it embodiments of the thought and sentiment of Grecian poetry, such as it never before possessed. For in 'Samson Agonistes' and 'Lycidas,'—full though they be of the classic spirit, behind that richness of Pagan lore and the Hebrew elevation of tone, there is ever present in the back-ground the strong soul of Milton, crowding along the multifarious imagery, and penetrating all with a deep harmony of his own. And Tennyson's 'Ulysses,' and 'Morte d'Arthur,' perfect in their kind, contain as much of his own as of the Hellenic spirit. It is Mr. Arnold's peculiar merit to have produced, not mere copies, nor even imitations, but living embodiments of antique poetry all but uncoloured by the feelings of modern times. He has breathed a breath of poetry over the dead bones of scholarship till it has become alive and beautiful. Some, we are aware, have regarded these results as nothing more than happy imitations, proving their author to be strong in the mimetic, but not in the original or inventive faculty. But such an opinion, so stated, does injustice to him. For this marriage of poetry with scholarship is something which mere imitation could never have effected. Such reproductions are indeed creations, and prove that among classical materials at least he works with original power. Else how could he have produced what is at once so rare and so beautiful? Why should it require an original poetic faculty to bid live anew the middle age with its shapes of old romance, which are so much nearer ourselves, if mere imitation is enough to re-animate a form of life so remote and difficult as classical antiquity. It may well be doubted whether Mr. Arnold has done wisely in taxing his best powers to reproduce the old classic excellence, but that having chosen this poetic field, he has brought thence some rare, almost unique results, it were prejudice to deny. The truth seems to be, that most readers, and many critics, having no deep feeling for the classic poets themselves, care still less for modern re-creations of their style, and so are tempted to underrate the power of mind employed in producing what they have no heart for; and this is a significant fact which Mr. Arnold would do well to take heed to.

But while we differ entirely from these critics in our estimate of the power required for such poems as 'Sohrab and Rustum,' and 'The Strayed Reveller,' we agree with them in thinking that no strength of imagination can turn back the world's sympathies to the shores of old Greece; and that the poet who tries to do so, while his own land and all Christendom lies fresh around him, is wasting himself on an unprofitable task. By devoting his efforts to subjects of this kind, Mr. Arnold has of necessity confined his audience to the small circle of scholars; and though he may have succeeded in pleasing *them*, he has cut himself off from that general popularity which true poets have sooner or later commanded. Mr. Arnold, we are sure, will not be content with that narrower success, while the other and higher goal stands unattained; and this volume seems to contain proofs of a power which, if rightly used, may yet land him there. But if he is ever to attain to thorough popularity, he must shake himself loose of the exclusive admiration in which the Greek poets have held him,—an admiration so intense, as to have in some degree blinded him to the real lesson which these poets teach.

In his preface he has pointed out two or three lessons to be gathered from their works,—'the all-importance of the choice of a subject, the necessity of accurate construction, the subordinate character of expression.' Truer lessons for a poet there could not be, none but that one self-taught lesson—that native music of soul, 'better than all treasures that in books are found.' But has Mr. Arnold really learned these lessons from his study of the classics? Not in the choice of his subjects. For Homer, and after him all the tragedians chose subjects which were deeply rooted in the hearts of their countrymen, and intertwined with the very fibres of their national existence. Had they done like Mr.

Arnold, they would have turned from the legends of old Achaia, and the ancient sympathies of their race, to choose some theme from Egyptian or Syrian antiquity. Nor, again, peculiarly in the construction of his poems. For the ancients had no classical models to fall back upon, but relied for their art on their own strong sense and clear judgment. And so will the modern poet, if his sense is as strong, and his judgment as clear. Even in expression Mr. Arnold does not seem to have read their lesson aright. For they did not mould themselves on any earlier style, but laid hold of the richest words and strongest idioms which the men of their own day employed in common conversation. But in Mr. Arnold's poems the style, though with many excellencies and full of promise, is too prominent, the classical expressions and allusions too abundant. Here, too, as in choice of his subjects, he will have to cleave his way through the classic cloud that still encompasses him, and hold on his independent path into the bracing air and open pastures of his own land. He must remember that the lessons which the old masters teach are of the spirit, not of the letter, and can hardly be reduced to any preciser shape than this most wide maxim: Let the modern poet act under his circumstances, for his countrymen, with his materials, as the classic poets did with theirs, so widely different.

Leaving the classic poems, we might pause over the romantic ones, 'Sir Tristram and Iseult,' and the 'Church of Brou,' or might express once more admiration of 'The Forsaken Merman,'—on the whole, the most universal favourite of all that Mr. Arnold has yet given to the world. But from these let us turn to 'The Scholar Gipsy,' one of the fresh additions which this volume contains. We would ask all lovers of poetry to read it, and see whether it does not touch their hearts with a sense of fresh beauty, such as one feels on first looking over a new kind of country. And we would ask Mr. Arnold to consider whether the acceptance this poem is sure to win, does not prove to him that it is better to forget all his poetic theories, ay, and Homer and Sophocles, Milton and Goethe too, and speak straight out of things which he has felt and tested on his own pulses. It may be that it derives some of its charm from the vividness with which it brings back old scenes and dear recollections; yet we cannot but think that every one with an open heart for nature, whether he has seen the neighbourhood of Oxford or not, will welcome its delightful pictures. The story is of an Oxford scholar in the 17th century, who was forced by poverty to leave his college, and at last to join a camp of gipsies. Some time after two of his former companions chanced to meet him in their ride. He told them how and why he had taken to this manner of life, that the gipsies with whom he lived were not wholly unlearned, but had a traditional learning of their own, and that he intended to remain with them till he had mastered their lore, and then to give some account of it to the world. In describing his haunts and way of life, all the peculiar traits of Oxford and Berkshire scenery, the habits of the country people, and the sights and sounds that meet one far and near, are portrayed with quite a delightful faithfulness and transparency. Of all the poems in the book, there is none that gives us so fresh and pure delight. A picture of a part of southern England that has been and will be dear to the young hearts of each succeeding generation, but which never till now has found its poetic expression. Here we have done for Oxford in poetry what Turner's picture from the fields above Ferry Hinxey has done in painting.

[Quotes ll. 71–80, 'For most, I know, thou lov'st', etc.]

We should not think much of the poetic taste of him whose heart did not own the natural beauty that is here. But what a pity that the author had not been content to let this portrait stand out in its own refreshingness, without doing his best to dash the dew from it by the painful contrast he draws of our own, as he thinks, unhealthy, unrestful age. Our age may be sickly enough,—the symptoms he describes may or may not exist,—but if they do, the more need that all who have any force in them, as Mr. Arnold undoubtedly has, should do their utmost to strengthen and restore, not farther to paralyze it by useless and unmanly lamentations. At all events, such mournings form no fit setting for otherwise so fair a picture, and, when Mr. Arnold republishes this poem, we are nearly sure that his better judgment will have wholly suppressed them.

Our author is a better and more interesting poet when he goes outwards to describe the situations and feelings of others, than when he turns inward upon himself. The volume closes with lyrics and sonnets, but these are of much less value than the longer poems, which are its chief contents. The lyrics entitled 'Switzerland,' in spite of their frequent felicity of expression, come to us like faded violets, so pale their colour, so languid the passion. If, indeed, passion was ever there, it has been held up so long, and contemplated so steadily by the intellect, that it has altogether evaporated. There is in them none of that strong gush of heart or depth of tenderness which alone give value to poems of the affections, and which can endear to us songs of less ability than these.

But no ability can give interest to poems about feeling, where feeling is not. Indeed, as a general rule, it might be said that there are but two kinds of lyrics which are really valuable. The one, wherein the poet, having felt more deeply, has expressed more happily than ever before was done, some thought, sentiment, or emotion, in which all men share. The other, in which some original and thoughtful man, in the solitary strength of his own genius, goes forth to explore new paths of meditative feeling, in treading which, a younger age, if not his own, will yet inhale fresher and deeper draughts of humanizing sentiment. Of the former kind, are the choicest songs of Burns, and the best of the Scottish and national lyrics of Campbell. To the latter order belong the lyrical ballads of Wordsworth, almost the earliest and most delightful of his poems. To neither of these good kinds do Mr. Arnold's lyrics belong; but it is not because we cannot refer them to any recognised standard, that we reject them, but because they seem entirely empty of human interest. For these our best wish is, that when another edition appears, they may be allowed to retire into the obscurity of private life.

Of the sonnets nothing need now be said, for they have been before the world for some years.—This only by the way, that the 'marble massiveness' of their style, so imposing at a distance, is not borne out, on a nearer approach, by corresponding solidity of thought or depth of wisdom.

But if from many of these shorter poems we are repelled by the blank dejection and morbid languor of their tone, or by the seeming wisdom of apathy, which is not wisdom, we cannot be deaf to some strains of nobler aspiration which here and there break through. The former tones are fewer in this than in the earlier volumes, the latter more numerous. May these grow till they have become full chorus! Of these latter kind are the two poems entitled 'The Future,' and 'Morality.' Let our quotations close with this last. It is a striking, if rather recondite expression of the old truth, that man's moral being is higher than nature's strength; that, as Sir Thomas Browne has it, 'there is surely a piece of divinity in us,—something that was before the elements, and owes no homage to the Sun.'

[Quotes 'Morality', in its entirety]

And now, before taking leave of these poems, we must advert to one thing which strikes us as their prevailing fault. We read them separately, and see many separate excellencies; but there is no one predominant interest to give life to the whole. High gifts, beautiful poems you do see; but one thing you miss—the one pervading poet's heart, that throb of feeling which is the true inspiration, the life of life to all true poetry, without which all artistic gifts are of little worth. Where this is present you cannot but feel its presence, not by self-revelations of the poet's own feelings, but by the living personality and interest which it breathes through whatever it touches. If you associate much with a man of strong character and deep heart, you cannot but feel what kind of man he is. So you cannot read poems which come from a strong poetic soul without their thrilling to your own. But when you have read these poems, and read with admiration, you are still at a loss to know what the author most lays to heart—what kind of country he has lived in— what scenery is dear to him—what part of past or present history he cares for—in what range of human feeling and action he is peculiarly at home. Certain characteristics they do contain—admiration for Greek Art and a uniformly artistic style; but these are not enough to stamp individuality on the poems. The two earlier volumes, it must be allowed, were pervaded by a strong sense of man's nothingness in presence of the great powers of nature—that effort and sorrow are alike vain—that our warm hopes and fears, faiths and aspirations, are crushed like moths beneath the omnipotence of deaf adamantine laws. But such a view of life can give birth to nothing great and noble in character, nor anything high or permanent in poetry. This last volume has much less of that blank dejection and fatalistic apathy which were the main tones of the former ones; and though it has hereby lost in unity of purpose, we gladly welcome the change. In some of the newer poems we seem to catch strains which may prelude a higher music, but they have not yet attained compass enough to set the tone of the book. They may grow to this—we trust they may. Meanwhile we cannot but remind Mr. Arnold that there is a difference between poetic gifts and the poet's heart. That he possesses the former no candid judge can doubt; of the existence of the latter in him he has as yet given less evidence. But it is the beat of this poetic pulse that gives unity of impression and undying interest to the works of the noblest poets. At the outset we noticed the difference between what we called the natural and the artistic poets; those chiefly remarkable for what they say; these for the manner in which they say it. And although in the great poet-kings the two qualities meet and combine, they are not the less in other men distinct and in danger of falling asunder. Where the nature is strong, and the heart full, the poet is apt to rely entirely on this, and to care little for the form to which he entrusts his thoughts. Where the sense of artistic beauty and power of expression predominate, their owner, intent on these, is ever ready to divorce himself from the warmth of life and human interests. This is Mr. Arnold's danger. If we are to judge from these poems, his interest in the poetic art would seem to be stronger than his interest in life, or in those living powers which move the souls of men, and are the fountains of real poetry and of all genuine art. Indeed it is only in proportion as it expresses these that any art is truly valuable. Before he again gives anything to the world, we hope that he will take honest counsel with himself, ask himself the simple question:— What is there which he cares about, for its own sake,— apart from its poetic capabilities, what side of human life, what aspects of nature, what of thought or passion is there, in which he is more at home, about which he feels more intensely than common men do? When he has found this, let him forget the ancient masters and all theories of poetry, and stick to his subject resolutely with his whole heart. For, after all that has been said about it, the soul alone is the true inspirer. Let him be true to this, and seek no other inspiration. And when he has found a self-prompted subject, let him turn on it his full strength of poetic gift and power of expression. These will manifest themselves all the more fully when employed on something which has a real base in human interests, and his future productions will awake a deeper response in other breasts when he speaks from out of the fulness of his own.

Criticism steps beyond its province when it prescribes limits to the poet, or attempts to dictate what his subject should be, or chains him down to the present. All ages, past, present, and future, are alike open to him. Which he is to choose his own instinct must decide. But some are more promising, because they have a deeper hold on men's minds than others. Therefore we cannot but doubt whether Mr. Arnold, or any man, will succeed in really interesting his countrymen by merely disinterring and reconstructing, however skilfully, the old Greek legends. And we are quite sure, that if he is ever to take permanent possession of men's thoughts it must be in the strength of some better, healthier spirit than the blank dejection of his early poems. Mr. Arnold must learn, if he has indeed to learn, that whatever are the faults or needs of our time, the heart has not yet died out of it; that if he thinks it bad, it is the duty of poets, and all thoughtful men, to do their part to mend it, not by weak-hearted lamentations, but by appealing to men's energies, their hopes, their moral aspirations. Let him be quite sure that these are still alive, if he can but arouse them, and that if he cannot the fault lies elsewhere than in his age. To arouse, to strengthen, to purify whatever is good in the men of his own and after times, this is the work which the true poet does. A noble work, if any is, and it takes a noble unworldly nature rightly to fulfil it.

'To console the afflicted, to add sunshine to daylight, by making the happy happier, to teach the young and gracious of every age to see, to think, and feel, and therefore to become more active and securely virtuous, this is their office, which I trust they will perform long after we (that is, all that is mortal of us) are mouldered in our graves.' It was thus that Wordsworth looked forward to the destiny of his own poems at the very time when all the world were combining to scorn them. This calm and invincible confidence was supported, not more by the consciousness of innate power than by the feeling that his poetry had left conventional taste behind it, and struck home into the essential harmony of things. For Mr. Arnold we can have no better wish than that his future efforts may be guided by as true and elevated a purpose, and win for him, according to his measure, as worthy a success.

10. Arnold in response to his critics

1854

(a) Preface to *Poems*, 2nd edition (1854), dated 1 June 1854.

Since many reviewers agreed about the limitations of the 1853 preface, Arnold was probably offering a general rebuttal—or apology. However, he meets specific charges in Froude, Aytoun, W. C. Roscoe, Goldwin Smith, Kingsley, as well as J. D. Coleridge, whom he answers in (b) below.

I have allowed the Preface to the former edition of these Poems to stand almost without change, because I still believe it to be, in the main, true. I must not, however, be supposed insensible to the force of much that has been alleged against portions of it, or unaware that it contains many things incompletely stated, many things which need limitation. It leaves, too, untouched the question, how far, and in what manner, the opinions there expressed respecting the choice of subjects apply to lyric poetry—that region of the poetical field which is chiefly cultivated at present. But neither do I propose at the present time to supply these deficiencies, nor indeed would this be the proper place for attempting it. On one or two points alone I wish to offer, in the briefest possible way, some explanation.

An objection has been ably urged to the classing together, as subjects equally belonging to a past time, Oedipus and Macbeth. And it is no doubt true that to Shakespeare, standing on the verge of the middle ages, the epoch of Macbeth was more familiar than that of Oedipus. But I was speaking of actions as they presented themselves to us moderns: and it will hardly be said that the European mind, in our day, has much more affinity with the times of Macbeth than with those of Oedipus. As moderns, it seems to me, we have no longer any direct affinity with the circumstances and feelings of either. As individuals, we are attracted towards this or that personage, we have a capacity for imagining him, irrespective of his times, solely according to a law of personal sympathy;

and those subjects for which we feel this personal attraction most strongly, we may hope to treat successfully. Alcestis or Joan of Arc, Charlemagne or Agamemnon—one of these is not really nearer to us now than another. Each can be made present only by an act of poetic imagination; but this man's imagination has an affinity for one of them, and that man's for another.

It has been said that I wish to limit the poet in his choice of subjects to the period of Greek and Roman antiquity; but it is not so. I only counsel him to choose for his subjects great actions, without regarding to what time they belong. Nor do I deny that the poetic faculty can and does manifest itself in treating the most trifling action, the most hopeless subject. But it is a pity that power should be wasted; and that the poet should be compelled to impart interest and force to his subject, instead of receiving them from it, and thereby doubling his impressiveness. There is, it has been excellently said, an immortal strength in the stories of great actions; the most gifted poet, then, may well be glad to supplement with it that mortal weakness, which, in presence of the vast spectacle of life and the world, he must for ever feel to be his individual portion.

Again, with respect to the study of the classical writers of antiquity; it has been said that we should emulate rather than imitate them. I make no objection; all I say is, let us study them. They can help to cure us of what is, it seems to me, the great vice of our intellect, manifesting itself in our incredible vagaries in literature, in art, in religion, in morals: namely, that it is *fantastic,* and wants *sanity.* Sanity—that is the great virtue of the ancient literature; the want of that is the great defect of the modern, in spite of all its variety and power. It is impossible to read carefully the great ancients, without losing something of our caprice and eccentricity; and to emulate them we must at least read them.

(b) From the note on 'Sohrab and Rustum', 1854.

Arnold knew that Coleridge had written the article for the *Christian Remembrancer* and was naturally displeased that a friend should accuse him, especially in a public medium, of plagiarism. Arnold also wrote a private letter to Coleridge, expressing much the same thing, and with absolutely no ill-temper. But A. P. Stanley made clear to Coleridge that the review was far too severe, the charges too pointed, to have come from a friend. The following passage is Arnold's conclusion to the note and comes after an explicit account of his sources for 'Sohrab and Rustum'.

A writer in the *Christian Remembrancer* (of the general tenour of whose remarks I have, assuredly, no right to complain) having made the discovery of this notice by M. Sainte-Beuve, has pointed out the passages in which I have made use of the extracts from M. Mohl's translation which it contains; has observed, apparently with blame, that I 'have not thought fit to offer a single syllable of acknowledgment to an author to whom I have been manifestly very largely indebted'; has complained of being 'under some embarrassment from not being sure how much of the treatment is Mr. Arnold's own'; and, finally has suggested that 'the whole work of M. Mohl may have been used throughout, and the study of antiquity carried so far as simply to reproduce an ancient poem as well as an ancient subject'.

It would have been more charitable, perhaps, had the reviewer, before making this goodnatured suggestion, ascertained, by reference to M. Mohl's work, how far it was confirmed by the fact.

The reader, however, is now in possession of the whole of the sources from which I have drawn the story of 'Sohrab and Rustum', and can determine, if he pleases, the exact amount of my obligation to M. Mohl. But I hope that it will not in future be supposed, if I am silent as to the sources from which a poem has been derived, that I am trying to conceal obligations, or to claim an absolute originality for all parts of it. When any man endeavours to *rémanier et reinventer à sa manière* a great story, which, as M. Sainte-Beuve says of that of 'Sohrab and Rustum', has *couru le monde*, it may be considered quite certain that he has not drawn all the details of his work out of his own head. The reader is not, I think, concerned to ask, from that sources these have been drawn; but only how the whole work, as it stands, affects him. Real plagiarism, such as the borrowing without acknowledgement of passages from other English poets—real dishonesty, such as the endeavouring to pass off the mere translation of a poem as an original work—are always certain enough to be discovered.

I must not be led on, from defending the morality of my imitation, to defend at length its aesthetics; but I cannot forbear adding, that it would be a most unfortunate scruple which should restrain an author, treating matter of history or tradition, from placing, where he can, in the mouths of his personages the very words of the old chronicle, or romance, or poem (when the poem embodies, as that of Ferdousi, the tradition of a people); and which should lead him to substitute for these any *eigene grossen Erfindungen*.[1] For my part, I only regret that I could not meet with a translation from Ferdousi's poem of the whole of the episode of 'Sohrab and Rustum'; with a prose translation, that is: for in a verse translation no original work is any longer recognizable. I should certainly have made all the use I could of it. The use of the tradition, above everything else, gives to a work that *naïveté,* that flavour of reality and truth, which is the very life of poetry.

[1] '[of his] own great inventions.'

11. George Eliot, unsigned review, *Westminster Review*

July 1855, lxiv, n.s. viii, 297–9

George Eliot (1819–80) had not, at the time of this review, begun her career as a novelist, but she had been contributing to the *Westminster*—for one period as editor—since 1850. In this review of several authors and of different types of literary works, her discussion of *Poems* is necessarily brief. But it is also discriminating and prophetic. Her reservations about Arnold are that the earlier poems seem superior to the later, so that Arnold does not seem to progress as an artist; and that his sense of rhythm is defective—a charge that was to become common. Her description of the slow but powerful effect of the poems, which seemed at first 'tame and prosaic', is emblematic of the whole development of Arnold's reputation.

The name of Matthew Arnold on a volume of Poems is a sufficient recommendation to the notice of all those who are careful to supply themselves with poetry of a new vintage, so we need not regret, except on our own account, that we have made rather a late acquaintance with his Second Series of Poems, published last quarter. If we had written of these poems after reading them only once, we should have given them a tepid kind of praise, but after reading them again and again, we have become their partizan, and are tempted to be intolerant of those who will not admit their beauty. Our first impression from a poem of Mr. Arnold's—and with some persons this is the sole impression—generally is, that it is rather tame and prosaic. The thought is always refined and unhackneyed, sometimes new and sublime, but he seems not to have found the winged word which carries the thought at once to the mind of the reader; his poems do not come to us like original melodies, which are beautiful facts that one never thinks of altering any more than a pine-tree or a river; we are haunted by the feeling that he might have said the same thing much better. But when, simply for the sake of converse with a nature so gifted and cultivated as Mr. Arnold's, we linger over a poem which contains some deep and fresh thought, we begin to perceive poetic beauties—felicities of expression and description, which are too quiet and subdued to be seized at the first glance. You must become familiar with his poems before you can appreciate them as poetry, just as in the early spring you must come very near to the woods before you can discern the delicate glossy or downy buds which distinguish their April from their winter clothing. He never attains the wonderful word-music of Tennyson, which lives with you like an Adelaide of Beethoven, or a *Preghiera* of Rossini; but his combinations and phrases are never common, they are fresh from the fountain, and call the reader's mind into new activity. Mr. Arnold's grand defect is want of rhythm—we mean of that rhythm which is music to an English ear. His imitations of the classical metres can no more win a place in our lasting national poetry than orange and olive-trees can flourish in our common English gardens; and his persistence in these imitations is, we think, a proof that he lacks that fine sense of word-music, that direct inspiration of song, as distinguished from speech, which is the crowning gift of the poet.

This Second Series is not equal, though it is a worthy companion, to the first; there is no poem in it so fine as 'Zohrab and Rustum,' or 'Tristan and Iseult;' but in putting the volume into the hands of a reader to whom Mr. Arnold's poems were new, we should point to 'Resignation,' and to 'The Last Glen,' and 'Typho' in 'The Harp-player on Ætna,' as favourable specimens of the author's power in two directions—the expression of exquisite sensibility united with deep thought, in which he reminds us of Wordsworth, and the revivifying of antique conceptions by freshly-felt descriptions of external nature and masterly indications of permanent human feeling, after the manner of Tennyson. We steal space for the sake of quoting two passages from 'Resignation:'—

> The Poet, to whose mighty heart
> Heaven doth a quicker pulse impart,
> Subdues that energy to scan
> Not his own course, but that of Man.

[Quotes additionally ll. 164–98; 261–78]

12. Other comments on the early volumes

(a) Unsigned notice in the *English Review*, March 1850

A still more helpless, cheerless doubter [than Clough] is 'A.,' author of *The Strayed Reveller, and other Poems*, whom, for the sake of his father's memory, we forbear to name more particularly. Yet, not surprised are we, such teaching should have led to such results: by the fruit we know the seed. Any thing more darkly melancholy, more painfully sombre, than the last poem in the volume entitled 'Resignation,' and addressed to 'Fausta,' we never remember to have seen. The poet, in the very heyday of his youthful spring, arrives at the conclusion, that all life, whether for ourselves or others' sakes, is vanity. He says:—

[Quotes 'Resignation', ll. 231-8, 'Blame thou not', etc. and 261-78, 'Enough, we live!' etc.]

This melancholy is deep indeed. The very first longer poem in the volume, 'Mycerinus,' is a kind of apotheosis of despair; it looks as if suggested by a father's fate. At the same time, it seems almost a profession of atheism! 'Emerson,' we learn from the sonnet on p. 52, is one of 'A.'s' great teachers: a 'god of his idolatry.' Poor worshipper, with such a god!—The reminiscences of Tennyson and Browning are manifold also in this volume. Thus 'A Modern Sappho' is a rather confused imitation, or reminiscence, of one of Browning's 'Dramatic Romances,' entitled 'The Laboratory;' and a very mystical affair, called 'The New Sirens, a Palisode,' is more Tennysonian than Tennyson himself. Even the most beautiful poem in the volume, 'The Forsaken Merman,' reminds us of Tennyson, but not unpleasantly: it is far superior to *that* poet's 'Merman' or 'Mermaid;' and, perhaps, equal to any of his lyrical creations. There is a musical cadence in the rhythm almost unrivalled. The same merit will be discovered in the somewhat aimless, yet lyrically beautiful poem, which gives its name to the volume.

Altogether, of these two new poets, 'A.' is, we think, the superior, being at once the more earnest and the more poetical; but each has real claims. 'A's' singing is like the musical wind wailing through the forest tops on the high mountains far away. 'Clough' resembles rather the monotonous heaving of the sea against a rock-bound shore. Both are very *sad;* and neither Oxford nor Cambridge need rejoice in their children.

(b) J. C. Shairp in a letter to Clough, 16 April 1853

I fear Mat's last book has made no impression on the public mind. I'm not much in the way of hearing but I've seen no one, except a few Oxford Rugbeans who have even read it. It does not much astonish me, for though I think there's great power in it, one regrets to see so much power thrown away upon so false and uninteresting (too) a view of life. Since you have gone from England, it's well you've gone to a hearty fresh young people, rather than into the 'blank dejection of European Capitols'. Anything that so takes the life from out things must be false. It's this I like about your things that though in theory you maintain the contrary, yet in fact the 'great human heart' will out and you can't hinder it: Stick to this. Mat, as I told him, disowns man's natural feelings, and they will disown his poetry. If there's nothing else in the world but blank dejection, it's not worth while setting them to music.

(c) Arnold to Clough in November 1853

[November 25]
My dear Clough
   Just read through Tennyson's Morte d'Arthur and Sohrab and Rustum one after the other, and you will see the difference in the *tissue* of the style of the two poems, and in its *movement*. I think the likeness, where there is likeness, (except in the two last lines which I own are a regular slip) proceeds from our both having imitated Homer. But never mind—you are a dear soul. I am in great hopes you will one day like the poem—really like it. There is no one to whose aperçus I attach the value I do to yours—but I think you are sometimes—with regard to *me* especially—a little cross and wilful.
   I send you two letters—not that you may see the praise of me in them (and I can sincerely say that praise of *myself*—talking about imagination—genius and so on—does not give me, at heart, the slightest flutter of pleasure—seeing people interested in what I have made, does—) but that you may see how heartily two very different people seem to have taken to Sohrab and Rustum. This is something, at any rate.

[November 30]
   I think the poem ['Sohrab and Rustum'] has, if not the *rapidity,* at least the *fluidity* of Homer: and that it is in this respect that it is un-Tennysonian: and that it is a sense of this which makes Froude and Blackett say it is a step in advance of Tennyson in this strain.
   A thousand things make one compose or not compose: composition seems to keep alive in me a *cheerfulness*—a sort of Tuchtigkeit, or natural soundness and valiancy, which I think the present age is fast losing—this is why I like it.
   I am glad you like the Gipsy Scholar—but what does it *do* for you? Homer *animates*—Shakespeare *animates*—in its poor way I think Sohrab and Rustum *animates*—the Gipsy Scholar at best awakens a pleasing melancholy. But this is not what we want.

> The complaining millions of men
> Darken in labour and pain—

what they want is something to *animate* and *ennoble* them—not merely to add zest to their melancholy or grace to their dreams.—I believe a feeling of this kind is the basis of my nature—and of my poetics.

You certainly do not seem to me sufficiently to desire and earnestly strive towards—assured knowledge—activity—happiness. You are too content to *fluctuate*—to be ever learning, never coming to the knowledge of the truth. This is why, with you, I feel it necessary to stiffen myself—and hold fast my rudder.

My poems, however, viewed *absolutely*, are certainly little or nothing.

(d) Harriet Martineau in the *Daily News*, 26 December 1853

That the keen and just observation, and power of reflecting upon the 'inner eye' things absent, which are privileges of the true poet, are wanting in Mr. Arnold, we infer, notwithstanding his frequent assembling of picturesque words and images, from such lines as the following:

> Pois'd on the top of a huge wave of Fate,
> Which hangs uncertain to which side to fall.

(There never was such a wave seen at Brighton, or elsewhere.)

> To gaze on the green sea of leaf *and bough*.

(There never was such a forest view beheld off any mound in Windsor or West Kentucky)
and even from the employment of single words such as 'beckon'd,' in page 21. 'Ere the parting kiss be *dry*' is the refrain of a love poem, but had better been altogether refrained from. We draw a similar conclusion from innumerable trite phrases and illustrations, such as 'quick as a flash;' 'thundering to earth' [a club]; 'her fingers slight, as the driven snow were white;' 'raven hair;' 'whispering honied nothings;' 'Fate's iron heel;' as also from the attempts at rich description of scenery, as in

the 'Dream,' page 178, and of a church, page 151, in both of which are good enough words, but no poetry. We may note, in passing, that the three lines on this page 151, 'And thou, O princess,' &c., are as glaring examples of want of truthful conception as could perhaps be anywhere found.

Among the other pieces is one called 'Mycerinus.' He, according to Herodotus, being a King of Egypt better than any of his predecessors, was told by an oracle that he had but six years longer to live. Mr. Arnold represents him as thereupon giving up all care of his kingdom with these words:

> Ye men of Egypt, ye have heard your king.
> I go, and I return not. But the will
> Of the great Gods is plain; and ye must bring
> Ill deeds, ill passions, zealous to fulfil
> Their pleasure, to their feet; and reap their praise,
> The praise of Gods, rich boon! and length of days.

and spending the remaining six years in continual revelries in his pleasure-gardens on the Nile, only intruded on by awful reminders of his approaching doom. The moral significance, here again, is either null, or very difficult to understand, or not salutary. 'Let us eat and drink, for to-morrow we die;' and the same remark applies to 'The Strayed Reveller,' which would seem to express, if anything, the pleasures of getting drunk. It has no story. The issues of those that have—of 'Tristram and Iseult,' 'Sohrab and Rustum,' and 'Mycerinus,' are each and all, unrelieved, undignified misfortune, the infliction (this is very noticeable) of a blind Fate: acting through a love-potion in one case; announced by a cruel oracle in another; and driving the Father and Son against each other—according to Sohrab's own words,

> Fage—Fate engag'd
> The strife, and hurl'd me on my father's spear.

in the third.

Have we really at this day amongst us one for whom the universe turns round that awful centre, of a blind necessity, grinding men and all things continually to dust?—that thought from which the Greek took refuge in poetic mythology and exquisite realism. But to recur; we find in Mr. Arnold's preface this paragraph:— 'What then are the situations, from the representation of which, though accurate, no poetical enjoyment can be derived? They are those in which the suffering finds no vent in action; in which a continuous state of mental distress is prolonged, unrelieved by incident, hope, or resistance; in which there is everything to be endured, nothing to be done. In such situations there is inevitably something morbid, in the description of them something monotonous.' Now, in the three principal pieces just named, what is the situation in which we, at least, leave Iseult, and Rustum, and Mycerinus, to which the whole in each case tends, and from which we carry away our general impression?—surely in 'a continuous state of mental distress, unrelieved by incident, hope, or resistance; in which there is everything to be endured, nothing to be done.' Theory and practice, in this respect more utterly at variance, could not, it seems to us, be found anywhere.

The shorter pieces are not remarkable, except, first, for the absurd servility to antique fashions which gives one lyric, about a young lady, the title of 'The Modern Sappho,' and another, about a nightingale, the very fresh one of 'Philomela,' whom Mr. Arnold hears on the banks of the Thames complaining of the ill-usage recorded by M. Lemprière; and, second, for the promise of metre which so many of them keep to the eye but wholly break to the ear. At this season, when charades and conundrums enliven the drawing-room, we offer the following, here printed without alteration or transposition of a word or comma, for the wits of the ingenious to exercise upon, in discovering how they could possibly have been arranged in the form or semblance of metre. *Imprimis,* the whole of the poem called 'Richmond Hill' (but we are not so cruel as to set out friends to look for the meaning of it—only the metre), as follows: 'Murmur of living! stir of existence! soul of the world! make, oh make yourselves felt to the dying Spirit of Youth! Come, like the breath of the Spring! leave not a human soul to grow old in darkness and pain. Only the living can feel you, but leave us not while we live!' Then these extracts: 'Mist clogs the sunshine. Smoky dwarf houses hem me round everywhere. A vague dejection weighs down my soul.' 'Time, so complain'd of, who to no one man shows partiality, brings round to all men some undimm'd hours.' 'What Bard, at the height of his vision, can deem of God, of the world, of the soul, with a plainness as near, as flashing as Moses felt, when he lay in the night by his flock on the starlit Arabian waste? can rise and obey the beck of the Spirit like him?'

Finally, we take leave of Mr. Arnold, with his cleverness and his scholarship, his somewhat superciliously announced theories of poetry, his attachment to ancient models, and his echoes (for all that) of the

Tennysonian cadences, in the conviction that, although he has written no common verses—nay, better than some men to-day of celebrity as 'poets'—he was not born a poet, and therefore never can be one. Many claim the rank; few show claims so plausible as his, because of the superiority of his general talents and culture; but his claims also want the genuine stamp. We say so, not without pain, yet distinctly.

(e) W. R. Roscoe in the *Prospective Review*, February 1854

This book must bring genuine pleasure to every one whose judgment it is worth a man's while to interest. Mr. Arnold measures himself too justly to claim a place among the kings of song, but below the topmost heights of Parnassus lie many pleasant ranges and happy pastures, among whose denizens he may enjoy a not ignoble rank. He starts from a vantage ground rare in these days. He possesses the uncommon and valuable conviction that poetic art has its nature and its rules which admit of being studied with advantage. Nor does he want the more intrinsic attributes of a poet. A keen and refined sense of beauty, sometimes finding its expression in phrases of exquisite felicity, a mind and artistic faculty, trained, and disciplined to reticence, and an imagination of considerable scope and power, are no mean qualifications.

There is artistic finish too in his verse (though as we wish hereafter to remark, not in his conceptions); not the finish of high polish, but the refined ease and grace of a taste pure by nature and yet conscientiously cultivated. Hence instead of congratulating ourselves that we have read him, we find a pleasure in actually reading him, and take him up again and again with undiminished freshness and enjoyment. Partly it is that he does not make too great a demand upon us; his light free air refreshes us. Instead of being hemmed in by that majesty and terror which make the vicinity of the Alps oppressive, we stroll with lighter hearts on breezy heaths and uplands. Like Wordsworth, Mr. Arnold owes part of his charm to the very absence of deep and engrossing feelings in his nature.

(f) Charles Kingsley in *Fraser's Magazine*, February 1854

One point seems questionable about ['Sohrab and Rustum'] and that is the end of it. Why, after all the human interest of the poem, are we to turn suddenly off to mere nature and nature-description, beautiful as that may be?

> But the majestic river floated on
> Out of the mist and hum of that low land
> Into the frosty starlight, and there moved
> Rejoicing, through the lone Chorasmian waste
> Under the solitary moon.

And so on, for some twelve or fourteen lines more, every one and all of them life-like, perfect, both as parts and as a whole: but why here?—why end with this? True, the poem began with the Oxus, and ends with it also; but is that right, even in an episode? If the poet cannot always shew how his subject arises out of eternity, he should surely shew how it returns to it again; there must be some solace; the mind must have something on which to rest, after the chances and changes of this mortal life; something to calm his excitement, without deadening his interest, and to make him feel that after all The Powers are just, that it is better with the righteous in his misery, than with the evil in his prosperity. Sophocles surely always does this; Shakspeare always. And if Mr. Arnold was not minded to do it here, he had far better have ended with

> And Rustum and his son were left alone,

so compelling the reader to work out the problem in his own mind, than have tried to turn our human interest and affection from them, by telling us about the Oxus. Who cares whither the Oxus goes, or what becomes of it, while Rustum is lying in the sand by his dead son, like one of 'Giamschid's fallen pillars in Persepolis?' The Oxus, and all the rivers on earth, yea all nature, and the sun and moon, if they intrude themselves at such a moment, are simply impertinences. Rustum and his son are greater than they: nearer to us than they. Our spirits are hovering lovingly round their spirits; and as for the Oxus and its going into the Aral Sea, or the Red Sea—Let it go! Surely Mr. Arnold has not fallen into this mistake of malice prepense? Surely this is not a remnant of that old fault of his, the affecting—(for no young man really does more than affect)—to believe that man is less than phenomenal nature, and a part of it, and that while the Oxus, and the stars, and the Aral Sea, go on right and fulfil their destinies, it is somewhat beneath a wise man to make himself unhappy about the puny little human beings who fight, and love, and do right and do wrong upon its banks? He would not surely wish us to believe that all the noble human pathos, and spiritual experience which he has been displaying throughout the poem, is at heart cold and unreal, a thing which has been put on for forty pages, and then pulled off again at the sight of any river in the world?

(g) D. G. Rossetti in a letter to William Allingham, 1855

I suppose there is no chance of your having written an unrhymed elegy on Currer Bell, called 'Haworth Churchyard', in this *Fraser*, and signed 'A.' There is some *thorough* appreciation of poor *Wuthering Heights* in it, but then the same stanza raves of Byron, so you can't have done it; not to add that it wouldn't be up to any known mark of yours, I think.

MEROPE

1857, dated 1858

13. 'J.C.' (John Conington?), review, *Fraser's Magazine*

June 1858, lvii, 691–701

Conington (1825–69) was a classical scholar, an editor of Greek and Latin literature, and an Oxford professor, who was temperamentally and by training inclined to respect Arnold's tragedy. Of the preface and the play he writes: 'The one is a brilliant specimen of a class of which we have many, though still too few, examples; the other is almost, if not altogether unique.' Conington begins his discussion with a pertinent and shrewd analysis of the preface, which has obvious application to the play. I have included this but omitted a leisurely discussion of the mythological basis of the play and what amounts to a plot summary.

This is an instalment, promptly and gracefully offered, of Mr. Arnold's debt to the University which, not twelve months ago, elected him to its Professorship of Poetry. It is indeed precisely what was to have been expected from his poetical antecedents. He had published enough to show that it was in his power to give new life to a chair which was especially instituted to promote the study of the poetry of classical antiquity. It was not merely that, in his Preface to the first volume which appeared with his name, he had given a delicate and discriminating exposition of the excellences of the classical school, but that some of his own happiest efforts were framed after classical models, and framed with a minute attention which was itself, to all intents and purposes, a lecture in criticism. The reader of the 'Fragment of an Antigone' could hardly help feeling that he understood Sophocles better; the reader of

'Sohrab and Rustum' could scarcely fail to gain a new insight into the conduct of the Homeric narrative and the structure of the Homeric simile. Such was the promise, and we are now in possession of what may fairly be called a substantial part of the performance. We have a Preface, which is itself a long lecture on classical poetry; and we have an entire tragedy, which is virtually equivalent to many more. Both are, in their way, remarkable; but the pretensions of the play are necessarily much beyond those of the preface. The one is a brilliant specimen of a class of which we have many, though still too few, examples; the other is almost, if not altogether, unique.

We are conscious that our description of Mr. Arnold's experiment does not altogether agree with that which he would himself put forward. We have treated it as an experiement in art made for the sake of criticism; he evidently intends it to be an experiment in art made for the sake of art. 'I desired,' such are the words of his Preface, 'to try how much of the effectiveness of the Greek poetical forms I could retain in an English poem, constructed under the conditions of those forms; of those forms, too, in their severest and most definite expression, in their application to dramatic poetry.' Elsewhere in the Preface he dwells on this severity of form as the secret of that peculiar excellence which has always impressed itself on the minds of the students of the Greek drama. 'Sophocles,' he remarks in a very discriminating passage, *apropos* of Mr. Lewes' critique of Goethe's *Iphigenia*, 'does not produce the sentiments of repose, of acquiescence, by inculcating it, by avoiding agitating circumstances: he produces it by exhibiting to us the most agitating matter under the conditions of the severest form.' He insists on the effect, not only of unity of plan in the action, and symmetry in the treatment of it, but of the minuter conformity of speech to speech in the dialogue, and strophe to antistrophe in the choral songs. He enlarges on the functions performed by the Chorus itself as a constituent element of the drama—first, as the 'ideal spectator,' expressing what the actual spectator would wish to feel; secondly, as affording to excited feeling the relief which Shakespeare seeks to supply by intermingling comedy with tragedy. All this he puts forth, not as an antiquary, or even as a philosophical critic, anxious to show that ancient art had its true and human side, but as an artist desirous to remedy the defects, and renovate the spirit of modern art by a recurrence to earlier and, in some respects, better times. He nowhere, indeed, commits himself to a formal comparison between the classical and the romantic, the old and the new; but he scarcely conceals that he is not exactly neutral in the controversy. The very sentence in which he appears to demand least for the ancients contains a claim which, if conceded, would involve the concession of all. 'The laws of Greek art . . . are not exclusive; they are for Greek dramatic art itself, but they do not pronounce other modes of dramatic art unlawful: they are, at most, *prophecies of the improbability of dramatic success under other conditions.*' The italics are Mr. Arnold's own, and they certainly add significance to what was already significant enough.

Now, we are not going to take the part of modern sciolism against ancient experience, and protest against a classical revival merely because it is classical. Our love of classical poetry is as warm as Mr. Arnold's: our opinion of the good which he is doing and may do, by fixing the attention of our younger poets on classical models, is strong and decided. But we wish to point out one or two considerations which seem to us, apart from popular ignorance and prejudice, effectually to preclude any attempt at restoring the classical drama as against the Shakespearian, or even side by side with it. The first is furnished to our hands by Mr. Arnold himself. In a passage not far from those which are extracted in the last paragraph, he admits clearly that the structure of the Greek drama was necessitated by certain circumstances which he proceeds to explain:—

The Greek theatres [he says] were vast, and open to the sky: the actors, masked, and in a somewhat stiff tragic costume, were to be regarded from a considerable distance: a solemn, clearly marked style of gesture, a sustained tone of declamation, were thus rendered necessary. Under these conditions, intricate byplay, rapid variations in the action, requiring great mobility, ever-changing shades of tone and gesture in the actor, were impossible. Broad and simple effects were, under these conditions, above all to be aimed at: a profound and clear impression was to be effected.

What is this but really to concede the whole point at issue? Certain things, which Mr. Arnold apparently admits to be good, and which a modern will be apt to say constitute almost the whole resemblance between the drama and human life, had to be sacrificed by the Greeks in consequence of the peculiar construction of their theatres. But is that any reason why they should be sacrificed by a nation which can enjoy them even in the theatre, and can unquestionably enjoy them in the closet? What becomes of the 'prophecy of the improbability of dramatic success under other conditions' than those of the Greek forms, when the circumstances of dramatic representation are changed? It is possible, no doubt, that the Greeks were in some sort gainers by their privations; that having, before all things, to aim at 'effecting a profound and clear impression,' they did produce it more unmistakeably than others who have fewer difficulties to contend with, just as a blind man will often acquire extraordinary powers of touch. It is possible; and yet when we think of Shakespeare, we can hardly say that modern art must necessarily fail in producing an impression of real and profound unity, while at the same time it confessedly creates that sense of variety which Greek art, as confessedly, does not attempt to compass. But in any case it seems strange to expect that modern dramatists should consult clearness of impression by writing in the manner best adapted to strike the eye and ear of spectators—ideal in another sense than Schlegel's —sitting at distances which are happily now impossible.

Again, it is forgotten that the Greek drama was not, even in Greece, a permanent institution. Mr. Arnold quotes a passage from Aristotle, where it is said that 'tragedy, after going through many changes, got the nature which suited it, and there it stopped.' Tragedy, with Aristotle's favour, did not stop as he would lead us to suppose. In one sense, indeed, it stopped—as a watch stops. It ceased to be cultivated with success, and it ceased to be cultivated at all. But its whole life was a course of change, and the change may be said to have gone on after its death. About the earlier changes there is indeed no dispute. The dialogue, it is admitted, gradually gained ground on the chorus: but it appears to be thought that about the time of Sophocles, a compromise came in, and that henceforth the principle of *uti possidetis*[1] was observed. But though Euripides did not abridge the quantum of space allowed to the chorus, he impaired its efficiency by making its songs less relevant to the play; and we know that after, if not during his time, the custom was introduced of singing insertions, as they were called—choral odes written for no one tragedy, and so capable of being used in any—a way of relieving the overwrought feelings of the spectator, which even Mr. Arnold would scarcely approve. We can hardly doubt that, if tragedy had continued, its next stage would have been that through which comedy passed—the chorus would have been dropped as a useless appendage. Really, however, we are not left to surmise: the change in question *did* take place. The last phase of Athenian tragedy had no chorus; for the last phase of Athenian tragedy was the new comedy. The fact was one which a Greek critic, living at the time, could hardly be expected to recognise; but the critics of Rome could see that Menander was the real successor of Euripides, though the Roman tragic poets tried to reorganise

[1] 'according to your abilities'.

the form that had already separated into its elements, and wrote lyrics that were either too simple or too difficult to be sung for choruses that had no longer any orchestra to dance in. Sophocles was not, as Mr. Arnold and others have thought him, the final law-giver of Athenian tragedy; he was one of a long line of dramatic improvers, beginning, it may be, with Thespis, but extending down to our own day.

But even if Greek tragedy could be regarded as having the fixity and permanence which would make it a proper object of imitation, there is a further reason why it is not likely, in any real sense, to be naturalized among us. Here, again, Mr. Arnold perceives the truth, though he does not appear to apply it. Speaking of *Samson Agonistes,* he observes with justice, that 'the forms of Greek tragedy are better adapted to Greek stories than to Hebrew or any other.' But it is not likely that the un-learned public can be made to appreciate Greek stories to any great extent. Even Grecian history is not capable of being made very popular, and Grecian mythology has a much worse chance with the million than Grecian history. It is not simply, as Mr. Arnold says in the first sentence of his Preface, that a subject is taken from classical antiquity. A historical subject from classical antiquity might be treated by a modern writer to a spirit which should appeal to modern readers. But mythological subjects are only known to us through the great imagina-tive writers, who have, in fact, half created them. We adopt their point of view; in short, we imitate them, not only in their form, but in their sentiments, and their whole manner of treatment. And these imitations are to be relished by persons to whom the originals are practically un-known. 'Sublime acquiescence in the course of fate' is to be taught by poets who could not feel towards fate as the Greeks did, even if they would. A national want is to be created or satisfied by a national drama, which is to be Greek in everything but language.

There are, however, in Mr. Arnold's statement of his own object, some points which we can cordially accept. He takes in fact, much the same ground which we have already intimated that we are most willing and most anxious to accord to him. He desires to satisfy the 'wide though ill-informed curiosity,' which he believes to prevail even in England 'on the subject of the so-called classical school,' and to give those who know and love Greek the opportunity of approaching Greek beauty through the more familiar and less resisting medium of their own language. Of this presumed curiosity we can say but little. It is most common, perhaps, among intelligent women, who have a taste for poetry, and are sorry not to have had the advantage of learning Greek. To such *Merope* may be confidently recommended, as likely to give them a better notion of a Greek play than anything which exists in English. In one sense, indeed, *Samson Agonistes* is a more truthful representative of the Greek drama, as placing us in something of the same position as a Greek play placed a Greek audience, appealing to religious associations which are acknowledged, and to a reflection of a reflection. But though neither the best translation nor the best imitation can offer the student any advantage as against the original, they may throw great light on it if used in combination with it. Scholars will always be glad to learn from scholars, and readers of poetry from men of poetical feeling. We once had the privilege of an interview with Hermann, when the conversation turned on Greek tragedy, and he spoke of having recently ordered an English work, which treated of Greek tragedy aesthetically—that work proving, on an appeal to his memoranda, to be the poetical prelections of one of Mr. Arnold's most eminent predecessors, Mr. Keble. So we are glad to notice that in the last number of the *Journal of Classical and Sacred Philology* Mr. Lightfoot, whom we know to be one of the most distinguished scholars in Cambridge, illustrates an interpretation of a passage in one of the choruses in the *Helen* of Euripides, by an extract from *Merope*.

But it is time to give some account of the play itself, and offer a few remarks upon it.

Wisely declining to enter into direct competition with any of the masterpieces of Greek tragedy by writing a drama on the same subject, Mr. Arnold has chosen a story which has not the disadvantage of being embarrassed by any previous associations in the mind of a modern reader, while it is known to have had great success when brought on the Athenian stage.

[Discusses the various myths and their treatment by the Greek tragedians, then details Arnold's plot]

No student of Greek tragedy, we think, will deny that Mr. Arnold has succeeded in producing an imitation sufficiently like to satisfy the curiosity of an English reader. In one sense, indeed, the fault of *Merope* is that the imitation is too close. No two of the extant Greek plays so far as we are aware, resemble each other so nearly as a great part of *Merope* resembles a great part of the *Electra* of Sophocles. The similarity of the stories, as we have already intimated, makes a certain degree of resemblance unavoidable: but Mr. Arnold has gone beyond this. He was perhaps not called upon to depart from Sophocles in the manner in which the supposed death of Æpytus is announced. Obvious as the imitation there is, it is no more than would naturally result from the coincidence of two writers conducting two very similar transactions under the ordinary forms of the Greek stage. But the scene which follows, the lyrical dialogue between Merope and the chorus, is an imitation of a very different kind. Mr. Arnold was not obliged to follow Sophocles, but he has followed him so minutely as to seem to do little more than set new words to an old tune. This, however, will be felt by those who know Sophocles, not by those who are ignorant of him. A graver question arises with reference to the management of the story. Mr. Arnold, as we have already intimated, has departed from the ancient tradition in at least one important point, while in another he has struck out a line of his own which, if not inconsistent with the legend, is contrary to the interpretation placed on it by other modern writers. He has done this to bring about certain results which he considers poetically and dramatically important; and there is no doubt that these results have their value. But the loss seems to us more than sufficient to compensate for the gain. Out of deference to modern feelings, Polyphontes is made, not the husband, but the suitor of Merope. There is nothing in the position itself which is contrary to Greek usage: Theoclymenus, in the *Helen* of Euripides, is a case in point: but the question still remains, why has the tradition been disturbed? Abstractedly it is quite true that a modern audience would be revolted by seeing a widow married to her husband's murderer: but a modern audience which could be collected to see a play imitated from the Greek would probably be able to repeat to itself the maxim that when we are in Greece we must do as the Greeks do. Mr. Arnold may plead that he is only exercising the same licence as the Greeks themselves did in softening the grosser and harsher forms of legend; but the plea, we think, will scarcely avail a modern writer. The Greeks seem scarcely to have looked historically at the stories which they dramatized: they invested them, not with the garb of the heroic age, but with the costume of their own day, whatever that might be; they did, in short, what Racine and Voltaire have done, the difference being, not in the principle, but in the result. But for ourselves there seems to be no medium between a modernization like the French, which destroys all antiquity, and a historical representation which takes the floating mass of Greek legend for granted, and simply builds upon it. The consequence of Mr. Arnold's undecided mode of treatment shows itself, we think, in Merope's character. She is not sufficiently antique: she is modern, reflective, even sentimental. The Greek Merope, animated at once by resentment for her husband and fear for her son, would not have shrunk from bloodshedding any more than the Greek Electra. How her endurance of Polyphontes as a husband would have been reconciled with her co-operation in his murder, we know not, but we may be sure that a Greek dramatist would have found, or made a way. Mr. Arnold's Merope is Greek in the brief interval during which she believes her son to be murdered, but it is precisely in that interval that she ceases to be herself. Readers of Greek plays are aware that scenes are not uncommon where a sort of rhetorical fight is maintained, one speaker counselling prudence, another boldness. In this, as in other respects, Mr. Arnold has followed his models: prudence and boldness are pitted against each other in various parts of the play. So the change in Merope is shown by making her change her side for once in this argumentative contention: elsewhere she censures others as rash, but on this occasion she has to be told that she is rash herself.

Connected with this treatment of the character of Merope is the treatment of the character of Polyphontes. Other writers, as we have seen, have made him repulsive. Mr. Arnold, seizing on a hint in Pausanias' version of the story, has chosen to invoke our sympathies for him. There is perhaps nothing in the character so produced which is itself alien from the Greek spirit, while the interest inspired is no doubt poetical and tragic. But the alteration has, we think been injurious to the general effect of the play in more respects than one. It has made the solution of the knot (to borrow a term from Aristotle) a very awkward one. The original legend was clear enough. Polyphontes has put a price on the head of Æpytus; the disguised Æpytus appears to claim it, declaring that he has killed the prince. The fiction is natural, and it is natural that Merope should believe it, and suppose her son to be her son's murderer. But Mr. Arnold precluded himself from dealing with the matter so simply. It is not clear whether his Polyphontes even desires the death of the prince: it is certain that he has taken no steps towards it. Æpytus accordingly has to come with a tale of accidental death, a result which Polyphontes may accept, though he would not have concurred in bringing it about. But this, though unobjectionable in itself, does not help towards the catastrophe, as there is nothing in it to make Merope mistake her son for her son's murderer. Another story, in consequence, has to be devised for her. Æpytus is made to have acted without taking into council the very person whom he would most naturally have consulted, the old retainer, who has for twenty years been the established organ of communication between him and his mother. The story of Æpytus' death has been spread and is believed in the country where the event is supposed to have occurred, and the old man believes it among the rest. Suspicion falls on the person whom Æpytus employed to give himself out as the eye-witness; but Æpytus is not aware of the suspicion. Æpytus and his agent are confounded, not in consequence of any deep-laid scheme, but by a mere accident; while we are left to wonder how it is that Polyphontes, whom we gather to be acquainted with the agent, should have made the mistake. Here is a train of events which could only be made intelligible by detailed treatment; but Mr. Arnold is compelled by the exigency of the play to dispose of them rapidly; and some study and comparison of parts are required to discover what is really intended. And all this, as we have said, is necessitated by his interpretation of the character of Polyphontes. But this is not all. The character itself is left in an obscurity which materially interferes with the symmetry and unity of the play. We do not complain that the judgment passed on a character by the other *dramatis personæ* is not the same as that which the poet intends his readers to pass. One of the chief elements, indeed, of tragic interest is the mutual misunderstanding which frequently prevails among the personages of the drama. Each holds a half-truth or half-right, yet each presses on against the other to a deadly solution: and the reader or spectator is expressly intended to overlook them both, and harmonize in his own moral feeling the claims of the conflicting parties. But Polyphontes is not simply the victim of a misconception which the reader's feeling is expected to rectify. His opponents differ between themselves: to Æpytus he is a mere murderer, usurper, and tyrant, who deserves *la mort sans phrase;* to Merope he is as she admits herself, an enigmatic character, for whom there is probably a good deal to be said, though not quite enough to exempt him from punishment. This moral complication, like the material complication of the plot, if introduced at all, ought to have been dealt with at length; but this again the general exigencies of the play prevent Mr. Arnold from doing. The result is, not that we are left to rectify a judgment which, however mistaken, we feel to have been unavoidably passed, but that we are compelled to doubt whether the judgment might not have been rectified in the first instance without the necessity of appeal to a higher court. Polyphontes' death is really the result, not of Merope's judgment, but of Æpytus's; yet we feel that Æpytus has had but slender means of judging as compared with his mother. What would our feelings have been if Æschylus or Sophocles had represented Clytæmnestra's death as virtually the work of Orestes alone, Electra feeling that her mother is partly in the right, and acquiescing in the assassination rather than approving it? And yet we have a kind of sympathy for Clytæmnestra which her executioners had not.

The chorus in general is managed with considerable judgment. The part it bears in the action is much the same as that which is sustained by the choruses in the genuine Greek plays, that of a sympathizing and right-minded confidant; and its songs harmonize with the events which are being transacted, without referring to them too closely. The vein of moral and political reflection which runs through the first ode might easily be paralleled, though the language is sometimes the language, not of Greek poetry, but of English philosophical prose.

> But, more than all, unplumbed,
> Unscathed, untrodden, is the heart of man.
> More than all secrets hid the way it keeps,
> *Nor any of our organs so obtuse,*
> *Inaccurate, and frail,*
> *As those with which we try to test*
> *Feelings and motives there.*

The second ode is founded, as we have said, on one of the Euripidean fragments; but it contains touches also from the *Œdipus Tyrannus* of Sophocles. The third we have heard objected to as simply telling a mythological story not connected with the piece; there are, however, instances in point in the last chorus of the *Iphigenia in Tauris,* which recounts the deeds of Apollo, and the last but one in the *Helen,* which describes the wanderings of Ceres in quest of Proserpine, though the latter has been supposed by some to be one of the 'insertions' of which we spoke in a former paragraph, an ode written to do duty in more plays than one, while others contend that both are purposely irrelevant, as a plot is going on, and persons are on the stage from whom it is desirable to conceal it. The fourth is in some respects Mr. Arnold's masterpiece, in point of execution; the symmetrical arrangement of the third strophe and antistrophe is a feat of marvellous and, indeed, superfluous ingenuity; but the story of the death of Hercules, which occupies a principal place in it, is rather far-fetched. 'The invariableness of justice' surely might have found a more appropriate illustration than an event which, though capable of being represented as the consequence of an error, is never, so far as we are aware, put forward prominently by any Greek writer in its retributive aspect. While we are on the subject, we will just raise the question whether there is any authority for Merope's sending the chorus from one part of the stage to another to fetch the axe—a business which, after all, is performed by the leader, not by the eleven or fourteen subordinates. Our memory does not serve us with a parallel, but we would not assert that one is not to be found.

Perhaps the most difficult part of the imitation of a Greek play is the language. A Greek story can be found ready to hand, and a mode of treatment, more or less Greek, seems to follow as a matter of course, though, as we have seen, there may be difficulties in working out the catastrophe clearly. But the language requires constant, pertinacious, unresting effort—the effort of combining English words into Greek phrases. It becomes almost necessary to compose the sentences in some kind of Greek; and then there is the labour—itself enough for a modern artist—to translate the Greek into English. If we say that Mr. Arnold's success in this respect is considerable, but not complete, we say, perhaps, all that could be expected under circumstances so peculiar as his. Had he striven to make every line and every word the reflex of some possible Greek model, the effect might have been to deprive his poem of almost everything which the English reader would recognise as poetical in expression. We think, however, that there are a few words which should have been avoided in any case, not simply as English, but as English of the most vulgar or the most modern stamp. We cannot reconcile ourselves to hearing that 'trials . . . *used* two generations of his (Hercules') offspring *up*.' 'Dumbfoundered' is a word which has yet to establish its right to exist in English at all; though, the verb 'to dumbfound' may be tolerated in a prologue by Dryden, or a humorous paper by Addison. Nor is it easy to feel, as Mr. Arnold doubtless wishes us to feel, that we are standing on the dim borderland which separates Grecian history from Grecian fable, when we hear Æpytus talk to Merope about 'electrifying the hearts' of the Messenians.

It remains to speak of the metrical characteristics of *Merope*. The subject is one to which Mr. Arnold invites attention in his Preface, asserting the superiority of the 'true oratorical rhythm' of Greek tragedy, which places the pause at the end of the line, to the Elizabethan habit of pausing in the middle, and pleading the necessity of inventing new English rhythms to represent the effect of the Greek choral measures. There can be no doubt that in imitating a Greek play he is right in adopting that type of the English iambic line which most nearly answers to the Greek; but many will be found, ourselves among the number, to doubt whether the stately monotony of Greek iambic rhythm is of itself preferable to the more broken and varied cadence which has generally been heard on the English stage, or whether the speeches in *Richard the Third* are finer pieces of oratory than the speeches in *Lear*. But questions like this cannot be opened at the end of an article.

[Opens the question, nevertheless, and introduces a few examples of Arnold's metrical 'blemishes']

In one respect, we are conscious that our remarks have failed to do justice to Mr. Arnold. The few and brief quotations which we have made have been intended to exhibit, not his excellences, but his defects. We had hoped to remedy this one-sidedness by giving specimens of the various kinds of success which he has achieved, but such specimens would necessarily extend to a considerable length, and our limits are, we fear, at an end. We trust, however, that our readers will repair the omission by studying the poem for themselves. Those who love Greek plays already, and those who wish to be taught to love them, will find themselves amply repaid; and even a modern reader who cares nothing for the antique, as such, will see much to admire in a brilliant piece of word-painting, like the description of the stag hunt which leads to the supposed death of Æpytus.

14. Other comments on *Merope*

(a) From the *Saturday Review*, 2 January 1858

Mr. Arnold has in many different ways invited the English public to return once more to the controversy between the classical and the romantic schools of poetry, and to reconsider the judgement which modern opinion has pronounced in favour of the latter. In the inaugural address which he recently delivered, on his appointment to the Professorship of Poetry at Oxford, he stated the results at which he had himself arrived; and he has now brought them to a practical issue by the publication of a tragedy composed after the Greek model. What he asks for is, not the admiration which all educated men bestow on the Greek drama as a masterpiece of the genius of the ancient world, but a recognition that this drama, which we call ancient, is essentially modern. He contrasted, in his Oxford Address, the literature of the age of Pericles with the literature of the age of Elizabeth—thus selecting the age when classical poetry was most perfect in Greece, and the age when romantic poetry was greatest and most exuberant in England. Diverging from poetry to history, he compared Thucydides with Sir Walter Raleigh, and called on his hearers to decide whether the calm wisdom and the nervous conciseness of the former, or the childish credulity and rambling prolixity of the latter were more nearly akin to what satisfies us in the productions of the nineteenth century. It would be easy to show that the illustration was not a fair one; but it is unnecessary to enter on the point, because the question is not one of details, of the style of particular writers, but of the whole cast, aim, and range of two different modes of human thought. The salient feature of ancient thought is simplicity—the salient feature of modern thought is complexity. Classical poetry may, after its kind, be equally perfect with romantic, but it is certainly not equally plastic. It will not contain all that the modern world has to throw into shape of poetry. Nor can it ever be popular in England. To relish it requires a special and most laborious cultivation, and to imitate it requires the abnegation of endless feelings which are most intimately a part of ourselves. *Merope* is a very skilful imitation, and abounds with touches of a refined and delicate taste. But the enjoyment it affords is almost exactly that afforded by a very good copy of Latin verses; and the readers who will care for the one will be almost as few as those who would care for the other. Nor is it possible for any literary adroitness to persuade us that a tragedy like *Merope* can express all the feelings of the modern world. We cannot be beguiled by the platitudes, however exquisite, in which the Chorus resigns itself to fate, into forgetting Christianity and the Hebrew poets. The Greek drama is dead; and so far as *Merope* is intended to give it a new life, we must think it a failure.

But if we may regard it as written with a somewhat different object, and for a rather narrower purpose, its value is great. *Merope* may be taken as a protest against the extremely subjective character of modern English poetry, and as also intended to recall to us the high degree in which simplicity and moderation contribute to the perfection of form.

(b) George Lewes in the *Leader*, 30 January 1858

There are two separate topics offered to the critic in this volume, one the tragedy itself, and the other the preface in which Mr. Arnold argues in favour of a restoration of the forms of Greek Drama. To do justice to either of these topics would require more space than any journal can allow; and to touch on them both would obviously be only to the disadvantage of both. We shall leave the preface and its theoretical discussions to the quiet meditation of the reader, whose attention is specially directed to it; and say a few words on the tragedy which that preface introduces.

Merope is the closest reproduction of the forms of Greek tragedy which, to our knowledge, has been yet attempted. Hitherto scholarly poets have been contented with an imitation of certain parts of the Greek form, or with such implied allusions as would gratify the scholarly reader, but no one has adopted that form in all its niceties and characteristics, as if submitting to all the conditions which affected the Grecian poet. Mr. Arnold now tries that experiment on the English public. Modern, intensely modern in spirit (as it ought to be) *Merope* is minutely antique in form. Not only are the more massive peculiarities of the Greek Drama reproduced, not only have we the simplicity of structure, slowness of movement, and choral interruptions, which were necessities in the Greek Drama, but we have also the simplicity of diction and the balanced seesaw of dialogue. In fact after a careful reading of *Merope* the English reader may congratulate himself on having made acquaintance with a Greek play. But this is, after all, a slight matter compared with poetic interest: a scholar might have achieved such a feat; but to write *Merope* something more than scholarship was required. We cannot but regard the form as a mistake; yet in spite of the gratuitous restraints which the author has laid upon himself in imitating where he should have been creating, we feel throughout the play a fine dramatic instinct moving a thoughtful and accomplished mind. The characters are not pure Greek, but very human, and moved by modern ideas. The language too is modern, of course, yet having much of the pregnant simplicity of the ancients, sometimes careless to a point remarkable in one so solicitous of ancient finish, but never meretricious or tricky. Let this portion of the early scene between Merope and the tyrant illustrate what we have said:—

[Quotes extensively from the play]

Unless we could give several columns to the analysis of the various phases of the artistic evolution of the subject chosen by Mr. Arnold we could offer no intelligible criticism of his work. The plot might be told in a few lines, as, indeed, is the case with all Greek plays, but the poetic treatment cannot be thus summarily indicated. We content ourselves therefore with heartily recommending the work to the reader's careful perusal and reperusal, for it is in our opinion a work eminently deserving of such study: with some blemishes in the versification, and with what seems to us an initial error in the adoption of an obsolete form, obsolete because the conditions which originally determined it have passed away, it is noble and pathetic in conception, elevated and elevating in execution.

(c) W. R. Roscoe in the *National Review*, April 1858

Mr. Arnold is no doubt following his own true bent when he devotes himself to what is called the classical school of literature. Certainly no living poet is so well qualified to familiarise the English mind (if that be possible) with the forms and substance of the Greek drama. The limits, as well as the quality, of his genius give him more than common facilities for such a task. His love of beauty is profound, and he loves best, perhaps by nature, and certainly from study, its more abstract manifestations, especially those of form. He uses the emotions as a field for the intellect, not the mind to subserve the heart, and his imagination is bound up with the former rather than the latter; it is a lamp that shines, not a fire that glows. He lays a cold hand on sensuous imagery; and there is a keen clear atmosphere about his pictures from nature, as if his muse had steeped his eyes in Attic air and sunshine. Thus gifted, he devotes himself to reproducing Greek poetry in an English dress, and presents us with an Athenian tragedy in our own language. We are not ungrateful for the gift. But Mr. Arnold is not content that we should accept it as a beautiful curiosity, or treat it as a rare exotic: he has written a preface to urge that such plants should be acclimatised; he boldly demands place in English literature for the forms of poetry which took their rise in Greek sacrificial observances, adapted themselves to Greek social habits, were limited by Greek ideas, and embodied Greek religion, Greek patriotism, and, above all, that which is most characteristic of a people,—the feelings with which it looks at the hidden arbiters of life, the controlling destinies of the world. That drama, which held these things as a wine holds its flavour and spirit, Mr. Arnold thinks should be studied in England; not studied to know it, but studied to reproduce it, that we may make the same kind of thing for ourselves. He thinks he can dig up the dusky olive from the plains of Attica, and plant it in our English wheat-fields; that he can take in its fullest development the most purely indigenous and the most intensely and narrowly national literature the world ever saw, and bid it find new springs of life some two thousand years later in a nation which has already found its expression in a dramatic literature evolved by itself. Did such an attempt ever succeed? A native literature in its infancy may take the impression of a foreign one; though even then, if it have strength to grow at all, it soon throws off, or carries only as a superficies, the marks of its early tutoring: but when did a foreign growth ever share the field with an indigenous one? A nation whose habits of thought were sufficiently congruous with those of some other, has plagiarised and adapted its literary productions: Terence went to Greece as Planché goes to Paris. But in these cases it is not a foreign form and spirit which is transferred, but the adapter merely studies his own idleness, or the poverty of his own resources, by borrowing a plot and a certain stock of wit and ideas; and his effort is to oust all that is specially foreign, or to transform it into a more familiar shape.

(d) John Nichols in *Undergraduate Papers*, 1858

Professor Arnold has given us a receipt for the production of good poems. He appears as the deliverer of the age from the faults of florid imagery, false method, weakness, and general inadequacy, which, according to his view, pervade our verses and vitiate our taste. He lays down rules for the drama after the fashion of the ancients, expounding the right sort of versification, the proper relation of parts, the duties of the chorus, the management of the catastrophe, and the spirit in which the whole should be read. He has embodied those rules in practice in presenting us with what is in form and feature a wonderfully close reproduction of an old Greek play. It is the right length, and involves the proper number of actors. The chorus breaks in just when it should, talking of ancient cities and impressing in antique song the moralities of ancient times. Aristotle's rules are nowhere contravened. The due proportion of storm and calm is preserved. The messenger rushes in at the right moment. The bloodshed all takes place behind the scenes. The unities are scrupulously observed. The theme is authorised by tradition and frequent use. The poem is throughout orderly, and correct, and regular; only, by some unfortunate accident, Mr. Arnold has omitted the poetry. Outline and feature are there, but the animating spirit that should inform the whole, the passion that is the soul of genius, the Promethean spark is wanting. It has some of the forms of a noble structure, but it is a palace of ice.

NEW POEMS AND *POEMS*

1867, 1869

---

15. Leslie Stephen (?), review, *Saturday Review*

7 September 1867, no. 619, 319–20

Stephen (1832–1904) was a regular contributor to various periodicals, including the *Fortnightly*, and he was to serve as editor of the *Cornhill Magazine*. There is some doubt about his authorship of this review of Arnold, which was not reprinted in later collections; but it is likely that he wrote it. Stephen expresses a common sense of nostalgia about the 1867 volume: 'Alas,' he says, 'why should his own Muse now wear a mien so little young, so little radiant?' He also has high praise for 'Empedocles', and talks about Arnold as a 'made' poet, 'exquisite' but 'unspontaneous'.

Those who know Mr. Arnold as the author of one of the most exquisite and delightful poems in the language will turn with eagerness to his new volume. To have written 'Sohrab and Rustum' was to win the lasting admiration and gratitude of every lover of poetry. The fine harmony of the verse, the stately imagery, the nobly tragical manner of the story, its sombre yet elevated pathos, fill the mind with that joy which it is the poet's chief glory to give. The writer's spirit has travelled in other ways since 'Sohrab and Rustum'—has left the serene and cheerful heights and come down among painful sunless places. The grey spirit of his time broods heavily over him, and instead of the light and joy of the poet, he is, like his own Empedocles, filled with the gloom and weariness of the baffled philosopher. From such a mood we may not expect the brightness and life that belong to the best poetry. Thought and feeling saturated and transfigured with Light—how can this, which is distinctively the work of the poet, come from a mind that is distressfully alive to a thousand problems and powerless to grasp a single solution? The poetic light shines in a tranquil air. There are natures, it is true—Shelley's for example—in which the rush and bound of the thought, in spite of intellectual distractions, seems to kindle light and heat by its own course. But Mr. Arnold is of another calibre. He is one of the poets who are made, who are not born. He is never impetuous, never ebullient. Nowhere even for a moment are we impressed with a sense of spontaneousness. And it is easy to see that this is the genuine result of an original want, and not of the discipline to which he has subjected himself in the severer forms of his favourite classics. Not to speak of the ancients, it is impossible to read pieces like *Athalie* or *Cinna*, whatever we may think of their dramatic merits, without being alive to the broad current of poetic feeling spontaneously flowing within the too rigid channels prescribed for it. If we remember how many poems which the world would not willingly let die have been the products of natures that, like Wordsworth's for example, became deeply poetic by culture and serene meditation, added to fine original susceptibilities, though not the finest, it is no too grievous disparagement to say of a poet that his verse is not the outcome of a spontaneously and ebulliently poetic mind. But it is a serious thing for such a mind to get into the distracting eddies of an epoch like ours, the critical hour of a great spiritual and intellectual interregnum. It is a serious thing for a mind not endowed with an ever-flowing fountain of poetic brightness, its own and inextinguishable, to fall among the shadows of a dim-believing age. We may get, as we do get in the present volume, gracious harmony of verse, delicately pensive moods, stately and grave thoughts, but of light and brightness we get too little, and of the cheerful inspiration of poetic joy scarcely any. There are occasional pieces and stanzas which must be excepted from this criticism, where we have glimpses of the old calmness and luminous objectivity. 'Thyrsis' is a poem of perfect delight, exquisite in grave tenderness of reminiscence, rich in breadth of western light, and breathing full the spirit of grey and ancient Oxford—

That sweet city, with her dreaming spires.

It is admirable, not merely for single touching lines and for single happy expressions and delicate strokes. Like 'The Scholar Gipsy', its companion-piece, in a former volume, it is remarkable for unity and completeness of conception—for that harmoniousness of composition which at once stirs and soothes, excites and satisfies the reader's mind, and which is the object and criterion of art. In 'Thyrsis' the poet projects his mind into the outer world with an effect that contrasts but too vividly with the self-brooding tone of the rest of the volume. One can only regret that the mood did not last longer, and has not been more frequent.

Let us turn to 'Empedocles on Etna', the most important piece in the volume. Empedocles, as the familiar legend tells us, was a Sicilian Greek who flourished probably about the middle of the fifth century before our era. Men revered him for his control over the winds and the rain, for his miraculous skill in the art of medicine, and for the loftiness of his wisdom. The manner of his death is told variously. Some say that he was drawn up in a shining chariot to the seats of the gods. Others tell that, wearied of the praises of men, and perplexed with his life, he plunged into the burning crater of Mount Etna. Mr. Arnold takes the latter legend. This is the whole story. And surely it is evident even to people far inferior to Mr. Arnold in fineness and depth of critical judgment—in which he has barely an equal—that the action here is incurably faulty as the base of a tragedy. He confessed, indeed, in one of his remarkable and instructive prefaces, written fourteen years ago, that he was sensible of the poetical weakness of such a situation as that of Empedocles. 'What,' he asked, 'are the situations from the repre-sentation of which, though accurate, no poetical enjoyment can be derived? They are those in which the suffering finds no vent in action; in which a continuous state of mental distress is prolonged, unrelieved by incident, hope, or resistance; in which there is everything to be en-dured, nothing to be done. In such situations there is inevitably some-thing morbid; in the description of them something monotonous.' Precisely. From the moment that Empedocles appears in the pass among the forests that clothe the sides of the fiery mountain, we are filled with mere profitless pain. We know that the catastrophe is certain, and that it is not of a kind that action can modify or prevent or retard. It may be said that we know the same thing in more than one tragedy of the highest order. Take the *Ajax* of Sophocles. Except in the first short dialogue between Ajax, still in his frenzy, and Athené, the misery of the hero is as monotonous—as little capable, that is, of being alleviated by any incident, hope or resistance—as is the fate of Empedocles himself. We know that the Greek hero is doomed, and that the sympathizing strains of Tecmessa and the mariners from Salamis, and his own pas-sionate and stern lamentations, cannot avert or delay the terrible climax. Does this, then, fall within the class of dramatic situations to which Empedocles belongs? On the contrary, there is a most important distinction. Ajax is the unhappy victim of the anger of the gods. We are horrified at his fate, but the horror is deeply penetrated by religious awe. The spectator prays that never upon him may the ire of Athené fall, and he trembles with devout pity for the ill-fated hero. With Empedocles the case is very different. In his dreadful end the gods have no part. The self-inflicted destruction of a philosopher, however sublime the exposition of the intellectual miseries and misgivings which have prompted the act, cannot affect us with anything but a helpless and unelevating distress. The graceful and musical verses which Mr. Arnold has put into the mouth of Callicles at the close of the tragedy are not able to transform the dreary pain with which we have pictured Empedocles plunging into the crater, into that mood of repose and resignation in which it should be the aim of the dramatist to leave us. For one thing, it may be said in passing, we have some difficulty to discover what idea it is that may be supposed to incorporate Callicles's song with what has gone before.

There is another consideration which points still more impressively to the unfitness of the story of Empedocles for dramatic treatment. It is fatally wanting in what may be called social interest, and without this social interest, the presence, directly or allusively, of love and human sympathies and human relations, it is impossible to affect the outside mind tragically. The sublimest philosopher declaiming on a mountaintop may teach one many wise and noble things, but noble declamation on life is not enough to kindle in one a warm and deep interest in the declaimer's fate. Man in speculative isolation cannot be dramatic. To be this, he must enter into the common field of human passion and affection. He will enter it in his own way, but if he simply stands aloof and finally meets or precipitates his fate without ever entering it at all, he is not a really tragical character, nor does his story afford a really tragical situation. Imagine *Hamlet* with everything omitted by particular desire *except* the Prince of Denmark—without Ophelia or Polonius or Gertrude. And who would care to listen to Faust's communings with his own spirit, or feel a tragical concern in his inexorable destiny, if he did not show himself human and did not participate in the common human passion?

Empedocles lived in the moment of the decline of the objective faith of the old Greek philosophy. Man had begun to turn from speculation as to the constitution and source of the Cosmos to speculation on the nature of his own mind; he had begun to doubt the trustworthiness of the senses and reason. It was a time of many questions and few answers.

Anger and impatience against the rising sophistry and scepticism were the moods most natural to a mind that could look back on days when Dialectic had not been discovered and Sophists were not. It is Mr. Arnold's own sympathy with such moods that has misled him to select so undramatic and impracticable a subject. In the second act, where Empedocles is left to soliloquize, the monotony is irredeemable. There is little ebb and flow, little alternation; no swift chasing of lights and shadows across the philosopher's soul, no fire ever and anon breaking through the profound gloom. The despair of the situation masters the poet, and the solemn energy which marks the long ode of Empedocles to Pausanias seems wholly to disappear in the second act. The nearest approach to that energy without which the reader refuses his ear is perhaps in the following lines:—

[Quotes ll. 235–57, 'And yet what days were those', etc.]

The rest of the passage is too long to transcribe here, but if the reader will refer to it, he will find there more than anywhere else something like that vivid, steady sustention of feeling without which the verse is not poetry, but only cunningly worked prose.

Notwithstanding its radical faultiness in point of situation, 'Empedocles on Etna' is a poem that nearly every verse-writer of our time might study with high advantage. This may be said of most of the pieces in the present volume. The characteristic excess of Mr. Arnold's poems is the characteristic defect of nearly all the verse that is now written. He overweights his poetry with thought. And this is precisely the quality in which most modern English poetry is thoroughly wanting. Of melodious verse, of graceful sentiment, of commonplace prettily put, we have enough and more than enough in the thousand imitators of the Laureate. In high-wrought and rapturous passion on the one hand, and, far different, in blowsy canting sentimentalism, as in *London Poems* and the like, we do not fail. But of bright, wide, large-eyed thought, Mr. Browning is the only great living poetic master, and his grievously bad art has unhappily destroyed, or at least profoundly impaired, what might have been the most robust and invigorating of the literary influences of the time. The sovereignty of the drawing-room school of poetry is practically supreme. Mr. Swinburne rises in hot rebellion against it from the side of Sense, and Mr. Arnold surveys it with cold displeasure from the remote altitudes of Reason. But each is weakened by *les défauts de ses qualités*. The truly recreative influence would be a fusion of the two—more passion penetrated with more reason. In a beautiful sonnet in the present volume Mr. Arnold has pointed out this very thing:—

[Quotes 'Austerity of Poetry' in its entirety]

Alas, why should his own Muse now wear a mien so little young, so little radiant?

16. A. C. Swinburne, review, *Fortnightly Review*

October 1867, n.s. ii, 414–45

Algernon Charles Swinburne (1837–1909) wrote a long and, characteristically, somewhat rambling review, and I have deleted, in addition to footnotes, passages concerned with Arnold and French culture and with British Philistia, which are largely digressive. Swinburne considers Arnold to be a great poet. Above all, the essay is a tribute to his greatness. As a poet, however, Swinburne is aware why he likes what he does, and he explains his praise by detailed reference to the poems. He writes both a sensitive appreciation and an apology for Arnold's type of verse. Swinburne was to be accused by several critics of praising too lavishly, and he himself later recanted, berating Arnold as an older man as he extols him here.

There are two things which most men begin by hating until they have won their way, and which when combined are more than doubly hateful to all in whose eyes they are not doubly admirable: perfection of work, and personality in the workman. As to perfection, it must be seen to be loved, and few have eyes to see it. To none but these few can it be acceptable at first; and only because these few are the final legislators of opinion, the tacit and patient law-givers of time, does it ever win acceptance. A strong personal tone of character stamped and ingrained into a man's work, if more offensive at first to the mass, is likelier to find favour before long in the sight of some small body or sect of students. If not repulsive, it must be attractive and impressive; and there are always mental cripples in plenty to catch at a strong man's staff and cut it down into a crutch for themselves. But the more love a man has for perfection, the more faith in form, the more instinct for art, the fewer will these early believers be, and the better worth having; the process of winning their suffrages will be slower, and surer the hold of them when won.

For some years the immediate fame of Mr. Matthew Arnold has been almost exclusively the fame of a prose writer. Those students could hardly find hearing—they have nowhere of late found expression that I know of—who, with all esteem and enjoyment of his essays, of their clearness, candour, beauty of sentiment and style, retained the opinion that, if justly judged, he must be judged by his verse, and not by his prose; certainly not by this alone; that future students would cleave to that with more of care and of love; that the most memorable quality about him was the quality of a poet. Not that they liked the prose less, but that they liked the verse more. His best essays ought to live longer than most, his best poems cannot but live as long as any, of their time. So it seemed to some who were accordingly more eager to receive and more careful to study a new book of his poems than most books they could have looked for; and since criticism of the rapid and limited kind possible to contemporaries can be no more than the sincere exposition of the writer's belief and of his reasons for it, I, as one of these, desire, with all deference but with all decision, to say what I think of this book, and why. For the honour of criticism, if it is to win or to retain honour at all, it must be well for the critic to explain clearly his personal point of view, instead of fighting behind the broad and crestless shield of a nameless friend or foe. The obscurest name and blazon are at least recognisable; but a mere voice is mere wind, though it affect to speak with the tongues and the authority of men and of angels.

First on this new stage is the figure of an old friend and teacher. Mr. Arnold says that the poem of 'Empedocles on Etna' was withdrawn before fifty copies of the first edition were sold. I must suppose then that one of these was the copy I had when a schoolboy—how snatched betimes from the wreck and washed across my way, I know not; but I remember well enough how then, as now, the songs of Callicles clove to my ear and memory. Early as this was, it was not my first knowledge

of the poet; the 'Reveller,' the 'Merman,' the 'New Sirens', I had
mainly by heart in a time of childhood just ignorant of teens. I do not
say I understood the latter poem in a literal or logical fashion, but I had
enjoyment enough of its music and colour and bright sadness as of a
rainy sunset or sundawn. A child with any ear or eye for the attraction
of verse or art can dispense with analysis, and rest content to apprehend it without comprehension; it were to be wished that adults
equally incapable would rest equally content. Here I must ask, as between brackets, if this beautiful poem is never to be reissued after the
example of its younger? No poet could afford to drop or destroy it; I
might at need call into court older and better judges to back my judgment in this; meantime 'I hope here be proofs' that, however inadequate may be my estimate of the poet on whom I am now to discourse,
it is not inadequate through want of intimacy with his work. At the risk
of egotism, I record it in sign of gratitude; I cannot count the hours of
pure and high pleasure, I cannot reckon the help and guidance in
thought and work, which I owe to him as to all other real and noble
artists, whose influence it was my fortune to feel when most susceptible
of influence, and least conscious of it, and most in want. In one of his
books, where he presses rather hard upon our school as upon one
devoid of spiritual or imaginative culture, he speaks of his poems as
known to no large circle—implies this at least, if I remember: he will
not care to be assured that to some boys at Eton Sohrab and Rustum,
Tristram and Iseult, have been close and common friends, their stream
of Oxus and bays of Brittany familiar almost as the well-loved Thames
weirs and reaches. However, of this poem of 'Empedocles' the world it
seems was untimely robbed, though I remember on searching to have
found a notice of it here and there. Certain fragments were then given
back by way of dole, chiefly in the second series of the author's revised
poems. But one, the largest, if not the brightest jewel, was withheld;
the one long and lofty chant of Empedocles. The reasons assigned by
Mr. Arnold in a former preface for cancelling the complete poem had
some weight: the subject-matter is oppressive, the scheme naked and
monotonous; the blank verse is not sonorous, not vital and various
enough; in spite of some noble interludes, it fails on the whole to do the
work and carry the weight wanted; its simplicity is stony and grey,
with dry flats and rough whinstones.

To the lyrics which serve as water-springs and pastures I shall have
to pay tribute of thanks in their turn; but first I would say something
of that strain of choral philosophy which falls here 'as the shadow of a

great rock in a weary land.' It is a model of grave, clear, solemn verse; the style plain and bare, but sufficient and strong; the thought deep, lucid, direct. We may say of it what the author has himself said of the wise and sublime verses of Epictetus, that 'the fortitude of that is for the strong, yet the few; even for them, the spiritual atmosphere with which it surrounds them is bleak and grey;' but the air is higher and purer, the ground firmer, the view clearer; we have a surer foothold on these cold hills of thought than in the moist fragrance of warmer air which steeps the meadows and marshes of sentiment and tradition.

> Thin, thin the pleasant human noises grow,
>   And faint the city gleams;
> Rare the lone pastoral huts; marvel not thou!
> The solemn peaks but to the stars are known,
> But to the stars, and the cold lunar beams;
> Alone the sun arises, and alone
>   Spring the great streams.

These noble verses of another poem clipped from Mr. Arnold's first book, and left hanging in fragments about one's memory—I here make my protest against its excision—may serve as types of the later, the more immediate and elaborate discourse of thought here embodied and attired in words of stately and simple harmony. It is no small or common comfort, after all the delicate and ingenious shuffling of other English poets about the edge of deep things, to come upon one who speaks with so large and clear and calm an utterance; who begins at the taproot and wellspring of the matter, leaving others to wade ankle-deep in still waters and weave river-flags or lake-lilies in lieu of stemming the stream. Nothing in verse or out of verse is more wearisome than the delivery of reluctant doubt, of half-hearted hope and half-incredulous faith. A man who suffers from the strong desire either to believe or disbelieve something he cannot, may be worthy of sympathy, is certainly worthy of pity, until he begins to speak; and if he tries to speak in verse, he misuses the implement of an artist. We have had evidences of religion, aspirations and suspirations of all kinds, melodious regrets and tortuous returns in favour or disfavour of this creed or that—all by way of poetic work; and all within the compass and shot-range of a single faith; all, at the widest, bounded north, south, east, and west by material rivers or hills, by an age or two since by a tradition or two: all leaving the spirit cramped and thirsty. We have had Christian sceptics, handcuffed fighters, tongue-tied orators, plume-plucked eagles; believers whose belief was a sentiment, and free-thinkers who saw nothing before Christ or beyond Judæa. To get at the bare rock is a relief after acres of such quaking ground.

Elsewhere, in minor poems, Mr. Arnold also has now and then given signs of an inclination for that sad task of sweeping up dead leaves fallen from the dying tree of belief; but has not wasted much time or strength on such sterile and stupid work. Here, at all events, he has wasted none; here is no melodious whine of retrospective and regretful scepticism; here are no cobwebs of plea and counterplea, no jungles of argument and brakes of analysis. 'Ask what most helps when known'; let be the oracular and the miraculous, and vex not the soul about their truth or falsehood; the soul, which oracles and miracles can neither make nor mar, can neither slay nor save.

> Once read thy own breast right,
>   And thou hast done with fears!
> Man gets no other light,
>   Search he a thousand years.
> Sink in thyself! there ask what ails thee, at that shrine!

This is the gospel of αὐτάρκεια, the creed of self-sufficience, which sees for man no clearer or deeper duty than that of intellectual self-reliance, self-dependence, self-respect; an evangel not to be cancelled or supplanted by any revelation of mystic or prophet or saint. Out of this counsel grows the exposition of obscure and afflictive things. Man's welfare—his highest sphere and state of spiritual well-doing and well-being—this indeed is his true aim; but not this is the aim of nature: the world has other work than this to do; and we, not it, must submit; submit, not by ceasing to attempt and achieve the best we can, but by ceasing to expect subservience to our own ends from all forces and influences of existing things; it is no reason or excuse for living basely instead of nobly, that we must live as the sons, not as the lords of nature. 'To tunes we did not call our being must keep chime;' but this bare truth we will not accept. Philosophy, as forcibly and clearly as religion, indicates the impediments of sin and self-will; 'we do not what we ought, what we ought not we do;' but there religion stops, as far as regards this world, and passes upward into a new world and life; philosophy has further to go without leaving her hold upon earth. Even were man pure, just, wise, instead of unwise, unjust, and impure, this would not affect the 'other existences that clash with ours.'

[Quotes 'Empedocles on Etna', ll. 247–61, 'Like us, the lightning fires', etc.]

Again, there are 'the ill-deeds of other men' to fill up the account against us of painful and perilous things. And we, instead of doing and bearing all we can under our conditions of life, must needs 'cheat our pains' like children after a fall who 'rate the senseless ground:'

[Quotes ll. 277–306, 'So, loathe to suffer mute', etc.]

Again, we must have comfortable Gods to bless, as well as these discomfortable to curse; 'kind Gods who perfect what man vainly tries;' we console ourselves for long labour and research and failure by trust in their sole and final and sufficient knowledge. Then comes the majestic stroke of reply, to rebuke and confute the feeble follies of inventive hope, the futile forgeries of unprofitable comfort; scornful and solemn as the forces themselves of nature.

> Fools! that in man's brief term
> He cannot all things view,
> Affords no ground to affirm
> That there are Gods who do!
> Nor does being weary prove that he has where to rest!

In like manner, when pleasure-seekers fail of pleasure in this world, they turn their hearts Godward, and thence in the end expect that joy which the world could not give; making sure to find happiness where the foiled student makes sure to find knowledge. Again the response from natural things unseen, or from the lips of their own wisest, confronts their fancies as before.

> Fools! that so often here
> Happiness mocked our prayer,
> I think, might make us fear
> A like event elsewhere!
> Make us, not fly to dreams, but moderate desire!

Nor, finally, when all is said, need the wise despair or repine because debarred from dreams of a distant and dubious happiness in a world outside of ours.

> Is it so small a thing
> To have enjoyed the sun,
> To have lived light in the spring,
> To have loved, to have thought, to have done?

The poorest villager feels that it is not so small a thing that he should not be loth to lose the little that life can yield him. Let the wiser man, like him, trust without fear the joys that are; life has room for effort and enjoyment, though at sight of the evil and sorrow it includes, one may have abjured false faith and foolish hope and fruitless fear.

The majesty and composure of thought and verse, the perfect clearness and competence of words, distinguish this from other poetry of the intellect, now more approved and applauded. The matter or argument is not less deep and close than clear and even in expression; although this lucidity and equality of style may diminish its material value in eyes used to the fog and ears trained to the clatter of the chaotic school. But a poem throughout so flowerless and pallid would miss much of the common charm of poetry, however imbued with the serene and severe splendour of snows and stars; and the special crown and praise of this one is its fine and gentle alternation of tone and colour. All around the central peak—bathed in airs high as heaven, and cloven with craters deep as hell—the tender slopes of hill and pasture close up and climb in gradual grace of undulation, full of sunbeams and showers, winds and birds. The lyric interludes of the 'Empedocles' are doubtless known by heart to many ignorant of their original setting, in which they are now again enchased. We have no poet comparable for power and perfection of landscape. This quality was never made more of by critics, sought after by poets with so much care; and our literature lies in full flowerage of landscape, like Egypt after the reflux of the Nile. We have galleries full of beautiful and ingenious studies, and an imperial academy of descriptive poets. The supreme charm of Mr. Arnold's work is a sense of right resulting in a spontaneous temperance which bears no mark of curb or snaffle, but obeys the hand with imperceptible submission and gracious reserve. Other and older poets are to the full as vivid, as incisive and impressive; others have a more pungent colour, a more trenchant outline; others as deep knowledge and as fervid enjoyment of natural things. But no one has in like measure that tender and final quality of touch which tempers the excessive light and suffuses the refluent shade; which as it were washes with soft air the sides of the earth, steeps with dew of quiet and dyes with colours of repose the ambient ardour of noon, the fiery affluence of evening. His verse bathes us with fresh radiance and light rain, when weary of the violence of summer and winter in which others dazzle and detain us; his spring wears here and there a golden waif of autumn, his autumn a rosy stray of spring. His tones and effects are pure, lucid, aërial; he knows by some fine impulse of temperance all rules of distance, of reference, of proportion; nothing is thrust or pressed upon our eyes, driven or beaten into our ears. For the instinctive selection of simple and effectual detail he is unmatched among English poets of the time, unless by Mr. Morris, whose landscape has much of the same quality, as clear, as noble, and as memorable—memorable for this especially, that you are not vexed or fretted by mere brilliance of point and sharpness of stroke, and such intemperate excellence as gives astonishment the precedence of admiration: such beauties as strike you and startle and go out. Of these it is superfluous to cite instances from the ablest of our countrymen's works; they are taught and teach that the most remote, the most elaborate, the most intricate and ingenious fashions of allusion and detail make up their best poetical style; they fill their verse with sharp-edged prettinesses, with shining surprises, and striking accidents that are anything but casual; upon every limb and feature you see marks of the chisel and the plane: there is a conscious complacency of polish which seems to rebuke emulation and challenge improvement. It is otherwise with the two we have named; they are not pruned and pared into excellence, they have not so much of pungency and point; but they have breadth and ease and purity, they have largeness and sureness of eyesight; they know what to give and to withhold, what to express and to suppress. Above all, they have *air*; you can breathe and move in their landscape, nor are you tripped up and caught at in passing by intrusive and singular and exceptional beauties which break up and distract the simple charm of general and single beauty, the large and musical unity of things. Their best verse is not brought straight or worked right; it falls straight because it cannot fall awry; it comes right because it cannot go wrong. And this wide and delicate sense of right makes the impression of their work so durable. The effect is never rubbed off or worn out; the hot suffering eastern life of 'The Sick King in Bokhara;' the basking pastures and blowing pines about the 'Church of Brou;' the morning field and midday moorland so fondly and fully and briefly painted in 'Resignation;' above all, to me at least, the simple and perfect sea-side in the 'Merman,'—'the sandy down where the sea-stocks bloom,' the white-walled town with narrow paved streets, the little grey church with rain-worn stones and small leaded panes, and blown about all the breath of wind and sound of waves—these come in and remain with us; these give to each poem the form and colour and attire it wants, and make it a distinct and complete achievement. The description does not adorn or decorate the thought; it is part of it; they have so grown into each other that they seem not welded together, but indivisible and twin-born.

169

Of the five songs of Callicles—whom we have left somewhat too long midway on Etna—that of Marsyas seems to me the highest and sweetest in tone, unless the first place be rather claimed for that of Cadmus and Harmonia. Others may prefer the first for its exquisite grace of scenery, or the last for its fresh breath and light, shed on softer places than the fiery cone of Etna—for its sweetness and calm, subduing, after all, the force of flames and darkness with the serenity of stars and song; but how fine in each one alike is the touch which relieves the scenery with personal life, Chiron's or Typho's or the sleeping shepherds' and passing Muses'. We have no word but the coarse and insufficient word *taste* to express that noble sense of harmony and high poetic propriety shown in the arrangement and composition of these lyrics; the first, full of the bright moist breath of well-watered glen and well-wooded ford, serving as prelude with its clear soft notes to the high monotone of Empedocles; the second when that has ceased upon the still keen air, rising with fuller swiftness from below. Nothing can be more deep and exquisite in poetical tact than this succession of harmonies, diverse without a discord. For the absolute loveliness of sound and colour in this and the next song there are no adequate words that would not seem violent; and violence is too far from this poetry to invade even the outlying province of commentary. It must be accepted as the 'warm bay among the green Illyrian hills' accepts the sunlight, as the frame of maiden flowers and enclosure of gentle grass accept the quiet presence of the sacred snakes. No ear can forget the cadence, no eye the colour; I am half shaken in my old preference of the next ode until I recall it from end to end:—

> That triumph of the sweet persuasive lyre,
>   That famous, final victory,
> When jealous Pan with Marsyas did conspire;
>   When, from far Parnassus' side,
>   Young Apollo, all the pride
>   Of the Phrygian flutes to tame,
>   To the Phrygian highlands came.

Verse stately as the step and radiant as the head of Apollo; not 'like to the night' this time, but coming as the morning to the hills. How clear it makes the distance between Parnassus and Phrygia, the beautiful scorn and severe youth of the God, leaving for these long reed-beds and ripped lakes and pine-clad ridges of hill the bays and olives of his Greece; how clear the presence of the listening Muses, the advent of the hurrying Mænads, the weeping Olympus, and the implacable repose of Apollo. No poet has ever come so near the perfect Greek; he has strung with a fresh chord the old Sophoclean lyre; he has brought back the Muses from Phrygia even to Colonus;

[Quotes several passages, with brief commentary, from Sophocles]

Even after his master, the disciple of Sophocles holds his high place; he has matched against the Attic of the Gods this Hyperborean dialect of ours, and has not earned the doom of Marsyas. Here is indeed the triumph of the lyre; and he has had to refashion it for himself among a nation and in an age of flute-players and horn-blowers.

For the rest, the scheme of this poem is somewhat meagre and inefficient. Dramatic or not, the figure of Empedocles as here conceived is noble, full of a high and serene interest; but the figure as here represented is a ghost, without form and void; and darkness is upon the face of the deep in which his life lies stagnant; and we look in vain for the spirit to move upon the face of the waters. Dimly and with something of discomfort and depression we perceive the shadow of the poet's design; we discern in rough and thin outline the likeness of the wise world-wearied man, worn down and worsted in the struggle of spirit against unwisdom and change and adverse force of men and things. But how he stands thus apart among the saints and sophists, whence and whither he comes and goes, what ruin lies behind or what revolution before, we hardly see at all. Not only do we contemplate a disembodied spirit, but a spirit of which we cannot determine how it was once embodied, what forms of thought or sense it once put on, what labour and what life it once went through. There is a poetry of the bodiless intellect which, without touching with finger-tip or wing-tip the edge of actual things, may be wise and sweet and fruitful and sublime; but at least we must see the light and feel the air which guides forward and buoys upward the naked fleshless feet of the spirit. Grant that we want no details of bodily life and terrene circumstance, no touch of local or temporal colour; we want at least an indication of the spiritual circumstance, the spiritual influence, without which this poetry would have no matter to work upon. 'Il fallait nous faire sentir l'entourage, l'habillement, le milieu respirable de cette âme nuageuse, de cet esprit fatigué.' After the full effusion of spirit in his one great utterance, Empedocles has little to bring forth but fragments and relics of the soul, shadows of thin suggestion and floating complaint. The manliness and depth, the clearness and sufficiency of thought, have passed from him; he is vague and weak, dissatisfied much as the commonest thinker is dissatisfied with whom all things have not gone well, to whom all things are visibly imperfect and sensibly obscure. Now, the prophet of nature who spoke to us and to Pausanias in the solemn modulation of his lyric speech was more than that. There needs no ghost come from the grave—there needs no philosopher scale the summit of Etna—to tell us this that we find here: that a man had better die than live who can neither live with other men as they do nor wholly suffice to himself; that power and cunning and folly are fellows, that they are lords of life in ages of men with minds vulgar and feeble, and overcome the great and simple servants of justice and the right; that the lord of our spirit and our song, the god of all singers and all seers, is an intolerable and severe god, dividing and secluding his elect from full enjoyment of what others enjoy, in the stress and severity of solitude,—sacrificing the weaker and sequestering the strong; that men on whom all these things beat and bear more heavily than they need can find no fulness of comfort or communion in the eternal elements made of like matter with us, but better made, nor in any beauty nor in any life of the laborious and sleepless soul of things; that even when all other components of our transient nature are duly and happily resolved into those durable elements, the insoluble and inevitable riddle of mind and thought must vex us to the last as at the first.

> We know all this, we know!
> Cam'st thou from heaven, O child
> Of light! but this to declare?
> Alas! to help us forget
> Such barren knowledge awhile,
> God gave the poet his song.

Not that such barren knowledge is ignoble or inadequate matter for poetry; only it must assume something of the dramatic form and circumstance which here are scantily supplied. Less scanty is the supply of noble verses such as these:—

> But we received the shock of mighty thoughts
> On simple minds with a pure natural joy;

verses in the highest tone of Wordsworth's, as clear and grave as his best, as close and full and majestic. The good and evil influence of that great poet, perverse theorist, and incomplete man, upon Mr. Arnold's work is so palpable and so strong as to be almost obtrusive in its effects. He is

the last worth reckoning whom the 'Excursion' is ever likely to mis-
guide. The incalculable power of Wordsworth on certain minds for a
certain time could not but be and could not but pass over. Part of this
singular power was doubtless owing to the might of will, the solid
individual weight of mind, which moulded his work into the form he
chose for it; part to the strong assumption and high self-reliance which
grew in him so close to self-confidence and presumption; part to the
sublimity and supremacy of his genius in its own climate and proper
atmosphere—one which forbids access to all others and escape to him,
since only there can he breathe and range, and he alone can breathe and
range there; part to the frequent vapour that wraps his head and the frequent dust that soils his feet, filling the simpler sort with admiration of
one so lofty at once and so familiar; in part, I fear, to the quality which
no other great poet ever shared or can share with him, to his inveterate
and invincible Philistinism, his full community of spirit and faith, in
certain things of import, with the vulgarest English mind—or that
which with the Philistine does duty for a mind. To those who, like
Shelley and Landor, could see and mark this indomitable dulness and
thickness of sense which made him mix with magnificent and flawless
verse the 'enormous folly' of 'those stupid staves,' his pupils could
always point out again the peculiar and unsurpassable grandeur and
splendour of his higher mood; and it was vain to reply that these could
be seen and enjoyed without condonation or excuse of his violent and
wearisome perversities. This is what makes his poetry such unwhole-
some and immoral reading for Philistines; they can turn round upon
their rebukers, and say, 'Here is one of us who, by your own admission,
is also one of the great poets;' and no man can give them the lie; and the
miserable men are confirmed in their faith and practice by the shameful
triumph.

It will be a curious problem for the critics of another age to work at,
and, if they can, to work out, this influence of men more or less imbued with the savour and spirit of Philistia upon the moral Samson who
has played for our behoof the part of Agonistes or protagonist in the
new Gaza where we live. From the son of his father and the pupil of his
teacher none would have looked for such efficient assault and battery of
the Philistine outworks; none but those who can appreciate the certain
and natural force, in a strong and well-tempered spirit, of loyal and unconscious reaction. I say reaction, and not revolt; he has assuredly
nothing of the bad, perhaps not enough of the good stuff which goes to
make a rebel. He is loyal, not to a fault, but to the full; yet no man's

habit of mind or work can be less like that which men trained in other schools expect from a scholar of Rydal or of Rugby. A profane alien in my hearing once defined him as 'David, the son of Goliath;' and when rebuked for the flat irreverence, avowed himself unable to understand how such a graft could have ever been set by the head gardener of the main hot-bed of Philistine saplings now flourishing in England. It is certain that the opinion put forth with such flippant folly of phrase is common to many of the profane, and not explicable by mere puerile prejudice or sentiment; and that students of Rugby or of Rydal, vocal and inarticulate, poetic and prosaic, are not seldom recognisable through certain qualities which, if any be, are undeniably Philistine. Whatever these schools have of good, their tendency is to cultivate all the merits recognised and suppress all the merits unrecognised in Ascalon or in Gath. I will not call up witnesses past or present from the realms of prose or verse, of practice or theory: it would be a task rather invidious than difficult.

Son of Goliath or son of Jesse, this David or Samson or Jephthah of our days, the man who has taught our hands to war and our fingers to fight against the Philistines, must as a poet have sat long and reverently at the feet of their Gamaliel. And as when there is a high and pure genius on either side a man cannot but get good from the man he admires, and as it was so in this case if ever in any, he must have got good from that source over and above the certain and common good which the sense of reverence does to us all. The joy of worship, the delight of admiration, is in itself so excellent and noble a thing that even error cannot make it unvenerable or unprofitable; no one need repent of reverence, though he find flaws or cavities in his idol; it has done him good to worship, though there were no godhead behind the shrine. To shut his eyes upon disproof and affirm the presence of a god found absent, this indeed is evil; but this is not an act of reverence or of worship; this is the brute fatuity of fear, wanting alike what is good and fruitful in belief, what is heroic and helpful in disbelief; witness (for the most part) the religious and political, moral and æsthetic scriptures of our own time, the huge canonical roll of the Philistine. Nothing can be more unlike such ignoble and sluggard idolatry than the reverence now expressed and now implied by Mr. Arnold for the doctrine and example of Wordsworth. His memorial verses at once praise and judge the great poet, then newly dead, better than any words of other men; they have the still clear note, the fresh breath as of the first fields and birds of spring awakened in a serene dawn, which is in Wordsworth's own verse. With wider eyes and keener, he has inherited the soothing force of speech and simple stroke of hand with which Wordsworth assuaged and healed the weariness and the wounds of his time; to his hands the same appeasing spells and sacred herbs that fell from the other's when they relaxed in death, have been committed by the gods of healing song. The elder physician of souls had indeed something too much of Æsculapius in him, something too little of Apollo his father; nevertheless the lineal and legitimate blood was apparent.

This elegy and the poem headed 'Resignation' are, in my eyes, the final flower of Mr. Arnold's poems after Wordsworth—as I take leave to qualify a certain division of his work. The second of these is an unspotted and unbroken model of high calm thought, couched in pure and faultless words; the words more equal and the vision more clear than his old teacher's, more just in view and more sure in grasp of nature and life. Imbued with the old faith at once in the necessity of things and in the endurance of man, it excels in beauty and in charm the kindred song of Empedocles; from first to last there rests upon it a serene spell, a sad supremacy of still music that softens and raises into wisdom the passionless and gentle pain of patience; the charm of earth and sorrowful magic of things everlasting; the spell that is upon the patient hills and immutable rocks, awake and asleep in 'the life of plants and stones and rain'; the life to which we too may subdue our souls and be wise. At times he writes simply as the elder poet might have written, without sensible imitation, but with absolute identity of style and sentiment; at times his larger tone of thought, his clearer accent of speech, attest the difference of the men. So perfect and sweet in speech, so sound and lucid in thought as the pupil is at his best, the master perhaps never was; and at his best the pupil is no more seen, and in his stead is a new master. He has nothing of Wordsworth's spirit of compromise with the nature of things, nothing of his moral fallacies and religious reservations; he can see the face of facts and read them with the large and frank insight of ancient poets; none of these ever had a more profound and serene sense of fate. But he has not grasped, and no man, I suppose, will ever grasp, the special and imperial sceptre of his elder. The incommunicable, the immitigable might of Wordsworth, when the god has indeed fallen upon him, cannot but be felt by all, and can but be felt by any; none can partake or catch it up. There are many men greater than he; there are men much greater; but what he has of greatness is his only. His concentration, his majesty, his pathos have no parallel; some have gone higher, many lower, none have touched precisely the same point as he; some poets have had more of all these qualities, and better; none have had exactly his gift. His pathos, for instance, cannot be matched against any other man's; it is trenchant, and not tender; it is an iron pathos. Take for example the most passionate of his poems, the 'Affliction of Margaret;' it is hard and fiery, dry and persistent as the agony of a lonely and a common soul which endures through life, a suffering which runs always in one groove without relief or shift. Because he is dull and dry and hard, when set by the side of a great lyrist or dramatist; because of these faults and defects, he is so intense and irresistible when his iron hand has hold of some chord which it knows how to play upon. How utterly unlike his is the pathos of Homer or Æschylus, Chaucer or Dante, Shakespeare or Hugo; all these greater poets feel the moisture and flame of the fever and the tears they paint; their pathos when sharpest is full of sensitive life, of subtle tenderness, of playing pulses and melting colours; his has but the downright and trenchant weight of swinging steel; he strikes like the German headsman, one stroke of a loaded sword. This could not be done even by the poets who could do more and better than this. His metre too is sublime, his choice or chance of language casual or chosen has miraculous effects in it, when he feels his foot firm on ground fit for him; otherwise his verse is often hard as wood and dry as dust and weak as water. In this as in other ways his influence has been now good and now bad. The grave cadence of such a poem as the 'Resignation,' in this point also one of Mr. Arnold's most noble and effective, bears with it a memory and a resonance of the master's music, such as we find again in the lovely single couplets and lines which now and then lift up the mind or lull it in the midst of less excellent verse; such for instance as these, which close a scale of lower melodies, in a poem not wholly or equally pleasurable: these are faultless verses, and full of the comfort of music, which tell us how, wafted at times from the far-off verge of the soul,

> As from an infinitely distant land,
> Come airs, and floating echoes, and convey
> A melancholy into all our day.

These have a subtle likeness to Wordsworth's purer notes, a likeness undefined and unborrowed; the use of words usually kept back for prose (such as 'convey') is a trick of Wordsworth's which, either makes or mars a passage; here the touch, it may be by accident, strikes the exact chord wanted, elicits the exact tone.

But indeed, as with all poets of his rank, so with Mr. Arnold, the technical beauty of his work is one with the spiritual; art, a poet's art above all others, cannot succeed in this and fail in that. Success or achievement of an exalted kind on the spiritual side ensures and enforces a like executive achievement or success; if the handiwork be flawed, there must also have been some distortion or defect of spirit, a short-coming or a misdirection of spiritual supply. There is no such thing as a dumb poet or a handless painter. The essence of an artist is that he should be articulate. It is the mere impudence of weakness to arrogate the name of poet or painter with no other claim than a susceptible and impressible sense of outward or inward beauty, producing an impotent desire to paint or sing. The poets that are made by nature are not many; and whatever 'vision' an aspirant may possess, he has not the 'divine faculty' if he cannot use his vision to any poetic purpose. There is no cant more pernicious to such as these, more wearisome to all other men, than that which asserts the reverse. It is a drug which weakens the feeble and intoxicates the drunken; which makes those swagger who have not learnt to walk, and teach who have not been taught to learn. Such talk as this of Wordsworth's is the poison of poor souls like David Gray. Men listen, and depart with the belief that they have this faculty or this vision which alone, they are told, makes the poet; and once im-bued with that belief, soon pass or slide from the inarticulate to the articulate stage of debility and disease. Inspiration foiled and impotent is a piteous thing enough, but friends and teachers of this sort make it ridiculous as well. A man can no more win a place among poets by dreaming of it or lusting after it than he can win by dream or desire a woman's beauty or a king's command; and those encourage him to fill his belly with the east wind who feign to accept the will for the deed, and treat inarticulate or inadequate pretenders as actual associates in art. The Muses can bear children and Apollo can give crowns to those only who are able to win the crown and beget the child; but in the school of theoretic sentiment it is apparently believed that this can be done by wishing.

Small things serve to give immediate proof or disproof of the requisite power. In music or in painting all men admit this for a truth; it is not less certain in poetry. There is nothing in either of the poets I speak of more distinctive and significant than the excellence of their best sonnets. These are almost equally noble in style, though the few highest of Wordsworth's remain out of reach of emulation, not out of sight of worship. Less adorable and sublime, not less admirable and durable, Mr. Arnold's hold their own in the same world of poetry with these. All in this new volume are full of beauty, sound and sweet fruits of thought and speech that have ripened and brought forth together; the poetry of religious thought when most pure and most large has borne no fairer than that one on the drawing in the Catacombs of the Good Shepherd bearing the young, not of a sheep, but of a goat; or that other on the survival of grace and spirit when the body of belief lies dead, headed (not happily) 'Anti-Desperation;' but all, I repeat, have a singular charm and clearness. I have used this word already more than once or twice; it comes nearest of all I can find to the thing I desire to express; that natural light of mind, that power of reception and reflection of things or thoughts, which I most admire in so much of Mr. Arnold's work. I mean by it much more than mere facility or transparency, more than brilliance, more than ease or excellence of style. It is a quality begotten by instinct upon culture; one which all artists of equal rank possess in equal measure.

There are in the English language three elegiac poems so great that they eclipse and efface all the elegiac poetry we know; all of Italian, all of Greek. It is only because the latest born is yet new to us that it can seem strange or rash to say so. The 'Thyrsis' of Mr. Arnold makes a third, with 'Lycidas' and 'Adonais'. It is not so easy as those may think who think by rote and praise by prescription, to strike the balance between them. The first however remains first, and must remain; its five opening lines are to me the most musical in all known realms of verse; there is nothing like them; and it is more various, more simple, more large and sublime than the others; lovelier and fuller it cannot be.

> The leader is fairest,
> But all are divine.

The least pathetic of the three is 'Adonais,' which indeed is hardly pathetic at all; it is passionate, subtle, splendid; but 'Thyrsis,' like 'Lycidas,' has a quiet and tender undertone which gives it something of sacred. Shelley brings fire from heaven, but these bring also 'the meed of some melodious tear.' There is a grace ineffable, a sweet sound and sweet savour of things past, in the old beautiful use of the language of shepherds, of flocks and pipes; the spirit is none the less sad and sincere because the body of the poem has put on this dear familiar raiment of romance; because the crude set naked sorrow is veiled and chastened with soft shadows and sounds of a 'land that is very far off;' because the verse remembers and retains a perfume and an echo of Grecian flutes and flowers,

Renews the golden world, and holds through all
The holy laws of homely pastoral,
Where flowers and founts, and nymphs and semi-gods,
And all the Graces find their old abodes.

Here, as in the 'Scholar Gipsy,' the beauty, the delicacy and affluence
of colour, the fragrance and the freedom as of wide wings of winds in
summer over meadow and moor, the freshness and expansion of the
light and the lucid air, the spring and the stream as of flowing and
welling water, enlarge and exalt the pleasure and power of the whole
poem. Such English-coloured verse no poet has written since Shakespeare, who chooses his field-flowers and hedgerow blossoms with the
same sure and loving hand, binds them in as simple and sweet an order.
All others, from Milton downward to Shelley and onward from him,
have gathered them singly or have mixed them with foreign buds and
alien bloom. No poem in any language can be more perfect as a model
of style, unsurpassable certainly, it may be unattainable. Any couplet,
any line proves it. No countryman of ours since Keats died has made or
has found words fall into such faultless folds and forms of harmonious
line. He is the most efficient, the surest-footed poet of our time, the
most to be relied on; what he does he is the safest to do well; more than
any other he unites personality and perfection; others are personal and
imperfect, perfect and impersonal; with them you must sometimes
choose between inharmonious freedom and harmonious bondage.
Above all, he knows what as a poet he should do, and simply does that;
the manner of his good work is never more or less than right. His verse
comes clean and full out of the mould, cast at a single jet; placed beside
much other verse of the time, it shows like a sculptor's work by an
enameller's. With all their wealth and warmth of flowers and lights,
these two twin poems are solid and pure as granite or as gold. Their
sweet sufficiency of music, so full and calm, buoys and bears up
throughout the imperial vessel of thought. Their sadness is not chill or
sterile, but as the sorrow of summer pausing with laden hands on the
middle height of the year, the watershed that divides the feeding fountains of autumn and of spring; a grave and fruitful sadness, the triumphant melancholy of full-blown flowers and souls full-grown. The
stanzas from the sixth to the fourteenth of 'Thyrsis,' and again from the
sixteenth to the twentieth, are, if possible, the most lovely in either
poem; the deepest in tone and amplest in colour: the choiceness and
sweetness of single lines and phrases most exquisite and frequent.

> O easy access to the hearer's grace,
> When Dorian shepherds sang to Proserpine!
> For she herself had trod Sicilian fields,
> She knew the Dorian water's gush divine,
> She knew each lily white which Enna yields,
> Each rose with blushing face;
> She loved the Dorian pipe, the Dorian strain.
> But, ah! of our poor Thames she never heard!
> Her foot the Cumnor cowslips never stirred;
> And we should tease her with our plaint in vain.

She has learnt to know them now, the river and the river-meadows, and access is as easy for an English as a Dorian prayer to the most gentle of all worshipped gods. It is a triumphal and memorial poem, a landmark in the high places of verse to which future travellers, studious of the fruits and features of the land, may turn and look up and see what English hands could rear.

This is probably the highest point of Mr. Arnold's poetry, though for myself I cannot wholly resign the old preference of things before familiar; of one poem in especial, good alike for children and men, the 'Forsaken Merman,' which has in it the pathos of natural things, the tune of the passion we fancy in the note of crying birds or winds weeping, shrill and sweet and estranged from us; the swift and winged wail of something lost midway between man's life and the life of things soulless, the wail overheard and caught up by the fitful northern fancy, filling with glad and sad spirits the untravelled ways of nature; the clear cry of a creature astray in the world, wild and gentle and mournful, heard in the sighing of weary waters before dawn under a low wind, in the rustle and whistle and whisper of leaves or grasses, in the long light breaths of twilight air heaving all the heather on the hills, in the coming and going of the sorrowful strong seas that bring delight and death, in the tender touch and recoil of the ripple from the sand; all the fanciful pitiful beauty of dreams and legends born in grey windy lands on shores and hill-sides whose life is quiet and wild. No man's hand has pressed from the bells and buds of the moors and downs, by cape or channel of the north, a sweeter honey than this. The song is a piece of the sea-wind, a stray breath of the air and bloom of the bays and hills; its mixture of mortal sorrow with the strange wild sense of a life that is not after mortal law—the childlike moan after lost love mingling with the pure outer note of a song not human—the look in it as of bright bewildered eyes with tears not theirs and alien wonder in the watch of them—the tender,

marvellous, simple beauty of the poem, its charm as of a sound or a
flower of the sea—set it and save it apart from all others in a niche of the
memory. This has all the inexplicable inevitable sweetness of a child's
or a bird's in its note: 'Thyrsis' has all the accomplished and adult beauty
of a male poem. In the volume which it crowns there is certainly no
new jewel of equal water. 'Palladium' is a fresh sample of the noble
purity and clearness which we find always and always praise in his
reflective poetry; its cool aërial colour, like that of a quiet sky between
full sunset and full moonrise, made ready for the muster of the stars,
swept clean of cloud and flame, and laved with limpid unruffled air from
western green to eastern grey; a sky the cenotaph of unburied sunlight,
the mould of moonlight unborn. 'A Southern Night' is steeped in later
air, as gentle and more shining; the stanzas on the Grande Chartreuse
are stamped with the impression of a solemn charm, and so the new
verses on Obermann, the new verses on Marguerite, strange to read for
those who remember reading the first at the time all the loves we read
of assume a form and ascend a throne in our thoughts, the old and the
new side by side, so that now this poem comes under our eyes like a
new lovesong of Petrarca to Laura, or Coleridge to Geneviève. It is
fine and high in tone, but not such as the famous verses, cited and
admired even by critics sparing of their priceless praise, beginning—

> Yes, in this sea of life enisled—

These in their profound and passionate calm strike deeper and sound
fuller than any other of the plaintive dejected songs of Switzerland.
'Dover Beach' marks another high point in the volume; it has a grand
choral cadence as of steady surges, regular in resonance, not fitful or
gusty, but antiphonal and reverberate. But nothing of new verse here
clings closer to the mind than the overture of that majestic fragment
from the chorus of a *Deljaneira*.

> O frivolous mind of man,
> Light ignorance, and hurrying unsure thoughts,
> Though man bewails you not,
> How I bewail you!

We must hope to have more of the tragedy in time; that must be a
noble statue which could match this massive fragment. The story of
Merope, though dramatic enough in detail, is upon the whole more of
a narrative romance than a tragic subject; and in Mr. Arnold's poem the
deepest note is that struck by the tyrant Polyphontes, whose austere and

patient figure is carved with Sophoclean skill of hand. It is a poem which
Milton might have praised, an august work, of steady aim and severe
success; but this of Deljaneira has in it a loftier promise and a larger
chance. Higher matter of tragedy there can be none; none more intense
and impressive, none fuller of keen and profound interest, none simpler
or statelier; none where the weight and gravity, the sweetness and
shapeliness of pure thought, could be better or closelier allied with the
warmth and width of common tenderness and passion. We must all hope
that the poet will keep to this clear air of the ancient heights, more
natural and wholesome for the spirit than the lowlands of depression
and dubiety where he has set before now a too frequent foot. This alone
I find profitless and painful in his work; this occasional habit of harking
back and loitering in mind among the sepulchres. Nothing is to be made
by an artist out of scepticism, half-hearted or double-hearted doubts
or creeds; nothing out of mere dejection and misty mental weather.
Tempest or calm you may put to use, but hardly a flat fog. In not a few
of his former poems, in some reprinted here, there is a sensible and
stagnant influence of moist vapour from those marshes of the mind
where weaker souls paddle and plunge and disappear. Above these
levels the sunnier fields and fresher uplands lie wide and warm; and
there the lord of the land should sit at peace among his good things. If
a spirit by nature clear and high, a harmonious and a shining soul, does
ever feel itself 'immured in the hot prison of the present,' its fit work is
not to hug but break its chain; and only by its own will or weakness
can it remain ill at ease in a thick and difficult air. Of such poetry I would
say what Joubert, as cited by Mr. Arnold, says of all coarse and violent
literature: it may be produced in any amount of supply to any excess
of effect, but it is no proper matter of pure art, and 'the soul says all the
while, You hurt me.' Deep-reaching doubt and 'large discourse' are
poetical; so is faith, so are sorrow and joy; but so are not the small
troubles of spirits that nibble and quibble about beliefs living or dead;
so are not those sickly moods which are warmed and weakened by
feeding on the sullen drugs of dejection; and the savour of this disease
and its medicines is enough to deaden the fresh air of poetry. Nothing
which leaves us depressed is a true work of art. We must have light
though it be lightning, and air though it be storm.

Where the thought goes wrong, the verse follows after it. In Mr.
Arnold's second book there was more of weak or barren matter, and
therefore more of feeble or faulty metre. Rhyme is the native condition
of lyric verse in English; a rhymeless lyric is a maimed thing, and halts

and stammers in the delivery of its message. There are some few in the language as good as rare; but the habit or rule is bad. The fragments of his 'Antigone' and 'Deljaneira' no reader can wish other than they are; and the chorus for example in *Merope* which tells of Areas and Callisto is a model of noble form and colour; but it does not fasten at once upon the memory like a song of Callicles, or like the 'Merman,' or like any such other. To throw away the natural grace of rhyme from a modern song is a wilful abdication of half the power and half the charm of verse. It is hard to realise and hopeless to reproduce the musical force of classic metres so recondite and exquisite as the choral parts of a Greek play. Even Milton could not; though with his god-like instinct and his god-like might of hand he made a kind of strange and enormous harmony by intermixture of assonance and rhyme with irregular blank verse, as in that last Titanic chorus of Samson which utters over the fallen Philistines the trumpet-blast and thunder of its triumph. But Milton, it may be said, even if he knew them, did not obey the laws of the choral scheme, and so forfeited the legitimate condition of its music. Who then has observed those laws and obtained that success which he did not? I scarcely think that Mr. Arnold has; and if ever man was qualified for the work it is he only. I have never seen other attempts at rhymeless choral metre which were not mere amorphous abortions of misshapen prose, halting on helpless broken limbs and feet. A poet of Mr. Arnold's high station cannot of course but write in verse, and in good verse as far as the kind will allow; but that is not far enough to attain the ultimate goal, to fill up the final measure of delight. We lose something of the glory and the joy of poetry, of which he has no reason and no right to defraud us. It is in no wise a question of scholarship, or in the presence of a scholar I should be silent; as it is, I must say how inexplicable it seems to me that Mr. Arnold, of all men, should be a patron of English hexameters. His own I have tried in vain to reduce by scansion into any metrical feet at all; they look like nothing on earth, and sound like anapæsts broken up and driven wrong; neither by ear nor by finger can I bring them to any reckoning. I am sure of one thing, that some of them begin with a pure and absolute anapæst; and how a hexameter can do this it passes my power to conceive. And at best what ugly bastards of verse are these self-styled hexameters! how human tongues or hands could utter or could write them, except by way of burlesque improvisation, I could never imagine, and never shall. Once only, to be candid— and I will for once show all possible loyalty and reverence to past authority—once only, as far as I know, in Dr. Hawtrey's elegant and fluent verse, has the riddle been resolved; the verses are faultless, are English, are hexametric; but that is simply a graceful interlude of pastime, a well-played stroke in a game of skill played with language. Such as pass elsewhere for English hexameters I do hope and suppose impossible to Eton. Mr. Clough's I will not presume to be serious attempts or studies in any manner of metre; they are admirable studies in graduated prose, full of fine sound and effect. Even Mr. Kingsley's 'Andromeda,' the one good poem extant in that pernicious metre, for all its spirit and splendour, for all the grace and glory and exultation of its rushing and ringing words, has not made possible the impossible thing. Nothing but loose rhymeless anapæsts can be made of the language in that way; and we hardly want these, having infinite command and resource of metre without them, and rhyme thrown in to turn the overweighted scale. I am unwilling to set my face against any doctrine or practice of a poet such as Mr. Arnold, but on this matter of metre I was moved to deliver my soul.

[Discusses for several pages Arnold's position as a critic, especially in relation to French literature and to English Philistia. Swinburne questions most of Arnold's positions on French literature and suggests that he squanders his talents in controversy]

There [in the realm of poetry], and not in the academies of the market-places of the Philistines, for peace or war; there, where all airs are full of the breath, and all fields of the feet of the gods; where the sea-wind that first waved the wet hair of one sea-born moves now only the ripples that remember her rising limbs; where the Muses are, and their mother. There is his place, who in such a place long since found Circe feasting and heard Apollo play; there, below the upper glens and well-springs of the Centaurs, above the scooped sea-shelves and flushing sands of the Sirens. Whatever now he say or do, he has been and will remain to us a lover and a giver of light; unwittingly, by impulse, for pure love of it; and such lead further and lighten otherwise than they know. All conscious help or guidance serves us less than unconscious leadership. In his best words there is often a craft and a charm; but in his best work there is always rest, and air, and a high relief; it satisfies, enlarges, refreshes with its cool full breath and serenity. On some men's nerves the temperature strikes somewhat cold; there are lungs that cannot breathe but in the air of a hothouse or a hospital. There is not much indeed of heat or flame in the Vestal of lunar light that shines from this hearth; but it does not burn down. His poetry is a pure temple, a white flower of marble, unfretted without by intricate and grotesque traceries, unvexed within by fumes of shaken censers or intoning of hoarse choristers, large and clear and cool, with many chapels in it and outer courts, full of quiet and of music. In the plainest air played here there is a sound of sincerity and skill; as in one little *Requiescat,* which without show of beauty or any thought or fancy leaves long upon the ear an impressure of simple, of earnest, of weary melody, wound up into a sense of rest. We do not always want to bathe our spirit in over-flowing waters or flaming fires of imagination; pathos and passion and aspiration and desire are not the only springs we seek for song. Sorrows and joys of thought or sense meet us here in white raiment and wearing maiden crowns. In each court or chapel there is a fresh fragrance of early mountain flowers which bring with them the wind and the sun and a sense of space and growth, all of them born in high places, washed and waved by upper airs and rains. Into each alike there falls on us as we turn a conscience of calm beauty, of cool and noble repose, of majestic work under melodious and lofty laws; we feel and accept the quiet sovereign-ties of happy harmony and loyal form, whose service for the artist is perfect freedom: it is good for us to be here. Nor are all these either of modern structure or of Greek; here is an Asiatic court, a Scandinavian there. And everywhere is the one ruling and royal quality of classic work, an assured and equal excellence of touch. Whether for Balder dead and the weeping gods in Asgard, or for the thought-sick heart-sore king of a weary land far east, blinded and vexed in spirit with the piteous pains and wrongs of other men, the same good care and wise charm of right words are used to give speed of wing and sureness of foot to the ministering verse. The stormy northern world of water and air and iron and snow, the mystic oppression of eastern light and cruel colour, in fiery continents and cities full of sickness and splendour and trouble tyrannies, alike yield up to him their spirit and their secret, to be rendered again in just and full expression. These are the trophies of his work and the gifts of his hand; through these and such as these things, his high and distinct seat is assured to him among English poets.

17. Isidore G. Ascher, review, *St. James's Magazine*

February 1868, xxi, 375–82

Ascher (1835–1914), who was born in Scotland, lived much of his life in Canada, where he won a certain reputation as a poet. By profession he was a lawyer. He later returned to England and contributed to various periodicals. Ascher sees Arnold as an essentially subjective and elegiac poet, whose 'thought . . . to some extent reflects and interprets . . . the tendencies of the day'. Ascher makes no discrimination between the early and later poems, and I have omitted his discussion of 'Empedocles', which is essentially restated in the comments on the other poems.

Nowadays one meets with so much that is turgid and commonplace in thought and expression, that a volume like the one we propose noticing is a positive *bonne bouche*. A calm, contemplative, serious book is this one of Mr. Arnold's, pervaded throughout by deep solemnity and an almost intense sadness. The key-note of his thoughts, sounded in the first poem, is heard to a greater or less extent in all the others.

'Empedocles on Etna' is hardly a dramatic poem, though it is called one by its author. There are no moving incidents in it; it lacks both the shadow and the substance of plot; nor have the characters any specific individuality; and though a tragedy, it hardly contains the elements of a tragedy. The mind of the hero is not fused with the ideas of his own time, but rather with modern ones. Banished from Agrigentum on account of the Sophists, 'a lonely man in triple gloom,' he lingers

> Alone
> On this charred, blackened, melancholy waste,
> Crowned by the awful peak, Etna's great mouth,

giving vent to his thoughts, which are very uniform in their strange sadness and plaintive despondency. He cannot live with men, nor with himself; and so he take his *quietus* by plunging into the crater. A bald story enough in the hands of any one but a poet; but Mr. Arnold extracts exquisite tones of thought and subtle plays of fancy from this rather barren episode; and yet in these portraitures of men, so oppressed by their thoughts as to be almost slaves to them, one naturally desires a little cheerfulness and hopefulness. The gloom of umbrageous shades, magnificent though they be, is apt to depress, unrelieved by the sunflecks.

[Discusses 'Empedocles', mainly in terms of the justification for suicide]

If there exists such a being as a man of cultured mind so stung by the wasps of misfortune, so pierced by the arrows of wretchedness, as to possess a wish to make an end of himself, in all seriousness, the poem of 'Empedocles of Etna' would be irresistible in its persuasion to urge him on to his mad act.

In the presence, as it were, of such a fine critic and true poet as Mr. Arnold, it may seem presumptuous on our part to point out what we consider his shortcomings. One of these is an over fondness to transcribe his moods and feelings into verse. All subjective poets, or those who make poetic capital from what is within them, instead of that which is without them, err in the same respect. It is this self-introspection, reflected in the description of the various heroes of Lord Byron's poems, that detracts somewhat from their wonderful merit. Our own moodiness may present itself to our minds in such a beautiful light as to be worth recording in a lyric. It may even wake similar feelings among those who, subject to despondency, may have read the dolorous verse; but to imagine and then pourtray the mood of another belongs to a higher poetic vision. It is not worth while occasionally for a poet to leave self out of the question?—for self is apt to grow wearisome, even when confined within the limits of melodious stanzas. Besides, the expression of a mood may be faithful and yet false. It may typify the poet's thought exactly, and yet be at variance with truth. In a piece called 'Youth's Agitations,' teeming with dolorous music, we are told that only one thing has been lent in common to youth and age—namely, discontent. Now, Mr. Arnold may fully believe this to be a truth. The idea also is so forcibly put as to impress readers of a different opinion with its supposed correctness. But is it a truth? The discontent of youth and age are not one. The wild recklessness of the boy, eager to leave his father's field, in order to find or make a way in life, is not the dissatisfaction of the old man who 'repines for what is not.' So we cannot help remarking that this poem is merely the offspring of a discontented mood of the poet.

In one of the finest of his poems, Mr. Arnold speaks of the

Haste half work and disarray

of our day, exemplified especially in works of art. This is a truth which must come home to most of us. With few exceptions, the magazine poetry of the day, and also some of our lately-published volumes of verse, lack the completeness of exquisite finish. Miss Jean Ingelow's 'Story of Doom' abounds in weak, slovenly passages, which the limits of this paper prevents us pointing out. Buchanan's *London Poems,* though largely imaginative, evincing often the spirit and expression of genius, are filled with commonplace sentiment and meagre verbiage. It seems as if the hurrying spirit of the age has so affected writers as to compel them to compose with undue haste. Instead of waiting for the tranquil approach of thought, they have snatched it anyhow from their brains, and then invested it with the easiest, and often worst possible dress. But we must except Mr. Arnold from these accusations. The tinsel of un-meaning smiles, the grand of extravagant hyperbole, the glare of riotous thoughts, have all no charms for him. If he does not often ascend to the heights of a sublime idea, at all events he never stoops to the level of a commonplace one. If he avoids the splendours of a too ornate diction, he takes care to eschew a puerile utterance. There is no ambiguity or incoherence in his book. If his Pegasus sometimes lacks courage, it never halts; if it is not very swift-footed, it does not suffer from lameness. Mr. Arnold is always lucid, concise, and pointed. His verse is always rounded with chastened elegance and refined simplicity. Everywhere there is evidence of painstaking effort never spent in vain. The poem which we now quote will prove the correctness of our remarks. It is, besides, a fair sample of Mr. Arnold's peculiar genius. Resonant with a sadly subdued wailing, it is still pregnant with apt wisdom delicately couched in clear language.

[Quotes 'A Wish' in its entirety]

The poetical student cannot fail to ponder long and thoughtfully upon the clear, well-defined thoughts, and harmonious grades of expression in these verses. The earnest pathos and solemnity pervading them will also deeply touch his heart. The philosophy of the poem may, perhaps, disappoint him; he may regret that it did not breathe a larger hope and fuller faith, but, unconsciously, he must acknowledge that its sentiments, sprinkled as they are with the waters of Marah, are very happily expressed.

When Mr. Arnold describes, he is almost fluent. He can reproduce the salient features of a scene, or an event, very faithfully and graphically. His colouring may not be rich, but the tones are always pure, and though he cannot invoke thoughts from nature's common objects, 'too deep for tears,' his refined mind still idealises his descriptions. For instance, how fine this description from 'Thyrsis;' the scene is chastened, by the hand of this artist, in words literally transfigured on paper:—

[Quotes 'Thyrsis', ll. 111–30, 'I know these slopes', etc.]

In the 'Epilogue to Lessing's Laocoön' Mr. Arnold treads on very high ground, and descants eloquently on the 'poet's sphere,' as compared with the world of the musician, the painter, and the sculptor. He proves to us that

> Beethoven, Raphael, cannot reach
> The charm which Homer, Shakspeare teach,

and that poetry is the highest art, since it comprises all the others. He convinces us that the poet is an artist, since he can mirror nature, and give it form and substance in his verse—a sculptor, on account of his being able to transmute all lovely images in his descriptions; and a musician, by reason of his being able to endow all with melodious epithet. Mr. Arnold, in this fine poem, pourtrays a spiritual insight into the poet's vocation. Unlike Tennyson, when he behoves mankind not to vex the poet's mind with shallow wit, since a poet's mind is not to be fathomed, Mr. Arnold strives to explain to us the reason why a poet's intellect surpasses others, dilating at length on his mission, how

> The movement he must tell of life,
> Its pain and pleasure, rest and strife;
> His eye must travel down, at full,
> The long, unpausing spectacle.

Of course, like Imlac's creation, Mr. Arnold's poet seems almost an impossible person, still many a poet's ideal bard, has appeared to benefit and charm the world, and no doubt, by-and-bye, when men can escape from the fever, hurry, and turmoil of this restless age, and allow themselves time for thought, a *vates*, even such as Mr. Arnold longs for, may, perhaps arise from the calm following the storm.

Mr. Arnold is very successful with his sonnets. These compositions especially suit his peculiar genius, inasmuch as their merit consists in their unity of aim, and their completeness of structure which, after all, is a narrow completeness. Their thoughts, compressed within such close limits, must be exhaustive. No grand poem will suffer the restraint of this composition; popular sentiment will not endure its trammels. 'To be, or not to be,' would lose its significance comprised in a sonnet. Dobell's and Smith's sonnets on the Crimean War were powerless to arrest the popular sympathies of the time. Thus, Mr. Arnold has had to draw out his ideas on Rachel into three sonnets, reflecting her life and disposition very clearly, in pointed and terse language. What nice observations and good reasoning are embodied in the one called 'West London;' and what fine ideas invests the one entitled 'Immortality,' though we question its general applicability—

> And he who flagged not in the earthly strife,
>   From strength to strength advancing—only he,
>   His soul well-knit, and all his battles won,
> Mounts, and that hardly, to eternal life.

This is consolatory to the hard-wrought, struggling individual who accomplishes something; but what of the tired wayfarer who, losing the battle, dies unhonoured and unknown, and whose soul, perhaps, is not so 'well-knit' as it might be. Is it not ordained for him to mount to eternal life? Fine as this sonnet is, we fear it is not cosmopolitan enough in its tendencies to suit the public. How much more pleasing and satisfactory is Mr. Addison's simple idea on this subject,

> Why shrinks the soul
> Back on itself, and startles at destruction?
> 'Tis the divinity that stirs within us;
> 'Tis heaven itself that points out a hereafter,
> And intimates eternity to man.

When Mr. Arnold descends to love lyrics, he can be as gay and sparkling as a troubadour, and as musical as the author of 'The Irish Melodies.' The poem called 'Calais Sands' is quite a gem in this way. Its beauties are not loosely strung, nor set at random; it is like all our author's compositions—studied, elegant, and chaste. Of course we should like the glow of earnestness, the fervour of passion, the warmth of spontaneousness in a love lyric; but the absence of these things still does not detract from the beauty of 'Calais Sands,' which has its own qualities to recommend it.

The limited space of a magazine paper does not permit us to enter more fully in detail into the characteristics of Mr. Arnold's new poems, which are well worth studying, specially on account of their peculiar thought—thought which to some extent reflects and interprets some of the tendencies of the day. Pervaded as they are with doubt, which sometimes borders on scepticism; with a cold questioning, which now and then touches on infidelity, the doubt is always real, never assumed, and the questions are poignant, and always suggestive; and even the gloom which haunts the thoughts never obscures them. Like Milton's 'visible darkness,' it is a very clear shadow, taking its rise, not always from the problems and mysteries of wretched and unfortunate lives, like the darkness lurking in Mr. Buchanan's writings, but, instead, emanates from the perturbed spirit of the writer. Such a book as the one we have attempted to notice hardly inspires hopefulness; but, on the other hand, it awakens reflection. The brightness and beauty of external nature do not often find their counterpart in human nature. The loveliness of the external world contrasts, alas, too often, with the terrible glooms of the world around us, and it is only right that in rendering the veil of self-complacency, which so often blinds our vision to the drear realities in our midst, we should look at life as it is, instead of dreaming of it as we should like it to be. The truths which our glance may reveal to us may be sad enough, Heaven knows; still better be alive to them than to the bright falsehoods of the optimist.

18. H. B. Forman, an attack on Arnold, *Tinsley's Magazine*

September 1868, iii, 146–55

Henry Buxton Forman (1842–1917) is remembered as an editor and critic of Keats and Shelley. His discussion of Arnold is largely unfavourable, and begins by taking Swinburne to task for indiscriminate praise. He accuses Arnold of many faults, especially of egotism, pointing to flaws in some poems and to what he considers total failure in others. Forman does have some grudging praise, but his is probably the sharpest attack on Arnold's poems by a contemporary.

The subject of Mr. Matthew Arnold is one on which so much has been said on various occasions by that gentleman himself, that it is by this time rather worn; and, indeed, if implicit reliance could be placed on all that has been thus said, it would be hardly necessary to discuss the subject further. It is the belief that Mr. Matthew Arnold's intense egotism has no sufficiently-rational basis that makes it seem desirable to dwell on some few points where his authority may be reasonably questioned. The strongly-implied belief in one's own importance and infallibility is not always a fair criterion of the amount of those qualities really existent in the self-devotee; and true modesty is as rare as the rare quality of true greatness, which it almost invariably accompanies. It is indeed a remarkable fact, that those possessed of the highest powers usually show a *minimum* of self-assertion, and are entirely lacking in that disagreeable, consequential pomposity of confidence which is so repelling,—while those who might reasonably mistrust themselves somewhat display no weak faltering or half-confidence in their own personal greatness.

For some years the immediate fame of Mr. Matthew Arnold has been almost exclusively the fame of a prose writer. Those students could hardly find hearing—they have nowhere of late found expression that I know of—who, with all esteem and enjoyment of his essays, of their clearness, candour, beauty of sentiment and style, retained the opinion that, if justly judged, he must be judged by his verse, and not by his prose—certainly not by this alone—that future students would cleave to that with more of care and of love; that the most memorable quality about him was the quality of a poet. Not that they liked the prose less, but that they liked the verse more. His best essays ought to live longer than most, his best poems cannot but live as long as any of their time.

These, reader, are the terms in which Mr. Arnold would be introduced if Mr. Swinburne were the critic; but, as such is not the case, we must take leave to qualify this introduction by means of a dissenting word or two. In the first place, we must range ourselves on the same side as the public, against whom Mr. Swinburne has pleased to pit his single self, as it would seem, from some inscrutable delight in mere dissentership; for what real charm that hot-blooded and fleshly author can find in the dry, cold, hard, bloodless productions of Mr. Arnold's muse, it is impossible to conceive. The public has tacitly decided that Mr. Matthew Arnold is a prose writer, not a poet; and Mr. Swinburne's one little voice, though it 'affect to speak with the tongues and the authority of men and of angels' (to use his own expression), is not likely to disturb this good judgment of the public, who have been so contemptuously regarded by himself and his lusty *protégé*—the great David Quixote—never weary of going forth with his little sling, and jerking his smooth little pebbles against the unfeeling and still-unpenetrated brow of an imperturbable giant, whom he is pleased to mistake for a Philistine —yea, even for Goliath of Gath!

In 'the best essays' of Mr. Arnold, no one can fail to find an elegance and muscularity of style that are at once pleasing and effective; and his prose is thoroughly prose—not pseudo-poetic, or overbedizened with ornamentation. From his poems, taken as a body, on the other hand, it is difficult to imagine how pleasure or profit is to be extracted; for the style is unpoetic in the extreme, and the sense of rhythm and sound faulty to the last degree. What can have induced Mr. Arnold to publish four volumes of verse is difficult to divine—certainly not the encouragement of the public, and certainly not any spontaneous and innate necessity of versified expression, if we may judge from the result. Perhaps a 'professor of poetry' is under a certain obligation to produce verse; and on that ground we might forgive a percentage of Mr. Arnold's 'poetical works.' But, when we are asked to recognise him as a poet, we must emphatically protest against any such abuse of language. A poet and a professor of poetry are two very different people; and the two titles are, to our thinking, almost of necessity mutually exclusive. Still, a professor of poetry must endeavour to distinguish himself in some way; and if his ambition is high, what is he to do? If he has not sufficient individuality of mind to originate new thoughts or new methods, the best way he can find out of his difficulty is to exclaim loudly against contemporaries for not reverting to some bygone method, instead of following the bent indicated by the current of contemporary thought; and, when the preaching is thoroughly preached, he may with complete consistency take up the task of attempting whatever *renaissance* his own imitative faculty may lead him to.

There have always been, and doubtless will always be, those who, with a certain amount of education and 'culture,' are quite unable to appreciate the grandeur of their own times, but devote their sympathies to other ages with too much exclusiveness. Every era is characterised by a more or less immense bulk of art-product, the *élite* only of which can possibly survive as of wide interest to all ages; and in the great Greek literature, as elsewhere, there existed innumerable works of minor importance which have been allowed to die. Those that survive are such as are broad and universal in their bearings and supreme in beauty; and every age produces some works of art based on sempiternal principles of human nature. Among the dead Greek tragedies were many founded on the Greek sentiment of uncompromising vengeance; and from these Mr. Arnold has dug up the subject of his tragedy *Merope*. The sentiment of this tragedy, as well as the scheme, are Greek; and the form is also imitated from the Greeks, as in the case of Mr. Swinburne's *Atalanta*. But, unfortunately, *Merope* has not any of the original poetic qualities which lend beauty to *Atalanta*, and is entirely lacking in artistic *vis*.

Mr. Arnold claims originality for some of the choric metres in *Merope;* and Heaven forbid that we should meet with their counterpart in the works of any who have gone before him, or in those of any who may come after! Here is a sample: Mr. Swinburne would perhaps say of it, 'verse thunderous as the footing of Æschylus, and pregnant as the thought of Shakespeare!' But we say of it, 'Read, and tremble at the thought of such prose, broken into little, unrhythmic, unmusical, unmeaning lengths, being thrust upon us in any appreciable quantity as poetry.'

> Did I then waver
> (O woman's judgment!)
> Misled by seeming
> Success of crime?

And ask, if sometimes
The gods, perhaps, allow'd you.
O lawless daring of the strong,
O self-will recklessly indulg'd?
Not time, not lightning,
Not rain, not thunder,
Efface the endless
Decrees of Heaven.
Make justice alter,
Revoke, assuage her sentence,
Which dooms dread ends to dreadful deeds,
And violent deaths to violent men.

In justice to Mr. Arnold, it should be stated that this chorus is duly completed by a second and third *strophe* and *anti-strophe* and an *epode*; all of which, *in justice to readers,* are omitted.

The obsolete subject and method will be shown to be sufficient to make the work a dead letter when it is pointed out that Mr. Arnold felt obliged to prefix an elaborate prefatory essay to justify and explain the tragedy. When such a necessity as this arises, the hope of finding beauty or propriety in the so-called work of art is indeed a fragile one. The essay ends with a passage which would be thoroughly sensible if we did not see through the veil of affected modesty:

I must have wearied my reader's patience, but I was desirous, in laying before him my tragedy, that it should not lose what benefit it can derive from the foregoing explanations. To his favourable reception of it there will still be obstacles enough, in its unfamiliar form, and in the incapacity of its author.

How much do I regret that the many poets of the present day who possess that capacity which I have not, should not have forestalled me in an endeavour far beyond my powers! . . . They would have lost nothing by such an attempt, and English literature would have gained much.

Only their silence could have emboldened to undertake it *one with inadequate time, inadequate knowledge, and a talent, alas! still more inadequate: one who brings to the task none of the requisite qualifications of genius or learning,* nothing but a passion for the great masters, and an effort to study them without fancifulness.

The italicised words, taken literally, are as true as anything that was ever spoken or written. But if really meant, why publish the book? And if merely written out of compliment to modesty, what an overstrained cant there is about them!

With a splendid dramatic form of our own, it would be hard if we modern English could not rest satisfied without going back for the disused forms of the ancients, suitable to their age and place, and indeed the natural outgrowth therefrom, but quite out of place now and here. Poetry, to be poetry at all, must be spontaneous; and the most natural current for spontaneous expression is the current which contemporary and immediately-antecedent thought has indicated, not an artificially-imposed method which the writer gets to think desirable from mere intellectual consideration of former products of it. In every age there are certain true poets who utter themselves with all the spontaneity of real art in antiquated methods and manners; but these are exceptional, and, in a sense, may be considered as born out of due season. Such poets will ever succeed in clothing new beauties on to the old forms—and new beauties for which they have to thank no one but themselves—in the same way that the greatest artists who adopt the contemporary methods have invariably been found to improve on them with additions and perfections from the store of their own individualities. We have bad taste enough (if it is to be considered bad taste) not only to prefer Shakespeare to all the great Greek dramatists and their followers, but also to prefer his form and method, as being not only more modern in its psychological adaptabilities, but more rich and beautiful intrinsically. This being our plight, what wonder if we state with confidence that the lasting dramatic works of the present age will be those executed in the still-living form and method which Shakespeare found and flushed with endless glories and perfections, and which other hands have since contributed to the beautifying of.

[Turns to the Preface to *Merope*, from which he moves to Arnold's concept of the Philistine and the discussion of Byron in the 'Heine' essay. He is sharply critical]

What Mr. Arnold says here, in the last few lines of the paragraph, in *plain* prose, he has elsewhere said in versified prose, under the title of 'Men of Genius.' The verses in question commence:

> Silent, the Lord of the world
> Eyes from the heavenly height,
> Girt by his far-shining train,
> Us, who with banners unfurl'd
> Fight life's many-chanc'd fight
> Madly below, in the plain.

Then we are told how the Lord sends 'his own' out to the battle, and how most of them fail:

Hardly, hardly shall one
Come, with countenance bright,
O'er the cloud-wrapt, perilous plain:
His Master's errand well done,
Safe through the smoke of the fight,
Back to his Master again.

If there is anything like the spontaneous utterance of a poetic soul in the dry crackle of leafless limbs flimsily attached to this bare trunk of an idea, we are sadly misled as to the meaning of 'poetry;' for it is impossible to trace in the composition anything further than the ghost of a thought, followed coldly out, and carefully written into verse form.

There is the same want of life and fervour about the great bulk of the author's volumes of verse; the chief cause of this is doubtless want of real poetic power; but this evil is evidently aggravated by Mr. Arnold's self-imposition of unsuitable forms and methods. Take, for instance, 'The Philosopher and the Stars:'

And you, ye stars!
Who slowly begin to marshal,
As of old, in the fields of heaven,
Your distant, melancholy lines—
Have you, too, surviv'd yourselves?
Are you, too, what I fear to become?
You, too, once liv'd;
You, too, mov'd joyfully
Among august companions
In an older world, peopled by gods,
In a mightier order,
The radiant, rejoicing, intelligent
Sons of Heaven!

And so on.

This is written in one of those irregular unrhymed metres which Heine used with so great effect, and is modelled so closely on the work of Heine that it strikes as a study in that method,—not as a genuine and spontaneous utterance of an original mind. Lack of spontaneity is nowhere more infallibly betrayed than in the awkward use of simile and metaphor. A simile to be effective should be direct and condensed; but with Mr. Arnold a long passage, entering into all sorts of details of the objects used for comparison, is frequently interpolated between two portions of the thing predicted concerning the actual subject of discourse. For instance, in 'Balder dead,' when the god Hermod has to

197

cross the bridge over 'Giall's stream,' to beg his brother Balder back from hell, the damsel keeping the bridge is introduced thus:

> Scant space that warder left for passers by;
> But, as when cowherds in October drive
> Their kine across a snowy mountain-pass
> To winter pasture on the southern side,
> And on the ridge a wagon chokes the way,
> Wedg'd in the snow, then painfully the hinds
> With goad and shouting urge their cattle past,
> Plunging through deep untrodden banks of snow
> To right and left, and warm steam fills the air;
> So on the bridge that damsel block'd the way,
> And question'd Hermod as he came.

The comparison of a damsel to a wagon is not specially poetical; and the minute details of drovers and cattle are vastly ineffective and irrelevant. There could be no object in setting a herd of oxen to stand as the type of Hermod, the swift and nimble god of the northern mythology; and, had there been, the details which swell up the eight lines of the simile would have been excessively ill-placed. This simile of cattle and drovers suggests a passage of the Laureate's in 'Aylmer's Field,' in which an admirable effect is given by an analogous comparison. When the miserable squire has been smitten by the sermon preached at him, and is following his fainting wife out of church, we are told in short direct phrase that he

> followed out
> Tall and erect; but in the middle aisle
> Reel'd, as a footsore ox in crowded ways
> Stumbling across the market to his death,
> Unpitied; for he groped as blind, and seem'd
> Always about to fall, grasping the pews.

There the simile is in proper artistic subordination to the incidents similised; and we do not for an instant lose sight of the man, while holding in our minds the touching association suggested in simile. But in the other complicated affair we have to go back and forward to satisfy ourselves who is to stand for the wagon and who for the cattle, and to search for inscrutable reasons why such and such small stupid detail was dabbed on. This is frequently the case with Mr. Arnold; and there are several instances in the same poem of 'Balder dead.' Another example occurs in that part of the poem where Hermod and Niord

visit the cavern of Thok, to beg her tears for Balder, the only condition
of whose release from hell is that everything weep for him:

> She spake; and to the cavern's depth she fled,
> Mocking: and Hermod knew their toil was vain.
> And as seafaring men, who long have wrought
> In the great deep for gain, at last come home,
> And towards evening see the headlands rise
> Of their own country, and can clear descry
> A fire of wither'd furze which boys have lit
> Upon the cliffs, or smoke of burning weeds
> Out of a till'd field inland,—then the wind
> Catches them, and drives out again to sea:
> And they go long days tossing up and down
> Over the gray sea ridges; and the glimpse
> Of port they had makes bitterer far their toil—
> So the gods' cross was bitterer for their joy.

The simile here is absurdly spun out; and this trick, as well as being in
itself objectionable, sometimes leads to entire loss of grammatical construction, as in the concluding lines of 'Balder dead:'

> And as a stork which idle boys have trapp'd,
> And tied *him* in a yard, at autumn sees
> Flocks of his kind pass flying o'er his head
> To warmer lands, and coasts that keep the sun;
> *He* strains to join their flight, and, from his shed,
> Follows them with a long complaining cry—
> So Hermod gazed, and yearned to join his kin.

The redundancy of personal pronouns here is rather too ludicrous: a
'professor of poetry' ought to know better than to flood us with nomina-
tives in this way, or to talk about 'A stork which idle boys have trapp'd
and tied *him*.'

Is it to be understood, then, that Mr. Arnold has written nothing
that can be called poetry? Not at all. Here and there we get unquestionably poetical ideas and undoubted pieces of real expression. But it is hard
to find anything like a complete poem. One entitled 'Obermann' opens
sweetly, with a real piece of landscape with real inner significance; and
the poetic mode of thought is sustained for several verses without
intermission:

[Quotes ll. 1–36]

This is poetry, and poetry, too, that bears reading over and over again; but after this the poem begins to fall away, and work out its time in rhymed prose, with occasional faint touches of poetry. What, for instance, can be more distinctly prose than this piece of rhyme?—

> But we, brought forth and rear'd in hours
> Of change, alarm, surprise,
> What shelter to grow ripe is ours?
> What leisure to grow wise?

Or, again, this scrap of doubtful philosophy:

> We, in some unknown Power's employ,
> Move on a rigorous line,
> Can neither, when we will, enjoy;
> Nor when we will, resign.

Such baldly-stated scraps of what is intended for thought are very frequent in Mr. Arnold's volumes, and they may be properly described as pseudo-epigrammatic; that is to say, they seem to have the intention of epigrams, without the necessary force and sprightliness. Here is a whole 'poem' in the same style:

[Quotes 'Too Late']

Of the performances of Mr. Arnold, those which are purely critical are the best; and the title of 'critic' is unquestionably that to which, if to any, he is entitled; but his criticism itself is far too narrow and far too fully saturated with the sense of his own personality to be popular or widely useful. The propensity for small wrangling and calling of names is largely exhibited in these writings; and the consequence has been that epithets have been applied to Mr. Arnold, and comments made upon him, not really more offensive intrinsically than his own epithets for and comments on others, but sometimes expressed with greater breadth than would be compatible with the cultivated style of the 'child of light' and intellectual agitator—the polished declaimer against the crass obliquities of the 'Philistines.' Mr. Arnold should not forget that the greater polish with which an insult is got up, the more offensive will it be; and, until he is prepared to withdraw the epithet of 'Philistine,' which he has scattered broadcast among his fellow-countrymen, he ought not to complain, as he does, that the editor of a journal more noted for *verve* and *empressement* of attack than for polite and subdued contemptuousness should allow him to be alluded to in the columns of that journal as an 'elegant Jeremiah' and a 'spurious Jeremiah;' nor is it quite reasonable to expect that the same or any other editor should discriminate nicely between those Jewish prophets whose style is admired by Mr. Arnold, and those whose style does not enjoy that distinction. The prevalent opinion will probably be, that whether Mr. Arnold admires the style of Jeremiah more or less than that of the other prophets, is of about the same importance to the British public as—well, as it is to Jeremiah himself.

19. Alfred Austin, on Arnold's poetic characteristics, *Temple Bar*

August 1869, xxviii, 35–45

Austin (1835–1914), was a barrister by training and poet laureate, one would think, by accident. With W. J. Courthope he edited the *National Review*, wrote for various periodicals, and wrote minor poetry, for which he was awarded the laureateship in 1896.

'The age is sick', Austin writes, 'with a surfeit of analysis.' And 'surely the Pegasus of the Poet, the freest possible gift to all mankind, should not be subjected to too rigorous an inspection.' After such a disclaimer, and after a rather laboured introduction, Austin discusses Arnold more or less as the spokesman for his age, at once exemplary and distinct, who more than Tennyson or any other poet embodies the doubts and aspirations of the time.

In the case of Mr. Matthew Arnold one experiences an additional repugnance to the undertaking we have conscientiously imposed on ourselves ['Criticism—or what is so termed'] because he himself evidently sees and feels—what is there that he does not see and feel?—the force of all the objections we have to make to contemporaneous verse (his own included), and likewise the uncritical temper in which it is usually mentioned. The sardonic lines we just now quoted show how strongly he disapproves the improper mentioning in the same breath of the giants of old with the pigmies of to-day; and those which he prefixes to the second volume of his *Poems* are of themselves enough to demonstrate in what estimation he holds the poetry, either actual or possible, of such an age as that in which it is his lot to live:

> Though the Muse be gone away,
> Though she move not earth to-day,
> Souls, erewhile who caught her word,
> Ah! still harp on what they heard.

He cannot bring himself to refrain from song, but he owns in his inmost heart that there is that without him, if not within him, which will prevent it from being such as was possible before the Muse had gone away. Again and again he recurs to this painful—this overwhelmingly sad conviction. In some of the most exquisite and pathetic lines he ever wrote, 'Stanzas from the Grande Chartreuse,' it is not only faiths that are dead and gone, but the paralysis which smites the lyre in the interval between their disappearance and some hoped-for palingenesis, that move him to this mournful strain:

[Quotes ll. 85–90, 'Wandering between two worlds', etc.]

He goes about the world, oppressed with the sense not only of the unjoyous, but of the unspiritual character of the times in which he has been given his brief span of life. Even when Empedocles is the supposed spokesman, it is still Mr. Arnold that speaks through him:

[Quotes ll. 239–45, 'And yet what days were those', etc.]

Mark the distinction he draws between being Thought's slaves and 'receiving the shock of thought,'—a distinction recalling Wordsworth's 'Thought was not; in enjoyment it expired,' quoted by us when protesting against Mr. Browning's deep thoughts being considered poetry —and a distinction which, moreover, eminently corroborates the position we have persistently maintained, whilst insisting on the specific nature of poetical genius. Burning to bring back such days, and to be no longer Thought's slave, Mr. Arnold confesses, with sad reiteration, the vanity of his desires. No amount of knowledge, no profundity of research, will give him the poet's strong, free, spontaneously soaring pinion. Indeed, they help only to weigh him down to the ground:

[Quotes 'Resignation', ll. 206–14, 'Deeper the poet sees', etc.]

Here again we meet with a striking confirmation of the contrast we have pointed out between deep thoughts and lofty thought—a contrast which, it is plain, haunts Mr. Arnold, and the consciousness of which is to him the explanation of his own comparative powerlessness, and of that of his poetical contemporaries. They are all hemmed in and cannot escape. They abide, and cannot mount to breathe the immortal air where Orpheus and where Homer are. The age, not great, but big and exacting, forbids them to get beyond its influences; and its most imperative influences are those which fasten men down, not those which lend them buoyancy. And what is worst and most grievous of all is that the poet's efforts to baffle them are bootless:

[Quotes 'The Buried Life', ll. 64–71, 'And long we try in vain', etc.]

Enormous is the power of the age over us; but it is 'stupefying,' and Mr. Arnold feels that it has, in a sense, benumbed him far more than it has benumbed all save the chosen few whom he resembles. In order not to be so affected by it, one must remain aloof from it. Yet with what result? Let Mr. Arnold himself answer in his 'Stanzas in Memory of Obermann.' After a laconic and somewhat unsatisfactory reference to Wordsworth as one of the only two spirits besides Obermann who have seen 'their way in this our troubled day,' he goes on to acknowledge—

> But Wordsworth's eyes avert their ken
> From half of human fate—

and to explain that if his spirit was freer from mists, and much clearer than ours, it was because—

> . . . though his manhood bore the blast
> Of a tremendous time,
> Yet in a tranquil world was passed
> His tenderer, youthful prime.

To us tranquillity and a tremendous time have both been denied; and we cannot avert our ken from what is now to be seen, even if we would:

[Quotes ll. 69–76, 'But we, brought forth', etc.]

It is ever with him the same complaint. The tree of knowledge of which we have been forced to partake, is no more the tree of song than it is the tree of life. We know all—or we think we do—but all that we can effect without our knowledge is to sigh under the burden of it. The age is sick with a surfeit of analysis, and Mr. Arnold is sick along with it.

Not content with half, we have grasped the whole; and, having got it, we have only proved the truth of the old admonition, that the half is often more than the whole. We should like to throw it away, but we cannot; so we keep harping on our disappointment.

[Contrasts the ages of Chaucer and Shakespeare with his own]

To use Mr. Tennyson's words, the most open and sensitive minds now amongst us

> . . . sit apart, holding no form of creed,
> But contemplating all.

We have emptied the heavens and the earth of everything but man and the indefinite unknowable, and stand very properly tolerant in the vacant space we have created. We have made a mental solitude, and call it peace. We mean no reproaches: we are simply stating facts. It is not our fault perhaps, but it is woefully our misfortune. Every thoughtful man and woman feels it; the age feels it; the poet feels it. He, more than any other, is unable to mistake the dead past for the living present; he, more than any other, is unable to mistake what have now proved to be mirages and phantoms for new births and solid promises of the future. 'For what availed it,' asks Mr. Arnold, in the poem from which we have once before quoted:

> For what availed it, all the noise
> And outcry of the former men?—
> Say, have their sons obtained more joys?
> Say, is life lighter now than then?

We have been in the Land of Promise which the fervour of our immediate sires pointed out, and fancied they had bequeathed us, and we have found it, some worse, none better, than the desert they bewailed. So, though we inherit the ruins they made, we have no fresh shelter for our heads; past and future alike fail us,

> For both were faiths, and both are gone.

Gone with them, too, says Mr. Arnold, is 'the nobleness of grief,' and he begs that the 'fret' may not be left now that the nobleness is taken away. He is almost ashamed of himself for singing at all. 'The best are silent now,' he says:

[Quotes 'Stanzas From the Grande Chartreuse', ll. 115–26, 'Achilles ponders in his tent', etc.]

What wonder, then, that in moments when they cannot be quite mute, not yet content themselves with bemoaning their impotence, Mr. Arnold, and others like him, should reproduce the literature of the past, and, as he says, now that 'the Muse be gone away,' try to 'harp on what they heard'? In a sonnet to a friend, beginning, 'Who prop, thou ask'st, in these bad days, my mind?' he answers, Homer and Epictetus:

> But be his
>> My special thanks . . .
>
> Who saw life steadily, and saw it whole:
> The mellow glory of the Attic stage,
> Singer of sweet Colonus and its child.

What must be the mental and spiritual condition of an age, when one of its poets turns away from it to seek his comfort and inspiration in the writings of Sophocles? That a student should do so, that a philosopher should do so, that a cynic should do so, were intelligible enough; but a poet! The Muse must, indeed, have fallen upon evil days, and evil tongues, before this could be; and that she has done so, is the explanation of the Poetry of the Period. We have seen how Mr. Swinburne too, when flying from the sensuous atmosphere of erotic lyricism, can find no refuge but in the 'mellow glory of the Attic stage;' and the 'something Greek about' Mr. Tennyson's idyllic manner, has been repeatedly noticed, even to the extent of some of the recent translators of Homer having founded their style upon it. We shall see directly how far the same remark is applicable to Mr. Morris; but Mr. Arnold saves us from all further necessity of investigation, by his 'special thanks,' and by the obvious echoes of those 'who prop his mind,' in three of his longest works: 'Empedocles on Etna,' 'Sohrab and Rustum,' and 'Balder Dead,' and in several shorter pieces. A very few examples will suffice to illustrate our meaning:

[Quotes 'Sohrab and Rustum', ll. 160–9, 'But as a troop of pedlars', etc.; 'Balder Dead', ll. 559–65, 'And as a stork', etc.; 'Empedocles on Etna', ll. 67–77, 'But an awful pleasure', etc.]

Why need we point out what these passages sufficiently indicate for themselves?—that they are the echo of an echo, written less by the Poet than by the Professor of Poetry; that the writer's mind is leaning upon props, and that here he is not himself? This may be the verse of the period, but we can scarcely call it the poetry of the period; it is too academical for that. It is the result and expression of culture, not of impulse. What Mr. Arnold is really like when his impulses master him, we have seen. 'Your creeds are dead,' he cries:

[Quotes 'Obermann Once More', ll. 229–32; 245–8]

It is in vain and idly that he ascends the 'blanched summit bare of Malatrait,' there to conclude with an ephemeral effort at being sanguine:

> Without a sound,
> Across the glimmering lake,
> High in the Valais depth profound
> I saw the morning break.

Such a conclusion is just as hollow, unsatisfactory, and—we speak objectively—as insincere, as the solution, which is no solution, given by Mr. Tennyson in 'The Two Voices,' when

> The sweet church-bells began to peal.

Unhappily, sweet church-bells are no longer any answer to a sad but edifying scepticism that is the martyr of its own candour; and Mr. Arnold proves to us over and over again that he has seen no morning break, and that only those now see it who, like Wordsworth,

> . . . avert their ken
> From half of human fate.

In his unrest he gazes at the star-sown vault of heaven, and he gets for answer:

> Would'st thou *be* as these are? *Live* as they!
> Unaffrighted by the silence round them,
> Undistracted by the sights they see.

But how soon is it before he hears another voice, saying:

> Calm's not life's crown, though calm is well.

What then is it? Mr. Arnold cannot tell us. Neither can the age in which he lives. Homer knew what it was: it was fighting, loving, and singing. Epictetus knew what it was: it was renunciation. Christ knew what it was: it was to leave all things and follow Him. Shakespeare knew what it was: it was, as with the singer of sweet Colonus and its child, to see life steadily, and see it whole. Byron knew what it was: it was to exhaust and then abuse it. But we? But Mr. Arnold?

> Ah! two desires toss about
> The poets' feverish blood!
> One drives him to the world without,
> And one to solitude.

No doubt they do in these days; but the days have been when they did not, and when one, and only one, feverish commanding desire, whatever it might happen to be, stirred the poets' blood and ruled it. Otherwise we should have inherited no greater poetry than now, alas! we can ourselves produce. Great ages, productive of great things, whatever else may characterise them, have always this one salient characteristic—that they have made up their minds. We have not made up ours, and we cannot make them up. Two desires toss us about, as they toss about our poet. The old injunction to steer the middle course is of no avail here. Mr. Tennyson has steered it, and we have as a consequence his golden mediocrity. Mr. Arnold has never been able to subdue himself to this pitch; and so, whilst Mr. Tennyson's verse is the resultant of the many social and spiritual forces of the time, Mr. Arnold's is fraught with the visible forces themselves, now in its lines expressing one, now another. Anon he makes an effort to submit.

[Quotes 'In Utrumque Paratus', ll. 36–42 (1869 ed. only) 'Be not too proud', etc.]

But this mood of humble optimism is ephemeral. He chafes at 'this stuff,' and owns the disease of a yearning for proud self-severance:

[Quotes 'In Memory of the author of "Obermann"', ll. 97–104, '*The glow*, he cries, *the thrill of life*', etc.]

This last assertion can be accepted only with a most important and pregnant qualification. There is no necessity for a man with high and noble aspirations to renounce his own life in order to live with the world's, if the aspirations of the world at the same time likewise happen to be high and noble. Granted a great age, and a man capable of being great in the direction in which the greatness of the age itself tends, what need of renunciation of one's life then? The age and the man will be one. No two desires will toss either about. They will pull strongly, and pull together. Even this age produces men to whom, not as men, indeed, but under some other connotation, the epithet 'great' may be applied. It produces great speculators, great contractors, great millionaires, great manipulators and mountebanks. But poets! Alas! none of these. How can it? It cannot give what it has not got; and it has not got

the divine *afflatus*. To live with it, the man who has must indeed renounce his own life; and his own individual possession of the divine
afflatus helps him not—save to gasp and to flutter. He can do little or
nothing, unless the age assists him. He might as well think to fly in
vacuum, swim without water, or breathe without air. Mr. Arnold has
tried, and feels that he has done that little or nothing—that he has failed;
that he had better have remained pondering, like Achilles in his tent;
that the wisest course would have been to keep silent:

> Silent—the best are silent now!

[Turns to a discussion of William Morris]

20. Other comments from the 1860s

(a) From the *Spectator*, 7 September 1867

Any one who, like ourselves, has always procured and read Mr.
Arnold's poems with eagerness, from the first series of *Poems by A.* to
this volume, will now be possessed of nearly every one of his poems in a
double form, and of two or three of them in a triple form,—a result
which, though it does not diminish their merit, is rather vexatious to the
possessor of books. Mr. Arnold says that 'Empedocles on Etna' cannot
be said to be republished in this volume, because it was withdrawn from
circulation before fifty copies of it were sold, but as the present writer,
at all events, was amongst the fifty buyers, he now finds himself in
possession of the whole poem, as well as of most of the others belonging
to the same volume, in a double shape, and of part of 'Empedocles on
Etna'—the exquisite verses called 'The Harp Player upon Etna'—in a
treble shape, which is a vexation that Mr. Arnold might perhaps have
spared his readers. Nothing is less pleasant to the true lover of a poem
than to have it in two or three different forms,—generally with minute
differences in phrase in each,—and always associated with a different

page, and different print, and different memories as regards the external shape of the volume in which it is contained. It dissipates to a certain extent the individuality of a poem to have it issued by its author in two or three distinct volumes, embedded in different company in each, and clipped or modified to suit its various settings. We feel now towards some of Mr. Arnold's poems as we might towards friends who had two or three different bodies, and who were fond of trying the permutations and combinations of bodies in which they could appear to us. If they came with an entirely new gait, or with different-coloured eyebrows, or a different voice and accent, we should feel inclined to beg them to keep as much the same in future as might be consistent with the law of growth and change in personal characteristics, and should be a little troubled to which form of friend to refer our own private feelings. So it is with Mr. Arnold's various editions of his poems. We always feel a certain amount of embarrassment, whether it is the form in *Poems by A*, or in the first or second series of Mr. Arnold's acknowledged poems, or in the 'new' poems that we are thinking of. It is a small matter to cavil at, but an injury of this kind thrice repeated vexes the best disciple. We should scarcely have expressed our chagrin had not Mr. Arnold quoted two or three lines as motto to one of his pieces from 'Lucretius, an Unpublished Tragedy,' and so refused us deliberately what we want, while giving us duplicates and triplicates of what we have. However, much as there is,—near half the volume,—which is not only known to the students of Mr. Arnold, but already in their possession in volumes of his poems, we are not really ungrateful for anything new which he gives us stamped with the peculiar mark of his genius, and there are several new and fine poems here, though from one of the finest (on Heine's grave) Mr. Arnold had quoted the finest passage, likening England to Atlas, 'the weary Titan with deaf ears and labour-dimmed eyes,' in that memorable address of his, a year and a half ago, to his 'countrymen.'

(b) 'Shirley' [Sir John Skelton] in *Fraser's Magazine*, November 1869

We owe an apology to Mr. Matthew Arnold. In an article, now some months old, we used *Merope*—rather unfairly perhaps—as a foil to *The Earthly Paradise*. The unfairness, if there was unfairness, consisted in this, that the article, which was originally meant to be an exhaustive criticism of Mr. Arnold, as well as of Mr. Morris, was, in point of fact, devoted almost exclusively to the latter. The result was that only one side of Mr. Arnold's poems was considered, and that side the weakest—his reproduction of the classical life in its tragic forms. Had we had space to enter into a complete analysis, we should have gone on to point out that he owns certain subtle gifts and graces of a modern kind, to which Mr. Morris can lay no claim, and which constitutes him, in a peculiar manner, the spokesman of the new generation. His irony, his subdued pathos, the union, Antinous-like, of sadness and scorn in his poetry, the severity of his culture, and the delicate sensitiveness of his insight, make him in many respects a representative man—the representative of a powerful but obscure force in our society, a force that would be more powerful if its aims were better defined and its attitude less critical. A man like Mr. Arnold could have been possible in no other age than our own, and yet his avowed relation to it is that of sharp antagonism.

Remarkable as Mr. Arnold's first volume of poems was (which contained among others very notable, the charming 'Tristram and Iseult,' most musical, most melancholy), there is nothing in it to compare, in point of far-reaching poetic faculty, with 'Dover Beach,' 'Rugby Chapel,' and 'Heine's Grave,' in his new volume. These are the strong words of a strong poet, who is himself affected—depressed and oppressed—by the malaria-taint that is all about him in the air—the subtle disease which paralyses our energies, and mars our work. We suffer from weariness not merely of the flesh but of the spirit. 'Dover Beach,' which gives expression to this complaint, is at once the finest and most despondent of these poems. . . .

21. R. H. Hutton, 'The Poetry of Matthew Arnold', *British Quarterly Review*

April 1872, lv, 313–47

Richard Holt Hutton (1826–97) was an extraordinarily diverse and prolific man of letters. He was an editor, theologian, academician, journalist. With Walter Bagehot he edited the *National Review* (1858–60), then edited the *Spectator* (1861–97), wherein he published several reviews of Arnold. For many years Hutton was Arnold's foremost apologist. This essay, reprinted often, elaborates the conviction that Arnold's poems are one long variation on a single theme, 'the divorce between the soul and the intellect'. Hutton compares Arnold with Wordsworth and Goethe, comments on his poetic 'recitative', and argues that he 'expresses powerfully' the 'spiritual weaknesses' of the age.

Hazlitt, writing of one of Wordsworth's latest and more classical poems, 'Laodamia,' describes it as having 'the sweetness, the gravity, the strength, the beauty, and the languor of death: calm contemplation and majestic pains.' There also, we have, in one of Hazlitt's terse and sententious criticisms, the aroma of the finest poems of Wordsworth's greatest poetical disciple—one, too, who is the disciple of Wordsworth, emphatically in his later rather than in his earlier phase; Wordsworth schooled into a grace and majesty not wholly meditative, but in part, at least, critical; Wordsworth the conscious artist as well as poet; not Wordsworth the rugged rhapsodist of spiritual simplicity and natural joy. 'The sweetness, the gravity, the strength, the beauty, and the languor of death,—calm contemplation and majestic pains,'—all these may be found in the most characteristic and most touching of Mr.

Arnold's poems; in the melancholy with which the sick King of Bokhara broods over the fate of the wretch whom his pity and power could
not save from the expiation he himself courted; in the gloomy resentment of Mycerinus against the unjust gods who cut short his effort to
reign justly over his people; in the despair of Empedocles on Etna, at
his failure to solve the riddle of the painful earth—his weariness of 'the
devouring flame of thought,' the naked, eternally restless mind whose
thirst he could not slake; in those fine lines written by a deathbed, in
which Mr. Arnold contrasts the hopes of youth with what he deems the
highest gain of manhood, 'calm'; in the noble sonnet which commemorates Sophocles as one whom 'business could not make dull nor
passion wild'; in the graphic 'Memorial Verses,' wherein he praises
Wordsworth for assuaging that dim trouble of humanity which
Goethe could only dissect and describe; in the melodious sadness of the
personal restrospects in 'Resignation,' 'A Southern Night,' and 'Self-
Dependence'; in the large concessions to Heine's satiric genius, made in
the verses composed at his tomb at Montmartre; in the consciously
hopeless cravings of 'The Scholar Gipsy' and 'Thyrsis' after a reconciliation between the intellect of man and the magic of Nature; and,
most characteristically of all, in the willing half-sympathy given by Mr.
Arnold to those ascetics of the Grande Chartreuse, whom his intellect
condemns, and in the even deeper enthusiasm with which he addresses,
in the midst of melancholy Alpine solitudes, that modern refugee from a
sick world, the author of 'Obermann,' delineates the intellectual weakness and dejection of the age, and feebly though poetically shadows
forth his own hopeless hope of a remedy. In all these poems alike, and
many others which I have not space to enumerate—in all, indeed, in
which Mr. Arnold's genius really gains a voice—there is 'the sweetness,
gravity, strength, beauty, and the languor of death,' blended in the
spirit of a calm contemplativeness which takes all the edge off anguish
and makes the poet's pains 'majestic'; for Mr. Arnold's poems are one
long variation on a single theme, the divorce between the soul and the
intellect, and the depth of spiritual regret and yearning which that
divorce produces. Yet there is a didactic keenness with the languor,
an eagerness of purpose with the despondency, which give half the
individual flavour to his lyrics. A note of confidence lends authority to
his scepticism; the tone of his sadness is self-contained, sure, and even
imperious, instead of showing the ordinary relaxation of loss; and the
reader of his poetry is apt to rise from it with the same curious questioning in his mind which Mr. Arnold has put into the mouth of

Nature, in the verses called 'Morality,'—a questioning after the origin of 'that severe, that earnest air,' which breathes through poetry of all but hopeless yearning and all but unmixed regret.

No doubt one kind of answer to this question is, that Mr. Arnold has inherited from the great teacher of Rugby and historian of the Punic War the lofty didactic impulse which marks all his prose and poetry alike, although the substance of the lessons he is so eager to give has sadly dwindled in the descent from father to son. But that is but one sort of answer, explaining rather the source of the peculiar strain in his temperament which has impressed a certain nervous depth and moral 'distinction' upon poetry of which the drift is uniformly a realistic melancholy, than the source from which he has fed the flame of his genius, and justified the calm egotism of its literary rescripts. Intellectually, Mr. Arnold's descent, as he himself is always foremost to acknowledge, is to be derived in almost equal degree from Goethe the critic and artist, and from Wordsworth the poet; both of them, observe, marked by the same character of clear, self-contained, thoughtful, heroic egotism. I say Goethe the critic and artist—for I recognise but little, in Goethe's deepest and most perfect vein of poetry, of that conscious self-culture and that lucidity of enthusiastic self-study, which lend the charm to his conversations, his novels, and his criticisms. And Mr. Arnold, even in his capacity of poet—I am not about to touch his essays, except so far as they throw a light on his poetry—is always aiming at self-culture; and singing, not songs of involuntary melody, but of carefully-attuned aspiration or regret. From both Goethe and Wordsworth, again, he has learned to treat his own individuality with a certain exaltation of touch, an air of Olympian dignity and grace, which lends the fascination of 'the grand style' to lyrics so sad that they might otherwise trail upon the earth too slack and limp a growth. Mr. Arnold has always impressed on his poems that air of aristocratic selectness and conscious exclusiveness which Goethe, even after being the popular poet of Germany, claimed for his own writings. Eckermann tells how, going to dine with Goethe one day in 1828, and finding him dressed in 'the black frockcoat and star in which I (Eckermann) always liked best to see him,' the stately old man took him aside into the window, apart from the rest of the dinner company, only to make the following confidence:—

'Dear child,' he said, 'I will confide something to you, which will at once give you a lift over many puzzles, and which may be an assistance to you throughout your whole life. *My writings cannot become popular*; any one who

213

thinks they can, and strives to make them so, is in error. They are not written for the masses, but only for individual men who themselves desire and seek something analogous, and who are pursuing similar lines of thought.'

One can well imagine Mr. Arnold at the same age, and dressed with similar care, wearing the order conferred upon him many years ago by the King of Italy for his services to the Duke of Genoa, making a precisely similar confidence to some 'young lion of the *Daily Telegraph*' engaged in the study of his writings, and disturbed at finding that his poems secure so much less recognition from the people than those of Tennyson or Morris. And he would be far more in the right than Goethe, for Goethe's songs are popular in their very essence; it is only those of his writings where his cool reflective spirit has found expression, like *Tasso,* or *Iphigenia,* or *Wilhelm Meister,* or *Faust,* to which his ingenuous confidence to Eckermann can properly apply. But a similar confession would apply to all Mr. Arnold's poems, for they draw their life entirely from the proud self-conscious zone of modern experience, and have scarcely given forth one single note of popular grief or joy. It would apply, too, for a different reason, to almost all Wordsworth's poems, not because Wordsworth belonged to the aristocratic school of modern culture—quite the reverse; but because he steeped himself in the rapture of a meditative solitude which puts him at a distance from all mankind, and makes him loom large, as it were, out of the magnifying folds of one of his own mountain mists .

But Mr. Arnold, in borrowing from Goethe the artist and critic, and from Wordsworth the poet, something of what I have called their style of clear heroic egotism, has not borrowed from either of them the characteristic motive and individuality which in them justifies that style. Had he done so he could not be the original poet he is. He is neither the poet of mere self-culture, nor the solitary interpreter of Nature, but something between the two; a careful student and graphic, as well as delicate, expositor of the spiritual pangs and restlessness of this age on the one hand, and of the refreshments and anodynes to be derived from Nature on the other. And he is more or less conscious, moreover, in spite of some youthful theories of the true function of poetry which he has had to disregard, that it is in the elaborate delineation of his own poetic individuality that these distresses and these consolations receive their reconciliation and their best chance of being practically combined. He feels that his poetic personality has a certain grandeur and meaning in it; that while he has something of Goethe's calm critical eye for human life and its confusions, he has also something of the meditative thirst and meditative pleasures of Wordsworth; and that the combination of these two poetic qualifications gives him a distinctive power of his own. 'Non me tua turbida terrent dicta,' he said once in his majestic way to his critics, 'Dii me terrent et Jupiter hostis.' There is no better key to his true poetical aims than this passage from the very characteristic poem, addressed in November, 1849, to the author of 'Obermann':—

[Quotes 'Obermann', ll. 45–64; 69–72; 77–80, 'Yet of the spirits who have reign'd', etc.]

Nevertheless, that is precisely the combination which Mr. Arnold has tried to attain for himself, and which he aims at illustrating, through himself, for others. He tries to combine a spirit 'free from mists, and sane, and clear,' with Wordsworth's 'sweet calm' and pleasure in the freshness of Nature. And if he has in any degree succeeded, he knows that the success will best be realised, as those great masters' greater successes were realised, in a delineation of his own poetic individuality. Accordingly, it is really self-delineation of a kind like to theirs, though self-delination of aims and aspirations about midway between theirs, which gives the charm to his poems. In all his poetical successes, it is easy to distinguish two distinct strands: first, the clear recognition (with Goethe) of our spiritual unrest, and the manful effort to control it; next, the clear recognition (with Wordsworth) of the balm to be found in sincere communion with Nature. To the treatment of both these elements indeed he has given a certain freshness and individuality of his own.

I will first indicate generally his treatment of the former point. His characteristic effort on this side has been to introduce into a delineation, at once consistent and various in its aspects, of the intellectual difficulties, hesitations, and distresses of cultivated minds in the nineteenth century, a vein of imperious serenity—what he himself calls 'sanity' of treatment—which may stimulate the mind to bear the pain of constantly disappointed hope. Yet, oddly enough, his early theory of poetry would have restrained him from giving us such a picture of moral and intellectual sufferings at all; and he did for a time suppress a poem, 'Empedocles on Etna,' which had already gained a certain reputation, and which, beneath a thin disguise of antiquity, discussed half the religious difficulties of modern days, simply because he declared it poetically faulty to choose a situation in which 'everything is to be endured, nothing to be done.' It was a condemnation of every successful poem he has written, emphatically so of the long expositions of our modern spiritual paralysis and fever in the two poems to the author of 'Obermann,' of the lines at Heine's grave, of the stanzas at the Grande Chartreuse; indeed, we may say, of all his poems except the classic play *Merope*, which probably Mr. Arnold himself regarded as a partial failure, since, though now restored, he kept it back for a long time from his complete editions.

'Empedocles on Etna,' according to Mr. Arnold in his preface to the edition of 1853, was poetically faulty because it was a picture of 'a continuous state of mental distress, unrelieved by incident or hope,' which is quite true, and not less true of almost all his other poems. But when he added that it was also unrelieved by *resistance*, he was unjust to himself. What alone renders all the delineation of spiritual bewilderment which pervades this poem endurable, is that there is a steady current of resistance, a uniform 'sanity' of self-control in the treatment of the painful symptoms so subtly described. Empedocles, in the course of his meditations on suicide on the slopes of Etna, no doubt dwells much on the feeble and false religious philosophy of the time, the credulous self-flatteries of human sophistry, and the sharp antagonism between clear self-knowledge and the superstitions of the age; but he also makes a vigorous appeal to the manliness, fortitude, and sobriety of spirit with which all the disappointment and failures of humanity ought to be met, asserts that it is the part of a man of true wisdom to curb immoderate desires, to bow to the might of forces he cannot control, and, while nursing no 'extravagant hope,' to yield to no despair. And when, after thus completely justifying his own 'sanity of soul,' he confesses himself unable to act as he approves, and leaps into the fiery crater, the reader feels that the blunder of the poet has not been in colouring the suffering too highly—for it is not highly coloured—but in selecting for the sufferer a man of too low a courage, and in making his acts a foil to his thoughts. So far from there being no resistance, no breakwater opposed to the flowing tides of mental suffering, Empedocles creates the sole interest of the poem by his manly swimming against that stream of despondency to which later he suddenly abandons himself without sufficient cause assigned. It is like the parable of the man who said 'I go not,' and then went, without giving any glimpse of the reason for his change of mind—a parable which, without any attempt to fill in the missing link, would certainly not be a sufficient subject for a poem. It seems to me striking enough that the very charm of Mr. Arnold's method in dealing with this hectic fever of the modern intellect,—for

Empedocles, if a true ancient, is certainly a still truer modern in his argument,—is due to his own inconsistency; is due, that is, to the fact that when his subject required him to paint and justify the last stages of moral despondency, and when his intellectual view was sceptical enough to be in sympathy with his subject, he could not help expending his chief strength in cutting away the moral ground from under his hero's feet, by insisting that the well-spring of despair was, after all, not in the hostility of Nature or of human circumstances, but in the license of immoderate desires and of insatiable self-will. And it is so throughout his poems. He cannot paint the restlessness of the soul—though he paints it vividly and well—without painting also the attitude of resistance to it, without giving the impression of a head held high above it, a nature that fixes the limits beyond which the corrosion of distrust and doubt shall not go, a deep speculative melancholy kept at bay, *not* by faith, but by a kind of imperious temperance of nature. This is the refrain of almost all his poems. He yields much to this melancholy—intellectually, we should say, almost everything—but morally, he bids it keep its distance, and forbids it to engulph him.

It is this singular equipoise between the doubts that devour him, and the intrepid sobriety that excites him to resistance, which gives the peculiar tone to Mr. Arnold's poems. He has not the impulse or *abandon* of nature for a pure lyric melancholy, such as Shelley could pour forth in words that almost make the heart weep, as, for instance, in the 'Lines Written in Dejection in Naples.' Again, Mr. Arnold has nothing of the proud faith that conquers melancholy, and that gives to the poems of Wordsworth their tone of rapture. Yet he hits a wonderful middle note between the two. The 'lyrical cry,' as he himself has finely designated the voice in which the true poetic exaltation of feeling expresses itself, is to be found in a multitude of places in his poems; but in him it neither utters the dejection of the wounded spirit, nor the joy of the victorious spirit, but rather the calm of a steadfast equanimity in conflict with an unconquerable, and yet also unconquering destiny—a firm mind, without either deep shadows of despair or high lights of faith, only the lucid dusk of an intellectual twilight. Perhaps there is no more characteristic specimen of the exact note of Mr. Arnold's 'lyrical cry' than the close of the fine poem called 'Resignation':—

[Quotes ll. 271–77, 'Enough, we live!' etc.]

Such is the general nature of the human strand in Mr. Arnold's poetry, the restless spiritual melancholy which he pictures, resists, and condemns. But there is another permanent strand in it, that due partly to his love for Wordsworth, and partly to his love for Nature, of whom Wordsworth was the greatest of modern priests. Mr. Arnold finds in the beauty and sublimity of natural scenes the best assuagement of intellectual unrest and moral perplexities. Nature is his balm for every woe. He does not find in her, as Wordsworth did, the key to any of life's mysteries, or the source of hope, but only the best kind of distraction, which, while it does not relax but rather elevates the tone of the spirit, and even furnishes it with a certain number of symbols for its thought and emotion, also lightens the burden of the mystery by its cooling and refreshing influence. The 'languor of death,' of which Hazlitt speaks, as characterising 'Laodamia,' and of which I have said that it is also characteristic of Mr. Arnold's poetry, drives him to Nature for relief; and though it generally haunts him even under Nature's sweetest spell, yet you can see that he finds the relief, that the languor is less, and the pulse stronger while he dwells on Nature's life. And it is this sense of pure refreshment in Nature, this ease of mind, which she brings him, this calm amid feverish strife, this dew after hot thought, that determines the style of his studies of Nature. His poetry of this kind is the sweetest, the most tranquillising, the most quieting of its sort to be found in English literature. In Wordsworth, Nature is the occasion, but his own mind always the *object*, of thought, whether, in reculling the 'host of golden daffodils,' he exercises 'that inward eye that is the bliss of solitude,' or finds in the teaching of a daisy the true medicine for discontent. You cannot plunge yourself in the poetry of Wordsworth without being mentally braced and refreshed; but then it takes an effort to enter into a world so unique, 'so solemn and serene,' and so far removed from that of ordinary life. Throw off the yoke of the world sufficiently to steep yourself in Wordsworth, and no doubt the refreshment is more complete and the flow of new strength more full than you can expect from the verse of Mr. Arnold; for Mr. Arnold's poetry of Nature is not like Wordsworth's, a newly-created meditative universe, distilled by the poet's mind out of Nature; it is a delicate transcript of Nature, painted in the clear, dewy water-colours of tranquil memory. What he says of his own debt to Wordsworth would, if it did not imply a more vivifying and animating influence than Mr. Arnold's poetry ever really exerts, be more nearly applicable to most men's debt to *him*:—

He laid us as we lay at birth,
On the cool flowery lap of earth;

Smiles broke from us, and we had ease.
The hills were round us, and the breeze
Went o'er the sun-lit fields again;
Our foreheads felt the wind and rain.
Our youth return'd; for there was shed
On spirits that had long been dead—
Spirits dried up and closely furl'd—
The freshness of the early world.

Now that does not strike me as by any means an accurate description of the influence of Wordsworth's poetry on the mind. Wordsworth does not restore us to the ease and freshness of our youth, he rather baptizes us in his own strong and unique spirit. He has a spell of his own, no doubt a cooling and refreshing one, but also a powerful and transforming one. It is due to the strong, keen, meditative simplicity of a mind that is as full of rapture as it is full of insight. It is Wordsworth himself, far more than the lark he watched, whose 'canopy of glorious light' snatches us out of ourselves, and from whom we learn to be true 'to the kindred points of heaven and home.' It is Wordsworth himself, far more than the cuckoo to which he listened 'till he did beget that golden time again,' who tells us the old enchanting tale 'of visionary hours.' The strength and freshness which Wordsworth gives us is not the strength and freshness of childhood or youth, but the strength and freshness of a poet on whom 'the power of hills' had rested till he lived in a purer world than ours. When Wordsworth says of the solitary reaper—

Alone she cuts and binds the grain,
And sings a melancholy strain.
Oh listen! for the vale profound
Is overflowing with the sound!

—the charm is far less in the song, of which he gives so thrilling a conception, than in those grateful 'impulses of deeper birth' springing out of his own heart, of which he tells us a still more thrilling story. Wordsworth is the last poet of whom I should say that he makes us children again. He gives us a new youth, not the old—a youth of deeper serenity, and of a far more truly spiritual joy. But, for that very reason, it takes an effort to plunge into him; the change from the busy and crowded levels of human life to his poetry is too great and sudden to be easily taken; it requires a regeneration of our senses as well as a change of scene. But with Mr. Arnold it is different. He does not create for us a new world out of the suggestions and influences of Nature: he only makes us feel keenly the beauty and delicacy of the spectacle which Nature, as she is in her gentler and more subdued moods, presents to us, and her strange power of resting and refreshing the mind wearied by small human responsibilities. His eye is always on the object itself, not on the spiritual lesson it discloses. And he paints in the most restful way. He never concentrates, like Tennyson, so that the imagination is at some pain to follow all the touches crowded into little space; he never disembodies, like Shelley, till it becomes an effort to apprehend essences so rare; it is seldom that he paints, like Byron, with a brush dipped as deeply in the glowing passions of his own heart as in the colours of the external world. He paints Nature, like the author of 'The Elegy in a Country Churchyard,' with the cool, liquid, rather weary tone of one who comes to the scenery to take a heart from it, instead of giving the heart to it; but he does it with infinitely more of the modern tenderness and insight for Nature than Gray possessed, and with far more flowing and continuous descriptive power—far less of that polished mosaic-work manner which makes Gray's verses read as if he had forgotten most of the preceding links before completing and enamelling the next link in the chain. In Mr. Arnold's studies of Nature you see the quiet external scene with exquisite lucidity, but you see also, instead of a mirror of laborious and almost painful elaboration, as you do in Gray, a tranquillised spirit, which reflects like a clear lake the features of the scene. Take, for example, this picture of a wet and stormy English spring and a soft deep English summer, from the lovely poem 'Thyrsis,' written in commemoration of Mr. Arnold's early friend, Arthur Hugh Clough:—

[Quotes ll. 51–70, 'So, some tempestuous morn', etc.]

It would be impossible to give with greater ease as well as delicacy a true picture of these scenes, and with it the subtler flavour of a real rest of spirit in them. The 'volleying' rain, the 'tossing' breeze, the 'vext' garden trees, and the grass strewn with shed May and chestnut blossom, call up the very life of a squally spring day in England, as do the 'high Midsummer pomps,' the 'roses that down the alleys shine afar,' the 'open, jasmine-muffled lattices,' the 'groups under the dreaming garden-trees,' and the white moon and star, the very life of an English midsummer night; and yet the whole has a tinge of careful tenderness and peace that tells you of the refreshment of these images to the writer. The 'vext garden trees' could have been spoken of as 'vext' only by one who had a true delight in their air of tranquillity, just as they could have been described as 'dreaming' in the midsummer moonlight only by one who had the deepest feeling for the visionary beauty of contrast between the white light streaming over them, and the black shade beneath. Again, 'roses that down the alleys shine afar,' is a line sufficiently betraying how deeply the fair perspective of an English garden is engraved on the poet's imagination, while the reproaches lavished on the 'too quick despairer' for the hasty neglect of so rich a feast of beauty, strikes the keynote to the feeling of the whole. Nor is this passage in any sense a peculiar instance of Mr. Arnold's flowing, lucid, and tender mode of painting Nature. In all his descriptive passages—and they are many and beautiful—it is the same. He is never sanguine and bright indeed, but the scene is always drawn with a gentle ease and grace, suggesting that it springs up in the poet's imagination with as rapid and natural a growth as the strokes which delineate it before your eyes, for he makes no heavy draft upon your imaginative power to follow him; you seem to be sharing with him the very vision which he paints; and as to moral effect, the impressions that these pictures make is something between wistful enjoyment, quiet yearning, and regretful peace; it is always one of rest, but always of a rest that is not fully satisfying—the rest of which the poet himself says, 'Calm's not life's crown, though calm is well.' And it is characteristic of Mr. Arnold, that in closing his longer poems, even when they are poems of narrative, he is very fond of ending with a passage of purely naturalistic description which shadows forth something more than it actually paints, and yet leaves the field of suggestion absolutely to the reader's own fancy. Thus, after painting the fatal conflict between Sohrab and Rustum, in which the famous old warrior Rustum gives the death-wound to his own son, in ignorance that he is his son, Mr. Arnold, after describing the tender farewell of Sohrab to his father when the discovery is made, concludes with this most beautiful passage, in which the accomplished geographer turns the half-scientific, half-poetical pleasure which he always betrays in defining a geographical course, to the purpose of providing a poetical anodyne for the pain which the tragic ending has, or ought to have, given:—

[Quotes the concluding lines, 'But the majestic river', etc., which he compares with description in 'The Scholar Gipsy', ll. 71–80, 'For most, I know', etc.]

It would be impossible to express the tenderness of feeling which scenery long loved and studied excites in the heart—not by its mere beauty, but by its associations also—with more perfect simplicity, and yet not without grandeur of movement and dignity of feeling. The latter effect is gained partly by the cadence of the verse, which in this poem is always perfectly musical and sedate, and partly by the character of the expression, for instance, by a tinge of gentle condescension (as in the expression 'the stripling Thames'), and the careful benignity of the whole detail. The simplicity is gained partly by the perfectly poetical and yet technical naturalness of the line, 'As the punt's rope chops round,' which is poetical, because it brings the peculiar motion so vividly before you; partly by the happy tenderness of the line, 'Fostering in thy lap a heap of flowers,' to convey the conscious pleasure of both tending and touching them; but mostly by the perfectly easy flow of the language, and the still lucidity of the verse. But Mr. Arnold hardly exercises the full magic of his characteristic power of poetical expression until he is in the mood in which some sad, though calm, emotion is the predominant thread of his thought, and natural beauty only the auxiliary to it; till he is in the mood in which, if his heart flies to his eyes, it is only to find some illustration for the enigmas pent up within it, some new image for the incommunicability of human joy and grief, for the pain that results from the division of the soul against itself, for the restlessness which yearns inconsistently for sympathy and for solitude, and rebounds like a shuttlecock from the one desire to the other. No line, for instance, in the whole range of English poetry is fuller of depth of expression than that which closes one of the poems to Marguerite, the poem which begins with the sad cry—

> Yes! in the sea of life enisled,
> With echoing straits between us thrown,
> Dotting the shoreless, watery wild,
> We mortal millions live *alone*.

—where Mr. Arnold ends his melancholy reverie by confessing that it was God's will which decreed this strange isolation—

> And bade betwixt their shores to be
> *The unplumb'd, salt, estranging sea.*

That last line is inexhaustible in beauty and force. Without any false emphasis or prolix dwelling on the matter, it shadows out to you the plunging deep-sea lead and the eerie cry of 'no soundings,' it recalls that saltness of the sea which takes from water every refreshing association, every quality that helps to slake thirst or supply sap, and then it concentrates all these dividing attributes, which strike a sort of lonely terror into the soul, into the one word 'estranging.' It is a line full of intensity, simplicity, and grandeur—a line to possess and haunt the imagination. And the same exceptional force of expression comes out not unfrequently under the shadow of similar emotions.

Nothing, for instance, can have more force of its peculiar kind than the description of the blended delight in Nature and disappointment in Man felt by the French recluse, the author of 'Obermann,' who fled from the world he disdained to brood over its maladies in French woods and Swiss huts—

> In the lone brakes of Fontainbleau,
> Or châlets near the Alpine snow.

There is a mixed simplicity and exaltation of feeling in the following lines, which few English poets have surpassed:—

[Quotes 'Obermann', ll. 13–16; 21–36, 'I turn thy leaves!' etc.]

Nor is the opening of this poem at all more characteristic of the special power of its author than its close. There is indeed something, more almost of *peroration* than of the last swell of a lyric emotion, in the poet's adieu to the hero of his reverie:—

> Farewell! Under the sky we part,
> In this stern Alpine dell.
> O unstrung will! O broken heart,
> A last, a last farewell!

And that leads me to remark how very near poetry of this order— the predominant emotion of which, however sad, is always sedate and stately in its movement—often approaches to the nobler rhetoric,—of which, indeed, grandeur of total effect, with simplicity of elementary structure, are the main conditions. The object of the verse I have just quoted seems to be almost as nearly one of persuasion, *i.e.* oratorical, as one of expression, *i.e.* poetical. It reads more like an indirect but conscious effort to subdue the reader's mind into a mood of compassionate admiration for the author of 'Obermann,' than a mere utterance of the poet's own feeling;—it is more eloquent than pathetic. And where, as often happens in other poems—in the very fine continuation of this same poem, for instance—Mr. Arnold's thread of sentiment is much more directly didactic than it is here (and this is especially the case in his pieces of unrhymed *recitative*, where the leading idea is usually a train of thought rather than feeling, and very frequently a train of very directly hortative or argumentative thought), the rhetorical often predominates greatly over the poetical vein, and seems to court direct comparison rather with the effusions of the improvisatore than with those of the singer. In such pieces the verse fails—when it does fail—as the inspiration of the improvisatore fails, more from a subsidence of the initial impulse, than from artistic exhaustion of the theme, or inadequate command of language to work out fully the conception of the imagination. Take, for instance, among the rhymed pieces, the eloquent indictment brought against Death, as if it involved a sort of breach of faith with the instinctive youthful hope for some fulness of earthly rapture, in the piece called 'Youth and Calm.' No one can read it without noticing the regularly mounting steps of an impassioned *speech*, rather than the imperceptibly graduated concentration of feeling natural to a lyrical poem:—

[Quotes 'Youth and Calm', in its entirety]

Only here, what *should* be the peroration is an anticlimax. The best illustrations, however, of the rhetorical cast of a good deal of Mr. Arnold's poetry are to be found in the *recitatives* which find so much favour in his sight, but in which the perfect simplicity and lucidity of structure of his rhymed poems are sometimes—not always—remarkably deficient. The music of rhymed verse always seems to bind him down to the simpler ranges of human experience. He does not resemble Shelley, who, like his own skylark, sings the more sweetly the higher he rises into the rarefied air of abstract essences. On the contrary, Mr. Arnold is always awakened to homelier feelings by the melody of verse, and is never so lucid and concrete as when he has to meet the exigencies of a complex stanza such as he uses in 'The Scholar-Gipsy,' and 'Thyrsis.' The little speech which I have just quoted on the contrast between the youthful hopes of earthly bliss and the sad calm of early death is rhetorical in structure, but it is the pathetic rhetoric of a troubled heart, descanting on the experience of almost every home. When, however, Mr. Arnold chooses the unrhymed dactylic or anapæstic metres for his oratory, though he is often extremely eloquent, and sometimes even rich in pictorial effect, he is apt to be cold and grandiose, and now and then even to be obscure—a sin of which he is rarely indeed guilty. The contrast may be best seen, though it would be impossible in any small space to illustrate it adequately, in the com-

parison between the second poem addressed to the author of 'Obermann' ('Obermann Once More,' vol. ii, p. 239), and the poem which
follows it, and closes the volumes, called 'The Future.' They are on
kindred subjects, the first tracing the signs of the immediate future of
modern religion; the second, the relation generally of the tendencies of
the Future to those of the Past. The Pantheistic vein of thought and
sentiment pervades both poems alike,—and it is one which, as I need
hardly say, runs counter to my own deepest convictions,—but there is a
vast difference between the two as poems. The former is full of human
yearning and pathos, of definite picture, and clear imagery; the latter is a
dim vapour of eloquent dissertation, in which, indeed, there are vaguely
seen some of the bright tints of the rainbow, but there is no warmth and
no clearness; it is grandiose without grandeur, nebulous without
mystery. Within moderate limits I do not know that I can give a finer
specimen at once of the frequently high oratory of these choric outbursts of Mr. Arnold's didactic genius, and also of the frequent tendency in them to overpass the impulse which gave them birth, than in
the deservedly celebrated lines at Heine's grave, in which Mr. Arnold
passes from criticism of the bitter German poet into a grand image for
this Philistine nation of ours—for its blindness and its strength; but unfortunately does not stop there, falling into bathos as he proceeds:—

[Quotes 'Heine's Grave', ll. 70–120, 'I chide thee not, that thy sharp',
etc.]

It would be hard to find a higher piece of pure pictorial oratory than
that description of England;—as regards style, Mr. Bright, if he held
with Mr. Arnold, which of course he does not, might almost have
delivered it in one of his greater speeches;—and hard, too, to find a
bathos deeper than the flat, harsh, somewhat stilted prose, not even
rhythmical, though it is printed in metre, which immediately follows,
especially the lines which Mr. Arnold italicises in the last two stanzas.
The same may be said of almost all his *recitative* pieces. They contain
fragments of high oratory, but they are coldly intellectual, and tend to a
grandiosity from which the fall to flat prose is not difficult.

And it is, indeed, Mr. Arnold's chief defect as a poet and artist that
the themes which interest him most are seldom living and organic
wholes, but are rather trains of thought sufficiently fascinating to the
imagination and to the feelings, but without definite form and organisation; in fact, subjects which necessarily lend themselves more easily
to the irregular rhythmic improvisations to which we have just re-

ferred, than to more perfect forms of verse. Even when he adopts these more perfect forms, it is rather for the sake of the pathos of elegiac moods than for the completeness they give to the framework of an artistic whole. Of all his so-called narrative-poems, most of which are, indeed, usually reflective rather than narrative, 'The Sick King in Bokhara' is the only one that strikes me as reaching anything like the higher levels of Mr. Arnold's force. 'Sohrab and Rustum,' polished and elegant as it is, is tame beyond anything that the story can account for. The long Homeric similes are often extremely beautiful, the subject itself is genuinely tragic, the style is classical; there is nothing to account for its tameness except the tameness itself. It is evident that the author felt no throbs of heart as he brought the gallant son into the fatal conflict with the gallant father. He looked on it with the polished interest of an Oxford scholar in an episode of Oriental tradition, but without the slightest touch of that animated sympathy and vivid suspense which Scott would have thrown into such a theme. It is not till we get to the beautiful description of the northward course of the Oxus, when Rustum is left with the corpse of his son lying beside him on the plain, enveloped in midnight and despair, that we feel the true charm of the poet, and then the story is over. 'Balder Dead' has to my ears even less interest than 'Sohrab and Rustum.' 'Tristram and Iseult' is a great advance on either, and is unquestionably a very fine fragment; but it has little title to the name of a narrative-poem at all. Mr. Arnold borrows the Arthurian legend only to give a beautiful picture of the shipwreck of unhappy passions in a double form, in the feverish and restless delirium of the dying knight, and in the hollow disappointed youth of Iseult of Brittany after she has survived her husband and her grander rival. Iseult of Ireland is hardly painted, except in face and form; she only kneels beside her lover's deathbed to die with him, and lend her outward image to the poet's picture. But it would be difficult to speak too highly of the exquisite and lucid painting of the scene of Tristram's death in the Breton Castle, beneath those 'ghost-like tapestries' on which are figured the green huntsman, with his bugle and hounds, so dear to the sylvan knight in lifetime, with the Irish queen kneeling, also dead, at his bedside, both of them—

> Cold, cold as those who lived and loved
> A thousand years ago;

or of Iseult of Brittany, of the white hands, in the subsequent part, living, after her husband's and rival's deaths, the joyless life of one who had sought, but found not, the happiness of love, and who survives in the happiness of her children as in a kind of moonlit dream:—

[Quotes ll. 68–75, 'Joy has not found her yet', etc.]

No picture could be sweeter or fairer. Mr. Arnold has a special gift for the delineation of these moods of passionless pain—of still moonlit craving that is never hot and never satisfied. But the beauty of the poem certainly does not lie in the strength of its narrative, but in its exquisite delineation of the feelings of death-chilled passion and of joyless calm. 'The Forsaken Merman'—a very delicate little poem of its kind—is again hardly in any sense a narrative-poem. It is a pretty fanciful song full of picture, of which the living pulse is the innocent childish heart-longing of a bewildered, instinctive, unmasterful love conscious of the existence of a rivalry in the claims of religious feelings into which it cannot enter, and yet full of painful yearning. This is always the type of feeling which Mr. Arnold paints most finely.

But far higher are the pretensions of 'The Sick King in Bokhara.' Slight as the subject is, the poem is full of life, and paints not merely a new phase of that painful calm or placid suffering in which Mr. Arnold so much excels, but the richness and stateliness, and also the prostration and fatalism, of Oriental life; and it is especially happy in portraying vividly the concrete simplicities of Eastern imagery when expressing desire and regret. The grave, business-like local colour of the opening is in itself full of promise:—

[Quotes ll. 1–9, 'O most just Vizier', etc.]

And then the story of the poor man who, in the intensity of his thirst, during the long drought, had secreted a pitcher of water for his own use, and when he found it drained had cursed those who drained it, his own mother amongst them, and who in his remorse called upon the King to give judgment upon him that he might be stoned and expiate his sin as the law demanded, and the delineation of the King's extreme reluctance, are given with the most genuine force and simplicity. The King's great desire to spare the man, and the orders given for that purpose, of which it is pithily said,

> As the King said, so was it done,

the man's indignation at this hesitation to judge and punish him, the King's loth consent at last, and the fanatical joy of the victim, are painted with something like the grand simplicity of the Hebrew Scriptures:—

Now the King charged us secretly:
'Stoned must he be, the law stands so.
Yet, if he seeks to fly, give way!
Hinder him not, but let him go.'

So saying, the King took a stone,
And cast it softly;—but the man,
With a great joy upon his face,
Kneel'd down, and cried not, neither ran.

And, perhaps, the most dramatic thing in the whole range of Mr. Arnold's poems is the scornful reproof administered by the old Vizier, when he has heard the story, to the King's weakness and softness of heart:—

[Quotes ll. 133–80, 'O King, in this I praise thee not', etc.]

Mr. Arnold has never achieved anything so truly dramatic as this poem. The reasoning, never in the abstract, but always by examples, which runs through it, the profound abasement of mind before the demands of the admitted conditions of social existence, the utter acquiescence of the sage old minister's intellect in the order of things as he knows it, the wonder and distress of the young King that his own urgent desire is of so little account when he would alleviate the lot of one human being whom he pities, and the kicking of his nature against the pricks of the iron circle which limits his royal power, are all painted with a brightness and care which would almost argue a special Oriental culture, though I do not suppose that Mr. Arnold has had any exceptional opportunities in that direction. Of the poems which are called narrative, this is in my opinion the only one, rightly so called, that is perfectly successful. And perhaps its perfect success is due to the curious correspondence between the elements of the story and the peculiar tendencies I have already noticed in Mr. Arnold's genius. The stately egotism of manner, which has here full swing and a great field, the dignified remorse which breeds so resolute a spirit of expiation in the sinner's mind, the sedate dignities of the King's helplessness, the contemptuous criticism of the Grand Vizier on the unreasonable excess of his master's sympathy with one who had no natural claims on him, and the extreme simplicity of the whole action, all seem to fit the subject specially for Mr. Arnold's treatment. At all events, as to the brilliant clearness and rich colouring of the completed whole, there can be no two opinions. It seems to me nearly the only case in which Mr. Arnold has chosen a subject distinct and perfect in its parts, and complete as a

whole—a subject of which you cannot say that he brought it to a conclusion chiefly because it must end somewhere, and had exhausted his
own interest in it. This piece is the one exception to the rule that Mr.
Arnold's best poems are not artistic wholes, which come to a necessary
and natural end because their structure is organically perfect, but rather
fragments of imaginative reverie, which begin where the poet begins to
meditate, and end when he has done.

It must not be supposed, however, that I regard the art of those of
Mr. Arnold's poems which are expressly elegiac and lyrical as generally
poor. On the contrary, as it is of the essence of pieces of this kind to
reflect absolutely the mood of the poet, to begin where he begins
and end where he ends, the only artistic demand which can possibly be
applicable to the *structure* of such pieces, is that it shall show you the
growth and subsidence of a vein of thought and emotion, and make no
abrupt demands on the sympathy of the reader. This, at all events in
almost all his rhymed pieces of a lyrical and elegiac nature, Mr. Arnold
effects with the greatest delicacy and modulation of feeling; in the others
he is not unfrequently stranded on bare prose, and compelled to leap
back with a very jerky movement into the tide of his emotion. But
from his highest moods of reverie he subsides, by the help of some
beautiful picture of scenery in harmony with the emotions he is
delineating, as in the lovely Alpine sketches of his 'Obermann,' or with
some graceful episode of illustration, like the beautiful comparison
between the wandering Scholar Gipsy's dread of the contagion of our
hesitating half-love of Nature, which hugs the shore of artificial civilisation and the old Tyrian skipper's wrath against the Greek coaster, who
troubled his realm by timid competition, and yet never dared to launch
out into the shoreless ocean. No art can be more perfect than that with
which Mr. Arnold closes the finer of his lyrical and elegiac poems—
poems, however, of which it is the very essence to reflect his own
reveries, not to paint any continuous whole.

When I come to ask what Mr. Arnold's poetry has done for this
generation, the answer must be that no one has expressed more powerfully and poetically its spiritual weaknesses, its craving for a passion that
it cannot feel, its admiration for a self-mastery that it cannot achieve,
its desire for a creed that it fails to accept, its sympathy with a faith
that it will not share, its aspiration for a peace that it does not know.
But Mr. Arnold does all this from the intellectual side,—sincerely and
delicately, but from the surface, and never from the centre. It is the
same with his criticisms. They are fine, they are keen, they are often

true, but they are always too much limited to the thin superficial layer of the moral nature of their subjects, and seem to take little comparative interest in the deeper individuality beneath. Read his essay on Heine, and you will see the critic engrossed with the relation of Heine to the political and social ideas of his day, and passing with comparative indifference over the true soul of Heine, the fountain both of his poetry and his cynicism. Read his fine lectures on translating Homer, and observe how exclusively the critic's mind is occupied with the form, as distinguished from the substance, of the Homeric poetry. Even when he concerns himself with the greatest modern poets, with Shakespeare (as in the preface to the earlier edition of his poems), or with Goethe in reiterated poetical criticisms, or when he, again and again in his poems, treats of Wordsworth, it is always the style and superficial doctrine of their poetry, not the individual character and unique genius, which occupy him. He will tell you whether a poet is 'sane and clear,' or stormy and fervent; whether he is 'rapid' and 'noble,' or loquacious and quaint; whether a thinker penetrates the husks of conventional thought which mislead the crowd; whether there is sweetness as well as lucidity in his aims; whether a descriptive writer has 'distinction' of style, or is admirable only for his vivacity; but he rarely goes to the individual heart of any of the subjects of his criticism;—he describes their style and class, but not their personality in that class; he *ranks* his men, but does not portray them; hardly even seems to find much interest in the *individual* roots of their character. And so, too, with his main poetical theme,—the spiritual weakness and languor and self-disdain of the age. He paints these characteristics in language which makes his poems a sort of natural voice for the experience of his contemporaries, a voice without which their intellectual life would be even more obscure and confused than it is; but still with a certain intellectual superficiality of touch which suggests the sympathetic observer rather than the wakeful sufferer, and which leaves an unfathomed depth beneath the layer of perturbed consciousness with which he deals—that is, beneath that plane wherein the spheres of the intellect and of the soul intersect, of which he has so carefully studied the currents and the tides. The sign of this limitation, of this exclusion, of this externality of touch, is the tinge of conscious intellectual majesty rearing its head above the storm with the 'Quos ego' of Virgil's god, that never forsakes these poems of Mr. Arnold's even when their 'lyrical cry' is most pathetic. It is this which identifies him with the sceptics, which renders his poems, pathetic as they often are, no adequate expression of the passionate craving of the soul for faith. There is always a tincture of pride in his confessed inability to believe—a self-congratulation that he is too clear-eyed to yield to the temptations of the heart. He asks with compassionate imperiousness for demonstration rather than conviction; conviction he will not take without demonstration. The true humility of the yearning for faith is far from Mr. Arnold's conception. The Poet Laureate's picture of himself, as

> Falling with my weight of cares
> Upon the world's great altar stairs
> That slope through darkness up to God,

is a very great contrast indeed to Mr. Arnold's grand air of tearful Virgilian regret as he gazes on the pale ascetic faces of the Carthusian monks, and delivers himself thus:—

> Wandering between two worlds, one dead,
> The other powerless to be born,
> With nowhere yet to rest my head,
> Like these, on earth I wait forlorn.
> Their faith, my tears, the world deride;
> I come to shed them at their side.

His vision of Christ and Christianity even, is wholly taken from the same standing-point of genuine but condescending sympathy. He can see how much greater the Christian Church was than the Roman world it subdued; but to him it is greater not through the truth of its belief, but through that vast capacity of belief which enabled it to accept what was not true,—in short, to feign a truth higher than the naked facts. No passage in Mr. Arnold's poems is, perhaps, so grand as the one which delineates this contrast, with its majestic though false and desolating assumption that it was the mighty *dreaming* power of the East, the power to create the objects of its own belief, which conquered the hard organisation of the West; and as no passage is so characteristic of Mr. Arnold's whole relation to the thought of his day, with it, though it is somewhat long, I will close my too voluminous extracts from his stately and fascinating poems:—

[Quotes 1867–9 version of 'Obermann Once More', ll. 81–92, 'Well nigh two thousand years have brought', etc.]

It would have been impossible to paint more grandly the hard pageantry of Roman civilisation, or more imaginatively the apparently magic victory of the brooding mystic over the armed conqueror. But when Mr. Arnold paints the 'patient deep *disdain*' of the East for physical might as the power by which it won its miraculous victory, he is inverting strangely the testimony of history,—indeed he is reading his own lofty intellectualism back into the past. The East has always been accused of bowing with even too deep a prostration of soul before the omnipotent flat of the Almighty. It was the Eastern delight in that semi-fatalism which gave Mahommed his strange spell over the Eastern imagination; nay, it was the same fascinated submission to the finger of sheer Power which is occasionally so intensely expressed even in the Hebrew prophets as to read to Christian ears as if God were above righteousness, and as if responsibility could be merged in obedience.

[Continues for another page to question Arnold's interpretation of history]

Mr. Arnold's poetry towers above the warmth of the faith it analyses and rejects, and gains thereby its air of mingled pride and sadness. He seems indeed, to take a chilling pride in his assertion that Christ is not risen; that

> On his grave, with shining eyes
> The Syrian stars look down;

an assertion which sends a quiver through the heart that has discovered for itself how weak is the life from which the trust in Christ is absent.

However, Mr. Arnold's poetry is no more the worse, *as poetry*, for its erroneous spiritual assumptions, than drama is the worse, as drama, for delineating men as they seem to each other to be, and not as they really are to the eye of God. And as the poet of the soul's melancholy hauteur and plaintive benignity, as the exponent of pity for the great excess of her wants beyond her gifts and graces, as the singer at once of the spirit's hunger, of the insufficiency of the food which the intellect provides for her cravings, and yet also of her fastidious rejection of more heavenly nutriment, Mr. Arnold will be read and remembered by every generation in which faith continues to be daunted by reason, and reason to seek, not without pangs of inexplicable compunction, to call in question the transcendental certainties of faith; in a word, he will be read and remembered, as I said in my opening sentence, as the poet who, more than any other of his day, has embodied in his verse 'the sweetness, the gravity, the strength, the beauty, and the languor of death.'

22. H. G. Hewlett, 'The Poems of Matthew Arnold', *Contemporary Review*

September 1874, xxiv, 539–67

Henry Gay Hewlett (1832–97), father of Maurice Hewlett, was a minor poet and historian, who served as Keeper of the Land Revenue Records for over thirty years. His books include *Shakespeare's Curse and Other Poems* and *The Heroes of Europe: A Biographical Outline of European History*. Hewlett places Arnold in a distinguished line of poet-critics—distinguished except that Mrs Browning is ranked with Wordsworth—and asserts that in Arnold's career it is time for more poetry. Hewlett is especially interested in the terms Hebrew and Hellene, which he applies as a guide to the poet's career.

Throughout the course of history analysis and synthesis have been observed to advance by alternate strides, the one accumulating Science, the other erecting Art. Equally alternate in its operations must be the activity of that mind which unites the opposite powers whereof Art and Science are the outcome. To be inspired and self-restrained, fervid and sceptical, at one and the same time, is an obvious impossibility; but to pass through these phases at successive periods, to reflect in the critical mood of to-day upon the passionate mood of yesterday, is an experience sufficiently familiar. To balance these moods skilfully, however, giving both free play, without suffering either to encroach upon the other's province, and correct the estimates of the visionary faculty without chilling its enthusiasm, is perhaps among the rarest of gifts. What is easier and more common is to keep the provinces entirely distinct, by not turning the critical faculty inward, but reserving its skill to dissect the productions of others. In this narrow sense, indeed, every poet must be more or less of a critic. Involuntarily, if not consciously, he criticizes what has been already achieved, and measures his own performance thereby. Attempts, therefore, to draw a strict line of demarcation between the poetical and critical functions, and represent their antagonism as internecine, are as futile as they are unjust, and only recoil upon the mischief-makers. The poet of our time who has avowed his high contempt of criticism, in a tone that curiously resembles the outcry of wounded irritability, asserts himself in the same breath the most unsparing critic of his fellow-craftsmen. The only justification of the assumption that the two spheres are necessarily hostile, lies in a distinction which the development of intellectual action has long since deprived of significance. It may be worth while to recal and insist upon it, if the era of decadence through which other literatures have had to pass should ever befall our own, and the rules by which the poet has been critically discovered to work be adopted as substitutes for his intuition. But this danger is happily as yet remote, and meanwhile we may be confident that by those rare seers, to whom the stereoscope and the microscope are equally familiar, their several uses are not likely to be confounded.

The number of our illustrious writers who have been at the same time poets and critics is not yet large. Milton, Dryden, Pope, Wordsworth, Shelley, Byron and Mrs. Browning, in the first rank; Sidney, Cowley, Prior, Young, Goldsmith, Cowper, Coleridge, Landor, and Scott, in the second rank, are nearly all that can be named among the dead. Of these the majority have been critics only of their fellows, and refrained from any systematic course of self-scrutiny. Wordsworth, Shelley, Byron, and Mrs. Browning, are eminent exceptions, being all intensely self-conscious; but the process of submitting the successive moods of their own minds to revision is comparatively rare with the three first. With Mrs. Browning it is frequent, but her thought is little more than transfigured emotion. Among living poets, Mr. Tennyson has devoted two masterpieces, 'The Two Voices' and 'In Memoriam,' to the task of critical introspection, but they reflect only a single facet of his many-sided genius. In one remarkable poem, 'Christmas-eve and Easter-day,' and an occasional prologue or epilogue, Mr. Browning may be supposed to make his own mind the subject of analysis, but the personal element in his writings is infinitesimal as compared with the dramatic. The poet next in order, who has carried to its fullest extent the tendency which his forerunners and contemporaries have but indicated, and made it his special distinction at once to give rein to imaginative impulse and maintain the restraint of critical supervision, is Mr. Matthew Arnold. If his poetical are less widely known than his

prose writings, they have already a recognized place in modern literature. They are free from certain blemishes and mannerisms which
impair the value of his essays to those who most highly esteem them.
The ironic humour that therein enlivens his gravest mood, and by
which he has achieved the well-nigh impossible feat of making theology
an entertaining study, is the only mental trait conspicuously absent
from his poetry; but the loss is atoned for by the discovery of other
merits for which those who know him only as a prose-writer would
never give him credit. Such differences as exist are manifestly superficial, and do not preclude a fundamental similarity. It is reasonable to
interpret one transcript of a writer's mind by another. In studying the
poems we have found such acquaintance as we possess with the essays
of service as an explanatory aid, and shall scarcely err in attempting to
trace a continuity of thought and purpose between the two.

Twenty, or even fifteen, years ago, Mr. Arnold might have been
claimed as a partizan by the Neo-Pagan school of thinkers. Not only
were his poems imbued with the purest classical spirit, but the elaborate
prefaces, in which he laid down the principles that had governed their
composition, betrayed his hostility to current modes of thought and
feeling, and indifference to the moral and spiritual forces most actively
working in modern society, under phrases of vague and sweeping condemnation, suggestive of a deeper aversion and a loftier disdain than
they were perhaps intended to convey. In the preface to his collected
poems (1853) he gives his reasons for rejecting the theory of modern
criticism and the practice of modern art as radically unsound.

[Discusses the 1853 Preface, some of the literary essays, *Culture and
Anarchy*, and the terms 'Hebrew' and 'Hellene']

Alike by the associations of his birth and training, and the natural bent
of his genius, Mr. Arnold is exceptionally qualified for the task which
he has undertaken. From both sides he is entitled to a respectful hearing,
as the son of a man whose acumen and erudition were not less esteemed
among 'Hellenizers,' than his moral nobleness and spiritual energy were
held in veneration among 'Hebraizers'—veneration which he did not
forfeit by the concessions he had the courage to make in the direction of
rational theology. That Mr. Arnold's training under such a father was
imbued with the spirit of Hebraism, might be taken for granted had he
not himself referred to it. What his intellectual training was he sufficiently indicates by his ironic allusion to his 'having been brought up at
Oxford in the bad old times when we were stuffed with Greek and

Aristotle.' The coincidence of such influences in early life is common to so many minds, that of itself it would confer no special advantage for the work of conciliation. We infer from the study of Mr. Arnold's poems, that he has acquired this advantage by having undergone the change just described, by a transfer of allegiance from one hostile banner to the other, and retirement from the strife into neutral ground without loss of sympathy with either combatant. The order in which his mind underwent this change, however, seems to have been the converse of that which he has since recommended us to follow. These poetic records of his progress show that Hellenism was at first the paramount influence; Hebraism being temporarily in abeyance, but gradually reasserting itself after a period of sceptical transition, which terminated in the ultimate vindication by each of its due share of authority. Speaking roughly, and with due latitude in the matter of dates, we may consider the Poems of his youth and the Prefaces of 1853–4 as on the same intellectual plane; the Poems of his early manhood as filling up the gap between the Prefaces and the Essays of 1865; the Poems of his maturity as explaining and justifying the tone of wise discernment and balanced conviction that characterizes his later Essays.

The interpretation thus put upon the poems will not be clear to readers who are content to accept them in their existing arrangement, and it is therefore necessary to revert to their original form and order. It must be obvious, however, that where we are dealing with successive transcripts of moods no rigorous limitation of dates can possibly be applicable. The least experienced in mental travail know how perpetually the lines of thought traverse and intermingle, how of two ideas, the one discarded yesterday may be the one accepted to-morrow, that the glimmer of light quickly obscured by mists may be the prevision of a revelation which finally commands assent. No other excuse is needed for freely extracting from these volumes any evidence of persistence, change, anticipation, relapse, or recurrence of idea that they may record, without carefully observing the consistency of the dates involved. Reserving for distinct consideration such as are obviously miscellaneous, we may tentatively group the poems into three divisions, corresponding with the periods of one-sidedness, transition, and equilibrium above noted. Each of these groups demands separate notice.

No one has more frankly admitted than Mr. Arnold in his later essays that Hellenism has its faulty side, 'a side of moral weakness and of relaxation or insensibility of the moral fibre.' Nor from his present stand-point, probably, would he hesitate to endorse Mr. Gladstone's opinion that it was based upon a 'principle of the sufficiency of this our human earthly life, without any capital regard to what is before us in futurity, or what is above and around us in the unseen world.' At a time, however, when the influence of Hellenism was paramount, no such apprehension of its deficiencies could be reasonably expected of him; and we cannot be surprised to find them reflected in the poems then composed. 'The Strayed Reveller' is a vivid presentment of the splendid dream-world which intoxication with the cup of Circean pleasure has the power of creating. How momentary the enchantment, how hideous the waking, the author of the original myth did not neglect to show; but of that side of the picture there is no trace in Mr. Arnold's transcript. It cannot be said to be needed, because like all his poems this is intrinsically pure. For the pollutions of the old world, which, to some Neo-Pagan artists seem to constitute its chief attractions, he has never shown the faintest relish. His silence, nevertheless, must be taken to imply that he was sensible of no defect in the conception. The poem ends as it began with the passionate cry of the Reveller for a fresh draught of delirious delight:—

> Faster, faster,
> O Circe, Goddess,
> Let the wild, thronging train
> The bright procession
> Of eddying forms
> Sweep through my soul!

'Empedocles on Etna' (now happily restored to the collected works) is an elaborate attempt to portray in dramatic contrast the three leading types of Hellenic character—the thoughtful, brooding intellect that found expression in philosophy; the sensuous, joyous imagination that embodied itself in art; the credulous, matter-of-fact stamp of minds that made up the public with which philosophers and artists had to deal. Mr. Arnold's idea of Empedocles represents him as a teacher who has outlived not only his popularity, but his self-confidence, a thinker weary of the fruitless search after causes, dissatisfied with every explanation of the Universe that can be proposed, and though able to see for others, like his simple follower Pausanias, the wisdom of acquiescence in the inevitable, and that the moderate expectations thus dictated ensure sufficient happiness for man's life, is unable to apply the lesson to himself, and seeks refuge from despair in suicide. Full of pathetic majesty is the soliloquy of the troubled spirit as it braces up its strength for death.

The retrospect of its bright youthful ambitions only deepens the sense of present gloom. Nor is the doubtful anticipation of the future more consoling, for Death may not be annihilation:—

[Quotes ll. 345–72, 'But mind—but thought', etc.]

His solitary gleam of comfort is that though he has

> Lived in wrath and gloom,
> Fierce, disputations, ever at war with man,
> Far from my own soul, far from warmth and light,

he has 'not grown easy in these bonds,' he has

> Loved no darkness, . . .
> Allowed no fear.

In the sense that it hath been granted him

> Not to die wholly, not to be all enslaved,

'the numbing cloud mounts off' his soul, and he breathes freely. In that moment, lest 'the mists of despondency' should again envelope it, he takes the plunge.

Finely contrasted with this agony of morbid self-consciousness is the healthy, æsthetic serenity of Callicles, the young harp-player whose love of natural beauty, and pity for the wounded spirit of Empedocles, have induced him to linger in one of the mountain-valleys within ear-shot, and minister the healing influence of music and song. A picture of the calm life which he desires for the sufferer is thus shadowed forth in his rendering of a Theban legend:—

[Quotes ll. 427–42, 'Far, from from here', etc.]

The verses assigned to Callicles illustrate in the most favourable aspect the writer's power of transmuting into English the manner of Greek lyrical poetry. Though not to be compared with the marvellous choric song in 'The Lotos-Eaters,' or even with some of the choruses in 'Atalanta in Calydon,' their gracious music must be confessed too exceptional with Mr. Arnold. His later attempts (in *Merope*) to represent accentually the choric rhythm of Greek tragedy are far less satisfactory, but these are avowedly experiments, made in default of finding English measures that produce the same effect; and criticism is frankly deprecated by the admission that 'where the ear is guided solely by its own feeling there is a continual risk of failure and of offence.' To an ordinary ear, we think, lyrical effect is best conveyed by regularity of metre and rhyme, as *e.g.*, in the concluding verses sung by Callicles in honour of the Muses:—

[Quotes ll. 457–68, 'Whose praise do they mention?' etc.]

Some passages are strikingly graphic, especially such as paint the strange contrasts of volcanic scenery. Callicles thus describes his resting-place:—

[Quotes ll. 41–56, 'For 'tis the last', etc.]

The scene from the edge of the crater is still more vividly portrayed as Empedocles gazes by night over the

[Quotes ll. 308–14, 'Sea of cloud', etc.]

Though the direct intrusion of his personality is precluded by the dramatic form, the choice of theme and method of handling are commonly sufficient to mark a dramatist's sympathy. As respects the theme, we have Mr. Arnold's admission that to one situated as Empedocles, 'modern problems have presented themselves; we hear already the doubts, we witness the discouragement of Hamlet and Faust' (Preface of 1853). The poem is temporarily excluded from his collected works, on the ground that its exhibition of unrelieved mental suffering is too painful, and a protest entered against the view that to attempt a representation of the state of one's own mind is a worthy poetic aim. This would not of itself amount to a confession that in the thoughts and feelings thus depicted the writer had been reflecting his own scepticism; but such a construction may be reasonably put upon it when we find him giving personal expression to similar thoughts and feelings in poems composed at the same time. We shall presently have to speak of the latter as a separate group, but any one may discover this similarity for himself who, after reading the soliloquies of Empedocles, compares the tone of 'A Summer-Night,' 'Self-Deception,' and 'The Scholar-Gipsy.' The persistence with which Mr. Arnold contrasts 'the disinterested objectivity' of Callicles with the subjective anguish of the philosopher may be taken to indicate his consolatory faith in the remedial virtues of Art. In 'Memorial Verses,' another poem of this period, we find Goethe singled out for admiration because he prescribed the same panacea for the ills of his own time. To a mind dominated by the influence of Hellenism, no other conclusion could so fitly suggest itself.

'Mycerinus,' though not belonging to the first group by its subject, strictly belongs to it in treatment. The legend told by Herodotus of the Egyptian King who, in the midst of his just and pure reign, was warned by an oracle that he had but six years to live, is here expanded into an impressive and painful picture. The spectacle of a man who, deeming long life to be the reward of just deeds, arraigns the Gods for withholding it, admonishes his subjects to pursue vice instead of virtue, if they would avoid his fate, and devotes his remaining years to a continuous revel, is one which perhaps no one but a Neo-Pagan artist, an imitator 'not to the manner born,' prone to exaggerate the defects as well as the merits of his idol, would select as a congenial theme. If Mr. Arnold is right in his view that the highest aim of Greek tragedy was to produce 'a sentiment of sublime acquiescence in the course of fate, and in the dispensations of human life,' Æschylus and Sophocles would no doubt have forborne the subject. A distinctively Christian artist might choose it to deduce a moral from it; an artist of complete culture might suffer it to point its own moral. Mr. Arnold does neither the one nor the other, but goes out of his way to thrust in a suggestion that throws no light on the positive darkness at which it is directed, and serves to obscure the true significance of the story. 'It may be,' he says, 'that the eye of Mycerinus on his joyless feast'

> Dwelt with mere outward seeming, he within
> Took measure of his soul, and knew its strength;
> And by that silent knowledge, day by day,
> Was calm'd, ennobled, comforted, sustained.

That motives can safely be detached from conduct, an heroic spirit consist with an ignoble life, is a tenet which the author of *Literature and Dogma* would assuredly refuse to sanction. Apart from its ethical flaw, the poem is a fine one, statuesque in conception, lofty in diction, and solemn in rhythm. The writer's adherence to the Greek 'principle,' to which Mr. Gladstone has referred, has been maintained, it need hardly be said, at the expense of historical fidelity; no doctrines being more deeply-rooted in Egyptian belief than those which are here ignored.

'Sohrab and Rustum' and 'Balder Dead,' narrative poems drawn respectively from Persian tradition and Scandinavian mythology, both belong to the first group in virtue of their Homeric treatment. We do not doubt that the author has done wisely to disregard as accidental the national peculiarities of the literatures that have furnished his themes, and obtain the advantage of following the world's greatest epical model by assuming all conceptions of an heroic age to be essentially similar. The simple flow of the narrative, unbroken by reflection, the breadth and ease of handling, the unrestrained expression of emotion, the diffuseness of the imagery drawn from natural objects, and the skilful use and repetition of sonorous names, remind one continually of Homer. The Eastern legend takes precedence of the Northern myth in right of its human interest, admitting a larger infusion of the pathos in which Mr. Arnold excels. It turns upon the fortunes of Sohrab, the unknown son of the great Persian warrior Rustum, who, in hope of winning a proud acknowledgment from his father, joined the hostile Tartar tribes, among whom he has attained high distinction, and, on the eve of a great battle, obtains leave from their general to challenge a Persian warrior to single combat. The challenge is accepted by Rustum, who fights in disguise. He and his son encounter on the sands beside the Oxus, each unknown to the other, but the former stirred by deep pity for the daring boy who rushes on death, the latter agitated by strange yearnings towards the majestic warrior who answers to his ideal of father. Rustum, believing that he has no son, repels Sohrab's eager appeal to disclose his name with a taunt that admits of but one rejoinder. The father is at first worsted, and once at the mercy of his son. In the second onset, carried away by excitement, he shouts his battle-cry—'Rustum!' —as he hurls his spear. The name puts Sohrab off his guard, and he falls mortally wounded. A threat extorted from his agony that Rustum will avenge him, brings about the recognition he has so long sought. To prove his parentage, he bares his arm imprinted with the seal which Rustum had given to his mother:—

[Quotes ll. 689–706, 'Rustum gazed, and gazed', etc.]

The death of the son in his father's arms, amid the awe-struck silence of the hosts as night falls, is told with simple solemnity. Not the least impressive touch of art is the recurring reference to the presence of the great river beside which the tragedy is enacted, that contrasts the calm dignity of its course with the unseemly turbulence of human passions, its unexhausted permanence with their transience and decay. The poet's faithfulness to his method of Greek conception is again shown in his treatment of death:—

> Unwillingly the spirit fled away,
> Regretting the warm mansion which it left,
> And youth, and bloom, and this delightful world.

The farewells of the dying son and the bereaved father contain nothing that betokens their conviction or desire of aught beyond the grave.

If Mr. Arnold fails to move his readers to equal interest in 'Balder Dead,' the subject rather than himself may be responsible. The delineation of beings so anomalous as the Gods of Scandinavian mythology is attended with difficulties that Art can scarcely hope to overcome, the sense of which has a tendency to restrain one's sympathy. Those who are not thus repelled by the subject will find the treatment throughout in admirable keeping, and some of the descriptive passages singularly pictorial.

The special aptitude of Mr. Arnold's genius, in its early phases of development, for dealing with themes drawn from Hellenic or cognate sources, is attested by the inadequacy of his attempts in other directions. His 'Tristram and Isolt,' a half-dramatic, half-narrative version of one of the most vivid and passionate stories in the Arthurian cycle of legends, is curiously tame and cold; its highest effects being attained in some graceful touches of sentiment and faithful landscape-painting. An unavoidable comparison with the superlative art of the master to whom the Arthurian cycle is consecrated might be thought to explain his failure in this instance, if it were not equally conspicuous in his treatment of a mediæval subject, such as 'The Church of Brou.' For genuine sympathy with a conception of post-Pagan or distinctively Christian art, he seems at this period to have been constitutionally indisposed, the spiritual conviction upon which such sympathy should be based being as yet wanting. The evidence of this deficiency must be mainly negative, but positive confirmation could scarcely be stronger than the language of the fine sonnet composed during the revolutionary crisis of 1848-9, when the springs of so many earnest natures were sounded to their depths:—

[Quotes 'To a Friend' in its entirety]

One has only to compare this confession with that put forth in the stanzas of 'In Memoriam,' written at the same period:—

> And all is well, though faith and form
> Be sundered in the night of fear, &c.

to appreciate the difference as respects a basis of moral confidence between the 'Hellenic' and the 'Hebrew' spirit.

No tenets could better harmonize with a belief in the essential objectivity of Art than those of the Stoics, the most practical and least subjective of the schools. But it was the historic destiny of Stoicism to fall before Scepticism, and a modern adherent could expect no otherwise for himself. Mr. Arnold had scarcely announced a sense of security in his fortress than it seemed to be shaken. Doubts as to the all-sufficiency of Greek art and Stoical ethics to sustain a soul in the 'bad times' of social anarchy obtrude themselves in the contemporary sonnets addressed to a Republican friend. They deprecate, indeed, all rash attempts to forestal the Divine determination of events, and preach the wisdom of patience as the only remedy for existing evils, but betray a feeling that is appreciably warmer than the due temperature of philosophic apathy:—

> If sadness at the long heart-wasting show
> Wherein earth's great ones are disquieted;
> If thoughts, not idle, while before me flow,
> The armies of the homeless and unfed—
> If these are yours, if this is what you are,
> Then am I yours, and what you feel I share.

In 'Resignation,' another poem of the same period, studiously calm as is the tenor of its individual counsels—

> Be passionate hopes not ill resigned,
> For quiet and a fearless mind; . . .
> For they, believe me, who await
> No gifts from chance have conquered Fate—

the surface is ever and anon disturbed by the welling-forth of emotional sympathy. It may be discerned in the description of the Gipsies, for whom—

> Time's busy touch,
> While it mends little troubles much; . . .
> They must live still; and yet, God knows,
> Crowded and keen the country grows!

and yet more clearly in the closing lines, which remind those who prefer at 'intemperate prayer' to Fate,

> For movement, for an ampler sphere,

how many there are who suffer dumbly:—

> Not milder is the general lot,
> Because our spirits have forgot
> In action's dizzying eddy hurled,
> The something that infects the world.

In such passages as these there are indications, however faint, that 'Hebraism,' though still in abeyance, was troubling the writer's spirit. They inaugurate a period of transition which brought to a close his exclusive subservience to Hellenic influences. The first step taken in that direction was the abandonment of his cherished aversion to subjective poetry. His extravagant protests against it in theory continued long after he had assented to the practice, and were probably due to the consciousness of his own bias for what he deemed a fatal weakness. Nothing operates upon a strenuous nature more effectually, perhaps, than such a consciousness as an inducement to over-act the tyrant. But the soul holds on its course in supreme unconcern for all theories and prepossessions whatsoever. Mr. Arnold became a subjective poet involuntarily, and because the pursuit of truth led him through the furnace of doubt. He has only added one more to the number of those who

> Learn in suffering what they teach in song.

The sensible decrease manifest from this time forth in the flow of his creative impulse, and the increase, *pari passu*, of introspection in its stead, are the first characteristics of this period of transition. The critical bent of his genius now unmistakeably asserts itself. Rarely is an impression upon the mental retina simply recorded, but has to be carefully analyzed, sifted, and reduced to a formula. So patiently is the process conducted, that the poet often seems to regard his subject as an entity apart, like a physician who, to watch the effect of an experiment upon himself, undertakes to regulate his own temperature and time his own pulse. In one or two poems, *e.g.*, 'Youth's Agitations' and 'Growing Old,' he attains to the ruthless calm of a vivisector. This tone of self-scrutiny is common to both the second and third groups of poems. The distinguishing note of the former is their reflection of the sceptical phase through which the writer was passing. Every thinker worthy of the name has to make such a passage at some time or other, but perhaps it was never undertaken by a larger number of sincere and vigorous minds in company than at the period to which these poems belong. John Sterling, Arthur Clough, Mr. Francis Newman, Mr. Froude, and others of the fellowship, have severally recorded their experience. The incidents doubtless vary in each case, but we remember no more graphic expression of the moral uneasiness and spiritual darkness, often verging on despair, which are among the commonest sequels of such a crisis, than Mr. Arnold has given in his 'Scholar-Gipsy.'

Its imaginative thread is found in a story told by Glanvil of an undergraduate at Oxford, forced by poverty to leave his studies and join a tribe of Gipsies, from whom he acquired a knowledge of their secret lore. Having been recognized and accosted during one of his wanderings by two former fellow-students, he recounted the story of his flight, and of the learning he had gained, declaring his intention at some favourable opportunity of making it known to the world. The peaceful nomadic life, which, by a graceful fiction, he is represented as still leading in the rural neighbourhood of Oxford, and the happy confidence with which he waits for a 'heaven-sent moment' to announce his revelation, serve as a pointed contrast to the chaotic unrest of which the University is a typical centre, the self-mistrust and hopelessness of regaining conviction from which the most thoughtful of its members suffer:—

[Quotes 'The Scholar-Gipsy', ll. 165–84; 191–6, 'O life unlike to ours!' etc.]

The tone of sad yearning and bitter dissatisfaction in which this poem is pitched is fortunately not long sustained; but with modified intensity it runs through all the poems belonging to Mr. Arnold's middle period. The 'Stanzas in memory of Obermann' (1849), are an expression of deep sympathy with the philosophic Senancour, who, saddened by the spectacle which his age presented, retired to solitary communion with Nature; an example which the poet, perplexed with the 'hopeless tangle' of his own time, would fain follow, but for the fate that drives him forth into the world:—

> Thou, sad guide, adieu!
> I go; Fate drives me, but I leave
> Half of my life with you.

In the 'Stanzas from the Grande Chartreuse,' the sense of his own neutral, transitionary attitude, between allegiance to authority that has ceased to control him and acceptance of a system that does not command his reverence, prompts him to sympathy with those adherents of an outworn faith who have the courage to retire from a world that disowns them, and for which they know themselves unfit:—

> Wandering between two worlds, one dead,
>   The other powerless to be born,
> With nowhere yet to rest my head;
>   Like these on earth I wait forlorn.
> Their faith, my tears, the world deride,
> I come to shed them at their side.

In the 'Memorial Verses' on the death of Wordsworth (1850) his feeling is embodied in a tribute of reverence to the great poetic thinkers who have not been conquered by the problems of their age, but in their several ways have evinced the consciousness of mastery. Byron presented the spectacle of defiant force which, however terrible to witness in its strife 'of passion with eternal law,' was majestic in virtue of its 'fiery life:'—

> He taught us little; but our soul
> Had *felt* him like the thunder's roll.

Goethe offered the nobler example of calm æsthetic wisdom:—

[Quotes 'Memorial Verses', ll. 19–28, 'He took the suffering human race', etc.]

Wordsworth, the last of the triad, fulfilled the noblest mission by recalling the soul to sympathy with Nature:—

[Quotes ll. 42–54, 'He, too, upon a wintry clime', etc.]

With his death, however, the hope of Europe seemed dead:—

[Quotes ll. 64–70, 'Others will teach us', etc.]

The same jaundiced mood that finds its sombre hues reflected in the world and, though solaced by the memory of the past, discerns no outlook of comfort in the present or the future, recurs in 'A Summernight;' but here the gracious influence which Wordsworth had worshipped effects a partial cure. Though the poet still carries about with him

> The old unquiet breast,
> Which never deadens into rest,
> Nor ever feels the fiery glow
> That whirls the spirit from itself away;

and questions if there can be any life for man but that of 'madman or slave,' one who defies his fate or is made captive by it, yet the moonlit, starry heaven suggests that there is a possible alternative:—

[Quotes 'A Summer Night', ll. 78–82; 86–92, 'Ye heavens whose pure dark regions', etc.]

In the lines written beside the grave of Dr. Arnold, in Rugby Chapel (1857), this glimmer of hope has brightened. He is remembered as one whose 'even cheerfulness' sustained him unwearied through a career of lofty and beneficent exertion, devoted to the service of the Father in whom he trusted and the brothers whom he loved. The son of such a man has assuredly warrant to

> Believe
> In the noble and great who are gone, . . .

Nor is the faith wholly vain that such souls may still appear amid their 'fainting dispirited race,' like angels in the hour of need:—

[Quotes 'Rugby Chapel', ll. 196–208, 'Ye alight in our van!' etc.]

Here again Hebraism is plainly struggling to the surface. But the example of one who solves the problem of life by the energetic discharge of a recognized duty is not enough to stimulate a spirit which doubt has paralyzed for action. An example that should suffice for this would be that of a man whose scepticism never let him rest, but urged him unceasingly forward in quest of a satisfactory solution. Such an one Mr. Arnold finds in Arthur Clough, to whose memory his 'Thyrsis' is dedicated. It forms a companion ode to 'The Scholar-Gipsy,' but is pitched in a more plaintive key. Since Milton's 'Lycidas' and Shelley's 'Adonais,' no more exquisite monody has been tuned in English to a classic strain. Borrowing the pastoral language of Theocritus, the poet bewails his fellow-shepherd with whom he had so often frequented the Scholar-gipsy's haunts, especially the neighbourhood of a great elm which they had associated with his wandering existence, and agreed to accept as a token that he still pursued it. Here Thyrsis and his friend had passed the spring of life, rejoicing in 'each simple joy the country yields,' assaying together their 'shepherd-pipes,' and cherishing aspirations which Fate and Time had combined to baffle. For Thyrsis 'a shadow lowered on the fields,' and he could not remain:—

> Some life of men unblest,
> He knew, which made him droop, and filled his head.
> He went; his piping took a troubled sound
> Of storms that rage outside our happy ground;
> He could not wait their passing, he is dead.

Upon his friend also the shadow has fallen:—

[Quotes 'Thyrsis', ll. 141–50, 'And long the way appears, etc.]

But accepting as a happy omen that 'the tree' still crowns the height, and the scholar-gipsy, 'by his own heart inspired,' still lives his peaceful life and waits for Heaven's opportunity, the poet calls to mind how Thyrsis, animated by the same ambition, followed the same unworldly course:—

[Quotes ll. 221–30, 'What though the music', etc.]

To his friend a like path lies open:—

> Then through the great town's harsh heart-wearying roar,
> Let in thy voice a whisper often come
>   To chase fatigue and fear.
> Why faintest thou? I wandered till I died:
> Roam on! the light we sought is shining still!

In the third group of Mr. Arnold's poems we include those which take the motive here suggested as a point of departure. They indicate a gradual process of recovery from the morbid mental condition in which those belonging to his middle period were written, an approximation to the tone of balanced conviction and healthy hopefulness that characterises his later Essays. Criticism is the form of poetic reflection which these symptoms of convalescence commonly take; the scene and subject of an unhealthy mood being recalled for analysis, and the partial or false view in which it originated corrected by subsequent experience. The poem of 'Obermann once more' thus forms an answer to the 'Stanzas in memory of Obermann,' written twenty years before. The spirit of the hermit-philosopher with whose despair he had sympathized, and whose solitude he had yearned to embrace, now monishes him to avoid the error of a 'frustrate life,' and to advance by courageous and cheerful enterprize the attainment of that brighter day which had begun to dawn upon the world:—

[Quotes 'Obermann Once More', ll. 281–8; 301–12, 'Despair not thou as I despaired', etc.]

The tone of these verses may be compared with that of a passage in the contemporary Essay, commencing, 'And is not the close and bounded intellectual horizon within which we have long lived and moved now lifting up? and are not new lights finding free passage to shine in upon us?' (*Culture and Anarchy*). The active intercourse with the world for which he felt himself unfitted, and undertook only under compulsion, could have given no better proof of its tonic virtue than by thus clearing his perception of the real state of society, and bracing his sense of the obligations of genius in regard to it.

The 'Memorial Verses' on the death of Wordsworth are in like manner reviewed and answered in 'The Youth of Nature,' written beside his grave. The 'sacred poet' may well be mourned by those to whom he was a priest, but with his death the hope of mankind does not die, for the 'loveliness, magic, and grace' of Nature, which he interpreted, transcend and outlast him.

[Quotes 'Youth of Nature', ll. 80–6, 'They are here', etc.]

The mood in which 'A Summer Night' was written is in the same way summoned for comparison with the feelings suggested under similar circumstances at a later period. The wound inflicted on the writer's affections by a recent sorrow, to which the poem of 'A Southern Night' is consecrated, has made him insensible to the pain of the intellectual trouble that formerly possessed him. The ideal life of man which, as figured in the purity of the starry heavens, once seemed so remote of attainment, now seems nearer to realization, in memory of the 'high-souled' 'gentle' lives whose loss he is deploring, in presence of the divine beauty of Nature to which they bore affinity:—

[Quotes 'A Southern Night', ll. 129–40, 'And what but gentleness untired', etc.]

The assertion by the affections of their mastery over the intellect in supplying a ground of confidence when its assurance fails, is the theme of 'Dover Beach.' Standing beside the shore from which the tide is ebbing, the 'eternal note of sadness' reminds him that—

[Quotes 'Dover Beach', ll. 21–8, 'The sea of faith' etc.]

But the reflection brings no longer the old sense that all is lost to him:—

> Ah, love, let us be true
> To one another!

The power of love to reveal man's inner nature to himself, of which his other faculties disclose no glimpse, is the subject of 'A Buried Life':—

[Quotes ll. 72–90; 96–8, 'Yet still, from time to time', etc.]

This and such a poem as 'The Future,' seem inspired by the conviction that our emotional and spiritual instincts, and the harmonies which imagination constructs upon them, impalpable as they are, afford a better guarantee of certitude concerning the mysterious problems of existence than we can obtain elsewhere. To how many of us a vague but tender trust in Love, an *abandon* of imaginative speculation, and sense of room for hope in the infinite possibilities of the universe, are incomparably more satisfying than the dogmatic affirmations of Theology, or the not less dogmatic negations of Science! The poet's voice acquires a fuller and deeper tone than is usual with him as the mystery of the future is thus unfolded to his yearning gaze:—

[Quotes 'The Future', ll. 71–87, 'Haply the river of Time', etc.]

The due limitation of the indulgence which should be given to the soul's *aberglaube* is rightly defined in Mr. Arnold's latest criticism. The tendency of such extra-belief 'to substitute itself for Science,' in cases where Science has something positive to affirm, is undoubtedly, as he points out, a fruitful source of superstition. But he is not less careful to allow that 'that which we hope, augur, imagine, is the poetry of life, and has the rights of poetry.' It fills up the gap which Science sternly seeks to widen and Theology vainly attempts to bridge over. Herein lies its value, and it is the recognition of this that constitutes the charm of these poems.

The criterion of inward assurance and the experimental sanction of happiness which our spiritual instincts possess, are possessed in a still greater degree by those moral intuitions, reliance on which, as the one verifiable basis of belief, is preached in *Literature and Dogma*. Such poems as 'Self-dependence,' and 'Palladium' attest that the talisman which the writer thus commends to the acceptance of all doubtful minds has been long cherished by his own. 'Severely clear,' he hears a cry from his own heart that answers to the cry of the 'self-poised' stars—

> Resolve to be thyself! and know that he
> Who finds himself loses his misery!

Like the Palladium that stood 'high 'mid rock and wood' above Troy, which could not fall whilst it was firm—

> Still doth the soul from its lone fastness high,
> Upon our life a ruling effluence send;
> And when it fails, fight as we will, we die,
> And while it lasts we cannot wholly end.

The gradual reassertion by Hebraism of that share of authority which had long been denied to its influence, and the attainment of an equilibrium between it and Hellenism is shown more or less distinctly in 'The Better Part,' 'Pis-aller,' 'Progress,' and 'East London.' To those for whom a creed affords the only stronghold of moral security he has no other gospel to preach: 'For God's sake, believe it then!' To those who find in the absence of supernatural control an excuse for lawlessness, he makes an inward appeal:—

> Hath man no second life? *Pitch this one high!*
> Sits there no judge in Heaven our sin to see?
> *More strictly then the inward judge obey!*
> Was Christ a man like us? *Ah! let us try*
> *If we then, too, can be such men as he!*

To those whom zeal for intellectual freedom impels to a rash iconoclasm he points the value of all religious safeguards:—

> Which has not taught weak wills how much they can?
> Which has not fallen on the dry heart like rain?
> Which has not cried to sunk, self-weary man,
> '*Thou must be born again!*'

Every reader of *Culture and Anarchy* will observe the coincidence of its teaching with the drift of the foregoing. The cultivation of a standard of 'right reason or best self,' so eloquently urged in this Essay, is enjoined as emphatically in 'Morality' and 'The Second Best.'

[Quotes several passages from both poems]

Varied expressions of that intelligent sympathy with the spirit and history of the Christian Church which gives force to Mr. Arnold's conciliatory efforts in *St. Paul and Protestantism*, will be found in two or three of his later sonnets. The simplification of religious ideas to which he has devoted his ultimate efforts is more than once referred to in his poems as a reform that cannot be averted:—

> Alone, self-poised, henceforward man
> Must labour! must resign
> His all too human creeds, and scan
> Simply the way Divine.

The moral Pantheism, as one may succinctly describe it, which driven from Personal Theism as an unverifiable hypothesis, finds solid ground in a conception of God as 'the Eternal Power, not ourselves, which makes for righteousness,' and the Christianity that finds in the method and secret of its founder, inwardness and self-renouncement, the truest philosophy, are not obscurely avowed in such passages as the following:—

[Quotes a number of passages from 'The Divinity', 'Immortality', and 'Worldly Place', all without comment]

The classification thus attempted of Mr. Arnold's chief poems into three groups, representing three stages of mental progress, has been admittedly conjectural, and may be open to correction in detail. If, however, as we believe, it substantially affords the clue to their interpretation, the student who accepts it as a whole can correct the details for himself. It could be wished that in some future edition the author would take the matter out of his critics' hands, and indicate the true order in which his poems should be studied. Their existing arrangement is not unlikely to mislead some readers, and to them these volumes must appear a strange miscellany, a mirror of moods in perpetual flux and reflux. A writer of thoroughly unstable mind is scarcely entitled to take the public into confidence, and can certainly expect no sympathy. One could only criticize to condemn the tendency of such a poem as 'Stanzas from the Grande Chartreuse,' if it were to be accepted as a definitive expression of conviction. A jeremiad which dismisses the time present as characterized by decayed Faith, and unvivifying Science, and avers that 'the kings of modern thought are dumb,' waiting for the future, till when it behoves them to follow the example of monastic seclusion, and 'die out with these last of the people who believe,' could only inspire irritation at the writer's morbid perverseness, or at best such regret as those eccentric utterances of Mr. Ruskin inspire, which seem to proclaim his alienation from the spirit of his age, and his resolution to neutralize the influence he has hitherto exerted upon it. Viewed, however, as one of many phases in an intellectual revolution, the mood here reflected cannot but excite the deepest sympathy, and we welcome its record as a valuable addition to psychological poetry.

The poems that cannot be assigned to one or other of the groups proposed are comparatively few. They do not manifest Mr. Arnold's possession of any qualifications hitherto unnoted; but to two of them, depth of feeling and faithful observation of Nature, they bear fuller testimony. In the series entitled 'Faded Leaves,' the swift process of a real love-tragedy is recorded with peculiar tenderness. Certain poems which in earlier editions were interspersed with the foregoing, have since been collected into a companion sermon entitled 'Switzerland.' The separation is judicious, as the latter mark with much delicacy the gradual awakening of the affections from an illusion not destined to last. Of the delineation of passion Mr. Arnold's poems scarcely afford an example. His 'Modern Sappho,' a study of a woman's heart, restrained by the height of its love from the low impulses of jealousy, might serve for a type of his own Muse. Her crystalline purity is not to be mistaken for coldness. It is not the flesh that is weak, but the spirit that is stronger.

Perhaps the most touching example of his pathetic vein is the lyric of 'The Forsaken Merman' to his children, as they relinquish their fruitless quest for the mortal bride and mother who has left them, and returned to earth:—

[Quotes ll. 10–29, 'Call her once before you go', etc,]

Mr. Arnold's skill in painting landscape has been shown in the extract given from 'Empedocles on Etna.' Many of the poems to which we have adverted as subjectively gloomy are brightened by occasional glimpses of that objective Nature which was the poet's first love. The touches that thus delineate the change of the seasons afford a relief which cannot be overlooked by the readers of 'The Scholar-Gipsy' and 'Thyrsis':—

[Quotes a number of passages from both poems]

If comparatively little stress has been laid upon Mr. Arnold's qualifications as an artist, it is because with him, as in a still greater degree with Mr. Browning, art has been made subordinate to thought. With Mr. Tennyson alone among the poets of our time—taking each at his best—one is sensible of that intimate harmony between spirit and form which not only forbids the separation of one from the other, but makes it inconceivable that the idea could be conveyed in more perfect language. The most quotable of Mr. Arnold's words are not so 'married' to music that it would seem profane to divorce them, nor does that music, except in rare moments, keep us under its spell. Art, nevertheless, has been a matter of real concern with him, as is abundantly evident from the careful construction and diction of his principal poems. A few harsh phrases or uneven lines count for nothing, where there is so pervading an impression of order, tune, and polish. Though not specially epigrammatic, he is an eminently luminous writer. How much historic light, for example, is concentrated in this verse on the attitude of Oriental faith during the domination of Rome:—

> The East bowed low before the blast
> In patient deep disdain;
> She let the legions thunder past,
> And plunged in thought again.

How truthful in its discernment and wide in its application is this reflection upon life's attrition:—

> This is the curse of life, that not
> Another, calmer train
> Of wiser thoughts and feelings blot
> Our passions from our brain;
> But each day brings its petty dust
> Our soon-choked souls to fill,
> And we forget because we must,
> And not because we will.

His lyrical scope is limited, but he has treated several forms with success, especially that which for want of a better name must still be called the 'regular ode.' In several minor lyrics he has justified his adoption of accentual rhythm by proofs of its musical capability that were wanting in the choruses of *Merope*. In his sonnets, though they are not always accurate in form, nor commended to our ear by his division of the octave and sestette into their component parts, the arrangement of the sentences is skilfully adjusted to the conditions imposed. In the management of the eight-syllable couplet, a metre too seldom employed in modern verse, he is extremely successful.

We may conclude with the hope that Mr. Arnold's prolonged absence upon foreign service does not imply (as one of his critics supposes) that he has relinquished the arena in which his first laurels were won. Consummate as is his mastery of English prose, and immediate as may be its efficacy of operation, the gifts which have gained for him the third place in the hierarchy of living poets cannot fail to ensure a more permanent influence. *Pace* Mr. Carlyle's authority, poetic speech is to be preferred to prose speech as a medium of utterance, if for no other reason than this, that it takes firmer hold of the hearer's memory. Music, condensation, grace, point, emphasis, are elements of eloquence that no teacher can afford to despise, and he can never blend them so perfectly as in poetry. For one apophthegm of our greatest prose writers, Bacon, Hooker, Hobbes, Milton, Taylor, Addison, Gibbon, Burke, that dwells in popular remembrance, Shakespere, Milton, Dryden, Pope, Goldsmith, Burns, Wordsworth, Byron, Shelley,

Tennyson, have uttered a hundred that recur perpetually and most forcibly when the nature is most deeply stirred. Enrolment in their number who have contributed more than any other teachers to supply food which the mind can most readily assimilate—

> Those rare souls
> Whose thoughts enrich the blood o' the world—

is an honour which no one can be indifferent about retaining who has once shown the ambition and the power to secure.

23. Anonymous reviewer on *Poems* (1877), *Saturday Review*

29 September 1877, xliv, 393–4

In this laudatory notice, the writer touches on a number of contemporary interests and raises important questions about Arnold's powers. He notices the fact of Arnold's growing popularity despite the poet's evident lack of interest in appealing to a wide public; he compares Arnold's response to nature with Wordsworth's, especially in 'Tintern Abbey'; tries to account for Arnold's 'unique gifts'; and laments that Arnold seems to consider his life as a poet complete. He wishes that *Last Essays* might be followed by *Last Poems*.

The appearance of an edition of Mr. Arnold's poems which the author calls complete, though it contains neither *Merope* nor 'Lucretius, an unpublished tragedy,' nor one or two small pieces of which we have a recollection, is an occasion that may well be turned to account by those who wish to determine in what his charm over them consists. For an exact appreciation of Mr. Arnold's genius, for the precise definition of his place in English poetry, perhaps the time is not yet come, but every year brings it nearer. Every year widens the circle of those who recognize in the author of 'The Strayed Reveller,' 'Empedocles on Etna,' and 'Thyrsis,' that 'lucidity of soul,' that Greek clearness of touch, which nearly thirty years ago a small band of readers discovered in the author of the *Poems by A*. Why this should be, why during the last generation a writer who employs no popular arts, and who neither paints nor plays upon any passion, should have so steadily advanced in favour, is a question that is difficult to answer. Perhaps one cause of the fact, so creditable to the reading class in England, may be that his *Essays in Criticism* have taught us to judge.

A mind so individual, so clearly marked off from other minds, defies all attempts which a mechanical criticism might make to refer it to the circumstances out of which it grew; but traces of certain influences are visible in the poems, and it is the critic's business to follow them out. It is natural that the poetry of one who believes so firmly in culture, and who defines one element of culture as 'much reading,' should be full of literary reminiscences—of titles, of phrases, of ideas that are derived from books. In the first place, Mr. Arnold is steeped in Greek poetry; the 'Fragment of an Antigone' reads not like a translation of Sophocles, but like what Sophocles might have written had he written in English; and 'The Strayed Reveller' is a voice from the world

Where Orpheus and where Homer are.

That severer reading, which has borne its fruit in Mr. Arnold's later writings, appears in such patristic studies as 'Stagirius'; and it goes without saying that the problems of the modern world have come to him complicated with the thoughts of those who have best expressed or faced them—Goethe, Byron, Wordsworth, and the great French writers of this century. When the *Poems by A*. first appeared, Wordsworth was still living, 'by England's lakes in grey old age'; and it is natural that one of the strongest of all the influences to be detected in these poems should be that of the old man in whose very presence their author may almost be said to have grown up. But the limits of this influence are clearly defined. The strength and the weakness of Wordsworth's poetry may alike be explained by his optimistic view of the theoretical relation between man and nature; by his belief (if we may so formulate it) that man's distance from happiness may be exactly measured by his distance from nature. 'He grew old in an age he condemned,' as Mr. Arnold says; and the reason why he condemned it was because he saw mankind turning away from the field and the mountain to unlovely industries, to the vast town 'hiding the face of earth for leagues,' to the 'many-windowed fabric huge,' with its enslaving labour. To Wordsworth happiness for high and low meant harmony with nature, in a sense different from the Greek sense; it meant Lucy 'hunting the waterfalls,' or the Cumberland shepherd keeping watch on the hills, or the poet meditating among the Borrowdale yew trees. What nature was to him in the different stages of his life is nowhere told more clearly than in the 'Lines composed above Tintern Abbey'—familiar lines which it will be worth while to recall, because, as it happens, they give us an admirable opportunity for what we have immediately in hand—a comparison of the two poets' ways of looking at nature. We do not know that any one has ever pointed out the curious resemblance, at least in externals, between these lines of Wordsworth's and one of the most central and representative of Mr. Arnold's poems, that called 'Resignation,' which, though it is included among the 'early poems,' is full of his most mature philosophy. 'Tintern Abbey,' it will be remembered, is a monologue of the poet on returning with his sister, after five years' absence, to the scene by the Wye, with the 'soft inland murmur' of its waters, its steep and lofty cliffs, its peaceful apple orchards. The silent influence of this scene has never been absent from him in the interval, has given him sweet sensations in hours of weariness, has passed into his 'purer mind' and softened all his actions, and has even contributed to

> that blessed mood
> In which the burthen of the mystery,
> In which the heavy and the weary weight
> Of all this unintelligible world
> Is lightened.

But the actual sight of the place has a more vivid effect, and brings home to him the difference between what nature was to him five years ago and what she is now. The time when 'the sounding cataract haunted him like a passion,' when 'like a roe he bounded o'er the mountains,' is gone; and now nature comes to him laden with 'the still sad music of humanity':—

[Quotes 'Tintern Abbey', ll. 93–111, 'And I have felt/A presence', etc.]

Such was external nature to Wordsworth; in his youth the satisfaction of an appetite that felt no need of 'a remoter charm by thought supplied,' and later, the satisfaction of that pantheistic belief which, at least during the middle years of his life, was undoubtedly his religion.

Mr. Arnold's poem 'Resignation' is framed like Wordsworth's; it is an address to 'Fausta,' suggested by their walking together the same mountain paths, by Wythburn and Watendlath, as they and their young kindred had trodden, a 'boisterous company,' ten years before. The scene before them is not so directly the subject of the poem as in Wordsworth's case, but it is introduced to help out the answer to the question that had been previously raised—the question as to which ideal is preferable, attainment or resignation, active joy or passive acquiescence. To fierce struggling natures, to the pilgrim bound for Mecca, to the Goth bound Romeward, to all 'whom labours self-ordain'd enthral,' death or attainment is the only alternative; but milder natures, those who are freed from passions, mourn not that they are bound to obey the eternal necessities, and

> Claim not every passing hour
> As handmaid to their striding power.

Which aim should ours be? See, Fausta, says the poet, the course we took ten years ago and are taking now (and the lines in which he paints it bring back to many more than Fausta the never-ending charm of those fair places), see, all is the same now as then, the hills, the July sunshine, the gentians, the brook, the rushes. Down below we met a tribe of gipsies. Do they ever, as chance brings them back to places they once knew, moralize on the changes of the times and their own increasing hardships? No, they 'rubbed through yesterday' and will rub through to-day. The poet, too (to take an instance from the other end of the scale), whatever he beholds—and he beholds everything, the courts of kings, the beauty of women, the crowded life of cities, the loveliness of morning meadows—whatever he beholds he 'bears to admire uncravingly':—

[Quotes 'Resignation', ll. 186–98, 'Leaned on his gate', etc.]

Do not reply that the gipsies, who feel not, and the poet, whose power of escape from life's iron round is his compensation, are below and above humanity. See, the world in which we live and move is eternal; it outlasts all passions, it outlasts even death. Then blame not him who, with this permanence of the world and the unreality of passion in mind, pronounces human care all vain. The noblest aim that we can have is, not to amuse, but to set free heart; to await no gifts from chance; to win room to see and hear, and so draw homeward to the general life. And, if this seems inadequate, what then?:—

[Quotes 'Resignation', ll. 261–78, 'Enough, we live!' etc.]

We have dwelt so long on these parallel poems because they so well represent the way in which natural objects, brought home to the mind by striking associations, affect these two poets. Nature is to Wordsworth 'the soul of all his moral being'; it is enough for him, it is alive for him, he sees no imperfections in it. To Mr. Arnold it is rather something to be acquiesced in, lavishly beautiful, no doubt, but wholly careless of man, and going relentlessly and independently on its eternal way. As he says in 'Empedocles on Etna':—

> Nature, with equal mind,
> Sees all her sons at play;
> Sees man control the wind,
> The wind sweeps man away;
> Allows the proudly-riding and the foundering bark;

and again, in one of the early sonnets:—

> Man must begin, know this, where Nature ends;
> Nature and man can never be fast friends;

and again, in 'Dover Beach':—

[Quotes ll. 29–37, 'Ah, love, let us be true', etc.]

Yet it must not be supposed that this attitude towards nature, against which Wordsworth would have protested, indicates a want of susceptibility to natural beauty. Those lines already quoted, where the poet's function is described, would be sufficient to refute this, if, indeed, every page of the poems did not refute it, if 'Obermann' were not keen with Alpine air, and 'Thyrsis' not the loveliest picture of the calm Thames landscape that a son of Oxford ever drew. To Wordsworth, for developing this sense in him, he gives ample acknowledgment:—

> But he was a priest to us all
> Of the wonder and bloom of the world,
> Which we saw with his eyes, and were glad.

It was Wordsworth, he says, who 'made us *feel*':—

[Quotes 'Memorial Verses', ll. 42–53, 'He too upon a wintry clime', etc.]

Never indeed was Stoic so open to impressions from without as this poet is; but then never did Stoic distinguish more clearly between that which comes from without and that which comes from within. No force of will or imagination can blend the two into one, or can absorb the individual soul into the essence which Wordsworth believed to 'run through all things.' Man will find his happiness, not by flinging himself in utter abandonment on the breast of nature, but by frankly recognizing his separation from her, his self-dependence, learning lessons from her, it is true, but taking his best and most abiding lessons from her severer aspects, from 'the cone of Jaman, pale and grey,' from the stars that go upon their course

> Unaffrighted by the silence round them,
> Undistracted by the sights they see.

If this idea were all, however, Mr. Arnold might be no more than a moralist; and whether a moralist is or not to be considered a poet depends on the form into which he throws his reflections. 'Poetry,' he himself says in one of his essays, 'is simply the most beautiful, impressive, and widely effective way of saying things.' Criticism of poetry, therefore, when it has decided that the things are worth saying, resolves itself into asking the question—Are they beautifully, impressively, effectively said? Indeed the world seems in this case to have answered affirmatively; for this demand for new editions can hardly be put down to a spread of quietism in our busy, passion-stirred times, and it must be the loveliness of the expression that wins readers at least as much as the ideas. 'Thyrsis' and 'The Scholar Gipsy' are indeed, so far as mere expression goes, absolutely perfect poems; by which we mean that the music of their sound and the details of their imagery are in absolute harmony with the train of ideas through which the poet wishes to lead us. What hand, again, has ever painted in such fashion the poetic atmosphere that may brood over the 'black Tartar tents' in 'the hush'd Chorasmian waste'? or who, save perhaps Byron in one song and Shelley now and then, has so rendered the silence of the sea deeps?—

> Sand-strewn caverns, cool and deep,
> Where the winds are all asleep,
> Where the pent lights quiver and gleam,
> Where the salt weed plays in the stream, . . .
> Where great whales come sailing by,
> Sail and sail, with unshut eye,
> Round the world for ever and aye.

An almost unique gift, too, of Mr. Arnold's is that power of which 'the bright procession of eddying forms' of 'The Strayed Reveller' is the most brilliant example, and which appears again in 'Philomela'—that power of seeing Greek scenes with the eyes of a Greek artist. But these instances of perfect literary expression are, it must be owned, not so much without exception in Mr. Arnold's verse as in his prose. In spontaneous music, in instinctive accuracy of ear, he must be placed below some three or four poets of our time. That anapæstic blank verse, for example, of which he is so fond, and of which so far as England is concerned, he seems to be the inventor—the metre of 'Heine's Grave' and of 'Rugby Chapel'—is dangerously easy to write in, and it would not be difficult to point out flaws of rhythm in those poems which are written in it. And here and there may be recognized, even in the latest edition, a slip of expression that has escaped the revising hand. Shall we repeat a long since uttered criticism of the last line of the magnificent sonnet on Shakespeare—that a brow can have no voice?

But why, after all (and this is our only serious indictment), why are these poems so soon 'complete'? Why has that pen remained for all these years, if not inactive, at least content with prose, which, however perfect, is confessedly *not* 'the most beautiful, impressive, and widely-effective way of saying things'? We should be glad indeed if we could hope from Mr. Arnold, now that he has closed that chapter of his literary activity of which *Literature and Dogma* was the beginning, that fresh individual experiences might find utterance—that *Last Essays* might be followed by *Last Poems*.

24. J. B. Brown, from 'Modern Creeds and Modern Poetry', *Ethics and Aesthetics of Modern Poetry*

1878, 43–7

James Buchan Brown (1832–1904) was a poet as well as critic (who used the pseudonym J. B. Selkirk), yet his concern here, as the titles indicate, is less with poetry as such than with poetry as it reflects an age of religious doubting. The concern is understandable from the author of *Bible Truths* (1862). Brown's comments, nevertheless, typify much of the contemporary response to Arnold's poetry and point to a recurrent tendency to see his work as a kind of negative index of belief. This is not to call Brown crude or insensitive. He compares Arnold with Tennyson in brief but intriguing remarks, suggesting that 'Stanzas From the Grande Chartreuse' and 'Dover Beach' parallel in their genesis and importance 'the laureate's immortal elegy'.

[A] perfectly natural feeling of regret towards a departing faith is not, however, confined to our philosophers and men of science. It gives tone and colour to much of our later sceptical poetry, as well as to a good deal of poetry which does not earn that epithet except from the extremely orthodox. It lies at the heart of some of the most eloquent passages of the laureate's immortal elegy, and is the principal source of the mournful and pathetic inspiration of Mr. Arnold.

In order to see how true this is with regard to Mr. Arnold's genius, it is only necessary to recall the *motif* of some of his finest poems. It is the secret root of the poet's own uneasiness which gives him the power to describe the majestic despair of Empedocles on Etna, and express the godlike discontent and impatience of a soul that has broken with the past, thrown off its philosophies as utterly inadequate to explain the riddle of the world, but yet has failed to accept the future, or find any satisfactory substitute for the faith it has rejected, an attitude of soul well described in one of the author's most characteristic poems, where he represents himself as

> Wandering between two worlds, one dead,
> The other powerless to be born.

This rupture between the old and new seems to present itself to him in every situation. He hears it in the winds and the woods, and the sea takes up the cry; standing by a moonlit shore at full tide, the old plaint breaks forth in a lyrical burst unsurpassed in modern poetry for grandeur and breadth:—

[Quotes 'Dover Beach', ll. 21–8, 'The sea of faith', etc.]

If Mr. Arnold's poetical theory be true, when speaking of Heine, he tells us that all genius is but the passing mood of the spirit in whom we have our being, he must himself have been selected for the melancholy mood, and set apart as the special exponent of the still sad music of humanity. Wherever his contemplation wanders; by 'Dover Beach,' or by 'Heine's Grave,' with the world-weary author of Obermann, or with the Carthusian ascetics of the Grand Chartreuse, the same deep undertone of sorrow is everywhere present. Through the thin dramatic disguise of the singer, in all these poems one can read between the lines the trouble of the poet's own soul:

> A fever in his pages burns
> Beneath the calm they feign;
> A wounded human spirit turns
> Here, on his bed of pain.

All his communings with nature and human nature take the same sad and sober colour. His gladdest notes are not all glad, but seem to be conceived in shadow and set in the same low and plaintive key. His quarrel in one of his poems with the calmness of old age, and with death itself, because it does not fulfil the ardent promises of youth, and takes him out of 'the daylight and the cheerful sun,' though singularly Greek in feeling, is yet made to ring with a sorrowful pathos palpably projected from the later faith. It is the song of a Greek soul singing under the cross and thorns of a half-accepted half-rejected Christianity.

Since the days of Elizabeth contemporaneous religious difficulties have never received the attention, and have never been more vigorously incorporated and reflected in English poetry, than in the present day, and since that day to this it has perhaps never been more needful that it should be so. In Mr. Tennyson and Mr. Arnold we have the interpreters of the spiritual troubles of an age fraught with issues less salient it may be, but certainly not less operative in time to come than those of the Reformation, and the spiritual interpretation of the times would hardly have been complete without them both. With them both the subject is pretty comprehensively discussed and illustrated. In Mr. Arnold we have all the languor and weariness of soul, all the restlessness and hankering solicitude of an age, whose creed is more or less at war with its convictions; an age which has wakened, or whose attention has been aroused, to the inadequacy of its older authorities and will no longer accept existing standards in matters of faith, although it may not as yet have got its feet on firmer ground; an age that turns its back on the formulæ of the past, but yet has no sufficiently formulated future it can fairly embrace; refusing, and even overthrowing the old foundations, it yet would seek some external basis for that kingdom of heaven within us, that faith which is not of man, neither received of men, nor taught.

An age, in short, which dispenses with the revelation written on the stony tables of authority, and which has outgrown the legal swaddling-bands of its historic and dogmatic parchment, and yet is hardly prepared to accept, without some guarantee outside itself, that ever abiding revelation written not on stone but on the fleshy tables of the human heart and conscience. If in the poetical genius of Mr. Arnold (his prose works are not here taken into consideration) we have the regretful exponent of a tottering theological system, the Jeremiah of a decadent Israel, in Mr. Tennyson as reflected at the height of his power in the pages of 'In Memoriam,' we have the prophet of the wider faith to come. For it is hardly too much to say that from the shadow projected from that divine poem, we have a more certain indication of what the theological future will be, in those questions it sets itself to solve, than in all the volumes of theology proper the century has produced.

25. More views from the 1870s

(a) William LeSueur in the *Canadian Monthly*, March 1872

The *New Poems* published by Mr. Arnold some five or six years ago have taken an altogether higher rank in general estimation than his earlier productions. The latter indeed have for some years past been but little seen or heard of; the *New Poems*, on the contrary, have been received with a degree of favour which almost amounts to 'popularity'. Popular, in a wide sense of the word, Mr. Arnold never can be, at least, as a poet. His thoughts are too remote from those of every-day life, and of the average of readers, to excite a wide enthusiasm, or even to be very generally intelligible. Moreover, the form in which he has chosen to cast a considerable portion of his poetry repels those readers—and they are many—who resent the employment by a writer of any garb they do not recognize at once as modern, national and familiar. A writer with whom they cannot at once feel perfectly at home they turn from with an angry impatience. He may give them vigorous thoughts and beautiful images, but all is of no avail to win their favour if his accent is either archaic or foreign. People of this kind Mr. Arnold is sure to offend. His admirers will be, on the one hand, those who find the forms he has chosen appropriate and pleasing; and, on the other, those whose intellectual sympathy with him is so strong that the presence of certain elements they do not quite understand is no bar to their enjoyment of the substance of what he has written.

(b) William Adams in the *Gentleman's Magazine*, April 1875

Mr. Matthew Arnold is not a popular poet. He is rarely quoted; nor are his pieces chosen by the public readers, or by the young men of elocution societies. It is worth inquiring why, whilst 'In Memoriam' and the 'Idylls' are the bosom friends of every thoughtful girl in the kingdom, and 'The May Queen' and 'The Charge of the Light Brigade' figure in almost every entertainment of the 'reading' kind, the author of 'Empedocles' is known only to the more cultivated readers of his generation, and even by them, perhaps, is more admired than loved. Much of this, no doubt, may be accounted for by Mr. Arnold's terrible contempt for the great body of his countrymen, who are glad, it may be, to repay his scorn and pity by neglecting his poetical productions. Much, too, may be accounted for by the generally melancholy tone in which his muse conveys her message, by the comparatively narrow range of his sympathies, by the want of variety in his choice of topics for treatment, and especially by the severe and sometimes almost pedantic classicism of his style and diction. It is even complained of Mr. Arnold that he is cold and heartless; but the people who make this remark can hardly have read much of his poetry, for it is not wanting in many places in real tenderness and enthusiasm. What probably prevents Mr. Arnold from thoroughly taking hold upon the popular attention is his unfortunate self-consciousness, his inability to forget, as a rule, that he is a poet, or, as it would probably be more correct to say in his case, a man of poetic sensibility, expressing himself, according to established usage, in the form of verse. I am sure that in his inmost heart he is moved by the strongest and the warmest feelings; but there is observable throughout his poetry the effort to keep these feelings under control, a striving after that philosophic calm of mind and temperament which in his opinion ought to mark the man of culture, but which results too often in making his poetry bear a suspicious resemblance to the baldest prose.

(c) Edmund Stedman in *Victorian Poets*, 1876

Certainly he is an illustrious example of the power of training and the human will. Lacking the ease of the lyrist, the boon of a melodious voice, he has, by a *tour de force*, composed poems which show little deficiency of either gift,—has won reputation, and impressed himself upon his age, as the apostle of culture, spiritual freedom, and classical restraint.

There is a passion of the voice and a passion of the brain. If Arnold, as a singer, lacks spontaneity, his intellectual processes, on the contrary, are spontaneous, and sometimes rise to a loftiness which no mere lyrist, without unusual mental faculty, can ever attain. His head not only predominates, but exalts his somewhat languid heart. A poet once sang of a woman,—

> Affections are as thoughts to her,

but thought with Arnold is poetical as affection, and in a measure supplies its place.

We cannot accept his implication that he was born too late, since by this very reflection of the unrest and bewilderment of our time he holds his representative position in the present survey. The generation listens with interest to a thinker of his speculative cast. He is the pensive, doubting Hamlet of modern verse, saying of himself: '*Dii me terrent, et Jupiter hostis!*[1] Two kinds of *dilettanti*, says Goethe, there are in poetry: he who neglects the indispensable mechanical part, and thinks he has done enough if he shows spirituality and feeling; and he who seeks to arrive at poetry by mere mechanism, in which he can acquire an artisan's readiness, and is without soul and matter. And he adds, that the first does the most harm to Art, and the last to himself.' Quite as frankly Arnold goes on to enroll himself among *dilettanti* of the latter class. These he places, inasmuch as they prefer Art to themselves, before those who, with less reverence, exhibit merely spirituality and feeling. Here, let me say, he is unjust to himself, for much of his verse combines beautiful and conscientious workmanship with the purest sentiment, and has nothing of dilettanteism about it. This often is where he for-

---

[1] 'The gods frighten me, and Jupiter the enemy.'

sakes his own theory, and writes subjectively. 'The Buried Life,' 'A Summer Night,' and a few other pieces in the same key, are to me the most poetical of his efforts, because they are the outpourings of his own heart, and show of what exalted tenderness and ideality he is capable. A note of ineffable sadness still arises through them all.

(d) From the *Spectator*, 1 July, 1877

Mr. Arnold has not only arranged this new edition of his poems with taste and judgment, but has done well in restoring many of the older readings for which he had in his last edition substituted others elaborated in colder moods than those in which the original poems had been conceived. Nothing is rarer in the poet than the gift to alter well and without betraying the colour or structure of the new cloth which is put into the old garment; and it is no grave charge to bring against Mr. Arnold that assuredly he did not possess it. It is easy to understand the drift of most of his alterations. He wanted, as far as possible, to introduce clearness of thought where he thought it wanting, and where in some cases at least it really *was* wanting. But in the effort to mend the clearness of the thought, Mr. Arnold frequently lost what is even more important,—the glow and force of expression by which alone poetry is discriminated from prose. Expressions of great beauty linger in the mind and raise it to the poetic mood, even though the passages in which they occur fail to embody any thought which is distinct and poetic, and it generally happens that in the effort to improve the general drift of an early poem, those gems of detail which abound in the work of youthful genius, are lost. Certainly any one who will compare the 'Lines to a Gipsy Child by the Sea-shore,' in the form in which Mr. Arnold published them in his last edition, with that in which they were first published, and to which (almost without exception) they are now restored, will recognise at once that in the effort to make the drift clearer and less ambitious, Mr. Arnold robbed us of many a vivid touch, and that, too, without really giving us any adequate compensa-

tion. A poet sometimes succeeds in mending bad detail, and in sub-
stituting what is noble of that kind for what is ignoble; but he hardly
ever succeeds in the effort to make the general scope of a poem clearer,
and the only practical choice for him is between excluding altogether
one defective in this respect, and giving it with its defects.

(e) From the *Contemporary Review*, January 1878

There is plenty for the literary critic and the psychologist to say about
Mr. Matthew Arnold, but none of it will be said in this brief notice,
except what is on all hands admitted, and yet needs to be emphasized in
detail: namely, that Mr. Arnold is, to adopt a familiar contrast of
Goethe's, a voice and not an echo. His manner and his thought are alike
his own; and the former, with all its quietness and even occasional
prosaic meanness, has a singular pungency of its own. But, not to nibble
at topics which might well make a feast for the muses, we must give a
word of welcome to this handsome and complete edition of the poems
which many of us know and love so well. We were very glad indeed
when Mr. Arnold announced his departure from a certain sphere of
strife and turmoil, and hoped, against hope, that he was going back to
'the two-topt mount divine'—a hope which we fear we must give up
now that we see the words 'complete edition,' though of course that is
not conclusive. But if he would only keep away from political and
social wranglings,—

> Not here, O Apollo!
> Are haunts meet for thee:
> But where Helicon breaks down
> In cliff to the sea,

we should at least recover to the full our old image of him in his singing
robes, and get rid of the other, in which he is, if not exactly a 'budge
doctor of the stoic fur,' something even less congenial and of a more
prickly rind. . . .

(f) From 'The Poetry of Doubt' in the *Church Quarterly*, April 1878

There is a vagueness about the matter, and a pellucid clearness about the form of these poems that render it almost necessary to employ little but the poet's own words in presenting his thought. The matter is the matter, cloudy, varying, and intangible, of nineteenth century speculation: the form is Greek in its exquisite lucidity and clearness. In reading these poems we are continually met by passages in which no word is superfluous, no phrase is jarring, but that which has to be expressed is expressed once for all. Such a stanza as

> But each day brings its petty dust
> Our soon-choked souls to fill,
> And we forget because we must,
> And not because we will,

takes us back from the age of word-painting and novel combinations in language and rhythm, of superabundant epithets and darkened meaning, to the age of Pope, or of Gray, when language was studied and yet clear, artificial and yet simple. Not Mr. Tennyson's richness of detail, not Mr. Browning's rugged power, not Mr. Swinburne's astonishing volume of words can afford to the jaded minds of modern readers the exquisite pleasure which is given by Mr. Arnold's self-restrained purity of language. And if, to correspond to this, there is not the 'sad lucidity of soul' which he so much desires, and asserts that 'fate' has given to the poet, we may ascribe the want in great measure to the 'hopeless tangle of our age,' though partly, no doubt, it is due to the vague and unsatisfactory character of the self-possession to which he strives to attain.

(g) Oscar Wilde in a letter to Helena Sickert, 2 October 1879

Though you are determined to go to Cambridge, I hope you will accept this volume of poems by a purely *Oxford* poet. I am sure you know Matthew Arnold already but still I have marked just a few of the things I like best in the collection. . . . 'Sohrab and Rustum' is a wonderfully stately epic, full of the spirit of Homer, and 'Thyrsis' and 'The Scholar Gipsy' are exquisite idylls, as artistic as 'Lycidas' or 'Adonais:' but indeed I think all is good in [them].

26. Walt Whitman, 'Our Eminent Visitors', *Critic* (New York)

17 November 1883, iii, 459–60

The author of *Leaves of Grass* (1819–92), predictably, did not care for Arnold's work. Elsewhere he explicitly criticizes Arnold's poems for their over-cultured, effete old-world qualities. Here his attack on the verse is implicit, part of a general indictment of most Englishmen coming to America. Whitman's irony lumps together Arnold, Wilde, Thackeray, Froude, and others, as if to say that on *one* side of the Atlantic at least they are much the same. Whitman's estimate of Arnold's verse is clear in the mention of Tennyson as the poet Whitman would have liked to see, and of Carlyle as the voice he would have preferred to hear.

Welcome to them each and all! They do good—the deepest, widest, most needed, good—though quite certainly not in the ways attempted —which have, at times, to the appreciative nostril, a scent of something irresistibly comic. Can there be anything more farcical, for instance, than the sight of a worthy gentleman, coming three or four thousand miles through wet and wind to speak complacently and at great length on matters of which he both entirely mistakes and knows nothing, before a crowd of auditors equally complacent and equally at fault?

Yet welcome and thanks, we say, to those we have, and have had, among us—and may the procession continue! We have had Dickens and Thackeray, Froude, Herbert Spencer, Oscar Wilde, Lord Coleridge —and now Matthew Arnold and Irving the actor. Some have come to make money—some for a 'good time'—some to help us along and give us advice—and some undoubtedly to investigate, *bona fide*, this great problem, democratic America, looming upon the world with such

cumulative power through a hundred years, now with evident intention (since the Secession War) to stay, and take a leading hand, for many
a century to come, in civilization's and humanity's eternal game. But
alas! in that very investigation—at any rate the method of that investigation—is where the deficit most surely and helplessly comes in. Let not
Lord Coleridge and Mr. Arnold, (to say nothing of the illustrious actor,)
imagine that when they have met and surveyed the etiquettical gather-
ings of our wealthy, distinguished, and sure-to-be-put-forward-on-
such-occasions citizens, (New York, Boston, Philadelphia, etc., have
certain stereotyped strings of them, continually lined and paraded like
the lists of dinner dishes at hotel tables—you are sure to get the same
over and over again—it is very amusing,)—and the bowing and introducing, the receptions at the swell clubs, the eating and drinking and
praising and praising back—and the next day riding about Central
Park, or doing 'the Public Institutions'—and so passing through, one
after another, the full-dress coteries of the Atlantic cities, all grammatical and cultured and correct, with the toned-down manners of the
gentlemen, and the kid-gloves, and luncheons and finger-glasses. Let not
our eminent visitors, we say, suppose that they have 'seen America,' or
captured any distinctive clew or purport thereof. Not a bit of it. Of the
pulse-beats that lie within and vitalize this Commonweal to-day—of
the hard-pan purports and idiosyncrasies pursued faithfully and
triumphantly by its bulk of men, generation after generation, super-
ficially unconscious of their own aims, yet none the less pressing on-
ward with deathless intuition age after age—those coteries will not
furnish the faintest scintilla. In the Old World the best flavor and
significance of a race may possibly need to be looked for in its 'upper
classes,' its gentries, its court, its *état major*. In the United States the rule
is reversed. Besides, the special marks of our grouping and design are
not going to be understood in a hurry. The lesson and scanning right
on the ground are difficult, I was going to say they are impossible to
foreigners—but I have occasionally found the clearest appreciation of
all coming from far-off quarters. Surely nothing could be more apt, not
only for our eminent visitors present and to come, but for home study,
than the following editorial criticism of the London *Times* on Mr.
Froude's visit and lectures here a few years ago, and the culminating
dinner given at Delmonico's:

We read the list [says *The Times*] of those who assembled to do honor to Mr.
Froude: there were Mr. Emerson, Mr. Beecher, Mr. Curtis, Mr. Bryant; we add
the names of those who sent letters of regret that they could not attend in

person—Mr. Longfellow, Mr. Whittier. They are names which are well known —almost as well known and as much honored in England as in America; and yet what must we say in the end? The American people outside this assemblage of writers is something vaster and greater than they, singly or together, can comprehend. It cannot be said of any or all of them that they can speak for their nation. We who look on at this distance are able perhaps on that account to see the more clearly that there are qualities of the American people which find no representation, no voice, among these their spokesmen. And what is true of them is true of the English class of whom Mr. Froude may be said to be the ambassador. Mr. Froude is master of a charming style. He has the gift of grace and the gift of sympathy. Taking any single character as the subject of his study, he may succeed after a very short time in so comprehending its workings as to be able to present a living figure to the intelligence and memory of his readers. But the movements of a nation, *the voiceless purpose of a people which cannot put its own thoughts into words, yet acts upon them in each successive generation,*—these things do not lie within his grasp. . . . . . The functions of literature such as he represents are limited in their action; the influence he can wield is artificial and restricted, and, while he and his hearers please and are pleased with pleasant periods, the great mass of national life will flow around them unmoved in its tides by action as powerless as that of the dwellers by the shore to direct the currents of the ocean.

A thought, here, that needs to be echoed, expanded, permanently treasured, by our literary classes and educators. How few think of it, though it is the impetus and background of our whole Nationality and popular life. In the present brief memorandum, I very likely for the first time awake 'the intelligent reader' to the idea and inquiry whether there isn't such a thing as the distinctive genius of our New World, universal, immanent, bringing to a head the best experience of the past—not specially literary or intellectual—not even merely 'good,' (in the Sunday School and Temperance Society sense,)—some invisible spine and great sympathetic to these States, resident only in the average People, in their practical life, in their physiology, in their emotions, in their nebulous yet fiery patriotism, in the armies (both sides) through the whole Secession War—an identity and character which indeed so far 'finds no voice among their spokesmen.'

To my mind America, vast and fruitful as it appears today, is even yet, for its most important results, entirely in the tentative state. (Its very formation-stir and whirling trials and essays more splendid and picturesque, to my thinking, than the accomplished growths and shows of other lands, through European history or Greece, or all the past.) Surely a New World literature, worthy the name, is not to be, if it ever comes, some fiction, or fancy, or bit of sentimentalism or polished work merely by itself or in abstraction. So long as such literature is no born branch and off-shoot of the Nationality, rooted and grown from its roots and fibred with its fibre, it can never answer any deep call or perennial need. Perhaps the untaught Republic is deeper, wiser, than its teachers. The best literature is always a result of something far greater than itself—is not the hero, but the portrait of the hero. Before there can be recorded history or poem there must be the transaction. Beyond the old masterpieces, the Iliad, the interminable Hindu epics, the Greek tragedies, even the Bible itself, range the immense facts of what must have preceded them, their *sine qua non*—the veritable poems and master-pieces, of which these are but shreds and cartoons.

For to-day and the States, I think the vividest, rapidest, most stu-pendous processes ever known, ever performed by man or nation, on the largest scales and in countless varieties, are now and here presented. Not as our poets and preachers are always conventionally putting it—but quite different. Some colossal foundry, the flaming of the fire, the melted metal, the pounding trip-hammers, the surging crowds of workmen shifting from point to point, the murky shadows, the rolling haze, the discord, the crudeness, the deafening din, the dis-order, the dross and clouds of dust, the waste and extravagance of material, the shafts of darted sunshine through the vast open roof-scuttles aloft—the mighty castings, many of them not yet fitted, per-haps delayed long, yet each in its due time, with definite place and use and meaning—such, more like, is a symbol of America.

After all of which, returning to our starting-point, we reiterate, and in the whole Land's name, a welcome to our eminent guests. Visits like theirs, and hospitalities, and hand-shaking, and face meeting face, and the distant brought near—what divine solvents they are! Travel, reci-procity, 'interviewing,' intercommunion of lands—what are they but Democracy's and the highest Law's best aids? O that our own country—that every land in the world—could annually, continually, receive the poets, thinkers, scientists, even the official magnates, of other lands, as honored guests. O that the United States, especially the West, could have had a good long visit and explorative jaunt, from the noble and melancholy Tourguéneff, before he died—or from Thomas Carlyle. Castelar, Tennyson, Victor Hugo—were they and we to come face to face, how is it possible but that the right and amicable understanding would ensue?

27. Henry James on Arnold's importance, *English Illustrated Magazine*

January 1884, i, 241–6

James (1843–1916) was an established novelist when he wrote this review. He confessed that his essay on Arnold was something of a puff, but the disclaimer seems if anything less sincere than the admiration expressed in the essay itself. James is writing here for an English rather than for an American audience, in part because 'Superior criticism, in the United States, is at present not written', and he may be proving to the English that they know not what they have. Still, his consideration of Arnold is careful and discriminate, and if James's criticisms are brief, they are not suppressed. Most of the essay is not about Arnold's verse, but this, apparently, is in deference to James's readers. He says: 'It was by his Poems that I first knew and admired him.'

It seems perhaps hardly fair that while Matthew Arnold is in America and exposed to the extremity of public attention in that country, a native of the United States should take up the tale in an English magazine and let him feel the force of American observation from the rear as well as from the front. But, on the other hand, what better occasion could there be for a transatlantic admirer of the distinguished critic to speak his mind, without considering too much the place or the vehicle, than this interesting moment of Mr. Arnold's visit to the great country of the Philistines? I know nothing, as I write these lines, of the fruits of this excursion; we have heard little, as yet, of Mr. Arnold's impressions of the United States, or of the impression made upon their inhabitants by Mr. Arnold. But I would much rather not wait for information on these points: the elements of the subject are already sufficiently rich, and I prefer to make my few remarks in independence of such knowledge. A personal acquaintance with American life may have offered to the author of *Culture and Anarchy* a confirmation strong of his worst pre-conceptions; it may, on the other hand, have been attended with all sorts of pleasant surprises. In either event it will have been a satisfaction to one of his American readers (at least) to put on record a sentiment unaffected by the amount of material he may have gathered on trans-atlantic shores for the most successful satirical work of these last years. Nothing could be more delightful than the news that Mr. Arnold has been gratified by what he has seen in the western world; but I am not sure that it would not be even more welcome to know that he has been disappointed—for such disappointments, even in a mind so little irri-table as his, are inspiring, and any record he should make of them would have a high value.

Neither of these consequences, however, would alter the fact that to an American in England, and indeed to any stranger, the author of the *Essays in Criticism*, of *Friendship's Garland*, of *Culture and Anarchy*, of the verses on Heine's grave, and of innumerable other delightful pages, speaks more directly than any other contemporary English writer, says more of these things which make him the visitor's intellectual com-panion, becomes in a singular way nearer and dearer. It is for this reason that it is always in order for such a visitor to join in a commem-oration of the charming critic. He discharges an office so valuable, a function so delicate, he interprets, explains, illuminates so many of the obscure problems presented by English life to the gaze of the alien; he woos and wins to comprehension, to sympathy, to admiration, this imperfectly initiated, this often slightly bewildered observer; he meets him half way, he appears to understand his feelings, he conducts him to a point of view as gracefully as a master of ceremonies would conduct him to a chair. It is being met half way that the German, the French-man, the American appreciates so highly, when he approaches the great spectacle of English life; it is one of the greatest luxuries the foreign inquirer can enjoy. To such a mind as his, projected from a distance, out of a set of circumstances so different, the striking, the discouraging, I may even say the exasperating thing in this revelation, is the uncon-sciousness of the people concerned in it, their serenity, their indiffer-ence, their tacit assumption that their form of life is the normal one. This may very well be, of course, but the stranger wants a proof of some kind. (The English, in foreign lands, I may say in parenthesis, receive a similar impression; but the English are not irritated—not irritable—like the transplanted foreigner.) This unconsciousness makes a huge blank surface, a mighty national wall, against which the perceptive, the critical effort of the presumptuous stranger wastes itself, until, after a little, he espies in the measureless spaces, a little aperture, a window which is suddenly thrown open, and at which a friendly and intelligent face is presented, the harbinger of a voice of greeting. With this agreeable apparition he communes—the voice is delightful, it has a hundred tones and modulations; and as he stands there the great dead screen seems to vibrate and grow transparent. In other words it is the fact that Mr. Arnold is, of all his countrymen, the most conscious of the national idiosyncrasies that endears him to the soul of the stranger. I may be doing him a poor service among his own people in saying this, I may be sacrificing him too much to my theory of the foreigner and his longing for sympathy. A man may very well not thank you for letting it be known that you have found him detached from the ranks of his compatriots. It would perhaps be discreet on the part of the Frenchman or the American not to say too loudly that to his sense Matthew Arnold is, among the English writers of our day, the least of a matter-of-course Englishman—the pair of eyes to which the English world rounds itself most naturally as a fact among many facts. This, however, is after all unnecessary; for what is so agreeable in his composition is that he is *en fin de compte* (as the foreigner might say) English of the English. Few writers have given such proof of this; few writers have had such opportunity to do so; for few writers have English affairs, the English character, the future, the development, the happiness, of England, been matters of such constant and explicit concern. It is not in the United States that Mr. Arnold will have struck people as not being a devoted child of the mother-country. He has assimilated certain continental ways of looking at things, his style has a kind of European accent, but he is full of English piety and English good-humour (in addition to an urbanity still more personal), and his spirit, in a word, is anchored in the deeps of the English past.

He is both a poet and a critic, but it is perhaps, primarily, because he is a representative of the critical spirit—apart from the accident of his having practised upon the maternal breast, as it were—that the sojourner, the spectator, has a kindness for the author of so many happy formulas, the propagator of so many capital instances. He, too, is necessarily critical, whatever his ultimate conclusion or reconciliation, and he takes courage and confidence from the sight of this brilliant writer, who knowing English life so much better than he can ever hope to do, is yet struck with so many of the same peculiarities, and makes so many of the same reflections. It is not the success of the critical effort at large that is most striking to-day to the attentive outsider; it is not the flexibility of English taste, the sureness of English judgment, the faculty of reproducing in their integrity the impressions made by works of art and literature, that most fixes the attention of those who look to see what the English mind is about. It may appear odd that an American should make this remark, proceeding as he does from a country in which high discernment in such matters has as yet only made a beginning. Superior criticism, in the United States, is at present not written; it is, like a great many superior things, only spoken; therefore I know not why a native of that country should take note of the desuetude of this sort of accomplishment in England, unless it be that in England he naturally expects great things. He is struck with the immense number of reviews that are published, with the number of vehicles for publicity, for discussion. But with the lightness of the English touch in handling literary and artistic questions he is not so much struck, nor with a corresponding interest in the manner, the meaning, the quality, of an artistic effort: corrupted (I should add) as he perhaps may be by communications still more foreign than those he has enjoyed on the other side of the Atlantic, and a good deal more forcible. For I am afraid that what I am coming to in saying that Matthew Arnold, as an English writer, is dear to the soul of the outsider, is the fact, (not equally visible, doubtless, to all judges) that he reminds the particular outsider who writes these lines (and who feels at moments that he has so little claim to the title), just the least bit of the great Sainte-Beuve. Many people do not care for Sainte-Beuve; they hold that his method was unscientific, his temper treacherous, his style tiresome, and that his subjects were too often uninteresting. But those who do care for him care for him deeply, and cultivate the belief, and the hope, that they shall never weary of him; so that as it is obviously only my limited personal sentiment that (with this little play of talk about the outsider in general) I venture to express, I may confess that the measure of my enjoyment of a critic is the degree to which he resembles Sainte-Beuve. This resemblance exists in Matthew Arnold, with many disparities and differences; not only does he always speak of the author of *Causeries* with esteem and admiration, but he strikes the lover of Sainte-Beuve as having really taken lessons from him, as possessing a part of his great quality—closeness of contact to his subject. I do not in the least mean by this that Mr. Arnold is an imitator, that he is a reflection, pale or intense, of another genius. He has a genius, a quality, all his own, and he has in some respects a largeness of horizon which Sainte-Beuve never reached. The horizon of Sainte-Beuve was French, and we know what infinite blue distances the French see there; but that of Matthew Arnold, as I have hinted, is European, more than European, inasmuch as it includes America. It ought to be enough for an American that Sainte-Beuve had no ideas at all about America; whereas Mr. Arnold has a great many, which he is engaged at the moment at which I write, in collating with the reality. Nevertheless, Sainte-Beuve, too, on his side, had his larger movement; he had of course his larger activity, which indeed it will appear to many that Mr. Arnold might have emulated if it had not been for a certain amount of misdirected effort. There is one side on which many readers will never altogether do justice to Matthew Arnold, the side on which we see him as the author of *St. Paul and Protestantism*, and even of many portions of *Literature and Dogma*. They will never cease to regret that he should have spent so much time and ingenuity in discussing the differences—several of which, after all, are so special, so arbitrary—between Dissenters and Anglicans, should not rather have given these earnest hours to the inter-pretation of literature. There is something dry and dusty in the atmos-phere of such discussions, which accords ill with the fresh tone of the man of letters, the artist. It must be added that in Mr. Arnold's case they are connected with something very important, his interest in religious ideas, his constant, characteristic sense of the reality of religion.

The union of this element with the other parts of his mind, his love of literature, of perfect expression, his interest in life at large, con-stitutes perhaps the originality of his character as a critic, and it certainly (to my sense) gives him that seriousness in which he has occa-sionally been asserted to be wanting. Nothing can exceed the taste, the temperance, with which he handles religious questions, and at the same time nothing can exceed the impression he gives of really caring for them. To his mind the religious life of humanity is the most important thing in the spectacle humanity offers us, and he holds that a due percep-tion of this fact is (in connection with other lights) the measure of the acuteness of a critic, the wisdom of a poet. He says in his essay on Marcus Aurelius an admirable thing—'The paramount virtue of reli-gion is that it has *lighted up* morality;' and such a phrase as that shows the extent to which he feels what he speaks of. To say that this feeling, taken in combination with his love of letters, of beauty, of all liberal things, constitutes an originality is not going too far, for the religious sentiment does not always render the service of opening the mind to human life at large. Ernest Renan, in France, is, as every one knows, the

great and brilliant representative of such a union; he has treated religion
as he might have treated one of the fine arts. Of him it may even be
said, that though he has never spoken of it but as the sovereign thing in
life, yet there is in him, as an interpreter of the conscience of man, a
certain dandyism, a slight fatuity, of worldly culture, of which Mr.
Arnold too has been accused, but from which (with the smaller assurance of an Englishman in such matters) he is much more exempt. Mr.
Arnold touches M. Renan on one side, as he touches Sainte-Beuve on
the other (I make this double *rapprochement* because he has been spoken
of more than once as the most Gallicised of English writers); and if he
has gone less into the details of literature than the one, he has gone more
than the other into the application of religion to questions of life. He
has applied it to the current problems of English society. He has endeavoured to light up with it, to use his own phrase, some of the duskiest
and most colourless of these. He has cultivated urbanity almost as
successfully as M. Renan, and he has cultivated reality rather more. As
I have spoken of the reader who has been a stranger in England feeling
that Mr. Arnold meets him half way, and yet of our author being at
bottom English of the English, I may add here, in confirmation of this,
that his theological pertinacity, as one may call it, his constant implication of the nearness of religion, his use of the Scriptures, his love of
biblical phraseology, are all so many deeply English notes. He has all
that taste for theology which characterises our race when our race is
left to its own devices; he evidently has read an immense number of
sermons. He is impregnated with the associations of Protestantism,
saturated with the Bible, and though he has little love for the Puritans,
no Puritan of them all was ever more ready on all occasions with a text
either from the Old Testament or from the New. The appreciative
stranger (whom I go on imagining) has to remind himself of the force
of these associations of Protestantism in order to explain Mr. Arnold's
fondness for certain quotations which doubtless need the fragrance that
experience and memory may happen to give them to reveal their full
charm. Nothing could be more English, more Anglican, for instance,
than our author's enjoyment of sundry phrases of Bishop Wilson—
phrases which to the uninitiated eye are often a little pale. This does not
take from the fact that Mr. Arnold has a real genius for quotation. His
pages are full, not only of his own good things, but of those of every
one else. More than any critic of the day he gives, from point to point,
an example of what he means. The felicity of his illustrations is extreme;
even if he sometimes makes them go a little further than they would

and sees in them a little more than is visible to the average reader. Of course, in his frequent reference to the Bible, what is free and happy and personal to himself is the use he makes of it.

If it were the purpose of these few pages to give in the smallest degree a history of Mr. Arnold's literary career, I ought promptly to have spoken of his Poems—I ought to enumerate his works in their order. It was by his Poems that I first knew and admired him, and many such readers—early or late admirers—will have kept them in a very safe corner of memory. As a poet, Matthew Arnold is really singular; he takes his place among the most fortunate writers of our day who have expressed themselves in verse, but his place is somewhat apart. He has an imagination of his own, but he is less complete, less inevitable, as he says in his essay on Wordsworth that that poet said of Goethe, than the others. His form at moments is less rich than it might be, and the Wordsworthian example may perhaps be accused here and there of having sterilized him. But this limited, just a little precarious, character of his inspiration adds to his value for people who like the quality of rareness in their pleasures, like sometimes to perceive just a little the effort of the poet, like to hear him take breath. It reminds them of the awkwardness of line which we see in certain charming painters of early schools (not that Mr. Arnold is early!) and which seems a condition of their grace and a sign of their freshness. Splendour, music, passion, breadth of movement and rhythm we find in him in no great abundance; what we do find is high distinction of feeling (to use his own word), a temperance, a kind of modesty of expression, which is at the same time an artistic resource—the complexion of his work; and a remarkable faculty for touching the chords which connect our feelings with the things that others have done and spoken. In other words, though there is in Mr. Arnold's poems a constant reference to nature, or to Wordsworth, which is almost the same thing, there is even a more implicit reference to civilisation, literature, and the intellectual experience of man. He is the poet of the man of culture, that accomplished being whom he long ago held up for our consideration. Above all he is the poet of his age, of the moment in which we live, of our 'modernity,' as the new school of criticism in France gives us perhaps license to say. When he speaks of the past, it is with the knowledge which only our own time has of it. With its cultivated simplicity, its aversion to cheap ornament, its slight abuse of meagreness for distinction's sake, his verse has a kind of minor magic and always goes to the point—the particular ache, or regret, or conjecture, to which poetry is supposed to address itself. It rests the mind, after a good deal of the other poetical work of the day—it rests the mind, and I think I may add that it nourishes it.

It was, as every one remembers, in the essay on *The Function of Criticism at the Present Time,* and that on *The Literary Influence of Academies,* that, in 1864, Mr. Arnold first appeared in the character in which since then he has won so much fame, and which he may really be said to have invented; that of the *general* critic, the commentator of English life, the observer and expostulator, the pleader with the Dissenters, the genial satirist. His manner, since this light, sweet prelude, has acquired much amplitude and confidence; but the suggestiveness, the delightful temper were there from the first. Those who have been enjoying Mr. Arnold these twenty years will remember how fresh and desirable his voice sounded at that moment; if since then the freshness has faded a little we must bear in mind that it is through him and through him only that we have grown familiar with certain ideas and terms which now form part of the common stock of allusion. When he began his critical career there were various things that needed immensely to be said and that no one appeared sufficiently detached, sufficiently independent and impartial to say. Mr. Arnold attempted to say them, and succeeded—so far as the saying goes—in a manner that left nothing to be desired. There is, of course, another measure of success in regard to such an attempt—the question of how far the critic has had an influence, produced an effect—how far he has acted upon the life, the feelings, the conduct of his audience. The effect of Mr. Arnold's writings is of course difficult to gauge; but it seems evident that the thoughts and judgments of Englishmen about a good many matters have been quickened and coloured by them. All criticism is better, lighter, more sympathetic, more informed, in consequence of certain things he has said. He has perceived and felt so many shy, disinterested truths that belonged to the office, to the limited specialty, of no one else; he has made them his care, made them his province and responsibility. This flattering unction Mr. Arnold may, I think, lay to his soul—that with all his lightness of form, with a certain jauntiness and irresponsibility of which he has been accused—as if he affected a candour and simplicity almost more than human—he has added to the interest of life, to the charm of knowledge, for a great many of those plain people among whom he so gracefully counts himself. As we know, in the number of the expressive phrases to which he has given circulation, none has had a wider currency than his application of Swift's phrase about sweetness and light. Assuredly it may be said that that note has reverberated, that it has done something—in the realm of discussion—towards making civility the fashion and facilitating the exchange of ideas. They appear to have become more accessible—they bristle rather less with mutual suspicion. Above all, the atmosphere has gained in clearness in the great middle region in which Philistinism is supposed to abide. Our author has hung it about—the grey confusion—with a multitude of little coloured lanterns, which not only have a charming, a really festive effect, but which also help the earnest explorer to find his way. It was in the volume entitled *Culture and Anarchy,* published in 1869, and perhaps his most ingenious and suggestive production, that he offered his most celebrated definitions, and exposed himself most to the penalties which the general critic is foredoomed to encounter. In some of his later books he has called down the displeasure of the Dissenters, but in the extremely witty volume to which I allude he made it a matter of honour with society at large to retaliate. But it has been Mr. Arnold's good fortune from the first that he has been fed and stimulated by criticism; his antagonist, in the phrase that he is fond of quoting from Burke, has ever been his helper. Rejoinder and refutation have always furnished him with texts and examples and offered a spring-board, as it were, to his polemical agility. He has had the further advantage, that though in his considerate, bantering way a disputant, having constantly to defend himself, as is inevitable for a man who frequently attacks, he has never lost his good humour, never shown a touch of the *odium theologicum,*[1] nor ceased to play fair. This incorrigible fondness for his joke doubtless has had something to do with the reproach sometimes made him that he is not serious, that he does not really care for the causes for which he pleads, that he is a talker, an artist even, a charming humorist, but not a philosopher, nor a reformer, nor a teacher. He has been charged with having no practical advice to offer. To these allegations he would perhaps plead guilty, for he has never pretended to have a body of doctrine nor to approach the public with an infallible nostrum. He has been the plain man that we have alluded to, he has been only a skirmisher and a suggester. It is certain that a good many fallacies and prejudices are limping about with one of his light darts still sticking to them. For myself, when I have heard it remarked that he is not practical, the answer has seemed to be that there is surely nothing more practical than to combine that degree of wit with that degree of good feeling, and that degree of reason with both of them. It is quite enough to the point to be one of the two or

[1] 'theological antipathy'.

three best English prose-writers of one's day. There is nothing more practical, in short, than, if one praises culture and desires to forward it, to speak in the tone and with the spirit and impartiality of culture. The Dissenters, I believe, hold that Mr. Arnold has not been impartial, accuse him of misrepresenting them, of making the absurd proposal that they shall come over to the Church merely because from the church-window, as it were, their chapels and conventicles interfere with the view. I do not pretend to judge this matter, or even to have followed closely enough to give an account of them the windings of that controversial episode, of which the atmosphere, it must be confessed, has at moments been more darkened than brightened with Biblical references and which occupies the middle years of the author's literary career. It is closed, and well closed, and Mr. Arnold has returned to literature and to studies which lie outside the controversial shadow. It is sufficient that, inveterate satirist, as he is, it is impossible to read a page of him without feeling that his satire is liberal and human. The much abused name of culture rings rather false in our ears, and the fear of seeming priggish checks it as it rises to our lips. The name matters little, however, for the idea is excellent, and the thing is still better. I shall not go so far as to say of Mr. Arnold that he invented it; but he made it more definite than it had been before—he vivified and lighted it up. We like today to see principles and convictions embodied in persons, represented by a certain literary or political face. There are so many abroad, all appealing to us and pressing towards us, that these salient incarnations help us to discriminate and save us much confusion. It is Mr. Arnold, therefore, that we think of when we figure to ourselves the best knowledge of what is being done in the world, the best appreciation of literature and life. It is in America especially that he will have had the responsibility of appearing as the cultivated man—it is in this capacity that he will have been attentively listened to. The curiosity with regard to culture is extreme in that country; if there is in some quarters a considerable uncertainty as to what it may consist of, there is everywhere a great wish to get hold of it, at least on trial. I will not say that Mr. Arnold's tact has absolutely never failed him. There was a certain want of it, for instance (the instance is small), in his quoting, in *Culture and Anarchy*, M. Renan's opinion on the tone of life in America, in support of his own contention that Philistinism was predominant there. This is a kind of authority that (in such a case) almost discredits the argument—M. Renan being constitutionally, and as it were officially, incapable of figuring to himself the aspect of society in the United States. In like manner Mr. Arnold may now and then have appeared to satisfy himself with a definition not quite perfect, as when he is content to describe poetry by saying that it is a criticism of life. That surely expresses but a portion of what poetry contains—it leaves unsaid much of the essence of the matter. Literature in general is a criticism of life—prose is a criticism of life. But poetry is a criticism of life in conditions so peculiar that they are the sign by which we know poetry. Lastly, I may venture to say that our author strikes me as having, especially in his later writings, pushed to an excess some of the idiosyncracies of his delightful style—his fondness for repetition, for ringing the changes on his text, his formula—a tendency in consequence of which his expression becomes at moments slightly wordy and fatiguing. This tendency, to give an example, is visible, I think, in the essay which serves as an introduction to Mr. Ward's collection of the English poets, and in that on Wordsworth, contained in the volume of Mr. Arnold's own selections from him. The defect, however, I should add, is nothing but an exaggeration of one of the author's best qualities—his ardent love of clearness, his patient persuasiveness. These are minor blemishes, and I allude to them mainly, I confess, because I fear I may have appeared to praise too grossly. Yet I have wished to praise, to express the high appreciation of all those who in England and America have in any degree attempted to care for literature. They owe Matthew Arnold a debt of gratitude for his admirable example, for having placed the standard of successful expression, of literary feeling and good manners, so high. They never tire of him—they read him again and again. They think the wit and humour of *Friendship's Garland* the most delicate possible, the luminosity of *Culture and Anarchy* almost dazzling, the eloquence of such a paper as the article on Lord Falkland in the *Mixed Essays* irresistible. They find him, in a word, more than any one else, the happily-proportioned, the truly distinguished man of letters. When there is a question of his efficacy, his influence, it seems to me enough to ask one's self what we should have done without him, to think how much we should have missed him, and how he has salted and seasoned our public conversation. In his absence the whole tone of discussion would have seemed more stupid, more literal. Without his irony to play over its surface, to clip it here and there of its occasional fustiness, the life of our Anglo-Saxon race would present a much greater appearance of insensibility.

28. W. E. Henley's appreciation, *Athenaeum*

22 August 1885, no. 3017, 229–30

William Ernest Henley (1849–1903), poet, essayist, editor, was born in the year that Arnold published *The Strayed Reveller,* yet Henley discusses Arnold as a modern, in some ways *the* modern poet. 'How many of the rarer qualities of art and inspiration are represented here, and here alone in modern work!' Henley's response to Arnold is a testimony to Arnold's impact rather than a careful scrutiny of the poetry: it is the grateful comment of a practising poet. Henley's praise of the 1885 edition represented a new direction for the *Athenaeum,* which had generally been cool to Arnold.

In every page of Arnold the poet there is something to return upon and to admire. There are faults, and these of a kind this present age is ill-disposed to condone. The rhymes are sometimes poor; the movement of the verse is sometimes uncertain and sometimes slow; the rhythms are obviously simple always; now and then the intention and effect are cold even to austerity, are bald to uncomeliness. But then, how many of the rarer qualities of art and inspiration are represented here, and here alone in modern work! There is little of that delight in material for material's sake which is held to be essential to the composition of a great artist; there is none of that rapture of sound and motion and none of that efflorescence of expression which are deemed inseparable from the endowment of the true singer. For any of those excesses in technical accomplishment, those ecstasies in the use of words, those effects of sound which are so rich and strange as to impress the hearer with something of their author's own emotion of creation—for any, indeed, of the characteristic attributes of modern poetry—you shall turn to him in vain. In matters of form this poet is no romantic but a classic to the marrow. He adores his Shakespeare, but he will none of his Shakespeare's fashions. For him the essentials are dignity of thought and sentiment and distinction of manner and utterance. It is no aim of his to

talk for talking's sake, to express what is but half felt and half understood, to embody vague emotions and nebulous fancies in language no
amount of richness can redeem from the reproach of being nebulous and
vague. In his scheme of art there is no place for excess, however magnificent and Shakespearean—for exuberance, however overpowering and
Hugoesque. Human and interesting in themselves, the ideas apparelled
in his verse are completely apprehended; natural in themselves, the
experiences he pictures are intimately felt and thoroughly perceived.
They have been resolved into their elements by the operation of an
almost Sophoclean faculty of selection, and the effect of their presentation is akin to that of a gallery of Greek marbles.

Other poets say anything—say everything that is in them. Browning
lived to realise the myth of the Inexhaustible Bottle; Mr. William
Morris is nothing if not fluent and copious; Mr. Swinburne has a facility
that would seem impossible if it were not a living fact; even the Laureate
is sometimes prodigal of unimportant details, of touches insignificant
and superfluous, of words for words' sake, of cadences that have no
reason of being save themselves. Matthew Arnold alone says only what
is worth saying. In other words, he selects: from his matter whatever is
impertinent is eliminated and only what is vital is permitted to remain.
Sometimes he goes a little astray, and his application of the principle on
which Sophocles and Homer wrought results in failure. But in these
instances it will always be found, I think, that the effect is due not to the
principle nor the poet's application of it but to the poet himself, who
has exceeded his commission, and attempted more than is in him to
accomplish. The case is rare with Arnold, one of whose qualities—and
by no means the least Hellenic of them—was a fine consciousness of his
limitations. But that he failed, and failed considerably, it were idle to
deny. There is *Merope* to bear witness to the fact; and of *Merope* what
is there to say? Evidently it is an imitation Greek play: an essay, that is,
in a form which ceased long since to have any active life, so that the
attempt to revive it—to create a soul under the ribs of very musty
death—is a blunder alike in sentiment and in art. As evidently Arnold is
no dramatist. Empedocles, the Strayed Reveller, even the Forsaken
Merman, all these are expressions of purely personal feeling—are so
many metamorphoses of Arnold. In *Merope* there is no such basis of
reality. The poet was never on a level with his argument. He knew
little or nothing of his characters—of Merope or Æpytus or Polyphontes, of Arcas or Laias or even the Messenger; at every step the
ground is seen shifting under his feet; he is comparatively void of matter,

and his application of the famous principle is labour lost. He is winnowing the wind; he is washing not gold but water.

It is other-guess work with 'Empedocles', the 'Dejaneira' fragment,
'Sohrab and Rustum', the 'Philomela', his better work in general, above
all with the unique and unapproached 'Balder Dead'. To me this last
stands alone in modern art for simple majesty of conception, sober
directness and potency of expression, sustained dignity of thought and
sentiment and style, the complete presentation of whatever is essential,
the stern avoidance of whatever is merely decorative: indeed for every
Homeric quality save rhythmical vitality and rapidity of movement.
Here, for example, is something of that choice yet ample suggestiveness—the only true realism because the only perfect ideal of realisation—
for which the similitudes of the 'Ionian father of his race' are pre-
eminently distinguished:—

> And as a spray of honeysuckle flowers
> Brushes across a tired traveller's face
> Who shuffles through the deep dew-moistened dust
> On a May evening, in the darken'd lanes,
> And starts him, that he thinks a ghost went by—
> So Hoder brushed by Hermod's side.

Here is Homer's direct and moving because most human and comprehensive touch in narrative:—

[Quotes 'Balder Dead', ll. 253–67, 'But from the hill of Lidskialf', etc.]

And here—to have done with evidence of what is known to every
one—here is the Homeric manner, large and majestic and impersonal,
of recording speech:—

[Quotes 'Balder Dead', ll. 236–44, 'Bethink ye, Gods', etc.]

One has but to contrast such living work as this with the 'mouldering
realm' of *Merope* to feel the difference with a sense of pain;

> For doleful are the ghosts, the troops of dead,
> Whom Hela with austere control presides;

while this in its plain, heroic completeness is touched with a stately life
that is a presage of immortality. It is evident, indeed, that Arnold wrote
'Balder Dead' in his most fortunate hour, and that *Merope* is his one
serious mistake in literature. For a genius thus peculiar and introspective
drama—the presentation of character through action—is impossible;
to a method thus reticent and severe drama—the expression of emotion

in action—is improper. 'Not here, O Apollo!' It is written that none shall bind his brows with the twin laurels of epos and drama. Shakespeare did not, nor could Homer; and how should Matthew Arnold?

29. Edward Clodd, 'Matthew Arnold's Poetry', *Gentleman's Magazine*

April 1886, cclx, 344–59

Clodd (1840–1930) was a banker with wide literary interests. In addition to writing several books, founding or presiding over literary societies—such as the Johnson Club and the Folk-Lore Society—he was known for his friendship with distinguished men of the time. In this essay he gives Arnold 'a first place among contemporary poets', comparing him with both Tennyson and Browning. His discussion moves from general assessment and a discussion of 'nature' in Arnold—with reference to Wordsworth and Darwin—to a specific commentary on what Clodd calls Arnold's 'most important poem', 'Empedocles'.

In his preface to 'Selections from Byron's Poetry,' Matthew Arnold doubts 'whether Shelley's delightful essays and letters will not resist the wear and tear of time better, and stand higher, than his poetry.' We may turn this sentence round, and, applying it to the acute critic himself, 'doubt whether his poetry will not resist the wear and tear of time better, and stand higher, than his delightful essays.' For delicate, brilliant, full of *verve* as they are, only those into which the controversial and the personal are not intruded will endure; the rest, despite the rapier style which makes its passes through our smug and vulgarised respectabilities, and which cuts away the base on which miracles and a materialised heaven alike rest, vainly attempting to save Christianity while surrendering whatever is distinctive in it, will share the relative impermanence of all such work, and have small interest for a later time. Probably Mr. Arnold's own sound instinct has, in the issue of his *Selected Prose Passages*, correctly anticipated the verdict of the future as to the place which *Literature and Dogma* and *God and the Bible* will occupy.

In the judgment of a slowly increasing number of thoughtful readers he is winning, as, in the judgment of a smaller circle, he has already won, no mean place among the masters of immortal song, and a first place among contemporary poets. Such an assessment of his position, thus stated at the outset, may sound like a challenge, since it at once invites that comparison between himself and other poets of our time which imports the din of controversy into a realm where we would fain listen only to the lyre of Apollo.

But, nevertheless, a mind like Matthew Arnold's, so individual that no poetic school of Paul, or Apollos, or Cephas can claim it, and flood the market with diluted imitations of the master, will have its unrelation to other minds best indicated by comparison, restricting this to Tennyson and Browning, not only for their eminence, but because they differ as much from each other as Matthew Arnold differs from them both.

The mellifluousness of Tennyson, the music of his verse, secures his work from oblivion. He is a supremely great artist, a brilliant colourist, a very Tintoretto among poets; and while this fair English landscape abides unsullied, he will be remembered as the word-painter in loveliest pictures of its varied moods, its chastened beauty. We wander through his verse as through a gallery of masterpieces, where colour vies with colour, yet with no garishness in general effect. Such is his treatment of all that he touches with cunning hand and faultless metre; but what lies beneath? Mr. Arnold, in speaking of Homer, says that the noble and profound application of ideas to life is the most essential part of poetic greatness; that a great poet receives his distinctive character of superiority from his application, under the conditions immutably fixed by laws of poetic beauty and poetic truth, to his subject, whatever it may be, of the ideas ' on man, on nature, and on human life' which he has acquired for himself. How loyal and thorough to his own rigid conditions Matthew Arnold has shown himself will be considered presently; but applying them to Tennyson, how stands it? Judged by this, his verse seems inadequate; though the words be strong, well-chosen, the fittest for the expression, 'tis 'a tale of little meaning' that they tell. The utterance is larger than the conception; the thought is often of a high average, but average only, at its best; it seldom sets us thinking, or has within it that element of suggestiveness which in poets of more philosophic sweep—Browning, Arnold, George Meredith—carries us into illimitable realms, lifts us to the summit of the mount of Transfiguration. For answer to the larger, profounder questions which seethe in men's minds to-day, we look in vain in the poetry of Tennyson. Pure and noble thought is there, high chivalric notes are struck in its sonorous, majestic music, but rarely the clear, sane, convincing words that shall infuse strength into souls fighting with their doubts. Even in the stately stanzas of 'In Memoriam,' through which we hear the changes rung on 'nature, man, and human life,' we hear mingled too often the notes of an unquiet mind. The tentative theology of Maurice, and the moribund philosophy of schools whose leaders still plead for some reserved place in man or nature where necessity shall have no sway, and law give place to chance, is in them.

Leslie Stephen's criticism on Byron and Shelley applies to Tennyson: 'the world seems to him awry, because he has not known how to accept the inevitable, nor to conform to the discipline of fact.' However intense the feeling, and however exquisite its expression, we are left in a state of intellectual and emotional discontent. While we enjoy his landscape-painting, whether of English meadow and upland, or of lands where 'it is always afternoon,' we feel that he has never penetrated to the arcana of Nature; that she is described, not interpreted; and with deepening experience of life, we can find no satisfaction in poetry whose philosophy is both inadequate and discredited.

In his sonnet on the 'Austerity of Poetry' Mr. Arnold describes the Muse as 'young, gay, radiant, adorned outside,' but with 'a hidden ground of thought and of austerity.'

Turning to Tennyson's great compeer, whatever his muse may lack in gaiety and radiance, she has no lack of austerity. Browning's rugged, healthy robustness is in sharpest contrast to Tennyson's never-limping, ever-limpid, rhythm. Musical and metrical as Browning has proved himself to be in sweet lyric and ringing verse, and masterly in his command of expression, for him the thought is everything, the grace and measured ease of expression secondary, the synthesis subordinate to the analysis. His gems tremble with the light of no common day, but their brilliancy owes nothing to the lapidary's art, nor is even the encrusting ore always removed. In their suggestiveness his poems remind us of the famous unfinished groups of Michael Angelo in the mausoleum of the Medici in San Lorenzo at Florence, only that the incompleteness of the statues was involuntary, while the unshapeliness of the written words is intentional. Both are alike the work of masterly anatomists, sympathetic in their tastes; for Michael Angelo was poet as well as sculptor and painter, and in much of the younger master's work there is an obtrusiveness of the anatomy which makes us desire the radiant, adorned outside of Mr. Arnold's muse, or at least more lucidity of treatment. The poet is not called upon to save us the trouble of thinking, but neither has he necessarily more to tell us, and that better worth the telling, because the language is obscure and the metre unshapely. Obscurity may cover mediocrity as well as the profounder truth. Not that there is anything mediocre in Browning; but with most of us leisure is scanty, if art is long, and we prefer our metaphysics in prose with honest labels on their backs, to thin disguise of them in different arrangement of type. That can be only rhyme or rhythm, or vapid verse, not poetry, which has no philosophy of life within it; but the philosophy must be touched with emotion, and though divine in essence, be made flesh, that it may dwell among men.

Unapproached as Browning is in power of psychological analysis and insight, it is not easy to find attached to his vigorous presentment of the problems of man and nature any solution of them in which a perplexed and fugitive age can rest.

Some quarter of a century after the brothers Tennyson had issued their anonymous volume, Matthew Arnold made his venture, veiling his identity under the initial 'A.' The *Strayed Reveller and other Poems*, published in 1849, was followed in 1852 by *Empedocles on Etna and other Poems*, by 'A.,' two years after the death of Wordsworth, the memorial verses upon whom are among its contents. Then, as the author himself tells us, when barely fifty copies of the volume had been sold, it was withdrawn, and, save in certain fragmentary portions, the great and noble poem which gave its name to the book was excluded from subsequent editions until that of 1867, chiefly on the ground that it lacked the action which could alone relieve the monotony of an attitude depicted as one of endurance and prolonged mental distress. Between the publication of the anonymous volumes and the publication within the last few months of the 'complete' edition in three volumes, the poems have been subjected to rearrangement and alteration. In work where there is no sheen or glitter one cannot speak of polishing and re-polishing; the alterations are mainly verbal, such as one might expect from a master craftsman and fastidious critic in revising his own work. Unlike any of his prominent contemporaries, Mr. Arnold has written no great or long-sustained work, which might be cause of regret if the length of a poem were the measure of its value. But in this, as in other matters, bigness is not greatness, as Emerson says, and diffuseness is often the accompaniment of flabbiness. 'The great artist can express his power within the limits of a coin or gem, the great poet will reveal his character through a sonnet or a song.' In running one's eye down the tables of contents of Mr. Arnold's poetry, one is struck with the apparent tameness of theme; the titles of the early and lyrical poems have the sobriety of the 'Christian Year,' and in the narrative and dramatic poems, wide as is the range from sick Bokhara's king to Balder dead, from the doomed Mycerinus to the wounded Tristram 'famous in Arthur's court of old,' we find no choice of subjects where the thrilling and romantic are the leading *motif*. Supreme artist as he is, master of a style pure, chaste, and well-nigh as faultless as work of man can be, severe in its simplicity, simple also in the main are the materials. Even where they have a studied commonplace look, as in an early poem, 'Lines written in Kensington Gardens,' there the presence of genius is manifest in the uplifting of the simple and familiar to a higher level, in the suggestiveness which is never exhausted, in the hiding of power within restfulness.

In truth, the first impression which the poems themselves, sober in their colouring, scarce a ripple in their movement, playing on no passion, scorning all tricks and catches, frugal of metaphor and imagery, give, is one of disappointment. It is like the oft-expressed feeling on first arriving within the walls of Rome, or on a first view of St. Peter's, whether we see the apparently small dome against a flushed sky from the Pincian Hill, or watch its recession as we approach it from the Piazza San Pietro; a feeling which wears away on nearer acquaintance, and departs altogether when the days spent among the ruins and treasured relics of the Eternal City have become happy memories. But, as the visits there, repeated again and again, deepen delight, so a closer study of Mr. Arnold's poetry deepens appreciation, and we are in the end held by an irresistible charm easy neither to describe nor to define. This powerlessness of definition is in itself evidence of the power of the thing which eludes it, or which would die under attempted dissection, as the sorrow of tears under chemical analysis, or the scent molecules of a flower in search for them among its scattered petals. Nevertheless, some analysis of the distinctive qualities of this passionless, yet stimulating, poetry must be attempted, if only to whet the appetite that it can never cloy.

Beauty of form, felicitous choice of measure, especially in the use of the anapest, grace and steadiness of movement—these are the external characteristics throughout. 'No countryman of ours,' says Swinburne, in his generous recognition of Matthew Arnold's high and distinct place, 'since Keats died has made or has found words fall into such faultless folds and forms of harmonious line. He is the most efficient, the surest-footed, poet of our time, the most to be relied on; more than any other, he unites personality and perfection.' In the subject-matter no 'provincial' note is struck. Mr. Arnold's reading has been wide and deep, and his sweep and range of history is correspondingly large and varied; the processions of the ages file before us in the 'Strayed Reveller'; the advent and varying fortunes of Christianity, in the sequel to Obermann; the Greek, through whose eyes he looks while losing not his own 'sad lucidity of soul,' the Asiatic, the Egyptian, the Scandinavian are there; 'the stormy northern world of water and air and iron and snow, the mystic oppression of Eastern light and cruel colour, in fiery continents and cities full of sickness and splendour and troubled tyrannies, alike yield up to him their spirit and their secret, to be rendered again in just and full expression.'

No surer test of Mr. Arnold's range and greatness and right assessment of men is supplied than in his elegiac poems. That on his friend Arthur Clough, entitled 'Thyrsis,' is placed by Mr. Swinburne, in which estimate most readers will agree, in equal rank with the 'Lycidas' of Milton and the 'Adonais' of Shelley. Wordsworth is the subject of two poems, the 'Youth of Nature' and 'Memorial Verses'; 'Rugby Chapel' enshrines the memory of the poet's father, through whom he believed

> In the noble and great who are gone;
> . . . Souls temper'd with fire,
> Fervent, heroic, and good,
> Helpers and friends of mankind;

'Westminster Abbey,' the memory of the chivalrous Dean to whom, a prey to unrest and weakness, death comes as 'crowning impotence.'

[Quotes 'Westminster Abbey', ll. 141–50, 'And truly he who here', etc.]

The Brontës, Heine, the living dead of the Grande Chartreuse monastery, whose peace he would fain possess while he pours on their faith the impassioned words of regret that he cannot share it; last, but not least, the obscure, serene, and gentle recluse, Senancour, the author of

'Obermann,' one of the few 'who possess their soul before they die'—these defile before us in sombre procession, while in 'Geists's Grave' and 'Poor Matthias' the pet dach-hound and canary have the tribute of enshrinement as sharers with us in one mysterious life and one unknown destiny.

Every philosopher is not, neither need he be, a poet; but every true poet must be a philosopher, dealing with 'nature, man, and human life,' and therefore dealing, as best he may, with the problem how to regulate that conduct which, as Mr. Arnold says in *Literature and Dogma*, makes up a great deal more than three fourths of life. And he is the greater poet whose imagination is most transfused with reason; who has the deepest truths to proclaim, as well as the strongest feelings to utter.

Dealing with the like materials, it is interesting to note, as the roll of English poets pass before us, how varied and progressive has been their interpretation of Nature; how the period of unquestioning delight has given place to that of reflection, and this in turn to the attempted solution of the problems pressed upon us in face of a universe whose component parts are weighed and measured and analysed. For this use of poetry 'in so dealing with things as to awaken in us a wonderfully full, new, and intimate sense of them, and of our relations with them, appealing to the whole man,' as science does, 'and not to a single faculty,' we are indebted to Wordsworth.

The sympathy with Nature, which had been fostered by observation in his boyhood, long satisfied an appetite that felt no need of a 'remoter charm by thought supplied'; but as he advanced in life and experience, he cared for Nature only as seen through human feeling, and made his poetry a didactic vehicle by which to expound his philosophy of the significance of the external world, and by which, in his own words, to 'console the afflicted, add sunshine to daylight by making the happy happier; and teach the gay and the gracious of every age to see, to think, and to feel, and therefore become more actively and securely virtuous.' Full of that imaginative sympathy by which the poet penetrates to the inner life of things, and in a single touch expresses their finer breath and spirit; as when he speaks of

> The silence that is in the starry sky,
> The sleep that is among the lonely hills;

he in the end conceived of Nature as responsive to his own moods, as laden with the 'still, sad music of humanity,' and talked of himself in this fashion to satiety.

This reading of oneself into externals, the 'pathetic fallacy,' as Ruskin terms it, is as pernicious as it is untrue. It is the survival of that fond delusion of an earth for whose sole benefit a sun, of whose rays that earth intercepts rather more than the two-thousand-millionth part, was created; and of man as the ultimate aim and end of the universe. Hence Wordsworth's attitude became that of a pantheistic optimist, to whom the contemplation of the presence

> Whose dwelling is the light of setting suns,
> And the round ocean and the living air,
> And the blue sky, and in the mind of man,

brings relief from the burden of mystery, enabling him to 'see into the life of things'; blinding him, however, to their dark side;

> But Wordsworth's eyes avert their ken
> From half of human fate.

His influence on Matthew Arnold is marked, and in the 'Memorial Verses' the worth of the man, and the debt to him, are acknowledged. 'We saw with his eyes and were glad.' But the master, 'growing old in an age he condemned' . . . an 'iron time of doubts, disputes, distractions, fears,' satisfied not the scholar, on whom the power of the *Zeitgeist* had fallen, and whose interpretation of Nature is the converse of the older bards. With the doctrine of the limitations and persistent lower instincts of Nature's highest creatures, and of the struggle for existence through which above seven hundred million human beings are every century pounded back to nothingness before they have known that they ever lived, the fittest being left to take their chance, Nature, to the truer modern insight, is the joyless, tearless, eyeless; away from and above humanity, careless, ignorant whether we laugh or weep, the infinite, unfeeling, isolated:

> The mystery she holds
> For him, inveterately he strains to see,
> And sight of his obtuseness is the key
> Among those folds.

> He may entreat, aspire,
> He may despair, and she has never heed.
> She, drinking his warm sweat, will soothe his need
> Not his desire.

First Principles and *The Origin of Species* have been published since Wordsworth died, and the poet has to make his reckoning with them, as Mr. Arnold, and, in less articulate fashion, Browning and George Meredith have done. To them Nature, with the larger knowledge gained concerning her works and ways, is the *unalterable*, to whom man, with whom 'she can never be fast friends,' must submit, to whose greatness he must yearn, following after whom he must tranquilly perform the tasks whose lasting fruit outgrows

> Far noisier schemes, accomplished in repose,
> Too great for haste, too high for rivalry.

This truer aspect does not dull the poet's eye to her beauty, but it chastens his descriptions; it does not lessen his awe, it increases his reverence; wherever he stands, his shoes are taken from off his feet as upon holy ground. And it is because Mr. Arnold is as alive to Nature's loveliness as to her rigidity that he is more self-restrained than the poet-painters of her prettinesses. Felicitous epithet, ever wisely economical of its adjectives, sets before us the essentials of the things portrayed. Where can be found a nobler roll of sonorous line than the description of the flow of Oxus to the Aral Sea, which closes the episode of 'Sohrab and Rustum'? In the 'Forsaken Merman', when the father's passion and sadness are stilled with departure of hope that the mother, sitting in the 'little grey church on the windy hill,' will answer the call of her children, 'wild with pain,' to return to the sea-caverns, what echoes of the sea-depths and vivid pictures of their inmates are here!

[Quotes 'The Forsaken Merman', ll. 30–45, 'Children dear, was it yesterday', etc.]

The Alpine air blows, the accents of the eternal tongue play, through the pine-branches in the 'Stanzas on Obermann' and 'A Dream'; the thunder of the avalanche and the hoarseness of the mountain torrent is in the lyrical group on 'Switzerland.'

We stand on Dover beach and

> . . . hear the grating roar
> Of pebbles which the waves draw back, and fling,
> At their return, up the high strand,
> Begin, and cease, and then again begin,
> With tremulous cadence slow, and bring
> The eternal note of sadness in,

the same note that Sophocles heard on the Ægean, the same that the age hears as the sea of faith retreats 'down the vast edges drear and naked shingles of the world.' Mr. Arnold finds frequent and happy suggestiveness in the hush and movement of the stars, and his apostrophe to the heavens in 'A Summer Night'—

> . . . Whose pure dark regions have no sign
> Of languor, though so calm and though so great,
> Are yet untroubled and unpassionate;
> Who, though so noble, share in the world's toil,
> And, though so task'd, keep free from dust and soil!

recalls the lines in Wordsworth's 'Ode to Duty'—

> Thou dost preserve the stars from wrong;
> And the most ancient Heavens through Thee are fresh and strong.

But save that the latter bard has a lyric to the cuckoo, no like reminder comes to us in this breath of sweet country air from 'Thrysis':—

[Quotes ll. 57–76, 'So have I heard the cuckoo's parting cry', etc.]

But we must pass to the essential significance of Mr. Arnold's poetry, that interpretation of Nature which determines his philosophy of life. Perhaps, amidst much variety of choice, the fittest representative poems for this purpose are 'Resignation,' which, included among the 'Early Poems,' has the germs of his matured thought, and the long chant to Pausanias in 'Empedocles on Etna.'

In 'Resignation,' Fausta, to whom the poem is addressed, reminds the poet, as they walk over Wythburn Fells to Watendlath, that they had trodden the same mountain paths ten years before with a 'boisterous company.' They sit down and survey the familiar whole, apparently unchanged.

> The self-same shadows now, as then,
> Play through this grassy upland glen;
> The loose dark stones on the green way
> Lie, strewn, it seems, where then they lay,

the wild brook, the rushes cool, the sailing foam, all are the same. There was a camp of gipsies hard by then; if chance brings them back to the old spot, do they moralise on harder times, stiffening joints, and the law growing stronger against vagabonds every day? No, they rubbed through yesterday, and will rub through to-morrow

> Till death arrive to supersede,
> For them, vicissitude and need.

The poet, by contrast, with quicker pulse, with energy to scan the many-sided life of humanity in city and village:—

[Quotes 'Resignation', ll. 186–98, 'Lean'd on his gate', etc.]

The poet, you reply, is more than man; the gipsy less. True, but the world outlasts them both, and were the scope of human affections widened,

[Quotes ll. 220–30, 'Man still would see', etc.]

The pilgrims, Mecca bound; the Goth, bound Romewards; the scarfed crusaders; these, and all whom labours self-ordained enthrall, set before them death or attainment; but milder natures, freed from passion, fret not that they are bound to submit to what they cannot alter in a world governed by necessity and outlasting all passion. Therefore blame not him who, knowing love as transient, or power as an unreal show, judges human care and restlessness as vain. Rather praise such an one, and make its life's aim not how to amuse, but to set free the heart, to conquer fate by awaiting no gifts from chance, to bow to what we cannot break and draw homeward to the general life. Such an attitude is not weakness or folly

> . . . . in His eye,
> To whom each moment in its race,
> Crowd as we will its neutral space,
> Is but a quiet watershed
> Whence, equally, the seas of life and death are fed.

The philosophy of acquiescence is not necessarily the philosophy of inactivity; we need not cry 'Kismet,' and fold listless hands; in the springs of eternal law and order man may renew his strength; in the freshness of Nature renew his youth, towards her greatness yearn while he rallies the good in the depths of himself. He need be neither madman nor slave, holding false way over a despotic sea, bent for some port, he knows not where, till the tempest strikes him and the wrecked helmsman disappears; or giving his life to unmeaning task-work, and dreaming of naught beyond it, till death reaches him, 'unfreed, having seen nothing, still unblest'; for the heavens above him declare

> How boundless might his soul's horizon be,
> How vast, yet of what clear transparency!
> How it were good to live there, and breathe free;
> How fair a lot to fill
> Is left to each man still!

Empedocles, the subject of Mr. Arnold's most important poem, flourished, as the phrase goes, in the fifth century B.C. He is one of the most imposing figures in Greek philosophy, but our knowledge of him is vague and shadowy. Lucretius, who adopted both his method and his philosophy, speaks of him in his immortal *De Rerum Natura* as 'the godlike genius whose verses cry with a loud voice, and set forth in such wise his glorious discoveries that he hardly seems born of a mortal stock.' The reputation which he acquired as statesman, orator, and physician among his fellow-Sicilians was so enhanced by the popular imagination that he was accredited with miraculous power and venerated as superhuman; in the current belief he had laid the winds that ruined the harvests, and brought back to life the woman Pantheia, who had long been in a death-like trance. According to one story, which has its variants among every people concerning the mysterious withdrawal of their demigods, he was taken from a feast held in his honour in a blaze of glory to the gods; according to another, he threw himself into the crater of Etna so that no trace of him might be left, and thereby the people believe in his translation to heaven; but the volcano rebuked his impious vanity by casting forth one of his sandals, and so revealing the manner of his death. Of his works, which were all in verse, only fragments remain, the most important being a didactic poem on Nature. The doctrines set forth in this are, with much that is wild and grotesque, curiously anticipatory here and there of the theory of evolution, of the doctrine of the forces and energies of nature, and of the oneness of the stuff of which all things, living and not living, are made.

Mr. Arnold lays the scene of his poem on Mount Etna, where Empedocles had promised to meet his friend Pausanias to tell him what it might profit him to know concerning current gossip about Pantheia's miraculous restoration to life. As they pass through a glen on the highest skirts of the woody region of the volcano, Pausanias asks the master to 'instruct him of Pantheia's story,' when Empedocles evades reply, and bids him listen to the song of Callicles, the sweetest harp-player in Catana. When this has ceased, Empedocles touches his own harp, and sings the chant which, with some few notes on the Empedoclean philosophy, contains what may be interpreted as Mr. Arnold's philosophy of 'Nature, man and human life.'

> The out-spread world to span
> A cord the gods first slung,
> And then the soul of man
> There, like a mirror, hung,
> And bade the winds through space impel the gusty toy.

There spins the soul, winning a thousand side-glimpses, yet never seeing the whole; while the gods laugh in their sleeve as man, purblind, 'dare stamp nothing false where he finds nothing sure.' Are we thus the toys of fate? I judge not, but much rests with man himself how best to meet doubt and be not fear's blind slave. Ask me not, Pausanias, how long Pantheia lay in trance, neither about miracles; 'tis pitiful trifling to inquire into the falsity or truth of these gossiping legends; 'ask what most helps when known,' how knowledge shall best aid right action, and the general weal be increased. We, feeling the burden of self, can have no relief from the nostrums of the several schools. The sophist sneers, bids us eat, drink, and be merry, and 'make up in the tavern the time wasted in the mosque'; the pious counsel us to forswear the world, the flesh, and the devil, each shouting that the truth is with him.

> And yet their oracle,
> Trumpet it as they will, is but the same as thine.

For the cure lies within, not without. The creeds of the schools are wearying logomachies; their revelations only supply the materials for the wrangling of the sects, and arrest the growth of the spiritual life:

> Once read thy own breast right,
> And thou hast done with fears;
> Man gets no other light
> Search he a thousand years.
> Sink in thyself! there ask what ails thee, at that shrine.

The neglect of this is why men have no calm. Lacking true perspective of things, right proportion, they make their *will* the measure of their *right*, nursing the delusion that they have claim to bliss, 'a title from the gods to welfare and repose.' Not that the thirst for these is to be condemned; the error is not in man's making them his aim, in seeking the best he can, but in thinking that the world, which 'is from of old,' exists only to insure them for him, who is a 'new-born stranger' here. This is no reason for living basely, for being content with low aims, but it is a reason for not expecting Nature to alter the conditions which are our limitations.

> Streams will not curb their pride
> The just man not to entomb,
> Nor lightnings go aside
> To give his virtues room;
> Nor is that wind less rough which blows a good man's barge.

Nature, with equal mind,
    Sees all her sons at play;
Sees man control the wind,
    The wind sweep man away;
Allows the proudly-riding and the foundering bark.

And not only this: though Nature harm us not, the ill deeds of other men darken life. So in face of vexations and hindrances of our lot, we create illusory causes. Like children who beat the stones they trip over, and who rate the senseless ground they fall upon, we people the void with gods on whom we charge our ills and all the world's evil. Or, reversing the scheme, when the lighter mood supervenes, and life brings joy, we postulate the existence of kind gods 'who perfect what man vainly tries.' We speculate about these figments of the brain, these products of our fears and hopes; we make them in our own image; we speculate about the world, about the things that have been; 'we search out dead men's words, and works of dead men's hands'; we shut the eye and muse 'how our own minds are made,' but we cannot overtake the secrets of the soul's origin and destiny. 'Our hair grows grey, our eyes are dimmed, our heat is tamed'; so, thinking that all knowledge must lie with the gods, we invoke oracle and revelation from them, arguing in our folly that our ignorance gives proof that omniscience is with them, 'that our being weary proves that we have where to rest.' Then, foiled in our search for knowledge, palled with pleasure, without resource enough to invent a new vice, as fleeting youth is spent, and *vanitas vanitatis* written on every rapture past and every dead passion, we create our illusion of another life, which shall redress the wrongs and compensate for the defects of this, and, learning no lesson of self-surrender, of sacrifice of illusions from the experience of life here, we appeal to the gods to give us with them the joy denied us on earth.

[Quotes with brief comments various stanzas from Empedocles' soliloquy in I, ii, 'Fools! that so often here', etc.]

For majesty and repose, for purity and lucidity of thought and expression, for insistence on the patient and willing subdual of the soul to immutable necessity, surely this poem has not its peer among any philosophic verse of our time—nay, since the tragedies of Sophocles and Æschylus. Mr. Arnold is not of the stuff of which heroes or martyrs are made, neither is there in his poetry the inspiration which makes a man die for a cause. But heroes and martyrs tarry not to reason, neither do they wait for the inspiration of poetry as stimulus to action; the world's crises evoke them, their lives are the response, and give material for epics to the singers of revolutions, through whose voice the many 'out of weakness are made strong.' The heroes and martyrs see the vision, and have faith in its accomplishment; the many, purblind and without capacity to nurture lofty ideals, desirous only to 'call their lands after their own names,' need most the incitement to rise above sordid aims into a larger, purer air which verse like Matthew Arnold's exhales.

The abiding qualities which render that verse so wholesome an influence in these times, and in all times of unquiet and practicalness, are its clearness, absolute freedom from sophisms, its frank, fearless attitude towards problems the recognition of whose insolubleness is no excuse for paralysis in thought or action; its nutritive suggestiveness, its pure emotion, without taint, 'its joy within its calm,' its healthiness in counselling introspection based upon faith in the sanity and essential goodness, and capacity for yet greater goodness, of humanity. Its philosophy lies in this—

> Yearn to the greatness of Nature,
> Rally the good in the depths of thyself.

30. Joseph Jacobs, obituary notice, *Athenaeum*

21 April 1888, no. 3156, 500–1

Jacobs (1845–1916) was a prominent member of the Jewish communities both in England and the United States. A student of folklore and a critic—he wrote a study of Tennyson—he was a prolific journalist who contributed to many periodicals. The following essay, for the *Athenaeum*, was later collected in *Literary Studies* (1895). Jacobs's obituary contains praise that may be excessive, but he was not alone in calling Arnold 'the poet and critic of an age of transition'. However, according to Jacobs, Arnold's influence as a poet is minimal, whereas his powers are great; and Jacobs joins the common inquiry into the limited nature of Arnold's appeal.

The terribly sudden death of Matthew Arnold has deprived England of an intellectual force of a high order. A striking and influential individuality is lost to English thought and letters. Matthew Arnold was the poet and critic of the age of transition which separates so widely the England of to-day from the England of the Reform Bill, or, to come down even later, from the England of the Great Exhibition. The changes in taste, in feeling, in the general attitude towards the fundamental problems of religion, of society, and of politics, have been enormous, and in all of them, except, perhaps, the last, Matthew Arnold has been an abiding influence. We shall never, perhaps, fully appreciate the way in which he softened the asperities of the conflicts which raged round him by his imperturbable good humour, and even by the mannerisms which diverted the stress of feeling. The solvent of his criticism was diluted to the exact strength where it could effect its purpose while giving least pain.

He began life as a poet, and in a measure remained one always, if we can divorce the poet from the technique of his art. His was a poetic force, a uniform recognition of the permanent power and reality of the ideal element in human character. His appeal was always to that, whether he were discussing Heine or Tolstoï, Irish affairs or Board schools. So far he was a poetic force in English thought and affairs. But in things specifically poetic he touched his readers less than any other Victorian poet of the first rank. Yet he is among the masters, his diction is unrivalled for purity and dignity, he strikes his notes with no faltering hand. Why then, is he not impressive? Because his problems and his moods are not poetic problems or poetic moods. Intellectual doubt has found its voice in Matthew Arnold's most sincere utterances, and doubt can never touch a wide circle. 'Obermann Once More' or 'The Scholar Gypsy' will answer to some moods of some men as few poems answer to the inmost depths. But the moods are rare among men, and the appeal of the poems must be as rare. Strangely enough, while Matthew Arnold deals most powerfully with one aspect of the inward conflict, he has been almost equally successful in the most objective form of poems, the heroic narrative. When he was urging with all his command of paradox that the English hexameter—the existence of which still remains to be proved—was the best medium into which to translate Homer, he himself was giving in his 'Sohrab and Rustum' the nearest analogue in English to the rapidity of action, plainness of thought, plainness of diction, and the nobleness of Homer. Yet even here we felt that something was wanting, as we feel in almost all attempts at reproduction of the Romance temper: it is not sincere, and cannot, therefore, be great. Where Matthew Arnold is sincere in his poetic work is when he gives expression to his 'yearning for the light,' and summons the spirit of renunciation to support him through the days of gloom.

These moods he reserved for expression in verse. In prose no one is less gloomy than he. If we might define him as a happy Heine, we should give the best point of view from which to survey his prose work, his criticism of life that underlies and involves all his criticism of books, of faiths, and of institutions. Like the German poet, he was armed with all the culture of his time—science does not count in such matters—and like him he played off the one side of his nature against the other. But the circumstances of his life saved him from the bitterness of Heine, while they intensified that tendency to good-humoured tolerance which gave to his work much power in some directions and robbed it of much in others.

It is usual to speak of Matthew Arnold as having revolutionised English criticism, by which is usually meant book-criticism. As a matter of fact he did very little in the way of 'judging' books, and what he did in this way was by no means always instructive or trustworthy. (His celebrated slip about Shelley's letters, the selections he made from Byron, may be recalled as instances of uncertain vision or imperfect appreciation. In introducing the methods of Sainte-Beuve into England, he transferred the interest in criticism from the books to the man.) What he did in criticism was to introduce the *causerie*, and with it the personal element. Instead of the 'we' of the older *régime*, the critic, even if he use the plural pronoun, professes to give no more than the manner in which a new work strikes his individuality. If this method has been the cause or occasion of much affectation in contemporary criticism, it has raised criticism into the sphere of literary art by giving it the personal element. The personality of Matthew Arnold was, with all its affectations and rather because his wit was so mild and free from caustic —the Puritan part of the nation felt that he too was on the side of the angels. He was so respectable, after all. Herein comes the great difference between him and Heine, who was not respectable at all and Renan, who always shows a hankering after the life of *les gais*. But Matthew Arnold was intensely sensitive and scrupulous in this regard, almost to the point of Podsnappery. Therefore the British public would allow him a hearing on the problems of life.

There was no affectation in all this. The Puritan in him came near the self-restraint of his father's Romans, or the artistic balance of life which he respected in the best Greeks. He was too much at east in Zion to be of the stuff of which prophets are made, yet there was something in him akin to the spirit of the old prophets. Hence it was that he was so influential with the Philistines; he was in a measure of them, though he saw their faults and narrownesses. Half humorously he recognised this in one of his books, and there can be little doubt of its truth and of its influence. Because he was of them, the Philistines, *i.e.* Nonconformists and Low Churchmen, listened to him, with the result that the Low Church is no more; and Nonconformity is Broad Church.

We have laid stress on the theological activity of Arnold because its importance is apt to be obscured by the fact that his particular way of putting his solution of theological difficulties is not likely to gain disciples. But for all that, the discussions have had as much effect on English theology as anything of the past quarter of a century, and he himself was in the right in laying stress upon his theological activity and its results as the most influential and most abiding part of his work.

A word or two may here be added on his general attitude towards politics. His appeal for detachment from party politics is part of a general tendency which seems to be dissevering everywhere the thinking part of the nations from active share in the politics of the democracy. The formation of a party of Independents, advocated by Mr. Lowell in the United States, is an instance of what we mean. By adopting this attitude Matthew Arnold showed less than his usual insight and sagacity. His influence in this direction cannot be said to have been for good.

He that is gone would not have been satisfied with any estimate of his life-work which did not take account of his strivings for educational reform, especially as regards middle-class schools. In English social arrangements he saw one great blot, the separation of classes which could be traced to school-days, and he argued, justly enough, that it would never cease till the enormous difference in the tone of boys' schools for the upper classes and of boys' schools for the middle classes was done away with. It cannot be said that his insistence on this point was effectual, though the improved tone of schools for middle-class girls may possibly be connected with it. But there can be little doubt of the brilliant suggestiveness of many of his interesting reports on education, which we trust will be now brought together in book form. Rarely have Bluebooks been made so enjoyable as those which contained Matthew Arnold's racy comments on things in general, and school things in particular.

He was a poet throughout, we have said, and he himself has defined a poet as a critic of life. Would that all poets were critics so genial! In that respect the style was the man, and no man was so charming to his intimates as Matthew Arnold. It may be suspected that when we come to know the private lives of the men of letters of this, or rather of the preceding generation, few will leave so pleasant an impression, few will seem so livable with as he. That easy temper which perhaps prevented him from giving his message in a more assured tone, or from giving a more assured message, made him a delightful companion. And a delightful companion he is, too, in his books, with their sub-acid egotisms, their easy flow of keen-sighted analysis, their sympathy with the ideal, and, above all, that determination to see things as in themselves they really are, which gives the virile strength that would otherwise be wanting. His books and he have done their work so well that they can never appeal to any later age with so much force as they have to this. But because they have had so direct an appeal to this, they must live as typical of our age and representative of it.

31. Frederic Myers, obituary, *Fortnightly Review*

May 1888, xliii, 719–28

Frederic W. H. Myers (1843–1901) was a respected critic, a poet, and a student of psychical phenomena (as in *Human Personality and Its Survival of Bodily Death*). His discussion of Arnold's poetry follows a brief analysis of Arnold's theology, appropriate from the author of *St. Paul* (1867) but not pertinent here. Myers outlines his views in relation to those of Swinburne (see No. 16), whom he finds right in spirit but mistaken in specific judgments; and he goes on to praise the elegiac poet, the sensitive writer of 'Dover Beach'. For 'we recognize that, whatever criticisms of details may be passed upon [Arnold], he belongs for us to that region in which our true being lies.'

Few men, if any, whom death could have taken from us would have been more perceptibly missed by a wider range of friends and readers than Mr. Matthew Arnold. Other men survive who command a more eager enthusiasm, or who are more actively important to the work of the world. But hardly any man was present in so many cultivated minds as an element of interest in life, an abiding possibility of stimulating and fruitful thought. His criticism of books and of life found wider acceptance in the English-speaking world than that offered by any other writer; and even the slight affectations or idiosyncrasies of his pellucid style had become so associated with the sense of intellectual enjoyment that few readers wished them away. And for those of us who were privileged to know him (and few men were more widely known) the keen interest, the sometimes half-smiling admiration of the general reader, was reinforced on its best and deepest side by our perception of his upright, manly, kindly soul. We saw that his manner was saved from any real arrogance by its tinge of self-mockery; that his playful superciliousness changed at once to grave attentive sympathy on any real appeal. And in his talk yet more strongly than in his books we felt the charm of that alert and open spirit, of that ready disinterested concern in almost every department of the thoughts and acts of men.

His business and achievements, indeed, were widely spread. He was an inspector of schools, a literary, social, and political essayist, a religious reformer, and a poet. To the *first* of these pursuits, widening into the study of state education generally, he probably gave the largest proportion of his time, and he became one of the most accomplished specialists in that direction whom England possessed; in the *second* pursuit he was the most brilliantly successful; to the *third,* as I believe, he devoted the most anxious and persistent thought; and by the *fourth* pursuit, as a poet, he will, we cannot doubt, be the longest remembered. We must not, however, speak as though these various activities were scattered or separate things. Rather they formed stages in a life-long endeavor—the endeavor to diffuse, in his favorite words, 'sweetness and light,' by the application to our pressing problems of his own special gifts, namely the tact and flexibility which spring from culture, and the insight gained by a wide miscellaneous acquaintance with men and things.

[Discusses Arnold's public stature and his 'religious attitudes' for two pages]

But on this [the religious] side, as on all sides of Matthew Arnold's nature, he has given us, so to say, an esoteric interpretation, a power of appeal to his inmost self. For his poetry runs parallel to, but deeper than, all his lines of prose expression; it reflects his culture in its Greek and mediæval tale and drama, his social energies in the 'criticism of life' which he judged to be the very function of poetry, and his religion in those melancholy stanzas in which his schemes of renewal, of conciliation, find no place, but which breathe with so pure a pathos the spirit of our unquiet age. And it is noteworthy that the poems are harmonious with themselves throughout. They belong mainly to his early life; but there is no marked difference of temper between the first utterances and the last. He told me once that his official work, though it did not check his prose-writing, checked his poetry; but it may be doubted whether even with complete leisure the poems would have come with much freer flow. 'The man mature,' as he says himself in his *Progress of Poesy* (rather less in 'the grand style' than Gray's)—

> The man mature with labor chops
> For the bright stream a channel grand,

> And sees not that the sacred drops
> Ran off and vanished out of hand.

Or let us rather say that his best poems were sufficient for their purpose already; they were the *suspiria* of moods which will not bear a too frequent iteration, the expression of thoughts and sentiments best seen, as it were, in a summer twilight, with vague outlines somewhat gravely fair.

It is impossible to speak of Matthew Arnold's poems without remembering Mr. Swinburne's eloquent praises, and hesitating to differ from that weighty verdict. But there would be no true respect in a mere half-hearted concurrence, and I cannot help admiring Matthew Arnold's poetry in some ways less, in some ways more, than his poet-critic admires it. And first I must say that his metrical and verbal effects seem to me, for good or for evil, mainly Wordsworthian, and that he often errs by too freely introducing Wordsworthian quaintnesses and prosaisms, without merging them in a flow of melody sufficient to upbear and excuse them. When Wordsworth says of ' The Danish Boy'—

> There sits he; in his face you spy
> No trace of a ferocious air;
> Nor even was a cloudless sky
> So steady or so fair,

there is a quaintness in the first two lines which, taken by itself, would be almost absurdity; but in the last two lines the dissonance is so sweetly resolved that it does but add a touch of *naïvéte* which probably not one reader in a thousand has paused to analyze. But in Matthew Arnold we cannot be confident that his prosaisms will be redeemed, or that adequate pains have been taken to avoid them. In the poem 'On Heine's Grave' we have the lines—

> But was it thou? I think
> Surely it was! that bard
> Unnamed, who, Goethe said,
> Had every other gift, but wanted love:
> Love, without which the tongue
> Even of angels sound amiss.

If this versified criticism (an odd one, by the way, to pass upon the author of some of the most exquisite love-songs ever written) were split up into fragments, according to the Horatian test, it might not be quite easy to discover in it the *disjecti membra poetae.*[1]

---

[1] 'torn limbs of the poet', i.e. his scattered remains.

Again, when Mr. Swinburne singles out the stanza from 'Empe-docles'—

> Fools! that in man's brief term
> He cannot all things view,
> Affords no ground to affirm
> That there are gods who do.

as a 'majestic stroke of reply,' 'scornful and solemn as the forces them-selves of nature,' one cannot help feeling that one of these lines at least affords no ground to affirm that the ode in which it occurs is 'a model of grave, clear, solemn verse;'—and suspecting that, had Mr. Swinburne wished to convert the world to this style, he had better first have burnt the manuscript of 'Atalanta in Calydon.' Surely, as an imitation from the Greek, the one poem stands to the other as the effort of a gifted amateur stands to the performance of a professional pianist.

Or take again a narrative poem, parts of which assuredly have much of beauty. I quote the brief description given by three poets of a single incident, the falling of Merlin into endless sleep. The last lines of Mat-thew Arnold's 'Tristram and Iseult' run as follows:—

[Quotes part iii, ll. 212–24, 'They sate them down together', etc.]

Now compare Tennyson's lines in 'Merlin and Vivien':—

> Then, in one moment, she put forth the charm
> Of woven paces and of waving hands,
> And in the hollow oak he lay as dead,
> And lost to life, and use, and name and fame.

Compare, too, Swinburne's lines in 'Tristram of Lyonnesse,' where the legend is taken in a different way. 'One there was,' says Tristram of Merlin,—

> Who sleeps and dies not, but with soft live breath
> Takes always all the deep delight of death,
> Through love's gift of a woman: but for me
> Love's hand is not the hand of Nimue,
> Love's word no still smooth murmur of the dove,
> No kiss of peace for me the kiss of love.

Surely a broad line is to be drawn between the first of these passages and the other two. The first is graceful and simple; but who would call it inimitable? And who, on the other hand, if he rightly apprehended the merit of the other passages, short as they are, could hope to rival the magic or the majesty which the Laureate can pour into one simple line?

the triumphant ease with which Mr. Swinburne rides over the language as a swan upon the waves?

But, if I may differ from Mr. Swinburne once again, and in a less carping tone, I see much more than he does to admire in 'the plaintive, dejected songs of Switzerland,' and the still sadder poems which touch on 'the small troubles of spirits that nibble and quibble about beliefs living or dead.'

The poems on Marguerite remind one of Goethe in their grave meditativeness, though they have not that greatness of Goethe's which can make even the flute-notes of a personal love-song stand out as from a vibrant orchestral background of the multitudinous passion of men. But they have a vein of sentiment—of pure and lovable sentiment—of which I hardly know like expression elsewhere. They embody the poet's mood as he looks back, with a yearning no longer selfish or even passionate, but which seems the mere intensification of the sense of kinship of all human souls, toward such hearts as have come near to him, and have been swept far from him again, by fault or accident, or the mere flow and stress of Fate. There is nothing that so brings home to him his mortal limitation. $M\acute{\eta}$ μοι γᾶν Πέλοπος[1]—it is not dominion, or wealth, or strength which the gentle soul desires—it is the power of infinitely loving; but alas! no infinite faculty can find harborage in the heart of man.

Lastly, the poems of the deepest, most intimate class—the elegies, and the poems, as one may call them, of cosmic meditation—are surely those by which Matthew Arnold lives most vitally now, by which we may best imagine him as living hereafter. We think of him as of one who to the Wordsworthian nearness to Nature added the solemn sadness of those who look on her with the consciousness that her secret is still unread. We think of him on Dover beach, hearing in imagination from 'the sea of faith'—

> Its melancholy, long, withdrawing roar,
> Retreating to the breath
> Of the night-wind down the vast edges drear
> And naked shingles of the world.

We think of his desire to see before his dying eyes—

> Bathed in the sacred dews of morn,
> The wide aerial landscape spread—
> The world which was ere I was born,
> The world which lasts when I am dead.

[1] 'not for the land of Pelops'.

We think of the new emotion which he gave to man's world-old gaze into the starlit heavens—

[Quotes 'A Summer Night', ll. 76–92, 'Plainness and clearness', etc.]

And we recognize that, whatever criticisms of detail may be passed upon this poet's work, he belongs for us to that region in which our true being lies; that he is made our closer friend by death; and that if there be aught within us which 'inhabiteth eternity,' by that we are akin to him.

32. H. D. Traill, obituary, *Contemporary Review*

June 1888, liii, 868–81

Henry Duff Traill (1842–1900) was a barrister, editor, journalist, and man of letters. He is perhaps best known for his *Social England,* but he was a political writer for the *Daily Telegraph,* editor of the *Observer* and of *Literature,* and author of various books. His essay on Arnold is an assessment of Arnold's achievement and a discussion, in response to obituary notices, of his stature and reasons for fame. Traill finds it absurd to argue—as Jacobs and others had done, and so many others were to do—that Arnold's fame would rest on the poetry. To illustrate his remarks he isolates what he considers to be Arnold's weaknesses or limitations, while admitting to being a devoted reader.

Critics are, perhaps, the only people in the world who do not need the advice addressed in the proverbial lore of more than one language to the physician. To call upon a critic to criticize himself would be quite superfluous. They are always doing it, in the act of criticizing others. At the same time they deserve no credit for it, as the operation is wholly unconscious, and for the most part absolutely involuntary. It has been liberally performed all round in the various obituary reviews of Mr. Matthew Arnold's literary genius and work, and no doubt a fresh example of it is about to be afforded to whoever shall read what I am about to write. No observer of the literary firmament can prevent 'personal equation' intruding into his efforts to fix the exact places of its celestial occupants. The best one can hope is to reduce the subjective element of error within as small dimensions as possible. It would, at any rate, be out of the question to hope for more than this in the case of Mr. Arnold. His work, both in prose and poetry, but in the former especially, was distinguished by characteristics of the strongest individuality; it displayed qualities which are as much overrated by some minds as they are depreciated by others; it enforced doctrines—the prose by precept, the poetry by example—on the soundness of which men have differed since the dawn of literature, and will probably continue to differ until literature is extinguished by Volapuk. To have reasoned opinions on literature at all is to hold strong convictions, or at any rate to feel strongly on the questions which Matthew Arnold's genius and teaching raised as with a standing challenge, and the critic who undertakes to review his literary work can hardly but be conscious of doing so from the standpoint, either of a convinced believer in his doctrines and method, or of a heretic hardened in their rejection. Such a one ought, perhaps, to be aware, therefore, that, in endeavouring to appraise the work of the departed poet and essayist, he runs a risk of supplying his readers with little else than an edifying disclosure of his own orthodoxy or heterodoxy from the Arnoldian point of view on the theories in question. It says much for the artless simplicity of the critical guild that this apprehension seems to weigh so little on their minds. Those who have adopted, equally with those who dissent from, Mr. Arnold's canons of art have in many instances assigned him his place in English literature with a noble unconsciousness of the fact that they have been merely sitting in judgment upon, and with judicial gravity deciding in favour of, their own prepossessions.

Mutely submitting to the obvious retort that I am about to afford an example of the precise foible in my own person, I propose at the outset to examine the comparative estimate of Mr. Arnold's poetic and prose work which has been formed and enunciated by the majority of his posthumous critics.

Now, the first reflection which suggests itself on this point might well be one of a somewhat painful character. It is only my intimate

personal conviction that no such thing as a literary counterpart of Mrs.
Candour is, or ever was, to be found among us—it is only this, I say,
which assures me of the good faith and good nature of many of the
obituary eulogies which I have read. 'It is as a poet rather than as a prose-
essayist,' runs the 'common form' of the euloigst, 'that Mr. Arnold will
be remembered;' and then the writer goes on to say—not 'in the same
breath;' he usually respires for two or three sentences before adding it—
that 'to the great body of his countrymen Mr. Arnold as a poet is almost
unknown.' He will be remembered, it seems, for those achievements
which have failed to attract the attention of the public which is to
remember him. Sometimes, it is true, the formula has been varied a
little, to the advantage of logic; and we have been told that the works
which failed to make Mr. Arnold known to the mass of his contemporaries will constitute his principal 'claim' to the 'remembrance of
posterity.' The critics who prefer this phrase are careful not to commit
themselves to the assertion that posterity will honour a draft which an
earlier generation had returned on the hands of the drawer marked with
the fatal superscription 'no effects.'

I am not so rash as to dispute the proposition that the poet was unknown to all but a very small fraction of those who were familiar
enough with the name of the literary critic, the essayist on politics and
manners, and, above all, perhaps, the amateur theologian. Indeed, the
facts and dates of the matter speak for themselves. It is considerably more
than thirty years since Mr. Arnold published his first two volumes of
poems—volumes which contain some of his best work. Fifteen or sixteen years had passed before his *Essays in Criticism* made their appearance, and it is safe to say that at that time very few, even of those who
were sufficiently struck with the contents of his book to take the trouble
to get its title correctly (the *varia lectio*[1] 'on' has not yet disappeared even
from library catalogues,), had made as much as a bowing acquaintance with Mr. Arnold's earlier muse, or had ever read a line of the *New
Poems* which had seen the light a year or so before. It was undoubtedly
the *Essays* that established his fame with that great world which can be
persuaded by 'persistent hammering,' as the author of *Our Noble Selves*
has it, to read and to admire the excellent in prose, but *not*, or very, very
rarely, the exquisite in verse. This great world was brought to perceive,
or to take for granted, in default of percipient power, that here was a
critic, not only of rare technical ability, but one possessed of original and
fertilizing conceptions on the subject of the critic's art, and the master,

[1] 'variant reading'.

above all, of a style which, whatever fault might be found with it on
other grounds, had become in his hands an instrument of marvellous
delicacy and power. Then the great world condescended to see what
this remarkable essayist and critic had written in rhyme and metre. And
in the course of time they had got by heart the last eighteen lines of
'Sohrab and Rustum' and the handsome compliment to Sophocles at
the end of the sonnet 'To a Friend,' and the description of our Titan of
empire, laden with 'the too vast orb of his fate,' and a few other elegant
extracts of an equally convenient and portable kind.

But the great world never got farther than that. They still continued,
and they still continue, to prefer their 'favourites'—the two or three
poets who have won their way to or beyond the place occupied for so
many years in lonely majesty, like the broken column of Ozymandias,
by the author of *Proverbial Philosophy*. They still prized, and prize above
all others, the three bards whom they have respectively learned to love,
been persuaded to admire, and taken at once and spontaneously to their
hearts—Lord Tennyson, Mr. Browning, and Mr. Lewis Morris. And
since Mr. Arnold as a poet and Mr. Arnold's poems were and are in this
position in the mind of the general public at the time of and since his
lamented death, it follows that, to declare, as has been declared in so
much recent criticism, that his future fame will depend upon his poetry,
must mean one of two things: either it is a polite way of saying that
Mr. Arnold is not destined to any future life at all in the popular recollection, or it amounts to a prediction that, sooner or later, the appreciation, now confined to a few, of his high excellence as a poet, will, as in
the case of his master, Wordsworth, dawn gradually upon the perceptions of the great body of his countrymen. It is possible that Mr. Arnold
himself entertained some expectation of the kind, and that his avowed
belief in the continuing growth of Wordsworth's fame and influence
was associated with a personal hope which would certainly not be
unjustifiable on the part of one so deeply imbued with the Wordsworthian spirit as himself.

It is ill dogmatizing on a question so obviously incapable of more
than a conjectural answer as this. No man's opinion as to what the public
taste of ten, twenty, fifty, a hundred years hence will be in the matter of
poetry, can be worth much more than that of his neighbours; and, for all
we know, the world may be reading Matthew Arnold with eager delight
a century hence, while Mr. Lewis Morris may have long sunk into neglect. The utmost one can say is that it is difficult to detect at present
any forerunning sign whatever of either development of the public

taste. I see no reason to doubt that poets who display Mr. Morris's triumphant address in adapting themselves to the poetical likings of so vast a multitude of their fellow-countrymen will always find innumerable admirers worthy of them. I do not believe that the singer will either get ahead of the listener or the listener of the singer, but that the two will be kept abreast of each other by the link of a quality which Horace, though with a slight difference of application, has described as 'golden.' On the other hand, I do not find any very convincing ground for the belief that the taste of any great multitudes of men in this or any other country will ever be powerfully attracted by poetry like that of Mr. Arnold. Even if the influence of Wordsworth should increase, instead of, as is at least as probable, diminishing, it does not follow that Mr. Arnold's would obtain additional acceptance on that account: for Wordsworth's appeal to the common mind is largely dependent upon a quality in his poetry which Mr. Arnold's is altogether without. Wordsworth lays firm hold of the religious instinct in man. His poetry, for all the mystical nature-worship that pervades it, was allied to a strongly and even almost narrowly personal Theistic creed. There is nothing in the poetry of his disciple to supply the place of this element, except that highly attenuated conception of the 'Something not ourselves which makes for righteousness,' so familiar to every student of the amateur theologian into which the poet and critic so unfortunately declined. It will be a long time before the mass of mankind are willing to accept the 'stream of tendency' as a substitute for their no doubt crude and self-contradictory conceptions of a personal Creator; and when, if ever, they do, they will probably have ceased to care for poetry of the Wordsworthian and Arnoldian type at all. Science relieved by sensuousness appears to be the ideal to which not only poetry, but art of all kinds, is tending at the present day, and if the movement is a real and persistent, and not a merely apparent or merely temporary one, the ultimate effect of that movement must be to crowd out all poetry set mainly in the contemplative key, to whatever tenderness of feeling and truth of æsthetic vision it may be allied. For, so long as this key is maintained by a poet, he will probably never be able to compete for the favour of the average man with those rivals who proceed upon the sound assumption that the average man wants, as Goethe said, not to be made to think, but merely to be made to feel.

In other words it seems to me almost self-evident that poetry in order to be popular—and I do not intend the word in any disparaging sense; I merely mean that poetry, in order to be the poetry of the many and

not of the few—must have something more than the power of delight-
ing the imaginative part of man: it must deeply move his emotional
part. The emotions stirred by it may be at any moral level you please,
however high, or however low; but the stir, the exaltation must be
there. Moreover, it must be a genuine troubling of the waters of the
spirit, and not merely an excitement of the æsthetic sensibilities dis-
charging itself along the channels of emotion. What makes Byron's
popularity so instructive is that we are so often in a position to say with
absolute certainty that the exaltation produced by his poetry is wholly
due to the former of these causes and not in the least to the latter. For the
form of the poetic utterance is sometimes so intolerably bad that we may
be quite sure that the power of the passage lies exclusively in the thing
uttered, and in our sympathy with the mood of the utterer. Lines which
lash Mr. Swinburne into fury will powerfully affect a reader of a less
exacting ear and a less fastidious taste. Mr. Arnold, so far as the faculty
of expression goes, may be said to stand in polar opposition to the
author of *Childe Harold,* and, just as a critical admirer of the latter can
almost always be sure that the pleasure given him by a passage of Byron is
of its essence and not of its form, so he can nearly as often and with as complete confidence say that the pleasure given by a poem of Mr. Arnold is
ultimately traceable to form rather than to essence. It is true that the pleasure is so intense and exquisite as to pass readily with those who are keenly
susceptible to such pleasure into emotional exaltation. No critic, no one
with any strong feeling for style, could find it in his heart to speak of Mr.
Arnold's poetry as 'cold.' To such a reader it is not and never can be that;
but it must be admitted, I think, that the glow which it takes in the mind
of such a reader is largely, if not wholly, self-generated. The flawless
perfection of Mr. Arnold's poetic work in its best specimens, the absolute sureness of his art when the artist is at his best, do much more than
charm and satisfy. They kindle enthusiasm; they elate and excite all who
are capable of being elated by mere beauty of form and mastery of workmanship; and it is easy for those upon whom this effect is produced to
fancy for the moment that their elation and excitement are in some way
associated with the matter rather than with the form of his poetry, and,
in fact, that *their* emotions have taken fire from *his* imagination.

My own impression—and I may perhaps trust it the more for feeling
the incomparable literary charm of Mr. Arnold's best work as intensely
as I do—my own impression is that the idea in question is a pure illusion;
and that it is because it *is* an illusion that Matthew Arnold will never be
more than 'the poet of a few.' It may sound paradoxical to say so of one

who was a genuine poet, and, on any intelligent estimate of him, a poet of no mean order, that he wrote without the genuine poetic impulse: but there is a sense, I think, in which every competent critic will understand what I mean. It would be difficult, I think, to point to any poem of Mr. Arnold's in which he is thoroughly possessed by, instead of merely possessing, his subject—any poem in which feeling and expression are so interfused that the critical and uncritical readers are brought abreast of each other in an equality, though not in an identity, of delighted emotion. Mr. Arnold's poetic imagination was vigorous, subtle, elevated—what you please: but I question whether it ever reached a temperature at which this fusion of form and matter can take place.

It is true, no doubt, that an exceptionally large proportion of Mr. Arnold's work was of such a character as to render the correctness of this judgment difficult to test. His lyrical poems were usually the expression of subdued emotional moods, and in his dramatic, or semi-dramatic, pieces, such as *Merope*, and, in a less degree, 'Empedocles in Etna,' he aimed deliberately at that reserve and repression which is the secret of the Greek tragedians, and which he was too much and too dogmatically inclined to impose upon all poetry whatsoever. Some small portion of his work however, was of a different character, and my point, I think, will appear with sufficient clearness in those poems in which the nature of the subject demands a more sustained ardour of imagination on the part of the poet than Mr. Arnold's subjects usually exacted from him. 'The Forsaken Merman' is a piece which I know to be admired by at least one critic for whose judgment I entertain a high respect; and, like everything else that came from the hand of its author, it contains beautiful passages. But surely, considered as an attempt to give poetic expression to the feelings of the deserted 'King of the Sea,' and to move the reader's sympathies therewith, it is not only a failure, but a failure which trembles throughout upon the verge of the comic. Mr. Arnold had far too keen a sense of the ridiculous to be insensible to the peculiar dangers of his subject, and must have been perfectly well aware of the essential conditions of success in dealing with it. He must have known that the idea of the Merman hovering, with his fishy offspring, about the little watering-place where the faithless wife and mother had taken up her abode, was one which, while it might be kept clear of the positively ludicrous by consummate tact and propriety of poetic treatment, would require much more than this to make it interesting and sympathetic. Art might avail to avoid the provocation of the smile of levity, but art alone would hardly avail in such a matter to convince incredulity. It was essential that the poet should believe most profoundly in, and should feel most intensely with, his own merman, to have any chance of producing a corresponding state of belief and feeling in the minds of his readers. But Mr. Arnold does not really believe in his forsaken merman a bit. He merely uses his subject as a canvas on which to paint a few such exquisite little marine pictures as that of the—

[Quotes 'The Forsaken Merman', ll. 35–45, 'Sand-strewn caverns', etc.]

Or he interprets the plaints of the forsaken merman in language which would be appropriate and touching enough in the mouth of Enoch Arden but which leave us quite cold as the utterances of an amphibious being in whom we find that the author has no more genuine belief than we have ourselves. I can understand people admiring the poem, as the critical friend to whom I have referred appears to admire it for its 'purple patches;' but I cannot understand any one admiring it as a whole, or failing to recognize it as a work of which the initial poetic impulse was not energetic enough to secure the adequate accomplishment.

And I venture to maintain that, with the few and partial exceptions above referred to, Mr. Arnold's poetry will be found full of positive or negative instances to the same effect throughout. It is not cold to the cultivated taste any more than the marbles of Phidias are cold, but to the natural man, to the man who has to be reached, if at all, through the emotions, rather than the æsthetic sensibilities, it *is* cold. The Horatian *Si vis me flere*, &c.[1], may or may not be a true maxim for the dramatic art, but it is assuredly true to this extent of the art poetic, that in all poetry which moves the common mind of humanity a certain thrill of agitation, a certain pulse of passion, is always to be felt. It would be absurd, of course, to deny that there are some short poems, and not a few passages perhaps here and there in longer poems, of Mr. Arnold's in which this throb and pulsation may be felt. But they are composed in his rarer—nay, in his very rare—moods. He does not feel and write at this temperature for long. Such pieces as 'Philomela' and 'The Strayed Reveller' are specimens of a very limited class. In much the larger majority of his poems, and in all the longer ones, the key is distinctly lower, and yet it is in these that his mere *technique* is far and away at its best. Take, for instance, that most perfect of all his poems—more perfect, it seems to me (though I suppose the opposite preference is more

---

[1] 'if you wish me to weep', etc.

common), than the 'Thyrsis 'itself—'The Scholar Gipsy;' and from this take the exquisite picture given in the following stanzas:—

[Quotes 'The Scholar Gipsy', ll. 71–110. 'For most I know thou lov'st retired ground', etc.]

That is pure essence of Arnold—a thoroughly typical example at once of his most characteristic manner and his most characteristic mood. No music could be sweeter; but how low, how plaintively minor is the key! Nothing could be more true and tender, nothing more deeply and sincerely felt than the mood which inspires it; but how alien, how incomprehensible to the mass of men? The very 'scholar-gipsy' himself, the aimless wanderer whom the poet meets in imagination at so many of the spots most familiar in the rural rambles of generations of Oxford students—what sort of a figure does he present to this age of ours? What chance is there of his seizing on the imagination of our 'strenuous time' (Heaven help it!) and of the multitude who have made it what it is? To that multitude this exquisite poem can be nothing more than a fantastic, and indeed reprehensible, glorification of 'mooning.' If it shows, as no one, I think, will dispute that it does show, Mr. Arnold, not only at his best but at his most characteristic best, I might venture, I think, to risk the case for my contention on this one poem alone. No other example of his work is needed, as no better could be found, to show that we have here a poet who has as little chance of finding his way to the hearts of the restless and emotion-seeking Many as he is assured of a perpetual place in those of the quiet and contemplative Few.

If the foregoing view of Mr. Matthew Arnold's genius and place as a poet be correct, we shall be justified, it seems to me, in regarding the early relapse of his Muse into silence without either surprise or regret. We shall not wonder that an impulse which was never strictly poetic in its character to the writing of poetry should have been soon exhausted, and we shall not deplore the reserve which he imposed upon himself from the moment when he became conscious that that impulse was spent. It is, in my opinion, an error of classification to include Mr. Arnold in the list of those poets with whom the critical faculty, strengthening with advancing years, has overgrown and killed the creative faculty. I am inclined to believe that the instinct of the critic—or, at any rate, of the thinker, the philosophizer, the theorist and moralist on life—was of earlier development in him than that of the poet. I do not say they begot the poet, for I cannot believe them capable in themselves of begetting anything higher than a verse-maker. But I strongly suspect that, before his poetic instinct began to respond to the impressions made upon it by the world without, the bent of reflective habit had so far fixed itself as seriously to limit his freedom of selection for poetic purposes from the impressions thus presenting themselves. It is not good for a poet that he should start with a ready-made philosophy of life. It is better that he should evolve it for himself—if indeed it is necessary for him to have one—at a later stage of his career. The ascent of Parnassus can be much more hopefully attempted without any such *impedimentum* in the knapsack of the mountaineer, and the article, moreover, can always be procured on the summit.

It was in this sense that I spoke of Mr. Arnold's impulse to poetry as not being in strictness of language a poetic impulse. I was far from intending to imply that he belonged to that unhappy class of self-deceivers who cut up their philosophy of life into lines of equal or ostensibly equal syllabic length, and occasionally, though not always, jingle the ends of them against each other. He was didactic only in the sense that his already formed philosophy of life, too rigidly prescribed the channels in which his poetic sensibilities were to flow, and forbade their replenishment from any new freshets of inspiration when at last they ran dry. It was to this that I at least am disposed to attribute that theory of his with respect to the functions of the poet which has provoked so much just opposition. His pronouncement upon poetry, that it should be 'a criticism of life,' is the eminently natural deliverance of a man who, though he was born both poet and critic, seems to have almost reached maturity in the latter character before he even began to essay his powers in the former. His own poetry from first to last had been far too much of a criticism of life—too much so at least for its popularity and for the vigour and permanence of its inspiration; and the dictum I have cited partook largely of the character of one of those after-thoughts by which the 'human nature in man' is apt to persuade him that any shortcomings of which he is conscious have followed inevitably from the nature of things. There is, of course, a sense in which it is true that poetry is and must be a criticism of life, but interpreted in that sense it becomes so absolutely uninforming and unfruitful that it would be unjust to suspect Mr. Arnold of having dealt with such insistence on a proposition of such futility. Poetry is only a criticism of life in the indirect fashion in which every human art, or for that matter every human science, is and must be so; and it would be just about as instructive and important to say that the execution of a song by Madame Patti is an illustration of the physical and physiological laws of vocalization.

The poet must describe life—either the life within him or the life without—in order to poetize, just as the singer must breathe to sing; but a poem is no more a critical deliverance on life than a song is a lecture on the respiratory functions. To attempt to impress any such character expressly and designedly on the poem is sure to be almost as fatal as it would be to intersperse the song with spoken observations on the structure and action of the 'vocal chords.'

This 'criticism of life' crotchet was, however, only one of a few critical perversities with which Mr. Arnold alternately amused and irritated his readers; and on these it is not necessary to dwell. It is more pleasant to dwell, as one can do, with admiration almost unqualified on his general work as a critic of literature. Much has been said since his death of the *Essays in Criticism* as an 'epoch-making book,' and, with a little care in defining the precise nature of the epoch which it did make, the phrase may be defended. It would be too much to say that the principles of criticism for which Mr. Arnold contended were new and original—or rather it would be the reverse of a compliment to say so, since it is literally certain that any fundamentally novel discovery on this ancient subject would turn out another Invention of the Mare's-nest. There is no critical canon in the *Essays* which has not been observed in and might not be illustrated from the practice of some critics for long before the *Essays* appeared. But it is quite true that these principles were at that time undergoing what from time to time in our literary history they have frequently undergone, a phase of neglect; and it is equally true that Mr. Arnold's lucid exposition of these principles, and the singularly fascinating style of the series of papers in which he illustrated them, gave a healthy stimulus and a true direction to English literary criticism, which during the twenty years now completed since the publication of the *Essays* it has on the whole preserved. And to credit any writer with such an achievement as this is undoubtedly to concede his claim to a permanent place in the history of English letters.

33. Mowbray Morris, unsigned essay, *Quarterly Review*

October 1888, clxviii, 398–426

Mowbray Walter Morris (1847–1911) was an established man of letters, contributor to periodicals, and editor of *Macmillan's Magazine*. His essay in the *Quarterly* is a general review of Arnold's major works. It is a long, careful discussion, first of the prose, then of the verse. The section here is the concluding half of the essay. Morris is sympathetic, though he finds Arnold limited as a poet; and like many later critics, he judges Arnold by application of the poet's own criteria. 'He has said that Gray's poetical production was checked and limited by the circumstances of his life and of the age into which he was born. Some such influence may, one fancies, have had power over Matthew Arnold.'

Many of Mr. Arnold's critics have indulged in speculations on his chance of literary immortality being founded in his prose or in his poetry. Such speculations may be interesting, but they are fruitless. In his lifetime there can hardly be question that his prose found many more readers than his poetry, because so large a part of his prose was concerned with subjects which will always secure readers more easily than poetry; subjects in some form always present to every age, but for which each age will and must choose its own point of view. When one talks, therefore, of literary immortality, it is clear that the subjects to which Mr. Arnold gave up so much of his time were but local and casual, and cannot have the quality of permanence. It is but a few months since the sad news of his death was fresh, yet even before that day how much of this part of his work had passed out of date, had become, if it was ever a power, a power of yesterday! And perhaps of all criticism this is the inevitable end. The critic does his work; he recalls the old laws from forgetfulness, he gives them fresh force and currency by applying them to the new occasions that his age provides; yet in doing this he but treads in other men's steps, and other men will in time tread in his. The last word in criticism—a phrase so much in vogue to-day—is never really spoken; men will always be finding new ways of spelling and pronouncing it. Literature, manners, theology, politics, in all these matters each age will provide its own criticism, because each age will find fresh occasions for the application of the old laws. And though, when the whirligig of Time brings round a crisis which has perplexed a former age, baffled or timorous spirits may turn back to the sages, who then cheered, rebuked and counselled, to extract some consolation for their present troubles, after all how poor and parcelled a form of immortality is that! To be the oracle of one age and the stop-gap of the next!

But with the poet it is not so. We cannot indeed say that the poet whom we prize highest will be prized highest by our children; we cannot say that the poet who has grown up among us till his song has become a part of our existence, will be even read by our children. But we do know that the genuine poets—*pii vates, et Phœbo digna locuti*[1]—will live while the world lasts. They are the true heirs of immortality. Whatever be the longest term of years allowed by our wise men for this terrestrial globe, so long will Homer and Virgil, Dante and Shakespeare and Milton be read. They are a part, and the most precious part, of the patrimony of the human race, never to be exhausted, never to be alienated. The kings of science will die and others will reign in their stead; history will be re-written, statecraft will become obsolete, creeds will perish; but the poet lives for ever. And his Valhalla grows never full; there is always room in it for whomsoever is worthy of room; for the great pre-eminent masters of song whose might is unquestioned, and for the lesser spirits who yet by virtue of the genuine touch have escaped oblivion. In the same hall where Homer and where Shakespeare are, sit, on lowlier thrones and robed in less abundant majesty, Catullus and Burns and Heine.

All poetry, all good literature, says Matthew Arnold, is at bottom a criticism of life. The phrase seems to have given much offence, and perhaps, as by criticism is now commonly understood the chatter of the journals on current productions, its use was unfortunate. Yet surely the significance he gave to the phrase is clear enough. The real permanence and value of poetry depends not on its fine passages, not on the grace of its language or the beauty of its melody, but on its eternal truth, on its relation to the eternal laws of human nature and human life,

---

[1] 'pious seers [poets] and such as speak things worthy of Phoebus'.

on what Mr. Arnold calls its 'profound application of ideas to life;' and what is this, using the word not in its bounded and local interpretation, but in its broad universal significance—what is this but a criticism of life? Beauty of language, of rhythm, of melody, these are certainly indispensable to the best poetry; without them the profoundest truth will not avail to reach beyond the power of prose. 'In poetry, the criticism of life has to be made conformably to the laws of poetic truth and poetic beauty. Truth and seriousness of substance and matter, felicity and perfection of diction and manner, as these are exhibited in the best poets, are what constitute a criticism of life made in conformity with the laws of poetic truth and poetic beauty.' When Mr. Arnold's unlucky phrase is thus qualified with his own words, its truth is surely unimpeachable. Readers, of course, there will always be who will take more pleasure, and genuine pleasure, in the lighter and more volatile beauties of poetry, as we may call them, than in its moral truths; and there is no doubt poetry which lives by the exquisite grace, felicity, and sweetness of its numbers. Many of the Elizabethan poets thus live, Herrick for example, and Wither. And of later poets Shelley lives mainly by his extraordinary gift of these qualities and his incomparable use of them. For sheer beauty of sound it would be hard, for example, to surpass such lines as these anywhere in English poetry:

> And the rose, like a nymph to the bath addrest,
> Which unveiled the depth of her glowing breast,
> Till, fold after fold, to the fainting air
> The soul of her beauty and love lay bare.

Yet how do they stand when placed beside such a passage as this?

> To-morrow, and to-morrow, and to-morrow,
> Creeps in this petty pace from day to day
> To the last syllable of recorded time,
> And all our yesterdays have lighted fools
> The way to dusty death.

If, then, we apply his own test to it, what is the criticism of life we find in Matthew Arnold's poetry? Is it just, clear, helpful in its application of ideas to life? One of the few lines of his which seem to have gained the currency of general quotation is that in which he sums up the merit of Sophocles's poetry,

> Who saw life steadily, and saw it whole.

327

Do we get the same impression from Mr. Arnold's poetry?

In one of his early pieces,—in the 'Memorial Verses' on Byron, Goethe, and Wordsworth, which for insight, comprehensiveness, and the skill with which the salient points of the subjects are selected and exhibited, may match with his best prose criticism—he thus marks the essential value of Wordsworth's poetry:

[Quotes 'Memorial Verses', ll. 58–70, 'Ah, since dark days still,' etc.]

It is true that he has elsewhere qualified this praise by the admission, that Wordsworth's view of life was partial, that there was a 'half of human fate' from which he kept his eyes resolutely averted. Wordsworth's view was not the 'wide and luminous' view of Goethe, but Goethe's course it is not now possible, or possible to but very few, to emulate. He had the priceless advantage of growing to manhood in a more tranquil world than that in which our birth was cast:

> But we, brought forth and reared in hours
> Of change, alarm, surprise,—
> What shelter to grow ripe is ours?
> What leisure to grow wise?

And in this conclusion Mr. Arnold seemed content to rest, content like his great master to put by 'the cloud of mortal destiny' since he could not confront it like Byron, nor steer his course through it like Goethe. But we never find assurance that he did put it by. The greater part of his poetry is occupied more or less explicitly with its enervating, engrossing influence, with protests against them, with exhortations to cast them off, and with confessions of man's general powerlessness to cast them off. His ideal of existence (as expressed in the poem called 'The Second Best') was moderation in all things, in study and leisure, in pleasure and suffering,—in a word, σωφροσύνη,[1] that peculiarly Greek notion which Socrates and Charmides discussed in the *palæstra* of Taureas, and which Plato has elsewhere defined as that general balance of body and soul which makes a man his own master. But in the press and hurry of modern life this is an impossible ideal; the best a man can do is to reject what cannot clear and console him, and to take for his watch-words, Hope, Light, Persistence. But yet the haunting doubt will rise, is this enough? Calm, he confesses, is well, but it is not life's crown. Men, ignorant or careless of their own comfort, will still immesh themselves in the doubts and self-torments of Hamlet. And they, too, lead to nothing: they but drive

[1] Roughly: 'the virtue of moderation'.

one round and round the eternal circle. 'Art still has truth', counselled Goethe; 'take refuge there.' But even art cannot wholly suffice, as Empedocles found,—Empedocles who, in Mr. Arnold's hands, becomes the embodiment of the modern spirit in the antique flesh. Nature sufficed for Wordsworth. In the contemplation of Nature he found not only the power to lighten 'the burden of the mystery,' but also a 'joy of elevated thoughts': in her presence the 'still, sad music of humanity' ceased to be harsh and grating, and sounded only to chasten and subdue. But the lesson Nature had for Wordsworth's pupil was not to rejoice, but to bear.

Even the great spirits on whom he had once rested, the 'masters of the mind' who had shown him in his younger days the 'high, white star of Truth,' seem to have failed him in his need. In the cloisters of the Grande Chartreuse he found, or thought he found, a momentary ease in the contemplation of the still, unvexed life of its inhabitants; yet this, too, but repeated the lesson of the stars and the hills and the waters,—that all man could do was to bear in silence the ills he could not cure. It is in the poem which commemorates his visit to the famous monastery of St. Bruno,—in the melancholy beauty of its cadences and grace of words perhaps the supreme example of the author's art—that we get the most complete, the most poetically as well as the most spiritually complete expression of this mood. It is idle to ask if, and how far it represents a genuine picture of the poet's mind. Such questions can never be answered, least of all by the poet himself. It has been the fashion to say that Byron could never be sincere, that he was always posing; but every man, who writes much about himself and his own relation to the world, must sometimes pose. Some will do so in more, some in less degree, with more or less consciousness, but all will do it in some degree. Of course, this mood of unrest and discontent, this world-sickness, as the Germans call it, is no new thing. It drove Empedocles to the only refuge he could find, but the young harp-player mocked at Pausanias's explanation of his friend's trouble.

> 'Tis not the times, 'tis not the sophists vex him;
> There is some root of suffering in himself,
> Some secret and unfollowed vein of woe,
> Which makes the time look black and sad to him.

No sufferer will ever be able to clearly distinguish between the two causes of his sickness, the external cause, and the cause at work within him; and few indeed are the physicians who will be able to distinguish for him. Hamlet and Faust felt the same sickness long before Obermann, long before the author of the lines to the memory of Obermann. And the time when Matthew Arnold was growing to manhood was a time of general stir and change everywhere, in religion, in politics, in society at home and abroad. The Oxford, to which young Arnold went from Rugby, was a house divided against itself. The wonderful man, whom we now call Cardinal Newman, was still a presence and a power there. 'He was close at hand to us at Oxford; he was preaching in St. Mary's pulpit every Sunday; he seemed about to transform and to renew what was for us the most national and natural institution in the world, the Church of England. Who could resist the charm of that spiritual apparition, gliding in the dim afternoon-light through the aisles of St. Mary's, rising into the pulpit, and then, in the most entrancing of voices, breaking the silence with words and thoughts which were a religious music,—subtle, sweet, mournful?' But the presence passed, and on too many minds the power worked only for confusion. He found sources of consolation denied to others, and a final refuge for his perplexities which they could not find. They were left, so this one says, waiting for 'the spark from heaven,' and faltering life away in new beginnings to end only in new disappointments.

> We others pine,
> And wish the long unhappy dream would end,
> And waive all claims to bliss, and try to bear;
> With close-lipped patience for our only friend,
> Sad patience too near neighbour to despair.

Clearly this is not the mood to engender a very profound or general application of ideas to life.

The author of 'Obermann' fled from the distracting world to the silence of the mountains. But they availed him not, or, like Empedocles, he could not bear them. He returned to Paris, and wrote for the newspapers. Is it altogether fanciful to picture Matthew Arnold like another de Senancour, like another Empedocles, finding the solitude and austerity of his poetic ideals unendurable, returning to the haunts of men, and once more, in a curious, yet withal somewhat contemptuous mood, interesting himself in their affairs; exchanging the young Apollo— 'though young, intolerably severe'—for Arminius and the Alderman-Colonel and Bottles, and those other companions of his latter years which we could, for our part, so well dispense with? At any rate the fact stands that, after his tenure of the Chair of Poetry at Oxford came to an end, Mr. Arnold, with the rare exceptions already noted, wrote no more poetry, and in literature generally may be said to have left the purer heights for the crowded levels of men.

But during the years of his poetical production he was at least staunch to his ideal. Whatever of genuineness, of native impulse and feeling there was in his attitude, at least he never changed it. This note of unrest, confusion, powerlessness—'the eternal note of sadness' which Sophocles 'heard long ago on the Ægæan'—runs through nearly all his poetry. It runs through 'Empedocles on Etna'—where the subject indeed seems to have been expressly chosen for the sake of the note—through the 'Stanzas from the Grande Chartreuse,' and the two poems to the author of 'Obermann,' through 'Resignation' and 'A Southern Night,' through 'Thyrsis' and 'The Scholar-Gipsy,' and through nearly all his shorter pieces. In 'Rugby Chapel,' indeed, it is hushed for awhile in proud and affectionate remembrance of the guide whom he had too early lost. But that beautiful tribute to the memory of his dead father breathes love and admiration only: it recognizes the value of such strong and cheerful souls, 'helpers and friends of mankind'; but it never seems in the least interested to discover the true secret of their cheerfulness and strength. All his most characteristic and finished work is, in a word, but an amplification of Wordsworth's famous couplet:—

> The world is too much with us; late and soon,
> Getting and spending, we lay waste our powers:

and it is curious to note that, deeply as Mr. Arnold had studied the old Pagan life and its literature, the side of it which seemed to have most attraction to him was not its old ideal, cheerful, sensuous side, beautifully as he has at times expressed it, but that which foreshadowed his own mood; the reflection that even the noblest and most successful effort that poetry has ever made as 'priestess of the imaginative reason, of the element by which the modern spirit, if it would live right, has chiefly to live,' was after all imperfect, that 'even of the life of Pindar's time, Pompeii was the inevitable bourne.' The joy of life, Empedocles is made to say, can only be felt by those 'who dwell on a firm basis of content.' The attraction he found in the Pagan life was not drawn from that period of its history when, more firmly perhaps than they have ever again rested or are destined to rest, men dwelt on such a basis, but from that period when their foundations had begun to fail them, when their minds had begun to take the ply of Hamlet and of Faust.

Tried, therefore, by his own supreme test, it seems impossible to call Matthew Arnold's poetry satisfactory. His criticism of life is not false, but it is partial and negative, and negative criticism alone can never be of any real service; it gives nothing to rest on, except for those souls who can enjoy 'the ecstasy of woe,' and, like Master Stephen, are content to get themselves stools to be melancholy upon. But poetry, Mr. Arnold has somewhere said, is made up of moral truths and natural magic. It is in the moral truths of course that the criticism of life lies, but the natural magic must be considered too.

We have said that Mr. Arnold did not probably feel the poetic impulse at any time very irresistibly. Nature, to use his fine phrase for Wordsworth, seems never to have taken the pen out of his hand and written for him. We are never impressed by him, as we are impressed by Byron, with the excellence of his sincerity and strength. Even on the rare occasions when he followed his own advice to young poets, and chose for his subject great human actions, and intense situations, as in 'Sohrab and Rustum' and 'Tristram and Iseult,' he rarely, if ever, so impresses us. Even in the scene between the dying Tristram and Iseult of Ireland—perhaps the intensest situation he has ever exhibited—it is but the memory of their passion which stirs the long-parted lovers; the 'anxious day' has come to evening. And in 'Sohrab and Rustum,' where the final situation is indisputably tragic and intense, it is not the human element which pleases most. Most readers have, we suspect, passed not without some sense of relief from the vision of Rustum bowed with muffled head over his dead son to the stately lines through which the majestic river moves along to its luminous home of waters—

> from whose floor the new-bathed stars
> Emerge, and shine upon the Aral Sea.

In 'The Sick King of Bokhara,' it is rather the colours of the Eastern picture that linger in our memory than the human figures: the night with wind and burning dust, the pool under the shade of the mulberry-trees, the high-heaped booths in the Registàn, the squares of coloured ice, 'with cherries served in drift of snow,' the enamelled mosques, the fretted brick-work tomb,

> Hard by a close of apricots,
> Upon the road to Samarcand,

are not these more real to us than the troubles of the repentant Moollah and of the young misdoubting King? Of course his advice on the choice of subjects needs some qualification, as he owned, when applied to lyric poetry; and it is in lyric poetry and elegiac, which in his hands is practically lyric, that his strength mainly lies: for narrative poetry he needed more swiftness, more directness and force. But even in lyric poetry the passionate mood did not suit him. 'Stormily-sweet' is the epithet he has given to Byron's cry; his own cry was often exquisitely sweet, but stormy,—never! His sentimental Sappho is but a faint reflex indeed of Phaon's high-hearted lover.

> They are gone—all is still! Foolish heart, dost thou quiver?
> Nothing stirs on the lawn but the quick lilac-shade.
> Far up shines the house, and beneath flows the river—
> Here lean my head on this cold balustrade!

These lines have left most readers, we suspect, very much in the case of the balustrade. Nor do the various poems to Marguerite move us much more; though they contain some beautiful passages, and notably one of the most impressive and felicitous lines Mr. Arnold ever wrote,—'the unplumb'd, salt, estranging sea.'

> Forgive me! forgive me!
> Ah, Marguerite, fain
> Would these arms reach to clasp thee!
> But see! 'tis in vain.

In vain, most assuredly!

> Not here, O Apollo,
> Are haunts meet for thee!

In one of his early essays Macaulay has well said that to Shelley of all modern poets the old terms *bard* and *inspiration* are most signally applicable:—'He was not an author, but a bard. His poetry seems not to have been an art, but an inspiration.' No one could truly say this of Matthew Arnold's poetry. It was an art, often a beautiful, an exquisite art, but an art always. Hardly ever, if ever, do we get from it that sense of inevitableness which Wordsworth complained was wanting in Goethe's poetry. His faults were never the faults of a great genius, exulting in the consciousness of its power and careless of those devices, by which lesser spirits seek to atone for the deficiencies of nature. 'I,' he has said,

> I, with little land to stir,
> Am the exacter labourer.

His poetry seems rather to have been the result of an exquisite sense for literature, stimulated by a careful and loving study and a rare perception of what is sound and beautiful in poetry, than a genuine poetic impulse. And his faults, when they come, come sometimes from his choice of a subject not truly poetical, or of a subject which needs a more quickening influence than that which stood in him for the genuine poetic impulse, for the accident of inspiration, as he somewhere calls it. On the other hand this perception of what was beautiful and sound in poetry, acting on his own native sense for style, rarely leaves him helpless. His sense for style and language, his distinction, to use one of his own favourite words, rarely desert him; and they help him over many passages where his imagination flags, and the subject is itself perhaps not very interesting. This sense is of course eminently conspicuous in his prose; but it is even more conspicuous in his best poetry. And besides, the inevitable restrictions of metre and rhythm seemed to have braced and purified it; in poetry he is far more seldom diffuse, he far more seldom repeats himself than in prose. Many are the passages in his prose, where the words convey the sense so perfectly that it seems impossible to add or take from them so much as a syllable, and where yet the sense suggested extends far beyond the mere verbal expression—passages admirably illustrating Marlowe's happy phrase, 'Infinite riches in a little room,'—yet nowhere in his prose has he anything to match on this side those lines in which he has summed up the mystery of Shakespeare:

> Others abide our question. Thou art free.
> We ask and ask—Thou smilest and art still,
> Out-topping knowledge.

This fine sense for language is never better seen than in his descriptions. In them he has touches of natural magic that it would be hard to match outside Shakespeare and Keats and Lord Tennyson; there indeed his words do almost seem inevitable; there truly do we get,

> All the charm of all the Muses
> Often flowering in a lonely word.

Such phrases as the 'warm, green-muffled Cumner hills,' or the 'wide fields of breezy grass, Where black-winged swallows haunt the glittering Thames,' leave nothing unsaid for all who know those pastoral slopes at whose feet Oxford lifts her 'dreaming spires' to their 'mild canopy of English air.' Perhaps the richest expression of this sense in his poetry is to be found in this passage from 'Thyrsis,' which is indeed, like its companion piece, 'The Scholar-Gipsy,' full of such exquisite bits of scenery.

[Quotes 'Thyrsis', ll. 51–76, 'So, some tempestuous moon', etc.]

We have said that for narrative poetry Mr. Arnold needed more swiftness, more directness and force. Yet he could, as he has said of Byron, make a single incident strikingly vivid and clear. Take from that incomparable chorus in 'Empedocles on Etna' which records the victory of Apollo over Marsyas, take the picture of,

> The red-snooded Phrygian girls,
> Whom the summer evening sees
> Flashing in the dance's whirls
> Underneath the starlit trees
> In the mountain villages.

or of the Mænads pleading with Apollo for the defeated Faun, from the same chorus:

[Quotes ll. 151–64, 'But the Mænads, who were there', etc.]

And though the note of passion is absent from his poetry, the note of pathos is frequent in it. He had not indeed what he has somewhere called the 'intolerable pathos' of Burns, nor the haunting melancholy of Shelley, nor the majestic sadness which breathes at moments through Milton's stateliest verse; his pathos was rather Virgilian in the tender grace of such lines as these, from 'Obermann Once More':

> Now he is dead! Far hence he lies
> In the lorn Syrian town;
> And on his grave with shining eyes,
> The Syrian stars look down.

Or of these, from 'A Southern Night';

> Mild o'er her grave, ye mountains, shine!
> Gently by his, ye waters glide!
> To that in you which is divine
> They were allied.

There is a peculiar exaltation of the mind, a fine frenzy, in reading those majestic bursts of song, which, like some mighty torrent, seem to burst irresistibly and, as it were, insensibly from the poet's soul. This sensation, this lifting of the feelings, Matthew Arnold's poetry does not give us. But in the measured grace, the trained harmonious expression of well-ordered thoughts, there is a charm and a contentment too; and in these qualities it is rarely wanting. Popular it has never been, as Byron's poetry was once popular, as Lord Tennyson's poetry is popular now. Nor is it ever likely to be popular hereafter. If destined to live, it will live, as in its author's own day, in the hearts of the few, and they will atone, by their close and unchanging devotion, for the more tumultuous but more fickle enthusiasm of the crowd. The number of those who are taken by the grave and so often melancholy beauty which stamps his verse never make the majority in any age; and for the rest, his subjects were as a rule too much outside the general groove of human interests to make them popular; his application of ideas to life was too partial and limited, though it would be hardly true, perhaps, to say that it was transitory, for the phase of life it touches has always in some degree existed and will exist. Great actions, noble personages, intense situations, —with these his poetry, whether from choice or necessity, rarely deals, and when it does, deals not in its best manner. The mood which inspired him, and which he in turn helped to foster, finds a different expression in every age, and needs a different physician. He has said that Gray's poetical production was checked and limited by the circumstances of his life and of the age into which he was born. Some such influence may, one fancies, have had power over Matthew Arnold; and this may help to account for the perversity and flippancy of some of his prose-writing. 'He could not do the thing he would.' Certainly one gets from even his best work a sense of something wanting, of insufficiency, a feeling that from a talent so fine and well-nurtured some wider and more active result should have issued. But it is vain to regret what a man was not, or to blame him for not being something other than he was. Vain is it also, we have said, to speculate on the chances of immortality, vainer still to predict it; and perhaps that part of a man's work for which his own age is most apt to predict immortality is soonest rejected. Yet if the quality of distinction is to hold in the future the place he has assigned to it, it should avail with Matthew Arnold. For it is this quality which marks all his best work, which singles him out from his contemporaries, and makes him not greater than them nor better, but something different from them. And for its sake he should keep the favour of those who can recognize and appreciate it, even should that day ever dawn when the mood he has so beautifully expressed has become in very truth 'a passed mode, an outworn theme.'

34. Rowland Prothero on Arnold's poetic career, *Edinburgh Review*

October 1888, clxviii, 337-73

Prothero (1851-1937), who accepted a peerage in 1919, was an editor, author, and administrator. His edition of Byron's *Letters and Journals* is well known, but Prothero also edited the *Quarterly Review*, wrote books on farming, entered Parliament, and served as President of the Board of Agriculture. His essay on Arnold is long, but it is acute and considered. Arnold, he thinks, made his appeal in spite of clear deficiencies as a poet because 'he expresses the unrest, the bewilderment, the perplexity of a doubting age'. Like Henry Hewlett, Prothero sees a gradual emergence of Hebraism in Arnold's poetry, but he goes further and is one of the first critics to speak of discernible stages in the poetic career.

Arnold the theologian and critic addressed a wider circle of readers than Arnold the poet. Yet his verse contains all that constitutes the permanent worth of his critical or theological writings, purified from the mannerisms and blemishes which mar the otherwise perfect beauty of his prose. A large section of his poetry consists almost entirely of criticism, whether social, moral, and religious—as in so many of his semi-didactic meditative compositions, or literary and æsthetic—as in his brilliant estimates of Byron, Heine, Goethe, Wordsworth, and in his exposition of the essential differences between the artistic spheres of musicians, painters, and poets. Whether his criticism assumed the form of prose or verse, he is rarely deserted by his innate faculty of felicitous diction, by his imaginative insight and interpretative instinct, by his sensitive delicacy of refinement, by his intellectual alertness, power of association, and promptitude to seize the best points of view. It is, however, in his verse that these gifts find their finest expression, because there the effect is heightened by a subdued emotional fervour. For the display of his ironic humour his poetry affords no scope; but with this exception all

337

the valuable elements of his prose writings are reproduced, while the half-cynical levity in the presence of venerable shrines, and the light banter, which some applaud for its pungency and others deprecate for its flippancy, are wholly absent. Nor is it only the mental gifts of the man that are best studied in his poetry. His inner character is there most truly mirrored. There we learn, what his prose sometimes teaches us to forget, that apparent levity is as little inconsistent with real earnestness as bluster is an irrefragable proof of intrepidity. There we find unplumbed springs of pathos and unsuspected currents of wistful affection which well up to the surface in his elegiac verse, and, breaking the superficial film of his serenity, afford us a glimpse into the hidden depths of his studiously veiled personality. His grave and mournful poetry never verges upon mockery; he is reverent to faiths which he cannot share; he views the world of folly and sorrow with melancholy tenderness; he utters no harsh, bitter, or uncharitable word. The disguise assumed in *Literature and Dogma* slips off him in 'Stanzas from the Grande Chartreuse.' Yet it may be objected—if this be so, if Arnold revealed his best intellectual gifts and the most human and loveable side of his character in his verse, how comes it that the lovers of his poetry are comparatively so few while the civilised world has applauded the keen thrusts of his incisive prose? The explanation is not far to seek, and it will be one object of the following pages to find the answer. For the present it will be enough to point to the total absence of enthusiasm for any one great master truth, the persistent melancholy of the tone, the apathetic indifference of the philosophy, the irresolution and impotence of the practical teaching. On the other hand, it must be throughout remembered that Arnold served his generation not only as a poet, but as a prose-writer and an educational reformer. Though both the latter fields lie outside our present scope, it would be manifestly unfair to judge him solely by his verse. As a prose-writer his compositions are in thought too closely and intimately connected with his verse to be completely severed from it, but the former will only be discussed so far as it throws light upon his poetry. As a school inspector he corrected the dreaminess of his poetry by a life of practical activity, distinguished for devotion to the harassing details of his immediate work, and for zeal in applying the comparative method to the study of educational principles.

Arnold's verse is, as we have said, a more truthful mirror of Arnold's mind and character than his prose. But it also commands attention by its intrinsic poetic worth. As the best material for a study of Arnold's mind, it is examined with most advantage by reference to the dates of the different compositions. Another arrangement than that of chronology will be adopted for the criticism of the literary value which the poetry in itself possesses, and the two different aspects will be contemplated, as far as possible, apart.

Examined as a reflection of Arnold's mind and character, and taken as a whole, the poems appear a sandheap of shifting judgements, of trembling opinions, of crumbling creeds. They strike the ear like a medley of conflicting cries which cannot be reduced from dissonance to harmony. This indefiniteness of utterance seems to be the expression of an instability of mood which goes far to explain the chilling reception of his first two volumes, and partially accounts for the comparative neglect of the main body of his poetry. Yet a chronological study of the various pieces may disclose definite stages of mental developement, reduce perplexity to some degree of order, and supply the motive to the distracting sounds of his uniformly mournful muse. Though Arnold was throughout life a critic first and a poet afterwards, three distinct epochs of intellectual progress seem to stand out with some degree of prominence. In the first he expresses the unrest, the bewilderment, the perplexity of a doubting age; in the second he has adopted paganism as his own model of artistic composition and his moral rule of life; in the third his æsthetic and moral stoicism is leavened by that Hebrew element which he affected to despise and strove prematurely to suppress.

In his first three volumes Arnold expresses with unequalled power and completeness the languor and self-disdain, the dissatisfaction and weariness of the age, the yearning for a creed, and the craving for peace which drove men like Sterling, F. H. Newman, Clough, and Froude to attempt the ascent of the Mount of Vision by new paths instead of the ancient beaten ways. His poetry cannot pretend to guide the tendencies of his day, or even to embody the results of its confused struggle; but it gathers up and reflects with minute fidelity the forces that were at work. His estimate of the age and its products is sardonic. He can no longer mistake the dead past for the living present. Fevered life beat in men's pulses, and urged them on from change to change with no fixed goal, no settle purpose, aiming at something they dimly felt, unable to rest satisfied with what was already achieved. The new age mocked their hopes with the unreality of a mirage; to their closer gaze the new birth that had been proclaimed faded into the misty shape of an unsubstantial phantom. Arnold's predecessors, upon whose destructive labours he and his contemporaries had entered, had pointed to a land of promise which lay beyond the wilderness of their pilgrimage, and to a more glorious temple destined to arise from the ruins of the building they had destroyed. But the most enterprising pioneers of discovery had not yet discerned the bounds of the trackless desert which still continued to rise on the limitless horizon of the one, and the other remained a ruined heap of stones which afforded shelter to no man, and from which no architect had yet begun to build. Modern thought was incoherent, tangled, confused. Those who should have been its kings sate dumb, but their silence was not the serenity of contentment; it was rather the stony apathy of passive endurance, the mute acquiescence of minds that had abandoned the struggle in despair. Old faiths were dead, and the morning of that more fortunate age when the world should be once more spiritual and joyous had not yet broken through the mists. Arnold saw the sundered blocks of the ancient life float by him like icebergs in a rolling sea, and the new order was not reconstituted from the scattered fragments of the old. To use a phrase of Harrington's which his father was fond of quoting, he was 'living in the days of the Gothic empire,' but into his own kingdom he had not yet entered. It was an age of hurry, change, alarm, surprise, without shelter to ripen thought or leisure to store genial wisdom.

> Like children bathing on the shore,
>   Buried a wave beneath,
> The second wave succeeds before
>   We have had time to breathe.

He feels himself 'a wanderer between two worlds, one dead, the other powerless to be born.' Life became more exacting in proportion as it ceased to be great; his limbs are paralysed, his senses stupefied, his spirits benumbed by its thousand nothings; his very soul is choked by its petty penetrating dust. Within him there is that which compels him to speak, without him that which stifles his utterance. He is himself Empedocles looking back regretfully upon the past.

> Then we could still enjoy, then neither thought
> Nor outward things were clos'd and dead to us,
> But we receiv'd the shock of mighty thoughts
> On simple minds with a pure natural joy.

Now all is changed. Like Empedocles again, he has become

> Thought's slave, and dead to every natural joy.

Once the stream of life flowed along a single channel, in a broad, un-broken majestic whole, straight for the Polar star. Now, dammed by beds of sand, chopped into eddies of blind uncertainty, choked by obstructing islands of matted drift, thwarted this way and that by con-flicting currents, the stream has forgotten its once bright speed, and flows sullenly along, a baffled, circuitous wanderer.

These are the feelings to which Arnold gave expression in his early poetry. The almost unvarying theme of his lyric verse is the divorce of the soul from the intellect, and the perplexity which the separation produces. Hope and buoyancy are banished. He can only attain the premature tranquillity which he sought by assuming an attitude of apathetic indifference. His poetry is dreary from the monotonous tone of despair. The two early volumes, and especially the first, are not merely melancholy, for if this were all, there would be nothing note-worthy. Melpomene is generally the favourite muse of youth. Tears come before laughter; and though children have a keen sense of the ludicrous, the comedy of life is more congenial to the pococurantism of men than to the reverent enthusiasm of boyhood. Wordsworth has said truly enough:—

> In youth we love the darksome lawn,
> Brushed by the owlet's wing;
> The twilight is preferred to dawn,
> And autumn to the spring.

But the persistent sadness of Arnold's early poetry is very different from the passing shadows of boyish melancholy. It is hopeless, callous to the issues of contemporary thought, to present and future alike indifferent. It breathes the settled atmosphere of blank dejection and morbid languor. He feels no humanitarian fervour, for the future is impene-trably dark; no glow of patriotism, since Attica, not England, is his country. Profoundly discontented as he was with present conditions, it might be supposed that the French Revolution of 1848 would have attracted his sympathies; but his musings on life prompt him to patience rather than to effort. He is hemmed in and overshadowed by the high impassable mountains of Necessity. If ever the fire of youthful turbu-lence flamed through his veins, his verse retains none of its heat and passion. Colour and scent have faded from his lyrics; his poems of senti-ment betray little feeling. Even in a love poem he cannot repress a sigh. He is never exuberant, never enthusiastic. In a word, he is never young. How curiously old, to take a simple instance, is the touch which he introduces in the last lines of this exquisitely fresh picture!

> Paint that lilac kerchief, bound
> Her soft face, her hair around;
> Tied under the archest chin
> Mischief ever ambush'd in.
> Let the fluttering fringes streak
> All the pale, sweet-rounded cheek,
> > Ere the parting hour go by,
> > Quick, thy tablets, Memory!

All his founts of joy seem frozen at their very source in the bleak winter of his surroundings. He saw no escape from the alternative of being either a slave or a madman. Modern life in its general aspect presented itself to his mind as a high-walled prison, glowing with the brazen heat of the fierce sun; and, confined within its narrow bounds, he saw men languidly give their lives to some unmeaning task-work, till death released them, as birth had found them, blind, unfreed, unblest. From this prison some few escaped, and launched forth upon the wide ocean of life; but these were struck by the tempest, and, in the intermittent glare of lightning flashes, were seen for a moment before they disappeared in the deepening gloom—wrecks driving through the waves—

> And the pale Master on his spar-strewn deck,
> With anguish'd face and flying hair,
> Grasping the rudder hard,
> Still bent to make some port, he knows not where,
> Still standing for some false impossible shore.

Nothing great is born of mere regrets, and the persistent lamentation upon the present world would be unmanly if the accompanying self-restraint were less rigorously maintained. Doubtless Arnold expressed a true, and not an affected, feeling of weariness; nor are we surprised at the sentiment, for he thought nothing of the world and much of himself. The limitations which he discovered without were really within; but his self-esteem encouraged him to seek them anywhere except in his own breast. And it is this contracted experience that makes his personal philosophy more interesting than valuable; he tells us little or nothing that by the width of its applicability will justify the meditations on life with which his volumes are crowded. Whatever teaching is there contained can only sadden his readers. It could not make them wiser. 'Empedocles on Etna' is not only the largest, but autobiographically the most important, poem in these early volumes. In his speech to Pausanias Empedocles strives to nerve his friend to show a braver front to life, to find energy and heart within himself. Man's wisdom is not to expect much happiness, but to take life as it is, and to make the best of it.

> I say, 'Fear not! Life still
> Leaves human effort scope!
> But since life teems with ill,
> Nurse no extravagant, hope.
> Because thou must not dream, thou need'st not then despair.'

Empedocles strikes the chord of self-government with a firm hand; but when he strives to awaken its music to cheer his own solitude, it snaps in two. Left to practise his own precepts, his philosophy tastes as ashes in his mouth. Alone, he yields to that very despondency against which he had eloquently invoked the manly sobriety of Pausanias. The physician illustrates in his own case the inefficacy of the medicine he prescribes. Weary of life, or rather of himself, this counsellor of fortitude in others finds that for his own smart the only anodyne is death. The conclusion of the poem suggests that Arnold knew his own creed to be worthless as a universal solvent, and the suggestion receives a general confirmation from the frosty coldness of his didactic poetry. His words do not burn themselves in on the brain with the heat of the summer solstice of conviction, but ring on the ear with the metallic hollowness of rhetoric, the wintry sententiousness of a man who strives to make his heart follow the guidance of his intellect. Teaching thus impotent and profitless was the best that Arnold had to offer; yet its transparent unsatisfactoriness naturally proved repellent to anxious questioners who were mocked with futile answers.

Apart from the coldness of his poetry, apart from the prevailing tone of melancholy, and the total absence of enthusiasm, apart also from the great inequality both in substance and mechanical execution which characterises the different compositions and which seemed to render the poet's future wholly uncertain, the irresolution and infirmity of the teaching would alone suffice to explain the chilling reception of the first two volumes. No predominant interest can be traced. The poet is informed by no great master truth. It is impossible to feel in living touch with the personality of a man who brings us nothing but haggard, hard negations. Wordsworth held that the office of the poet was 'to console the afflicted, to add sunshine to daylight by making the happy happier, to teach the young and gracious of every age to see, to think and feel, and therefore to become more active and securely victorious.' If Wordsworth was right—and it is difficult to say that he is wrong— Arnold fell lamentably short of the ideal. While he disturbs our peace by his persistent melancholy, he offers nothing to brace our energies, clear our mental vision, revive our sinking courage. He shuns the present, but does not lean upon the future, and refuses to trust wholly to the past. A man who has lost his way can never be a guide.

Arnold's third volume (1853) is a great advance upon its two anonymous predecessors. In strength of substance, manliness of tone, healthiness of feeling, the *Poems*, to which his name was for the first time appended, were superior to any of his previous efforts. He had shown in the early volumes his love of form and his keen sense of its absence from English literature. Out of this feeling is now developed a theory of art, if not of life. Devotion to classic form may be powerless to create that infectious certainty, that direct energy, that passionate fervour, which are the living breath of great poets. But any belief is better than none, and here the æsthetic theory was the complement of a moral creed. In the preface to the poems of 1853 Arnold insists that poets must seek their inspiration in the past, for action is the only theme of poetry, and it is in the past alone that action is found. Art is objective, and when this is forgotten, as it is by modern poets, all work is hopelessly vitiated. The choice of a good subject is indispensable, for without a worthy theme success is unattainable. Arnold carries his adoration of the antique to the verge of fanaticism. He establishes the rules of classic composition as the Median laws of poetry for all times and all conditions; he exults over their principles with the one-sided zeal of the archæologist, ignores the differences between the ancient Hellas and modern England, takes the classics for his masters, and, in deference to their decisions, excludes 'Empedocles on Etna' from his republished poems.

The æsthetic problem which Arnold solved by taking refuge in ancient Greece is only a different mode of stating the moral difficulty by which he was confronted. Among conditions which afforded him no guidance in conduct or in composition, what was the best model to follow in art and in life? His moral prop is identical with his artistic prop. To insist upon calm, patience, apathy, endurance, acceptance of fate, submission to the omnipotence of adamantine laws, is to state the æsthetic principles of classsicism from their moral side. With Arnold, as with the Stoics, his philosophy was the offspring of the union of the religious consciousness of the East with the intellectual culture of the West. With him, as with them, it was bred from despair in the presence of waning faiths. Like them, he sought in passionlessness a refuge from the turmoil of the world; like them, his conception of a personal God is shadowy, even if it exists at all; like them, he concerns himself more with the problems of the present life than the mysteries of the hereafter. Like them, he often leans towards materialism, though consistently with the practice of his teachers he concerns himself rather with ethical than with physical questions. In his views of life, of death, of necessity, of fate, of equanimity, of the relations of man with nature, he was in sympathy with the pagan world, not with the modern conditions of existence. His moral feelings as well as his intellectual instincts inclined him towards the classical school; but the impulse of his æsthetic paganism came from his ethical principles rather than his artistic theories. Neither his religious philosophy nor his æsthetic criticism rested on an assured basis of conviction; both were exaggerated in expression as their real hold on his mind relaxed, until the one became cynical and the other paradoxical.

Arnold's moral Stoicism was, as we believe, the parent of his devotion to the rigid principles of classic art. From his father he had inherited his moral ardour and sterling honesty, the lofty didactic impulse which breathes an earnest, serious air through all his teaching, and the fine historical sense which in 'Sohrab and Rustum' delineated with vivid force the distinctive lineaments of the earth's surface, or penetrated, as in 'Obermann once more,' with keen insight into the moral causes which sapped the strength of the Roman empire. But Dr. Arnold's most fatal error in dealing with the young was his insistence upon the duty of moral thoughtfulness, and the self-scrutinising habit was formed in the son before he was strong enough to support the weary burden of himself. In the 'Stanzas from the Grande Chartreuse,' he has told us how the change from faith to doubt began which ended in the temporary extinction of his religious consciousness before the absorbing passion of intellectual culture. He asks himself what spirit has guided him 'to the Carthusians' world-famed home'—

> For rigorous teachers seized my youth,
>   And purged its faith, and trimmed its fire,
> Show'd me the high white star of Truth,
>   There bade me gaze, and there aspire;
> Even now their whispers pierce the gloom;
>   *What dost thou in this living tomb?*

His poetry leaves little or no clue to the names of those who were his guides at the outset of his mental career. But it tells us who were the thinkers on whom his mind rested with most confidence after he had started on his journey. His mental props in the 'bad age' in which he found his lot was cast were two of the great poets of ancient Greece—Homer, 'the clearest-souled of men,' and Sophocles, 'the even-balanced;' Epictetus, 'the halting slave' of Epaphroditus, who taught Arrian at Nicopolis; Marcus Aurelius, 'the imperial sage, purest of men;' Emerson, whose 'oracular voice' the world refused to hear; Goethe, 'the physician of the iron age,' and Wordsworth. The influence of Homer was rather artistic than ethical; but the other six writers were his masters in his philosophy of calm resignation and self-culture. Sophocles was the preacher of quiet submission to the will of the gods. Epictetus taught that the will is the only possession which a man can really call his own, and that external to it nothing can be called either bad or good. Marcus Aurelius meditated upon that implicit obedience to the legislative faculty within the breast of man by which alone true equanimity can be secured. Emerson preached that the only revelation is that prompting which every individual receives, and that absolute conformity to inward impulse is the most perfect liberty, and makes men not only godlike, but gods. And though Goethe and Wordsworth travelled by widely diverging roads, the point which both reached was the same. The isolation of self-culture which in the Sage of Weimar was the conscious object of intellectual pride was in Wordsworth the inoffensive egotism of one who found self-cultivation to be the first and most important field for his energies.

A Stoic by circumstance and by training, Arnold accepted the materialism, though not in its grossest form, on which his ethical philosophy was based. Physical problems exercised his mind but slightly; yet a vague pantheism, always latent, and sometimes, as in the last stanzas of 'Heine's Grave,' confessed, pervades his poetry. Arnold is indeed inconsistent with himself, as though he was still struggling with the results of an early training. He has altogether abandoned, if he ever held, the proud mediæval view of the relations of man to nature which George Herbert expressed in the well-known lines—

> Man is one world, and hath
> Another to attend him.

His attitude is rather that of a pupil at the feet of a teacher, a disciple hanging on the lips of a master. Nature is his model, his guide, his consoler.

[Quotes 'A Summer Night', ll. 78–92, 'Ye heavens', etc.]

He does not even cling to the belief that the moral being of man is higher than nature's strength, or say with Sir Thomas Browne, 'There is surely a divinity within us—something that was before the elements, and owes no homage to the sun.' For a moment he is impressed with the belief that the struggles and the aspirations and the progressive desires of men raise them above the inanimate creation. He makes Nature herself ask the question.

> 'Ah, child!' she cries, 'that strife divine,
> Whence was it, for it is not mine?'

But the feeling is only transitory. Although in many respects a child of Wordsworth, he does not share his parent's confidence that while all things around him pass and change, man alone abideth for ever. He is rather impressed by a sense of human mutability in the presence of the permanence of nature.

> Race after race, man after man,
> Have thought that my secret was theirs,
> Have dreamed that I lived but for them,
> That they were my glory and joy;
> They are dust, they are changed, they are gone!
> I remain.

His most consistent attitude is that of a pantheist believing in a God, immanent in nature but impersonal, a Spirit in whom we exist, the calm Soul of all things, who alone is all things in one.

It is suggested, though it is impossible to prove, that Arnold's theory of the art of poetic composition was framed to support his moral theory of life. On any other supposition it is difficult to explain the inconsistency between his principles and his practice. If his criticism expresses his true and deliberate opinion, the contradiction which his own poetry gives to his æsthetic rules is inexplicable. Both his theories of art and of life were born of his passion of the brain, of his mental struggles, his intellectual impatience, his moral despair. Upon both he insisted with increased extravagance long after they had ceased to afford him true support. Who in 1853 would have ventured to predict that Matthew Arnold, the living embodiment of the classic spirit, would desert the 'disinterested objectivity' of Greek art for continued self-scrutiny and subjective introspection, would descend from the serene heights of his self-contained, impassive Stoicism to busy himself with the current questions of modern life—would throw aside his fatalistic passionlessness to assume the task of reconciling faith and reason, science and theology? The progress of this change is the interesting spectacle in Arnold's later development. The Hebrew spirit disputed the absolute sway of Hellenism, the religious consciousness strove with the intellectual culture, and conquered its right to a balance of power.

The full history of the change can only be read in his prose works; but it left its mark on the principles and the practice of his poetic composition. He ceased to write poetry, or wrote it in defiance of his own rules. Arnold's theory of art was, like his theory of life, one-sided and insufficient. To disinter the bones of Greek legends from the sepulchre of ages and to clothe them with their own flesh and blood is not necessarily an imitative work. If scholar and poet combine, as they did in Arnold, the result is the creative effort of a living reproduction. Though the materials are classic, and therefore secondhand, the poet's treatment of them is original. Yet no strength of imagination can turn the world's sympathies back to the alien shores of ancient Greece, and so long as Arnold remained true to his æsthetic theory, the circle of his readers was necessarily limited in its range. No one knew better than Arnold himself that to seek subjects exclusively in the past is to evade the conditions under which alone great poetry is possible. Verse inspired by bygone days can never earn the praise of adequacy. Poetry is only adequate when it expresses the grandest views that are possible concerning man and his destiny, respecting his relations with the world above him and around him. Poetry so written employs the best material of the age; it gives us noble reflections of the noblest features of its day, and so doing rears for itself a monument imperishable as time. Anything but this must be condemned as inadequate, and in practice Arnold recognises the deficiency of his theory. But the further he receded from his artistic rules, the more extravagantly did he defend their principles. And it is this defence of a theory of art, constructed, as we believe, in the first instance because the Attic pagan world suited Arnold's instincts, aspirations, and training better than the modern Christian view of life, that imparts such crotchety viewiness to the bulk of his prose criticism. He is perpetually defending positions which he feels are paradoxical.

Nor was he better satisfied with his moral prop. As his theory of the art of poetic composition ignored the conditions of modern society, so his theory of life starved the heart to feed the intellect. He was too tenderhearted for his creed. He felt that in the human breast there ought to reign an inward peace which no turmoil can disturb. But he craves

something more than stern self-suppression, more even than the gentler
ideal which Marcus Aurelius, who grew a better man as he became a
worse Stoic, conceived of his hard philosophy. Arnold cannot close his
eyes and ears to human suffering; he is saddened at the thought of the
vast armies of the homeless and unfed; he shudders to think how keen
and crowded the country grows. He cannot live like the stars of heaven
undistracted by the sights they see, unaffrighted by the vast silence of
their surroundings. It was impossible for him, though he might study
self-culture at the feet of the Sage of Weimar, to become nothing but a
reasoning self-sufficient creature, self-poised, self-centred—an intellectual all-in-all. He had neither the refined selfishness nor the cold
temperament, nor, it must be added, the wide and luminous view,
which enabled Goethe to attain the serene heights of philosophic calm.
The sensuous side of his nature always stirred strongly within him, and
it attracted him to nature's solitudes, drew him towards scholar-
gipsies, anchorites like the Carthusians, recluses like Sénancour. It suggested to him the doubt whether the Tree of Knowledge is indeed the
Tree of Life, whether there may not be an excess of over-culture,
whether the contact with Mother Earth will not give new vigour to the
intellectual athlete. Yet he knows the calm is not 'life's crown,' and he
cannot reconcile his conception of human duty with an exclusive isolation, or withhold his interest from the problems of contemporary life.
The Vizier to the sick King of Bokhara, with his hard, unsympathetic,
practical common-sense, can banish sorrow for the unalterable. But
Arnold himself rather resembles the kindly Oriental potentate, who in
the plenitude of power cannot shut his eyes to the injustice of the world,
or cease to lament his impotence to lessen by a single drop the great
ocean of sin and sorrow. The tenderness of his nature revolts from the
isolated selfishness of his creed, and the emphasis which he continually
lays on this aspect of isolation shows how such a prospect chilled him to
the bone. It is the feeling which he has embalmed in four of his most
familiar lines—

> Yes; in the sea of life enisl'd,
> With echoing straits between us thrown,
> Dotting the shoreless watery wild,
> We mortal millions live *alone*.

The marble coldness of his assumed impassiveness is often flushed with
emotional colour. In these transient flashes he forgets that he is a man
of culture and of philosophic calm; and it is in these momentary outbursts which break down the barriers of his proud self-consciousness

that he has written the lines which have most readily passed into the familiar currency of speech. The temporary glow seems to prove that Arnold, except in a set composition like 'Sohrab and Rustum,' never wholly extinguished the flame of Hebrew fire which irradiated his father with an 'ardour divine,' and still made him shine as a beacon of hope to the son, though many years had passed since the head master of Rugby had trodden

> In the summer morning, the road
> Of death, at a call unforeseen
> Sudden.

His poetry after 1854, with the exception of *Merope*, which he wrote rather as Professor of Poetry than as a poet, shows that artistically and morally the exclusive domination of the Hellenic spirit was overthrown. He had ceased merely to endure and acquiesce in the present. He began to hope of the future. In the lines 'In Memory of the Author of "Obermann"' he had lamented that fate drove him forth among the crowded haunts of men, leaving half of himself behind in the solitude of the anchorite's retreat. But the rough contact with the rude world which he disdained proved a wise though stern physician. As though to correct his former lamentations, he reserves for 'Obermann once more,' written twenty years later, his most explicit utterances of hope. Musing on the changes of time he sits among the hills that rise above the Castle of Chillon at the Vevey end of the Lake of Geneva, where Sénancour's mountain-chalet had once stood in the midst of solitudes which now were populated. As night ran gently down over hill and wood, the shade of Obermann stood before him on the grass, and thus addressed the wayworn man who in his youth had called the shy recluse his master:—

[Quotes 'Obermann Once More', ll. 277–92, 'Oh, thou who, ere thy flying span', etc.]

It is not suggested that Arnold ever attained the complete repose which he sought, still less that he approximated to the principles of orthodox Christianity. His note is still the Eternal Pain of his own Philomela. But so far as his peculiar temperament permitted, his search was rewarded, if not by peace, at least by hope. What he found it would be difficult to discover from his verse. Self-knowledge is still the summary of his creed. There is no revelation from without. But

> Once read thy own breast right,
> And thou hast done with fears;
> Man gets no other light,
> Search he a thousand years.

And such self-knowledge leads to self-dependence, and self-dependence to equanimity.

> Resolve to be thyself; and know that he
> Who finds himself loses his misery!

Yet beyond all doubt the direction in which he turned in such a poem as 'Dover Beach,' one of his later compositions, promised richer fruit than the cold soil which he had so assiduously cultivated. The affections of the heart reveal more of the possibilities of the future than the dogmas of the doubts of the intellect.

[Quotes 'Dover Beach', ll. 29–37, 'Ah, love, let us be true', etc.]

Arnold's search for truth is eager, sincere, indefatigable. He seeks to attain a knowledge of what perfection is by turning upon all matters, however sacred or venerable, if only they claim belief or call for action, a current of fresh, free thought. He pursues his ideal on every side of his nature, striving to see things as they are, and refusing to view them through the medium of traditional thought and feeling. He tolerates no fixed mental habits, allows no immoveable notions. He aims at a complete moral and intellectual deliverance which shall enable him to possess his own soul. Did he ever attain his object? So far as his verse is concerned, the answer must be in the negative. It is the poetry of a man whose sorrow is lifelong. In it we see reflected a mind ardently bent on the culture of all that was best and purest in itself, strenuously set to pursue the true and right. Why, then, did he fail to attain to any perception of truth which, whether orthodox or not, completely satisfied his mind? Some persons might reply that the object, the manner, and the method of the search sufficiently answer the question. But we have no intention of embarking upon the vexed seas of theological controversy. Our question relates solely to Arnold's mental and moral disposition. How far, in fact, might discontent be predicated as the necessary result of his character? The comparative failure cannot be attributed to moral defects. His loftiness of purpose is apparent from the first; the pure atmosphere which he breathes imparts an Olympian dignity even to his earliest efforts. He never mistook voluptuousness for beauty, and thus seems to have escaped a stage through which most youthful poets have passed. But though his mind was keen to seek, it was weak to find. He wanted the width of grasp which alone comprehends the breadth of genial wisdom. His chief intellectual defect—and it is a fault which not only detracts from the value of his criticism both of life and art, but mars the beauty of some of his poetry—is an incapacity to grasp large wholes in their general aspect. It is this limitation, rather than any special degree of materialism in his surroundings, which prevents him from attaining that composed strength and ardour of conviction, without which he could not write the highest poetry. His criticism, for instance, is powerful in its details, rather than in its leading ideas; it contains truths, but not the whole truth, and the theories which it supports are almost always one-sided. Instead of including in his view of poetry both mechanism and feeling, he exalts the mechanical element above the soul. So too in moral questions he neglects the heart to pamper the intellect. So, lastly, his poems, though delicately and purely finished, are weak in conception; they are deficient in organic completeness. He might, as it would seem, have attained the narrow, unhesitating satisfaction of the fanatic, if he was thus excluded from the broader wisdom of more comprehensive minds. Yet from this sphere of contentment he was debarred, not only by keenness of vision, but by his liberal fairness and width of sympathies. It is impossible to conceive two beings more different than Heine, the child of the Revolution, stained with every moral fault that did not unfit him to be 'a brilliant leader of the war of the liberation of humanity,' and Eugénie de Guérin, a Catholic of the Catholics, of whose nature love and religion were the mainsprings, and who gained an imperishable name in literature through the rare qualities of her soul. Yet into these two opposite characters he has thrown himself with sympathetic large-mindedness.

Both the strength and the weakness of his intellect thus combined to deny him the glow of conviction. He was the martyr of his own candour. Neither in æsthetics nor morals could he surrender his allegiance unreservedly to the past or to the present. He had none of the negative capacity of Tennyson, who continued to faintly trust in the larger hope. Neither could he adopt the practical advice of Browning, to shun 'the exhausted air-bell of the critic,' and cleave to that form of worship with which he was most familiar. He was unable to rejoice in the triumphs of modern thought, for scientific discoveries, whether of geology, chemistry, or physiology, exercised over him no potent charm Yet he refused to withdraw altogether from the activities of the world, to forget with Morris—

> . . . six counties overhung with smoke,
> Forget the snorting steam and piston-stroke,
> Forget the spreading of the hideous town,—

and dream his life away in some cool sequestered Temple the of ancient
or the mediæval world. He had broken too completely with the older
creed to feel that enthusiasm for faith which nerved Clough to continue his search for the light that somewhere was yet shining. But, on
the other hand, he was totally without sympathy with the aggressive
paganism of Swinburne, who, in the insolence of his iconoclastic zeal,
exults at the prospect of the passing away of the kingdom of the
Galilean. The illusion of Shelley's ardent faith in the future of a regenerated world melts before his 'sad lucidity of soul;' and he shrinks
with the shudder of scholarly refinement and of intellectual exclusiveness from contact with that democracy whose advent Whitman salutes
with his 'barbaric yawp over the roofs of the world.' Yet at the same
time he is too intellectual to glow with the fervent rapture of faith
which was the secret of Wordsworth's meditative calm, and he is too
limited in his experience and his perceptions to attain to Goethe's wide
view of life. Thus it seemed inevitable that he should bear with him as
long as he lived—

> . . . the old unquiet breast
> That neither deadens into rest,
> Nor ever feels the fiery glow
> That whirls the spirit from itself away,
> But fluctuates to and fro,
> Never by passion quite possess'd,
> And never quite benumb'd by the world.

It is as the representative of the highest type of agnosticism, as an
embodiment of the honesty, narrowness, and discontent of modern
doubt, that Arnold's mind and character arrest attention. His poetry,
read between the lines, is a vividly written page from the mental
history of the past half-century. It is the diary of the inner life-experi-
ences of an open doubter who has pursued culture at the expense of
faith, but who is no propagandist of scepticism, and looks back with
tender sadness on the shrines where once he worshipped. This dominant feeling of his mind is expressed in one of the most beautiful and
pathetic of his elegiac poems, 'Stanzas from the Grande Chartreuse.' No
life can be conceived more calculated to encourage this train of thought
than that of the austere Carthusian brotherhood in the famous monastery

whose site St. Bruno chose with such consummate skill. All the surroundings speak of complete severance from the outer world: the
steep winding ascent along a path literally scooped in the sides of lime-
stone cliffs, which, fringed with ragged pines, seem to meet several
hundred feet above, and almost exclude the sky; the sudden opening
out, as the defile ends on the green plateau where the Chartreuse itself
is reached; the intense oppressive silence of the courts and corridors;
the austere bareness of the tomblike cells; the grave solemnity of the
midnight service with its cowled and ghostly figures bowed in the
stern struggle of penitential prayer. To this spot Arnold is drawn by no
disloyalty to his modern teachers, yet he asks himself the question—

> And what am I, that I am here?

and the answer follows—

[Quotes 'Grand Chartreuse', ll. 73–90, 'Forgive me, masters of the
mind', etc.]

The comparative neglect of Arnold's poetry cannot be attributed to
the self-scrutiny and the introspection with which it is charged. In proportion as the present world takes little thought beyond the body, it
likes to be talked to about the soul. Reduced to its ultimate cause, the
failure of Arnold as a poet is due to the fact that he has nothing definite
to say, and that what he does say lacks the warmth of conviction. He
has parted from the older faith, but he has no new Gospel to substitute.
He has not made up his mind. Even his classic fervour is, in its most
extreme form, the expression of his moral difficulties rather than of his
artistic principles. Without enthusiasm for the future, without respect
for the present, half-hearted in his devotion to the past, his poetry is cold
and unimpassioned, and his teaching indefinite and indistinct. He has
cut himself too completely adrift from the spiritual things of the invisible world to be the spokesman of those who still struggle with
hesitations and difficulties. He is too reverential to the faith which he
has left, too mistrustful of that which is to succeed, to be the prophet of
the iconoclast. And this absence of any one overmastering impulse is to
be traced to the peculiar constitution of his mind, to his own limitations and endowments, and not to any excessive proportion of materialism in the conditions of his day. As a thinker Arnold was lucid rather
than deep, piercing rather than capacious. Intellectually too keen for a
twilight atmosphere where faith cannot be discriminated from doubt,
too honest to profess belief which he did not feel, too eager in his search
for truth to spare the most venerable traditions from enquiry, too

narrow in his perceptions to grasp the large views of genial wisdom, too open-minded for fanaticism, too sympathetic for philosophic calm, too active to be a dreamer, too definite for mysticism, he seemed inevitably destined to wander between two worlds—a citizen of neither.

The study of Arnold's mind as revealed in his poetry prepares the way for an appreciation of the value of the poetry itself. His verse divides itself into two broad divisions: one objective, consisting of narrative and dramatic poems dealing with external subjects, historical actions, romantic or classical legends; the other subjective, including lyric and elegiac poems of personal reflection and sentiment. In rather more than half his poetical compositions he contradicts his own principles of art. And it is difficult to explain this inconsistency except on the suggested supposition that his extravagant classicism was the offspring, not of his critical faculties, but of his moral perplexities. Yet though these broad divisions of Arnold's poetry may be appealed to in confirmation and illustration of the preceding study of his mind, for critical purposes it will be most convenient to adopt a more detailed arrangement into lyric, dramatic, elegiac, and narrative, to examine each group in this order, and to conclude with some observations of a general character.

The matter of Arnold's lyric poetry has been discussed at length in the preceding pages. It only remains to criticise the form of its expression. Large portions consist of prose cut into lines of uneven length, deceiving the eye with the outward semblance of verse, but cheating the ear of the promised melody. Its intellectual qualities, its acute self-scrutiny, its deep psychological meditation, ensure it an independent value which is wholly irrespective of its poetical claims. Yet judged as lyric poetry, it is so elaborately charged with material, so studiously burdened with meaning, so economically packed with thought, that it has lost every trace of the easy spontaneity, the headlong speed, the tyrannous impulse which are essentially associated with this class of verse composition. Arnold analyses himself as Man rather than as a man—as humanity, not as an individual; and this representative character gives to his outpourings the cold dignity of impersonality which robs it of its last trace of involuntariness. Even in his most personal lyrics, he seems to keep his fingers on his pulse; and there is a pride in his self-consciousness which resents sympathy as an insult. There is strength, but it is the strength of culture and of self-restraint, not the force of passion or of tenderness. The true lyric cry never bursts from the intellect alone. Arnold is too composed in his mental melancholy to surrender himself to that abandonment of sadness which impelled Shelley to relieve the intensity of his pent-up misery with the 'Lines written in Dejection at Naples;' and, on the other hand, he never reaches that rapture of faith which inspired Wordsworth's fervent 'Ode to Immortality.' His equanimity neither conquers nor is conquered by melancholy; it knows neither the elation of victory, nor the despair of defeat. And there is often a coldness in his manner, transcending the self-restraint of firm resolve and approaching the self-congratulation of keen-witted egotism, which unpleasantly suggests the external touch of the intellectual observer instead of the inward pain of suffering endurance.

Much of his lyric poetry is merely criticism, and often little more than prose criticism. When he deals with literary subjects, his love of art warms him into the glow of enthusiasm, as in the fine 'Epilogue to Lessing's Laocoön' or the exquisite passage from the 'Youth of Nature,' which affords one of the best specimens of the lyrical blank verse that he may be said to have invented.

[Quotes ll. 59–74, 'For, oh! is it you', etc.]

The whole of the reply of Nature would well repay quotation, but all who are likely to read these pages will probably be familiar with a passage which closes with lines that we have elsewhere quoted. In the sphere of social, moral, or religious criticism Arnold's inspiration uniformly deserts him. The positive teaching which is contained in this portion of his lyric poetry is not in itself valuable; although his maxims are pronounced with the solemnity of a lawgiver, they seem to be enunciated to convince himself rather than to guide others.

As a teacher he rarely rises above rhetoric; his verse proceeds step by step in the effort of persuasion, but it does not grow closer or more concentrated in feeling. His self-consciousness leads him to forget his poetic sensibility, and continually reminds him that he is a passionless Stoic. Hence, in dealing with these subjects, he repeatedly drops into prose, relieved by such powerful and finely sustained metaphors as that already quoted from 'A Summer Night,' in which he condenses the tragedy of modern life. It is only in the rare moments when, forgetting the conscious artist and the didactic moralist, he allows his verse to become the natural medium of his utterances, the simple transcript of his contemplative or meditative moods, that he rises into poetry.

His metrical gifts are not great. His short songs are deficient in fluency as well as prosaic in manner. Blank verse and graver movements are best suited to his serious purpose. His experiments seem to be almost a confession that lyric poetry is an uncongenial element. He appears to seek in the mechanical structure of his verse some compensation for the want of spontaneity and passion. Yet his lyrical blank verse, as we have shown, is sometimes of extraordinary beauty, and his Greek studies enabled him to imitate with success the free unfettered movements of the classic choruses. On the other hand, some of his unrhymed rhythmic novelties appear to be so harsh and unmelodious as to betray a defective ear. The effect of such lines as these from *Merope*—

> Thou confessest the prize
> In the rushing, thundering, mad,
> Cloud-enveloped, obscure,
> Unapplauded, unsung
> Race of calamity, mine?—

is not inaptly represented by the Bishop of Derry as the sound of a stick drawn by a city *gamin* sharply across the area railings.

A poet so intensely subjective, so absorbed in self-scrutiny and introspection, is rarely able to throw himself into the minds of other men, and in dramatic poetry Arnold achieves no great success. Yet, intellectually and autobiographically, 'Empedocles on Etna' is a striking poem. In Empedocles, Pausanias, and Callicles, Arnold depicts three types of the Hellenic mind, the philosophical, the practical and credulous, and the artistic. But it is with the first that he is mainly concerned. Although the form of the poem necessarily prevents the direct intrusion of the poet's personality, yet the choice of the subject is plainly dictated by the problems which were exercising his own mind. Written after Arnold had abandoned his inherited creeds, and before he had definitely promulgated his theory that the ancient world affords the best models both of art and morals, 'Empedocles' was excluded from his collected poems when the poet was at the height of his Hellenic enthusiasm. Possibly Arnold's rejection of the poem as a faulty subject may be critically just, for the exhibition of conquest is indisputably a more fitting theme for poets than the representation of defeat. Yet the real weakness of the poem consists less in the failure to relieve discontent by hope, incident, or resistance, than in the sudden change which Empedocles exhibits from fortitude to despondency. And for this reason it is difficult to suppose that the omission of the poem was wholly due to the alleged cause. Underneath the assigned artistic ground for its exclusion seems to lie the feeling that the catastrophe of the drama expressly contradicts the poet's own philosophy, and explicitly denies the adequacy of the moral theory, which, as we have endeavoured to

357

show, was the true parent of his æsthetic principles. The greater part of Arnold's lyric poetry breathes the same sentiment of mental despondency which is dramatically expressed in 'Empedocles on Etna,' and falls within the same condemnation; but unlike the hero of his drama, the poet himself, while yielding to intellectual melancholy, maintained the moral struggle with unflinching resolution. As an Essay on Life the poem is profoundly unsatisfactory, nor is the central figure sufficiently broad and massive to attain to the true classic dignity. On the other hand, the faults of the conception and the hollowness of the philosophy are more than redeemed by the exquisite beauty of such lyrics as these:—

[Quotes 'Empedocles on Etna', ll. 437–68, 'What forms are these coming', etc.]

Merope is a drama and not merely a dramatic poem; but it is rather an experiment in tragic composition than a tragedy. The central part of the play is one of those recognitions which always arrested the attention of a Greek audience. Merope believes her son Ægyptus to have been murdered, and determines to avenge his death. Axe in hand she approaches the couch where the supposed murderer is lying. Just as the fatal blow is about to fall she recognises in the sleeping victim her living son.

Merope forcibly illustrates the narrowness of view which mars the value of Arnold's criticism. He seized, with that instinctive acuteness which always characterises the details of his brilliant *aperçus littéraires*, upon the salient fact that English dramatists are prone to neglect clearness of outline, symmetry of form, propriety of detail and expression. But his inability to grasp whole truths led him to suppose that an alien literature which had originated in forgotten ceremonials and obsolete sacrificial observances, which depended for its life on a dead religion, on faded traditions, and extinct ideas, could supplant the native literature in which England had expressed her own national spirit. No one would deny that the classic drama pays more heed to justness of proportion and unity of impression than the so-called romantic school. But it might be argued with equal force that the Greek dramatists had not arrived at a conception of the full capacities of their art, and that they sacrificed variety to clearness, richness to simplicity, because of the exigencies of their rudimentary scenic representations. Greek actors were necessarily obliged to forego all that rapid interchange of voice and gesture and that minute and varied by-play which help the modern stage to reproduce human life with such fidelity. So, too, the Greek dramatist is above all things and essentially a narrator. The naked presentation of incidents, each of which in itself was profoundly significant because man was little more than an instrument in the iron hands of overruling Destiny, was the main object which he set before himself. But the range of the romantic school is far more varied and more complex. Nor need we search beyond this complicated subject-matter to discover the true cause of the relative want of symmetry which is conspicuous on the modern stage. The nineteenth-century drama cannot be reduced within the rigid lines of the Greek tragedians except by restricting its liberty, limiting its range, and adopting artificial conventions. 'Merope' was not, however, written merely to exemplify the artistic beauty of symmetrical form and unity of impression. It is an attempt to establish his theory that the organic and living growth of the English drama ought to be replaced by the dead forms of the classic stage.

But apart from the narrow critical principles which *Merope* was written to illustrate, there are defects in the choice and the treatment of the subject which bring out Arnold's deficiency in large conceptions. From the moment that Merope recognises her son the interest evaporates, and the subsequent story of Polyphontes fails to arrest attention. We cannot but think that a Greek tragedian would have allowed Merope to strike the fatal blow; he would have made the mother kill her own son, and delayed the recognition till it was too late. There is no tragedy in a happy ending, and the melodramatic touch of the escape is out of keeping with the severity of the Greek drama. Nor is Arnold true to the character of his heroine when he makes her hesitate respecting the assassination of Polyphontes. An Electra, burning to avenge the death of a husband and tortured by fears for a son's life, would have waded knee-deep in blood without a thought of pity. So, too, the treatment of the character of Polyphontes is essentially modern, and therefore wholly unsatisfactory. Greek tragedians knew too well the limitations of their stage to ask moral conundrums; they would not have attempted to depict the conflict of good and evil within the breast of Polyphontes. But Arnold, judging by modern canons of taste, felt that the fate of a person of mixed character commands more sympathy than that of a man who is wholly bad. He therefore endeavoured to shade off the good and bad elements into one another so as to show his hero to be compounded of the high-minded patriot and the self-seeking usurper. The rigid forms of the Greek drama frustrated his design; the elements refuse to blend; Polyphontes is painted with mathematical exactitude, one side white, the other black; and the impossibility of developing character in a classic tragedy might have convinced Arnold of the inadequacy of his artistic theories.

Arnold's strength is far better displayed in short narrative poems. Tennyson excels in the same class of composition, but the two poets are not exactly rivals in the same field. Arnold's narrative poetry has an abstract Wordsworthian tinge; less gorgeous, highly tinted, and picturesque than that of the present Poet Laureate, it is purer, clearer, and more statuesque. The one uses rich colours; the other paints with cool washes.

Arnold chooses his stories both from romantic and classic sources, and his treatment, though always measured, necessarily varies with his subject. To the more ornate class belong 'The Church of Brou,' 'Mycerinus,' 'The Sick King of Bokhara,' 'The Forsaken Merman,' and 'Tristram and Iseult;' to the simpler and more purely classic style of treatment belong 'Balder Dead' and 'Sohrab and Rustum.' In the first he is a painter, in the second a sculptor. The figures which he carves from the marble of his classic quarries are austerely cold; but the brighter hues of the East, or of the middle ages, or of fairyland lend some richness of colouring to the severe purity of his style.

The most important of the romantic poems is 'Tristram and Iseult;' yet many will prefer the genial wisdom of 'The Sick King of Bokhara,' or the exquisite pathos of 'The Forsaken Merman.' The latter is, in our opinion, the most perfect of his narrative poems. The words are so felicitously chosen, the metre is so skilfully handled, that sound and meaning are wedded in perfect harmony. The piece, like 'The Sick King of Bokhara,' is complete in itself; it is too short to be defective in conception, while the free rein which Arnold gives to the tenderness of his nature here supplies the force and swiftness of movement in which he so often fails. It enshrines that feeling of separation to the pathos of which Arnold was peculiarly sensitive, and the grief of the forsaken Merman and his children is depicted with touching grace. The following lines are familiar, but they will bear quotation:—

[Quotes 'The Forsaken Merman', ll. 10–29, 'Call her once', etc.]

The same feeling which inspired 'The Forsaken Mermaid' is expressed in 'Tristram and Iseult.' Tristram and Iseult of Ireland tread the dark road of death together hand in hand. She who is left behind bears the full burden of the pain of separation, and it is on the picture of the joyless calm of the widowed Iseult of Brittany that Arnold expends all his strength. But here the touching beauty of the picture is marred by the irrelevancy of its details and the weakness of its composition. The poem is more beautiful in its parts than as a whole. The connecting links are so slender that the construction falls to pieces. The unnecessary introduction of the story of Merlin mars the unity of impression; scene-painting predominates over the figures of the actors; and the inter-change of the dramatic and narrative elements strikes us as a defect of form which might have been easily overcome. Nor again does the exquisite picture of the children compensate for a departure from the original form of the legend which alienates our sympathy from Tris-tram. With far truer instinct the older chronicler relates that Tristram even on his marriage night was faithful to his love, and that Ysoude les Blanches Mains remained a pure virgin.

The subject of 'Balder Dead' is too remote to arrest sympathy, and 'Sohrab and Rustum' is the finest specimen of Arnold's Homeric manner. It is indeed a marvellously close reproduction of the classic style. The simple flow of the narrative, the reticence from personal re-flection, the skilful repetition of sonorous names remind the student at every turn of the poet's ancient model. The subject is one of those terrible situations which require delicate and refined handling. It strikes a note so high that it is with difficulty sustained. In the solemnising presence of a venerable cathedral we resent the disturbance of our soli-tude by the intrusive gabble of a verger. So also such an incident as the death of a son at the hands of a father suggests thoughts to the mind which make the poet's presentation of the scene, if it is not in faultless taste, appear officious. From this danger Arnold's refined instincts preserve him. There is not a word too much but from first to last the story is told with true Homeric simplicity. The poet knows that he has something to say, and is not afraid to be homely, while the even stately roll of the noble blank verse is the fitting embodiment of the strong and masculine tone of feeling. The environment of the poem with the wide steppes and plains of Central Asia and the wild free-ranging life of the Tartar hordes is skilfully conveyed with the force of graphic suggestion. Little fault can be found with the language. Yet surely the simile used to describe the feelings of Rustum as he eyes Sohrab coming towards him from the Tartar tents is out of keeping.

> As some rich woman, on a winter's mourn,
> Eyes through her silken curtains the poor drudge
> Who with numb blacken'd fingers makes her fire—

At cock-crow, on a starlit winter's morn,
When the frost flowers the whiten'd window panes—
And wonders how she lives, and what the thoughts
Of that poor drudge may be; so Rustum ey'd
The unknown adventurous youth.

The idea of the half-starved seamstress is so entirely modern that it strikes a jarring note. Another point, which is at least open to dispute, is the relevancy of the concluding portion of the poem. The description of the Oxus is in itself one of the most beautiful passages that Arnold ever wrote; yet we doubt whether the suggestion that the great river flows quietly onwards, undisturbed by the love and hate of men, is not in false taste, and whether the poem would not have ended more appropriately with—

So on the bloody sand Sohrab lay dead.

But this introduction of nature as the solace to overwrought feeling is eminently characteristic of the poet. The description of the Oxus resembles the vision which closes 'Empedocles on Etna,' or the spectacle of the untroubled heavens which in 'A Summer Night' consoles the poet for the hard alternatives of modern life. Thus the passage illustrates his peculiar attitude towards Nature, upon which something remains to be said. Both the harmony of the metaphor of the drudge, and the relevancy of the conclusion, are questions of taste upon which it is impossible to dogmatise. Even if both are, as we think, out of keeping with the general structure of the poem, they do not seriously detract from its general merits. But the grave defect of 'Sohrab and Rustum' remains to be mentioned. It is a fine picture after the Homeric manner; but it has the academic coldness of a reproduction, and the general effect is tame because Arnold does not attempt to give us a stirring battle-piece of his own. With what fire and spirit Scott would have treated the theme! And it must be confessed that the poem does not contain that amplitude of matter which is the excuse and the compensation for the measured movement of the ancient school.

Both the poems which we have called classic are written in an heroic blank verse that is always melodious and is rarely disfigured by weak endings. Such a passage as the burning of the ship in 'Balder Dead' is a fine specimen of Arnold's mastery of the metre. But the fault of his blank verse is its monotony of cadence. Arnold sacrifices variety to the rigid metrical principles of his masters. Like them he refused to divide his lines in the middle—with the inevitable result that his movements are fettered.

Elegiac poetry is most congenial to Arnold's mind. In grief for the loss of friends he was not hampered by those artistic rules to which he clung with paradoxical tenacity but without the grip of sincere conviction. In this mood his best poetry is written; in it he is himself; and of recent years in it alone he sang. To this class belong 'The Scholar Gipsy,' 'Thyrsis,' 'A Southern Night,' 'Obermann once more,' 'Stanzas from the Grande Chartreuse,' 'Heine's Grave,' 'Memorial Verses, 'Rugby Chapel,' 'Requiescat,' 'Westminster Abbey,' 'Geist's Grave,' and 'Poor Mathias.' In these poems Arnold finds full and legitimate scope for the tenderness which is one of the strongest of his poetic gifts, and for the deep sense of the pathos of separation which gives its charm to 'The Forsaken Merman' or 'Tristram and Iseult.' In them we find an intensity of feeling which elsewhere we seek in vain. In them he gives free rein to his heart, and no longer starves it by a laborious search for premature tranquillity or for academic correctness.

It may seem extravagant to rank 'Thyrsis' with the four great poems in which English poets have enshrined the memory of departed friends. But though it is less elaborate and ornate than 'Lycidas' or 'In Memoriam,' and less aflame with fiery scorn than 'Adonais,' it is more spontaneous and more tenderly regretful than any of its rivals, and leaves a deeper impression of the personal loss which the poet has sustained. Both 'Thryrsis' and 'The Scholar Gipsy' are too well known to bear the large quotations that would be necessary to establish their claim to rank among great memorial poems. As a specimen of his simple elegiac poetry, we quote the whole of 'Requiescat,' familiar though it is to students of Arnold's verse.

[Quotes 'Requiescat' in its entirety]

Objection may be taken—and, in our opinion, rightly taken—to the fourth line of the first stanza, because it intrudes a new element into the poem. But with this possible exception nothing can be simpler in its language or more quietly direct than the treatment. No analysis of character and no moralising are required to produce the impression. The pathetic effect is given by the plainest presentation of the situation. 'Requiescat,' as the pure expression of a single feeling, illustrates Arnold's Homeric style of elegiac poetry. More elaborate and more reflective is 'A Southern Night;' yet in the modern manner it is almost equally perfect. It contains a beautiful picture which supplies the keynote to the whole poem, and which we shall venture to extract. His brother died at Gibraltar on his voyage home from India, and Arnold recalls the scene.

[Quotes 'A Summer Night', ll. 29–48, 'Slow to a stop, at morning grey', etc.]

If we except the best of his elegiac compositions, none of Arnold's verse reaches the highest class of poetry. His achievements will not, in our opinion, raise him above the rank of minor poets. He is, in fact, a nineteenth-century Gray. He is less remarkable for what he says than for his manner of saying it, and he is never so completely a child of nature as to forget the form in which he clothes his thoughts. Yet in the austere earnestness of his tone and in the breadth of his simple style, he is essentially an imaginative, rather than a fanciful, poet. Dissatisfied with the mere adornment of ideas, he calls up images which more incline to vastness and sublimity than to filigree and definiteness. He esteems the solid worth of a single stone above the number and variety of the sparkling jewels into which it may be cut. He is not rapid, exuberant, or profuse, but stately, measured, self-restrained. His aim is unity of impression, sustained power, simplicity of effect.

Though Arnold is not a born poet, and writes rather for recreation than from impulse, he claims a high place among learned and artistic versifiers. His poetry possesses a decided, definite, and distinctive charm which never palls upon the appetite. It is not rich, generous, full-bodied, strengthening; but it is never cloying, and always pure, clean-tasted, and refreshing. Much of his early verse is vitiated by the affected quietism of his moral creed, or the professorial coldness of his æsthetic theories. His most affecting and imperishable lines are those which he wrote when the social preacher or the conscious artist was temporarily forgotten in the tender-hearted, affectionate man. Apart from these outbursts of true feeling, the general merits of his poetry must be, in the main, described by negatives, or, in other words, by the conspicuous absence of the most salient faults of other writers. It is essentially the poetry of a refined, high-bred gentleman.

Arnold never assumes the airs and affectations which are the vulgarities of poets. His artistic finish is, in fact, the graceful ease of a taste which is naturally pure, but it has also been sedulously cultivated. He never attempts to hide the barrenness of his thought by the luxuriance of his rhymes, or veils his nakedness in the involutions of studied obscurity. He never affects a false intensity of expression, or strains unnaturally after far-fetched epithets, and consequently his lines show no trace of spasmodic weakness. His muse is transparently honest; he nowhere pretends to express more than he feels, or strives at more than he can fully accomplish. Too dignified to be pretentious, too proud to be assuming, he neither apes profundity nor seeks to create an impression by startling phrases. He says what he has to say clearly and decisively, without any false show of word-daubing, never haunted by the fear that paralyses smaller men, and against which Sainte-Beuve cautioned Baudelaire—the fear *d'être trop commun*. He is careful to subordinate his details to the whole; with praiseworthy self-restraint he keeps his picturesque passages within bounds, and, even when he describes a garden, allots no inordinate space to the colouring of his flowers. It would be difficult in all his poetry to find a single ornament which has been pinned on merely as a spangle. He never paints for painting's sake, but uses similes and metaphors to help forward the central idea of his poem. His work is characterised by self-control and reticence, and his strong, decided, telling strokes bring out the exact point which most materially assists the development of his thought or of his narrative. An admirable illustration of his thorough self-discipline, braced and elevated by the study of Hellenic models, is seen in the introduction of the comparison of the two eagles to illustrate Rustum's ignorance of the desolation which his own hand had wrought by the death of his son. We refer our readers to the passage in 'Sohrab and Rustum,' and ask them to observe how Arnold's abstention from word-painting fixes the mind upon the one point that the comparison is designed to illustrate. The same restraint is visible in his use of language. He is always careful in his diction; he does not bewilder with the false gaudiness of perpetual metaphor, or dazzle with the unnatural sparkle of constant antithesis. Every epithet has its meaning, and many are so felicitously chosen that they are in their application condensed pictures. Merits such as these, though in the main of a negative character, are yet great. If Arnold lacks fire and spirit, he rarely halts or stumbles. Seeing how near he came to making himself a poet, he may be excused for the belief that poets need not be born. Yet the emphasis which he laid upon form and method was extravagant, and, as a basis of criticism, one-sided. The glowing stream of verse that pours forth from men who are aflame with some overmastering impulse forms its own channels, fusing thought and expression into one mould. But mere mechanics are not poets, and elaborate construction, though it may be less wearisome, is infinitely more hopeless than brilliant bursts of ill-assorted imagery.

Arnold's classical poetry has given us such embodiments of the Hellenic style as English literature had never before possessed. Behind the pagan lore and Hebrew elevation of 'Lycidas' or 'Samson Agonistes' speaks the voice of Milton, and it is the immanence of his strong soul that gives to both their depth of harmony. So, too, through the classic paintings of 'Hyperion' or 'Ulysses,' glows the youthful exuberance of Keats, or the warm richness of Tennyson's picturesque mind. But Arnold, without Milton's strength, Keats's gorgeous imagination, or Tennyson's pictorial fire, has succeeded—where they have relatively failed—in embodying the pure classic spirit in a statuesque form, almost entirely uncoloured by modern feeling. But he achieved this imitative success by the felicity of his artistic taste, and not by the ardour of his poetic soul. It is not as the skilful reproducer of classic methods, nor yet as the reflector of a confused, complex, and sceptical era, still less as the teacher of an indistinct ethical philosophy, that Arnold makes his strongest claim to be considered a poet; rather it is as the wistful memorialist of the pangs of loss and separation, and as the direct transcriber of the restfulness which belongs to the gentler moods of Nature. Weary of the struggle with himself, and of the contemplation of great currents of life, he turns his jaded eyes towards some human friend or on the inanimate world, and in their society seeks repose. For the English people he professed contempt; for English scenery he had conceived a passionate love, which inspired him to write passages of descriptive verse in a manner peculiarly his own, and with a power which, in the special and limited field of its exercise, is unrivalled. In his elegiac verse he allows free play to the two strongest feelings of which he was capable, and it is the union of both in the same compositions which constitutes the affecting truth and simple charm of this class of his poetry. Here he is most nearly a great poet, because he is most simply himself.

In Arnold's descriptive poetry Wordsworth was his master, but the pupil is entirely independent of the teacher. Wordsworth directed Arnold to the source where he found the truest anodyne for his intellectual pain. Worn out by the anxieties of human life, he flies to Nature for calm and quiet, and he finds them there. It was the combination of delight in Nature and disappointment in Man that first attracted him to Sénancour. His 'Wish' is only a poetical expansion of a prose passage from 'Obermann.' Arnold asks that when the winnowing wings of approaching death are clearing the mist that broods over the borders of the undiscovered future, he shall not be pestered by all that makes the angel's coming hideous.

Bring none of these! but let me be,
  While all around in silence lies,
Moved to the window near, and see
  Once more before my dying eyes,

Bathed in the sacred dews of morn,
  The wide aerial landscape spread,
The world which was ere I was born,
  The world which lasts when I am dead.

So too wishes Obermann:—

Si j'arrive à la vieillesse, si un jour, plein de pensées encore, mais renonçant à parler aux hommes, j'ai auprès de moi un ami pour recevoir mes adieux à la terre, qu'on place ma chaise sur l'herbe courte et que de tranquilles marguerites soient là devant moi, sous le soleil, sous le ciel immense, afin qu'en laissant la vie qui passe, je retrouve quelque chose de l'illusion infinie.

It is this sense of the soothing power of Nature which is always predominant in Arnold's mind. The attitude which he assumes to her is widely different from that of Wordsworth, and the gifts which she bestows on her worshippers are dissimilar. Wordsworth, seeking an interpretation of the mysteries by which he was surrounded, regards Nature through the medium of his own thoughts, and in describing her he gives us a new creation evolved from the influences of the inanimate world upon his own thoughts. He asks us to put ourselves in his place, to view the universe with his eyes, to behold it, not as it is, but as he sees it. To Arnold, on the other hand, Nature teaches no lessons, unlocks no mysteries of life. He does not seek her solitudes to learn the interpretation of oracles. She gives him the boon which he asks, and that boon is tranquillity, not knowledge. She cools the fever of his thoughts, distracts his mind from its saddening anxieties, and ministers relief rather than peace. To Arnold she offers a febrifuge, to Wordsworth a draught of intoxicating joy. And as Arnold's attitude is simpler than that of Wordsworth, so is his method of description. He exacts no labour from his reader to follow the course of his imaginative thought, but comes into direct contact with Nature, sees things as they are, and with his eye undistracted from its object transcribes the scene before him. He makes us share his picture, and so subtly suggests the rest which he himself enjoys that we become partners of his repose, and feel the cool breath of the same fresh free air upon our faces. Wordsworth, ever eager to decipher the riddles of human life in the hieroglyphics of Nature, elevates and invigorates minds which are capable of making the necessary

367

initial effort. Arnold sinks like a tired child upon the lap of Nature, and, reposing on her bosom, imparts to others his own restfulness. Many quotations might be made to illustrate the simplicity, the directness, and the repose of his descriptive passages. We will conclude our imperfect study of one of the most charming of our minor poets with four quotations as specimens of Arnold's treatment of Nature. The first is taken from 'The Scholar Gipsy:—'

[Quotes ll. 71–80, 'For most, I know, thou lov'st', etc.]

Our second quotation is made from 'Thyrsis;' and here the same characteristics of precision and directness reappear, combined with a simplicity which those who compare the description with Tennyson's picture of the garden in 'Maud' will scarcely fail to appreciate:—

[Quotes ll, 61–76, 'So come tempestuous morn', etc.]

Or compare this beautiful stanza from the same poem with the gorgeously imaginative picture which the same scenery inspired in Shelley's 'Alastor:'—

[Quotes ll. 121–30, 'Where is the girl', etc.]

The last quotation is taken from 'Lines written in Kensington Gardens,' and it is chosen out of many similar passages because it breathes the subtle air of that rest which Arnold sought and found in the society of Nature, even in the midst of a great city.

[Quotes ll. 1–16, 'In this lone open glade I lie', etc.]

35. Edward Dowden on Arnold as poet, *Atalanta*

September 1889, ii, 809–13

Dowden (1843–1914) was a Professor of English in Trinity College, Dublin. He is best known for his *Life of Shelley* (1886), which prompted Arnold's famous review. Dowden's is almost a textbook reading of Arnold as a 'poet of ideas'. He 'strike[s] at once for the centre' of the poems by applying to Arnold the notion of poetry as 'criticism of life'. Dowden's assessment can be no more subtle than his wholesale acceptance of Arnold's tag, but as criticism of 'content', his essay is efficient, clear, and in its focus characteristic of the time.

The work of Matthew Arnold as a critic of literature, politics, and social life would afford ample material for a separate study. I purpose here to speak only of his work as a poet—work of an earlier date and perhaps or a more enduring value than his work as a critic; and in the consideration of his poetry I purpose to apply some of his own principles, some of his own tests. He himself maintained that the poet is essentially a higher and deeper kind of critic, a critic of life who is eminently endowed with imagination and a love for what is beautiful and noble. 'It is important,' he said, 'to hold fast to this: that poetry is at bottom a criticism of life; that the greatness of a poet lies in his powerful and beautiful application of ideas to life—to the question: How to live.' And elsewhere he asserted, that for poetry 'the idea is everything,' and that its great function is to interpret life for us, to console us, to sustain us.

Instead, therefore, of wandering on the surface of his poems, I will strike at once for the centre, and put the question—What are the ideas which he has applied with power or beauty to life? How has he interpreted life for us? What sustenance, what consolation do we find in his verse?

His poems fall into two principal groups—those poems in which he expresses his own thoughts and feelings, whether directly or in connection with some subject that calls them forth, and those poems which are impersonal, which deal with themes viewed and handled of course in his own peculiar manner, but belonging rather to the universal life and passion of the world than to his own individual heart and soul. To this latter—the objective—class belong such poems as the Eastern epic episode 'Sohrab and Rustum,' the Scandinavian epic episode 'Balder Dead,' the drama of *Merope* designed after classical Greek models, the mediæval romance of 'Tristram and Iseult,' and that pathetic idyll of the sea-sands and the sea, a kind of domestic tragedy of life below the waves, 'The Forsaken Merman.' But the poems of Matthew Arnold which directly or indirectly embody his personal thoughts and feelings form the great body of his work, and in some respects the most characteristic part of that work. And it is in them we shall find with least difficulty the ideas which he applies to life, his interpretation of its meaning, and what he contributes as a poet to sustain us or to console.

One contrast runs through many of these personal poems of Matthew Arnold, and leads us to what may justly be called his central thought as a spiritual teacher in verse—the contrast between the life whose springs are inward of the soul and the life of division and distraction, of fever and unrest, which is drawn hither and thither by the influences of the world, its pleasures and passions, its business, greeds, ambitions, casual attractions, conflicting opinions, and trivial cares and strifes. Drawn hither and thither by these; and not by these alone, but also by all the various objects that claim our purer sympathies from day to day, and the various intellectual lights and cross lights that lead us or mislead us away from the true objects of the soul. Especially in these latter days of ours, when no dominant faith or doctrine of life imposes itself on the minds of men, when there is around us a chaos of creeds, and when men lie open through their finer intellectual sensitiveness to so many diverse influences, is it difficult to find one's true way. We are beset on this side and on that, and lose ourselves striving and toiling in the world and wave of men. We are as Hector contending on the plain around Troy in the heat and dust of battle. But the city of Ilium was safe so long as the sacred image, the Palladium, stood in its temple high amid rock and wood by the upper streams of Simois, where the moonbeams and the sunlight fall clear. And have we, asks the poet, no Palladium? Yes, we have, though we visit it too rarely and but for moments, and this Palladium of ours is the soul—

> Still doth the soul, from its lone fastness high,
> Upon our life a ruling effluence send;
> And when it fails, fight as we will, we die,
> And while it lasts we cannot wholly end.

It is the loss of this Palladium, the soul, that each of us should fear before all else.

To lose one's soul means for Matthew Arnold to live a life without unity, a life of cares, hopes, fears, desires, opinions, business, passions, which come into existence and cease to exist with the accidents of each successive day and hour. To live too fast, to be perpetually harassed, to be dulled by toil or to be made wild with passion, to adapt ourselves to every view of truth in turn, and never to see truth with lucidity and as a whole, to yield to the chance allurements of the time and place, and never to possess our souls before we die—this is the condition of many of us, especially in these days of crowded and hurrying action, these days of moral trouble and spiritual doubt, and it is no better than a death in life. On the other hand, to be self-poised and harmonious, to 'see life steadily and see it whole,' to escape from the torment of conflicting desires, to gain a high serenity, a wide and luminous view—this is the rare attainment of chosen spirits and the very life of life. And how may the evil be avoided and the good be gained and held fast? Not by any external aids, replies Matthew Arnold, not by the outward machinery of life, not by creeds that fail and philosophies that fade and pass away, not by dreaming of some more fortunate sphere than that in which we are placed; not thus, but by insight and moral vigour, by tending the growth of the godlike seeds within us, by rallying the good in the depths of ourselves—

> The aids to noble life are all within.

Such is his stoical moral teaching.

We cannot hope, as Matthew Arnold admits, that it will be granted to many of us to attain the wide view of Goethe, the joyous calm of Wordsworth; but we may at least aim at what he describes as the 'Second Best.' We must needs live to some extent a life of strain; we cannot escape from intellectual distractions; we cannot but be pestered by idle wishes which demand their gratification. Still it is something, it is indeed much, if we can thread our way not wholly without a purpose, if we can in the main choose what will aid our best life, and can make wise rejection of what will not serve the soul. 'No small profit,' says the poet, 'that man earns,

Who through all he meets can steer him,
Can reject what cannot clear him,
Cling to what can truly cheer him;
　Who each day more truly learns
That an impulse from the distance
Of his deepest, best existence
To the words 'Hope, Light, Persistence,'
　Strongly sets and truly burns.'

This is not the best, but it is the second best, and it is what each of us by fidelity to the promptings of his highest self may hope to attain. And with the Hope which lives within us and grows clearer and simpler as the years go by, what if we also come to possess something of Resignation? This also is a part of intellectual and spiritual clearness which comes with maturing years. We started with so many passionate hopes that were not a part of our true selves, and that could not be fulfilled. Better than these is a heart set free from vain desires and vain fears, a heart at rest in tranquil and resigned self-possession—

Be passionate hopes not ill resigned
For quiet, and a fearless mind.
And though fate grudge to thee and me
The poet's rapt security,
Yet they, believe me, who await
No gifts from chance, have conquered fate.

In such a calm as this there is something pathetic; yet it may be cheered by the words 'Hope, Light, Persistence,' though the hope and light have something autumnal in their calmness and their cool, and the quiet persistence be little like the eager energy of youth.

　But advancing years will not of themselves bring us clearness and poise. Matthew Arnold in his poetry was not one who sang the praises of old age. Youth with its thwarting currents of desire, its heats and agitations, its vain expense of passions may leave us, and yet no wider view, no stronger self-possession may be ours. We may have dwindled rather than have grown; we may have lost our faculty of joy and have gained nothing, finding at last that the only thing common to youth and age is discontent. (See 'Youth's Agitation' and 'Growing Old.') Death indeed will at last bring deliverance from the distraction and turmoil, and we speak as if there were a certain calm and poise attained in death—

372

Her life was turning, turning,
In mazes of heat and sound;
But for peace her soul was yearning,
And now peace laps her round.

But the crown of life is not a barren calm, though calm is well ('Youth and Calm'); it is that vital calm of self-poised joy which comes to us when the soul is living its truest and highest life. Neither mere lapse of time nor the touch of death will bring this to us; it can only be gained by 'rallying the good in the depths of ourselves.'

'Arnold,' writes a thoughtful critic, 'is never quite at his best except when he is delineating a mood of regret, and then his best consists not in yielding to it, but in the resistance he makes to it.' The pain and trouble expressed in his poetry arise from his sense of the many dangers to which the higher life is exposed through external distractions, 'bandied to and fro, like a sea-wave'—and from our own infirmity; the resistance to that pain comes from a consciousness of the strength and virtue of the soul, and a knowledge that it can at worst retire into a stronghold unbreachable by the world. If the world boasts her conquests over so many spirits once fiery with the ardour of reform, let each one of us, as the world's foe, resist with only the more determined energy—

Hast thou so rare a poison?—let me be
Keener to slay thee, lest thou poison me.

Even if the highest aids of the soul were to fail, still the soul could make a retreat upon itself and there find strength enough for noble life; even if Heaven were proved a dream, still to live nobly and not the life of the brute were best for man—

Hath man no second life? *Pitch this one high!*
Sits there no judge in Heaven our sin to see?
More strictly, then, the inward judge obey!
Was Christ a man like us?—*Ah! let us try
If we then, too, can be such men as He!*

Much may be taken from us, but at the worst we can make this our aim —to 'think clear, feel deep, bear fruit well.' (Last lines of 'Progress'.)

No English poet has given us more exquisite pictures of English landscape than Matthew Arnold. I cannot linger over their charm, but in accordance with the limited purpose of this paper, I must put the question—How is external nature, its glory, its beauty, its perennial life, conceived by Arnold in relation to the life of the soul? We know what

373

strength and joy flowed into Wordsworth's spirit from his communion with nature: is it so with Matthew Arnold? Assuredly not in a like degree. With a heart fretted and heated by the agitations of the world, he turns to nature more often for calm than for joy; with the tangle and tease of the world upon his spirit, cabined, cribbed, confined in the hot alleys of life, he turns to the gracious mountain lines, to the vastness of the sea, to the star-sown vault of heaven, to the calm radiance of the moon, and enjoys a sense of expansion and repose. The spaces of the upper air and sky remain

> A world above man's head, to let him see
> How boundless might his soul's horizons be,
> How vast, yet of what clear transparency.

At times it causes despondency and almost despair to contrast the everlasting wonder and bloom of the world with the faded, ignoble lives of ourselves and so many of our fellows. But in the end nature leads us back to the soul, and there we find the deep and inexhaustible source of strength. Would we be calm and full of undecaying power like the stars and the waters, which fulfil their functions with toil unsevered from tranquillity? Let us *live* as they, unaffrighted, undistracted, self-poised, pouring all their energies each into its own peculiar task. ('Quiet Work' and 'Self-Dependence.') Thus from nature we return to the soul, and hear its still small voice as if it were an echo from the mighty sum of things—

> Resolve to be thyself; and know that he
> Who finds himself, loses his misery.

Labouring as nature labours, with a sure aim, in obedience to an inward law, and free from vain turmoil, we shall ennoble even the hardest taskwork. In faith founded upon our former hour of insight, we shall persist in our toil even through darkness and amid manifold infirmities—

> For tasks in hours of insight will'd
> Can be through hours of gloom fulfill'd.

Nay, even the noisiest pleasures, though they may not serve us, may yet be harmless if amid their tumult we secretly keep close to the soul. Mycerinus, the just king of ancient Egypt, who even in fiery youth sat, self-governed, at the feet of Law, learned the doom of the gods, that after six short years he should die; and the just law-giver, the contemplator of divine things, under so great a shock seemed to lose his insight and balance, giving himself up to noisy revelry. Yet it may be that there were moments when he still possessed his soul, when 'he, within,—

> Took measure of his soul and knew its strength,
> And by that silent knowledge, day by day,
> Was calm'd, ennobled, comforted, sustain'd.'

And thus he may have been enabled to advance with a smooth brow and clear laughter towards his death.

When we have learnt the lesson of external nature, the lesson of 'toil unsevered from tranquillity,' we can then lift up our hearts and say that in a certain sense man is greater than nature, for it is the prerogative of man to be all that which we imply by the word *humane*—to be gentle, to choose the right, to love, and to adore. 'Man,' says Matthew Arnold, 'must begin where Nature ends,' he has all that nature has, but more—

> And in that *more* lie all his hopes of good.

A similar thought is expressed in Goethe's noble poem, *Das Göttliche*.

But deeper than our own power of choosing what is right, our own power of threading our way amid the confusion of the world, there may be implanted within us a law which determines our course. Let us not fret too much if we have sometimes been diverted from our aim—

> If some fair coast has lured us to make stay,
> Or some friend hailed us to keep company.

Let us know for our comfort that 'man cannot, though he would, live chance's slave.' We are each of us as a ship that pursues its labouring way through the ocean waves; all seems to change around us every moment, and all does indeed change, but may it not be that we steer across the sea of life, 'as chartered by some unknown powers,' leaving behind only

> The joys which were not for our use designed,
> The friends to whom we had no natural right,
> The homes that were not destined to be ours.

This inward law impressed upon our being is elsewhere spoken of by Matthew Arnold as 'the Buried Life,'—the life that lies deep within us, our hidden self, from which we often wander, yet which we do not ever wholly forsake. There are moments of lull in the hot race of life when a man becomes aware of this buried life, and 'thinks he knows

> The hills where his life rose,
> And the sea where it goes.'

Sometimes it is a gentle voice, or a beloved hand laid on ours which thus recalls us to our truer self. Passionate love of man and woman is not sung by Matthew Arnold; he distrusts all eager passions lest they may be erroneous; but the love which is tender, mild, lucid, is felt by him as at least a possible aid to the highest spiritual life.

More, however, than is ever likely to be gained through love of man for woman (for, after all, is not each human being isolated, an island encircled by some 'unplumb'd, salt, estranging sea'?) may be gained from the great teachers of a moral wisdom which each of us may indeed make his own. Matthew Arnold thinks with especial reverence of the Stoic moralist Epictetus; of Sophocles, with his steady and luminous view of life; of Wordsworth and Goethe; of Emerson, whose appeal is always to what is divine in the spirit of each of us; and of his generous and heroic father, the master of Rugby, that strong soul, radiant in its vigour, whose life was no 'eddy of purposeless dust,' who would not reach the goal alone, but would fain bring with him others that might have wandered or fallen by the way, poor stragglers that might have dropped from the ranks (see 'Rugby Chapel,' 'To a Friend,' and 'Sonnet written in Emerson's Essays'). These are the heroes of the spiritual life, and from these we may each derive something of light, hope, courage, guidance, calm.

These are the heroes of the spiritual life; but Matthew Arnold is also deeply interested in fugitives from the world, and shy recluses who desert the highways of men in order to seek after the life of the soul in solitude. Such are his Scholar Gipsy, his Obermann, his Empedocles, and the monks of the Grande Chartreuse in that poem which records his visit to their refuge and spiritual asylum amid the snows. No poems of the writer are more characteristic, more beautiful in utterance, more deep in meaning, than these which tell of his sympathy with the fugitives. Around the Oxford student, who left his collegiate seclusion for the more delicate seclusion of a shy wanderer by wood and stream in search of the hidden wisdom, the poet has thrown an inexpressible charm. How unlike his life to ours! We, tiring our wits upon a thousand schemes, fluctuating idly, striving, and not knowing for what we strive; half living, each of us, a hundred different lives; he, having *one* aim, *one* business, *one* desire, 'nursing his project in unclouded joy.' Less happy in the period in which he lived was Obermann, the fugitive to Alpine solitudes; yet he too, and even in our century of trouble, attained to see his way, and could look forward calmly to eternity as his everlasting refuge. The Carthusian monks possess their souls, but in a way which perhaps belongs rather to a past age than to our own, and which is certainly unattainable by one who has taken into his being all the diverse influences of modern thought and culture. Greatest of Matthew Arnold's fugitives is the philosopher Empedocles, the slave of thought, who has lost in tangled intellectual processes the life and the joy of the soul. As he climbs the heights of Etna, his spirit is somewhat attuned to harmony by the divine songs of the boy Callicles, and meditating much on the past history of his soul, he recovers, at least for a moment, insight and the poise of self-dependence, and in the same moment he flings himself into the seething crater to mingle his being with the living forces of nature. And for us too there may be a source of energy and strength, not in the force and fury of Etna, but in some general movement of higher spiritual life towards which the world is tending, and into which we can cast ourselves—

> One common wave of thought and joy
> Lifting mankind again!

This may be; it is our hope that it will be; but should we never feel the buoyant strength of that common wave of thought and joy, at least there remains for each of us his individual soul and its watchword of 'Hope, Light, Persistence.'

Such, keeping very close to the text, is an interpretation of Matthew Arnold's poetry as a criticism of life. I could wish that space allowed me to compare it with what seems to me the higher and wiser criticism of life to be found in the poetry of Robert Browning.

36. More comments from the 1880s

(a) C. E. Tyrer in the *Manchester Quarterly*, January 1883

There is perhaps no living writer who quite equals Mr. Arnold in the simplicity and clearness of his style, with the exception of another Oxford poet and thinker, who has brought charm of style and mastery of language to the service of a very different school of thought—John Henry Newman. Perhaps, if we would characterize by a single word this quality of Mr. Arnold's poetry, we may describe it as 'sculpturesque' —a term applied to it, I think, by a writer in *The Spectator*.

There is another quality in Matthew Arnold, which is perhaps still more precious than his classicality of style and language—that quality which he himself has called 'natural magic.' It is something as different as possible from mere description, which, whether in prose or verse, is in general, perhaps, the most tedious and unprofitable of all reading. The true poet does not describe nature—he in a manner reproduces her charm.

. . . .

'Poetry,' said the German mystic Novalis, 'heals the wounds which the understanding makes.' There was never perhaps a time in which the understanding has inflicted more wounds on the heart and the spirit of man than that in which we live, and it is especially in an age of unrest like the present that we need the soothing agencies of art and poetry.

> This strange disease of modern life
> With its sick hurry, its divided aims,

has touched our poet deeply, but his remedy for our discontent, for our imperious demand for happiness, is but such stoical comfort as we may gather from the chant of Empedocles:—

> In vain our pent wills fret
> And would the world subdue,
> Limits we did not set
> Condition all we do:
> Born into life we are, and life must be our mould.

378

Indeed, the philosopher of Agrigentum may not unfitly symbolize our modern thinker, pondering sadly on the deep things of life, while to him in his solitude there rise, as from the voice and harp of the boy Callicles, the healing influences of music and of song. There is a haunting sadness about much of Mr. Arnold's verse, that but too faithfully images the mood of many of the most thoughtful men among us.

(b) Anonymous critic on 'The Poetry of Despair', *London Quarterly Review*, April 1885

[Matthew Arnold's] poetry is virtually the confession that his culture has failed. In him the personal note is supreme; it is the problem of his own life which fascinates us. He can strike chords of great power and sweetness, and sometimes of deep tenderness, but he is greatest as a poet when he expresses his own heartfelt mournfulness and yearning. The two worlds he stands between are the old world of faith which is dead, and the new world of culture which is 'powerless to be born.' He cannot hide his sorrow, it is ever before him; he cannot disguise the fact that his culture has failed to satisfy him. In one of his most notable poems, which, perhaps, more than any other, distils the very essence of the disturbed religious spirit of the age, he cries with an exceeding bitter cry after that Cross which he has declared a vanished myth, and that assured creed which he had dismissed as a beautiful imposture. He confesses the cruel conflict that is within him, the devoutness which has survived his doubts, the religious yearnings which are not quenched by his denials. In this respect his position is unique; he sings as one believing in his unbelief, and he is only saved from utter despair by this devoutness which he has not dared to destroy. But beyond that, the most memorable feature of his poetry is its acknowledgment—wrung from him rather than confessed—that his lack of faith has sapped the very courses of his thought, and that culture in its utmost beauty and refinement has proved itself but shifting sand when the storms have beaten and the winds of trouble blown. He sees with dismay and despair the hopeless tangle of the age. . . .

(c) Anonymous critic on 'The Poet of Elegy', *Spectator*, 18 July
1885

Gray will always, we suppose, hold, by virtue rather of earlier claim
than of prior right, the first nominal place amongst our elegiac poets.
The 'Elegy in a Country Churchyard' is so beautiful and so simple, so
entirely devoid of anything that is 'caviare to the general,' and reflects so
perfectly that mood of gentle regret which is neither too gloomy for
fascination nor too intense for a quietly imaginative heart, that it has
almost stamped him on the national mind as the elegiac poet of our
country. But the present writer at least is convinced that neither the
'Elegy in a Country Churchyard,' nor the 'Ode on a Distant Prospect of
Eton College,' beautiful as each is, touches so high a point in the elegiac
poetry of our country as some half-dozen of Matthew Arnold's poems.
Just glance over the edition of his poems in three volumes which Messrs.
Macmillan have just issued; you will be struck by the fact that *all* the
finest poems in all three, even though professing to be lyric, or dramatic,
or narrative, are in their finest passages and happiest thoughts essentially
poems of elegy,—by which we mean poems of exquisite regret,—and
not, in fact, poems of longing, or of passion, or of character, or of heroic
venture. Even the beautiful early poem on the Church of Brou is essentially elegiac. 'Youth and Calm,' again, contains the very heart of
elegy:—

[Quotes 'Youth and Calm' in its entirety]

That is an early poem (and we take leave to print it as it was first published, and not as it has been re-edited by its author), and one in which
the elegiac tone is not perhaps hit with the perfect felicity of later years;
but still it has the very life of the poet in it, and marks as distinctly as
Goethe's early songs marked, the region in which the verse of the poet
who produced it was destined to excel. It is the same with the rather
enigmatic but still most powerful early lines addressed 'To a Gipsy Child
by the Seashore.' It is the same again with the touching lines entitled
'Resignation,'—also an early poem,—which in its close gives us another
and most pathetic variation on the note of exquisite regret:—

[Quotes ll. 261–78, 'Enough we live', etc.]

380

Even of the narrative poems, far the most effective parts are written in the elegiac mood. There is nothing so fine in 'Sohrab and Rustum' as the beautiful elegiac close describing the course of the Oxus to the Aral Sea. The 'Sick King in Bokhara' is one of the most beautiful of these poems; but the beauty in it is chiefly the beauty of the regret with which the King pities and commemorates the sorrow he could not cure. The whole tone of 'Tristram and Iseult' is elegiac, a chastened review of passion spent and past, not of passion strong and present. And it is the same with 'The Forsaken Merman.'

Or take the poems which Mr. Arnold himself calls lyric and you will find that all the more effective of them are really elegiac in tone. Is not the poem on isolation, in which the deep regret is poured forth that 'we mortal millions live alone,'—that it is a God who

> ——bade betwixt their shores to be
> The unplumb'd, salt, estranging sea,

much more truly elegiac than lyric? Shelley, the great poet of desire, is the true type of a lyric poet. Tennyson is great alike in reflection, in regret, and in description, and sometimes in lyrical feeling. But Matthew Arnold is hardly a lyric poet. His face is never turned to the future. His noblest feeling is always for the past. If he ever tries to delineate the new age, he only succeeds in breaking into praise of the age which is passed away.

(d) Richard Le Gallienne's commemorative poem in the *Academy*,
21 April 1888

MATTHEW ARNOLD.
Died April 15, 1888.
Within that wood where thine own scholar strays,
  O! Poet, thou art passed, and at its bound
  Hollow and sere we cry, yet win no sound
But the dark muttering of the forest maze
We may not tread, nor pierce with any gaze;
  And hardly love dare whisper thou hast found
  That nestful moonlit slope of pastoral ground
Set in dark dingles of the songful ways.

Gone! they have called our shepherd from the hill,
  Passed is the sunny sadness of his song,
    That song which sang of sight and yet was brave
  To lay the ghosts of seeing, subtly strong
    To wean from tears and from the troughs to save;
And who shall teach us now that he is still!

(e) Vida Scudder: an American view in the *Andover Review*,
September 1888

Arnold's attitude towards Nature is curiously distinctive. He never, like
Shelley, ascribes to natural forces, to wind and bird and river, the emotions of his own restless soul; yet he never loses the consciousness of self.
He has no part in the contemplative and impersonal rapture of Wordsworth. Never for a moment can he identify himself with the joy of the
blossom, merge his own life till thought expires in the glory of the

rising sun. He remains aloof, an unimpassioned spectator; noting, indeed, with tender truthfulness every detail; but feeling keenly that between his life and the life of Nature there is a great gulf fixed. Of the passion and wild joy of the natural world, indeed, he is hardly conscious; it is the grandeur of accomplished Duty, of unflinching obedience to Law, which constitute for him the glory of ocean and river and mountain. Thus severe, steadfast, and grand are the aspects that he renders. He is the poet of the sea; the sea, with its infinite yet obedient freedom, with its freshness and its calm. He is the poet of the moonlight, of the tranquil and unclouded heaven suffused with a radiance clearer than that of day; and in this glory of the night he finds example and warning for his restless soul:—

[Quotes 'A Summer Night', ll. 1–15, 'In the deserted, moon-blanched street', etc.]

He is above all the poet of the high mountains. Not even Shelley nor Wordsworth has rendered like him their distinctive majesty; the fullness of mysterious suggestion in the Romantic writers could ill convey purity so august and so serene. But Arnold, with his constant tone of remoteness, has perfectly recorded the isolated grandeur of the hills; that grandeur, terrestrial not celestial, yet possessing an eternal strength, an immutable and untainted glory. Again and again does Arnold instinctively turn to the mountains. The lover, tossed by the hot storms of passion, hears above them all the murmured summons of the untouched heights; the soul exhausted by the struggles of the revolution flees for refuge to the solitude of those pastures which yet cannot release it from its individual pain:—

[Quotes 'Obermann', ll. 25–32, 'Yes, though the virgin mountain air,' etc.]

(f) Augustine Birrell in *Scribner's Magazine*, November 1888

Mr. Arnold, to those who cared for him at all, was the most *useful* poet of his day. He lived much nearer us than poets of his distinction usually do. He was neither a prophet nor a recluse. He lived neither above us, nor away from us. There are two ways of being a recluse—a poet may live remote from men, or he may live in a crowded street but remote from their thoughts. Mr. Arnold did neither, and consequently his verse tells and tingles. None of it is thrown away. His readers feel that he bore the same yoke as themselves. Theirs is a common bondage with his. Beautiful, surpassingly beautiful some of Mr. Arnold's poetry is, but we seize upon the *thought* first and delight in the *form* afterwards. No doubt the form is an extraordinary comfort, for the thoughts are often, as thoughts so widely spread could not fail to be, the very thoughts that are too frequently expressed rudely, crudely, indelicately. To open Mr. Arnold's poems is to escape from a heated atmosphere and a company not wholly free from offence even though composed of those who share our opinions—from loud-mouthed random-talking men into a well-shaded retreat which seems able to impart, even to our feverish persuasions and crude conclusions, something of the coolness of falling water, something of the music of rustling trees. This union of thought, substantive thought, with beauty of form—of strength with elegance, is rare. I doubt very much whether Mr. Arnold ever realised the devotedness his verse inspired in the minds of thousands of his countrymen and countrywomen, both in the old world and the new.

(g) Charles Eliot Norton in *Proceedings of the American Academy of Arts and Sciences,* 1888

[Arnold's first volume] had no great success, and in the later collection and reprint of his Poems a large part of the contents of this volume is omitted. But a discerning critic might have recognized in it the qualities of a new, strong, individual genius. The hand had not yet attained full mastery over the instrument, but its touch was one of exceptional sensibility and refinement. The sentiment of the Poems was instinct with the modern spirit, but their form was largely shaped on the models of classic tradition. Arnold's poetry was the poetry of a scholar, but of a scholar in closest sympathy with the sentiment and emotions of his own generation.

37. Lionel Johnson on *Poetical Works* (1891), *Academy*

10 January 1891, no. 975, 31–2

Johnson (1867–1902), though best remembered as a poet, was also a periodical essayist and a remarkable critic. *The Art of Thomas Hardy* (1896) is an especially fine and sensitive study. Johnson, like his contemporary Oscar Wilde, was an Oxford man and partial to scholarly verse, and though, unlike Wilde, Johnson does not praise Arnold for his Oxford poems, he similarly recognizes a congenial poet. He finds, as George Eliot and J. D. Coleridge had in the early fifties, that Arnold's sense of melody is deficient. Generally, he acknowledges Arnold's faults in 'technique' and in 'conception', but the poems 'possess the secret of great verse, its power of haunting the memory, and of profoundly satisfying it'. He concludes the review with a brief comparison of Arnold and Verlaine.

The publication of Arnold's poems, at a low price, in a single volume, is an act of such merit that we are scarcely permitted to criticise the bibliographical details of this book. It is enough to say that it is a little heavier than is comfortable; something handier, and less awkward, would have been more acceptable. But we have all Arnold's poems, and the best of his portraits, in one volume; let us be satisfied with that, and grateful for it.

There are two poems, not hitherto included: the elegy on Kaiser, and the 'Horatian Echo.' The first contains that just and pleasant satire upon the Laureate, and upon his follower, which we enjoyed a few years ago:

What, Kaiser dead? The heavy news
Post-haste to Cobham calls the Muse,
From where in Farringford she brews
    The ode sublime,
Or with Pen-bryn's bold bard pursues
    A rival rhyme.

The 'Horatian Echo,' which enriched the *Hobby Horse* last year, contains, among many felicities of expression, two exquisite stanzas:

[Quotes ll. 25–36, 'Of little threads', etc.]

    The complete poems of Arnold are little more than one hundred in
number. Of these, only five are of considerable length; yet, taken together, they do not fill half this volume of five hundred pages. So careful and discreet an achievement, during some forty years, ought to come
close upon perfection; and this it does. But of Arnold's rare and happy
qualities we will speak later; let us first have done with his few and
venial faults. In reading this volume through, two things, now and
again, are noticeable. There are lines, phrases, and constructions, not
perfectly polished; and there are poems, or stanzas, not perfectly
musical. That is, there are faults of exclusion and of conception. Arnold,
as Lord Coleridge tells us, had a most imperfect ear for music. Now,
while no one questions his wonderful ear for the cadence of verse, it is
equally true that his sense for melody sometimes failed him. Within
one short poem occur two such discordant lines as 'There the pines slope,
the cloud-strips,' and 'Where the high woods strip sadly.' It explains
Arnold's avowed preference for the rhythm of

        Siehst sehr sterbeblässlich aus,[1]

over the rhythm of

        Que dit le ciel à l'aube, et la flamme à la flamme?

Again, the construction is at times forced, as in

        That furtive mien, that scowling eye,
        Of hair that red and tufted fell—

where the second line 'is only poetry because it is not prose.' These
technical faults are few, and they are less troublesome than the foolish
affectations of much modern workmanship. The second fault, faults of
conception, is more serious. Arnold rarely fails to write in a spirit of
singular loftiness and beauty; he is rarely neglectful of his own precept:

---

[1] [you] 'look deathly pale'.

> Such, poets, is your bride, the Muse! young, gay,
> Radiant, adorn'd outside; a hidden ground
> Of thought and of austerity within.

But, at times, the thought is unadorned and the austerity far from radiant. To take an example:

> 'Religious fervours! ardour misapplied!
> Hence, hence,' they cry, 'ye do but keep man blind!
> But keep him self-immersed, preoccupied,
> And lame the active mind!'

Contrast that, in its nakedness, with the ornament and the radiance of the preceding poem: a poem full, too, of austere thought:

> So, in its lovely moonlight, lives the soul.
> Mountains surround it, and sweet virgin air;
> Cold plashing, past it, crystal waters roll;
> We visit it by moments, ah, too rare!

At once we feel that the first lines are not interesting, not heightened, not touched with emotion; that the second are no less beautiful than elevated.

These things are worth a few words, because the admirers of Arnold are in danger of being held his worshippers also, unless they show themselves aware of his faults. Arnold, great and admirable as he is, is no more perfect than is Gray, Milton, or Sophocles; but he stands above the first, and the others were his most successful masters.

Arnold's poems are of two kinds: there are the narrative poems, whether dramatic or otherwise; and the lyrical, emotional, or meditative poems. Now, it is observable that Arnold is at his best in poems neither long nor short: in poems equal in length to the average Hebrew psalm, the average Greek ode. No doubt there are exceptions: 'Sohrab and Rustum' among the longer poems, 'Requiescat' among the shorter, are nearly faultless. But, for the most part, it is in such poems as 'Thyrsis,' 'A Summer Night,' 'Stanzas from the Grande Chartreuse,' that we find the true Arnold; not in 'Balder Dead,' 'Progress,' 'Revolutions.' In other words, Arnold, to use his own phrase, had not 'the architectonics of poetry, the faculty which presides at the evolution of works like the *Agamemnon* or *Lear*.' Nor was he in the literal sense a singer, such as was Heine or Catullus. Rather, his quality was meditative; he accepted, at least in practice, Wordsworth's definition of poetry, that it is 'emotion remembered in tranquillity.' But it may be objected that Arnold is genial, exultant, even rapturous; that he wrote nothing in the least like "The

Excursion.' That is true; but let us consider a little more curiously. Arnold was fond of national distinctions, qualities of race and temperament. Were one to distinguish Arnold's own qualities, the conclusion might be of this kind. From the Greek culture, he took a delight in the beauty of life and of fine imagination; from the Hebrew genius, a sense of reverence and meditation; from the French, a certain grace and lucidity of spirit; from the German, a steady seriousness of mind. By descent he was, in part, a Celt: that gave him a 'natural magic' of emotion and of soul; while from his English origin, he took that daring common sense which enabled him to hold in harmony these various qualities. Trained in those chosen places of beauty and high tradition, Winchester and Oxford, with the all strength of his father's influence at Rugby, he was always attached to the English ideal: to the ideals of Milton and of Burke. A scholar, a man of the world, a government official, his affections were not narrow, not provincial; but they were not cosmopolitan, not unsettled. His heart was at home in the quiet dignity and peace of an English life, among the great books of antiquity, and the great thoughts of 'all time and all existence.' Hence came his limitations; not from prejudice, nor from ignorance, but from a scrupulous precision and delicacy of taste. No one loved France more than he; no one abhorred more than he 'the great goddess Aselgeia.' He reverenced the German seriousness, depth, moderation of life and thought; he disliked and ridiculed pedantry, awkwardness, want of humour and of grace. In all his criticisms, the same balance between excess and deficiency appears: he was a true Aristotelian. And so, when it is said that Arnold was not a poet of profound philosophy, not a thinker of consistency, or not a man whom we can classify at all, the only answer is a *distinguo*.[1] It was Arnold's work to find beauty and truth in life, to apprehend the meaning and moral worth of things, to discriminate the trivial from the grave, and to show how the serene and ardent life is better than the mean and restless. His poetry, then, is not didactic; but meditative, in the classical sense, it is. Lord Coleridge—in those papers which make us regret that he has 'to law given up what was made for mankind'—is of opinion that Arnold's meditative poems are not destined to live, 'not from any defect of their own, but from the inherent mortality of their subjects.' Yet, surely these poems are more than records of a transitory emotion, the phase and habit of an age. Such a description would apply to Clough; his mournful, homesick, desultory poems are indeed touched with decay, because they are composed without care, in no wide spirit

[1] 'I distinguish.'

of contemplation; reading them we do not think of 'Sophocles by the Aegaean,' nor of the *lacrimae rerum*.[1] But Arnold's thoughts and emotions are profoundly human; we cannot say of them, that only an Oxford man, under such and such influences, at such and such a time, could have felt them in youth and expressed them in after life. True, their immediate tone is that of one 'touched by the Zeit-Geist' in the latter end of the nineteenth century; but their fundamental character is common to all times. For Arnold is human; and what is humanism but the belief that nothing which has ever interested living men and women can wholly lose its vitality: no language they have spoken, no oracle beside which they have hushed their voices, no dream which has once been entertained by actual human minds, nothing about which they have ever been passionate, or expended time and zeal?

Arnold, if this be so, was himself a true humanist, and no true humanist will ever forget him. No doubt the *Christian Year* or the *Essay on Man* have lost their charm and their significance; but we read the one as the memorial of a great phase of sentiment, and the other for its brilliant setting of a very tarnished theory. Much more will Arnold live in these grave and lovely poems, which have so little in them of merely transient feeling. Whatever be the future estimate of Arnold's poems, there is no doubt of their singular charm now. They possess the secret of great verse, its power of haunting the memory, and of profoundly satisfying it. Sad as are some of them, their melancholy is true to nature, and leaves us calm; rejoicing as are others, they never soar out of sight, away from life. But they give a view of nature and of life as contemplated by a mind of great sympathy and insight, acquainted with the choice spirits of ancient civility, and with the living emotions of our own age. No hymn to Dolores can so touch us as the lines 'To Marguerite': the feverish, antiquarian rhetoric of the one may thrill the nerves and leave us tired; the pure beauty and the austere passion of the other appeals to every faculty in us, and leaves a sense of the beauty of human sorrow. Paradoxical as it may sound, there is something very hieratic about Arnold; his apprehension of the beauty of holiness, his love for what is clear and lofty in the pleasures of thought, his constant service of meditation.

> Ah, les Voix, montez donc, mourantes que vous êtes,
> Sentences, mots en voix, metaphores mal faites,
> Toute la rhétorique en fuite des péchés,
> Ah, les Voix, montez donc, mourantes que vous êtes!

[1] 'tears for (or in) things'.

390

Arnold would not have like M. Verlaine's poetry; but those lines
express much of Arnold's mind. The false worship of words, the conventional acceptance of phrases, all the spurious wisdom in the world,
he fought against, and conquered much of it; and there is no one left
to take his place in the struggle against vulgarity and imposture. No
voice like his to sing as he sang of calm and peace among the turbulent
sounds of modern life.

38. Mrs Oliphant, 'Of the Younger Poets', *The Victorian Age of English Literature*

1892, 430–6

Mrs Margaret Oliphant (1828–97), an indefatigable writer of
novels, biographies, and various other books, successfully maintained herself and her family by her pen, as her *Autobiography*
(1899) records. A popular writer, she understandably considered
Arnold an overbred specialist, snobbish in his choice of material,
shamefully limited in his appeal. She can find few virtues in his
work, though she acknowledges his labours, but is fluent on his
limitations. Predictably, she contrasts Arnold with Browning,
whom she finds vigorous and readable, able to win the attention
of a general audience. Her position contrasts markedly with that
of Oscar Wilde, Hopkins, and Lionel Johnson.

The younger section of the poets who have illustrated this age could not
be headed by any name so appropriate as that of Matthew Arnold—
younger not so much in time, for he was not more than a dozen years
in age after Lord Tennyson—but because not only of much later publication, but of a mind and temper which never got far beyond the Academic circle, or remembered that the atmosphere of the classics is not
that most familiar and dear to all men. It is perhaps this atmosphere

more than anything else which has prevented him and others of his brethren from ever penetrating into the heart of the country, and which forms a kind of argument against that careful training which it is now the fashion to claim for every literary workman—the 'woodnotes wild,' which once were chiefly believed in as the voice of poetry, having lost their acceptance among those growing theories of development and descent which would make of every poet a well defined and recognisable product of the influences surrounding him. If this could be said with truth of any group of poets, it might be of Matthew Arnold, Clough, Swinburne, and some later names—to their advantage no doubt in the way of perfect versification, but to their great disadvantage in respect to nature and life. The intellectual difficulties of a highly organised age, and that 'doubt,' unkindly and unmusical spirit, which has been converted into a patron saint or demon by the fashion of the time, are not poetical founts of inspiration, and the old Helicon has run somewhat dry for the general reader. Matthew Arnold (1822–1888), the son of Dr. Arnold of Rugby, and occupied for the greater part of his life in the service of the country, as H. M. Inspector of Schools, is the poet of the Universities,—of the intellectual classes who derive their chief life therefrom, either at first hand or in reflection; he has not in him the mixture of common life and feeling which can conciliate that inner circle with the wider one of the general world, or the warm inspiration of passion and emotional nature which goes to the common heart. The old audience to which the old poets appealed, the *donne che hanno intelletto d'amore*,[1] are left out, unless perhaps when they belong to Girton; so are the children, except those precocious beings who lisp in Greek. The audience which is left him is perhaps the one which he would have preferred, just as Dr. Isaac Watts would no doubt have preferred his audience of the chapels and nurseries; but it is a limited audience, and not that of the greatest poets.

It would be difficult, however, to find a man who made a more prominent appearance on the stage of general literature in his time. His essays, critical and otherwise, kept him very distinctly before the world; and this, and other partly-artificial reasons, raised his name to such a point of general knowledge and acquaintance that a selection of his poems was made and published in his lifetime, an honour which falls to few poets. These we may take as his own selection of what he thought most likely to live. And we find among them the two poems on which most of those who esteem him most highly are willing to rest his fame,—

[1] 'ladies who have a knowledge of love'.

'Thyrsis' and the 'Scholar Gipsy,' both of them comparatively short, and so much more individual than most of his poetical works as to touch a chord of sympathy wanting in many of the others. The extreme diffuseness of much of this poetry is indeed one of the faults which will always keep it outside the popular heart. There is something in the flow of even rhyme, page after page, long, fluent, smooth, looking as if it might go on forever, which appalls the reader. Life is not long enough, as the word goes, for 'Empedocles on Etna.' Mr. Browning in his 'Cleon' has given us the spirit and fine concentrated essence of a philosopher of antiquity in a few pages. In the hands of Mr. Arnold this revelation takes almost a book and with how much less success! The same thing may be said of other poems, of which even the conception appears to be taken from an elder poet, but so amplified as to turn a fine suggestion into weariness. Wordsworth put his 'Yarrow' and 'Yarrow Revisited' (which indeed are not on the highest level of his poetry) into poems which a child might learn by heart without difficulty; but when Mr. Arnold visits the scene of Obermann again and again, each pilgrimage is so flooded with endless streams of verse that the attention of the reader is drowned and carried away like a straw on the tide. The same is the case in the poems called 'Switzerland,' and addressed to a certain Marguerite, which probably would never have been thought of had not Wordsworth dedicated a lovely string of little lyrics to Lucy, lines not only of the greatest beauty, but so brief that they lodge where they fall in the willing memory, and cannot be forgotten. The lesser singer draws out his much lighter theme into link after link of unmemorable verse. That the elder poet should influence the younger even to the point of actual suggestion is a thing perfectly natural and sanctioned by all the tenets of the time, which demand indeed that one should be the descendent and outcome of the other. Perhaps it is also a law of development that the successor should be more lengthy in proportion as he is less strong.

To return, however, to the special poems which we have selected as the most living and individual of Matthew Arnold's poetry, both the 'Scholar Gipsy' and 'Thyrsis' are full of the atmosphere of Oxford and of youth. They are indeed rather two different parts of the same poem than independent inspirations, though the latter embodies rather the regretful looking back of the elder man upon those early scenes, than the actual musings of the young one. Their music and freshness and reality interest all readers; yet we can more readily imagine these poems to be conned over and repeated to each other, with that enthusiasm which adopts and dwells upon every word, by those who 'wear the gown,' than by any other class. The scenery of the academic city with all its spires and towers, the centre of all thought, the fresh and fragrant hillsides and dewy fields surrounding it: the mild mystery of the wandering scholar, a musing and pensive shadow to be half seen by dreaming eyes about all those familiar haunts, are set before us with many beautiful touches. The vision is entirely harmonious with the scene; there is no conflict in it, or force of opposing life, no tragedy, no passion. The shade of the Scholar Gipsy is not one that expiates any doom. He roams about the places he loved, pondering the past, amid all the soft reflections of the evening, dim, pensive, but not unhappy, a wanderer by choice, fulfilling the gentle dream of fate that pleased him best. When that visionary figure gives place to the more real one of Thyrsis who is gone, and all the landscape fills with the brighter vision of the friend who but now was here, and the vacancy which he will never fill again, a warmer interest, yet the same, envelops the hillside and the fields. Yet there is no passion even of grief in the lament. Thyrsis is not mourned like Lycidas or Adonais. He is gone, yet he is there, and there too is still the dewy, dim and fragrant nature, the evening and the prevailing softness of the clouds—'One tree yet crowns the hill, One Scholar travels yet the loved hillside'—All is calm and pensive, a sorrow of the mind, a wistful regret. The two poems naturally hang together, two parts of one elegy, mildly mournful, nothing like despair in either, the friend shading into the more distant vision, the shadow becoming more distinct in the friend, and both full of charm—the atmosphere of the evening, the breath of Nature, the City close at hand with all its teeming young life—and wandering figures here and there, roaming as Thyrsis roamed in his time, keeping up the long continuance, which is never more dreamy nor more persistent than in such a place, where the generations follow each other so quickly, with so little interval between. These are poems of Oxford, of a phase of life which has become very prominent in recent times—but also of a purely vague emotion, a visionary sentiment which touches no depths.

39. George Saintsbury, 'Corrected Impressions', *Collected Essays and Papers*

1895, ii, 266–75

Saintsbury (1845–1933), who wrote about so many literary matters and literary men, was to write the first full, or at least book-length, study of Arnold, a rather breezy life-and-letters, in 1899. The essay included here, which touches first on Arnold's stature as a critic, offers the essential viewpoint of the longer study and expresses Saintsbury's reluctant admiration. He finds Arnold's prose less than satisfying, the more so because Arnold's 'powers' are so evident, but he feels that Arnold has improved the tone of English criticism. His argument suggests at first the superiority of the verse, and for Saintsbury it *is* superior. But it is also badly flawed. Saintsbury's remarks on 'Resignation' are typical: 'It is not faultless; it has lapses, flatness, *clichés*, but it is one of the greatest lyric dirges in English.'

Among the subjects of these papers there is hardly one in regard to whom I can speak in the tone of 'How it struck a contemporary,' to the same extent as I can with regard to Mr Matthew Arnold. Not of course that I can claim to have been a contemporary of Mr Arnold's in the strict sense; for he had taken his degree before I was born, and was an author before I was able to spell. But I can lay claim to having seen the birth of his popularity, its whole career till his death, the stationary state which preceded and succeeded that death, and something like a commencement of the usual depreciation and spoliation which so surely follows. For Mr Arnold's reputation made no very early or general way with the public, however high it may have been with his private friends, and with a small circle of (chiefly University) readers of poetry. A University Professorship has not very often been the occasion of attracting public attention to a man in England; but it may be said with some confidence that the remarkable *Lectures on Translating Homer* were the first which drew to Mr Arnold the notice of the world. He was then nearly forty, and he was several years over that Age of Wisdom when the *French Eton* and still more the *Essays in Criticism* fascinated the public with a double mannerism of speech and thought in prose, and set it inquiring about the author's verse.

Most young men of twenty who had any taste for English letters when the *Essays* appeared fell in love with them, I believe, at once and desperately, with the more or less natural consequence of getting used to them, if not positively disliking them, afterwards. My own admiration for them was, to the best of my remembrance, a good deal more lukewarm at first; and though it has never got any colder since, and has, I think, a little increased in temperature, it never has been, and I do not think it ever will be, at boiling point. I may give some reasons for this later, for the moment let us be historical.

It was undoubtedly one of those happy coincidences which, according to the optimist, happen to all of us who really deserve them, that just after the reading public had awakened to the sense that there was a very piquant and remarkable writer of English prose wrapped in the coat of one whom it had hitherto regarded, if at all, as a composer of elegant, but rather academic verse, the great political change of 1867 happened, and a reign of sharp social and political changes began. I do not think myself that the revolution of 1868–1874 has ever been fully estimated, and I have always thought it half an advantage and half a disadvantage that I was myself resident out of London during the whole of that time. The looker-on sees the drift of the game more clearly, but he appreciates the motives and aims of those who take part in it less fully than the players. During these years Mr Arnold seemed to have a great part before him. Everything (following his father's famous definition of Liberalism) 'was an open question,' and the Apostle of Culture with his bland conviction, first, that most things were wrong in England, and, secondly, that he was born to set them right, and with a singularly stimulating and piquant style to help him, had an unusually clear field.

As a matter of fact, Mr Arnold did help to produce a considerable effect on the public. But it was an effect chiefly negative as far as that public was concerned, and it cannot be said to have been altogether happy as regards himself. To the finest flowers of his production, such as the delightful whimsy of *Friendship's Garland*, little attention was paid: the good public, Populace, Philistines, and Barbarians alike, could not make out what the devil Mr Arnold was driving at. His formulas, after pleasing for a while, were seen to be rather empty things; his actual politics, if he had any (a point on which I have always entertained doubts), appeared to be totally unpractical; and he had not the chance which Mr Mill and Mr Morley enjoyed or suffered, of showing whether a sojourn in the House could practicalise them. Unluckily too for him, he allowed his energies to drift almost wholly into the strange anti-theological kind of theology which occupied him for nearly ten years, which at first brought on him much odium and never attained for him much reputation, which appears to me, I confess, to have palpably stiffened and dulled his once marvellous lissomeness and brilliancy of thought, and which is now abandoned to cheap beginners in undogmatism alike by the orthodox and the unorthodox of some mental calibre.

Then for another ten years Mr Arnold settled slowly back again, under the disadvantages just referred to, into his proper line of poet, literary and miscellaneous essayist, and mild satirist of society. Once in verse, in the exquisite lines entitled *Westminster Abbey* (I would they had had a better subject, not than the Abbey, but than Dean Stanley), once or twice in prose, as in the famous charge on the Shelleyites and other things, the Apostle of Sweetness and Light appeared at his very best; and perhaps he was never, except in the wondrous muddleheadedness of the *Irish Essays*, far below it. But in all the works of this time, though the positive dulness of the phase of which *St Paul and Protestantism* is perhaps the Nadir never reappeared, there is, to me at least, a sense of two drawbacks. There is a failing *fineness* of power in a man whose power had at its best been nothing if not fine, a growing heaviness of touch, a sleight of words that becomes a trick, a damnable iteration, an occasional passage from agreeable impertinence to something else that is not agreeable. And there is, on the other hand, an obvious disgust and dissatisfaction at the very results which he had hoped and helped to attain. It was impossible that Mr Arnold should accept democracy with anything but the wryest of faces; and he must have found the new Pharisees of undogmatism whom his religious musings had brought about suggestive of another work by the same author as *Religious Musings,*—the *Ode to a Young Ass*. The Young Ass has begun to kick at Mr Arnold now, I see, as the fashion of him passeth away.

But it was never possible for any competent person, however much he might find to dislike in this fascinating and irritating writer, to fail in recognition of his extraordinary powers. One might wince at the almost unbelievable faults of taste which he, *arbiter elegantiarum*[1] as he was, would not unfrequently commit; frown at the gaudy tricks of a mannerism quite as bad as those which he was never weary of denouncing; demur to his misleading and snip-snap phrases about 'criticism of life,' 'lucidity,' 'grand style,' and what not. There were a great many things that he did not know or did not fancy; and like most of us, no doubt, he was very apt to think that what he did not know was not worth the knowing, and that only very poor and unhappy creatures could like what he did not fancy.

Now all these things are specially bad preparations for the task of the critic; and perhaps Mr Arnold's critical abilities, if not overrated, were wrongly estimated. It was difficult to praise too highly the expression of his criticism when it was at its best; but it was easy to set the substance too high. Even his subtlety and his acuteness, two faculties in regard to which I suppose his admirers would put him highest, were rather more apparent than real, and were constantly blunted and fettered by the extraordinary narrowness and crotchettiness of his range of sympathies. He was always stumbling over his own formulas; and he not unfrequently violated his own canons. At least I am myself quite unable to reconcile that doctrine of confining ourselves to 'the best,' which it seems rules out the *Chanson de Roland* and makes Shelley more remarkable as a letter-writer than as a poet, with the attention paid to Senancour and the Guérins.

The real value of Mr Arnold as a critic—apart from his indirect merit of providing much delightful English prose shot with wit and humour, and enclosing endless sweetmeats if not solids of sense—consisted chiefly in the comparative novelty of the style of literary appreciation which he adopted, and in the stimulus which he accordingly gave to literary study. Since Hazlitt, we had been deficient in critics who put appreciation before codification; and Hazlitt himself was notoriously untrustworthy through caprice. The following of Sainte-Beuve saved Mr Arnold from both errors to some extent, but to some extent only. Though well read, he was not extremely learned; and though acute, he was the very reverse of judicial. He had fortunately been brought up on classical literature, to which he pinned his faith; and it is impossible that anyone with this advantage should be a literary heretic of the worst description. But he constantly committed the fault of Shylock in regard to his classics. What was not in the classical bond, what 'was not so expressed,' could not be good, could not at least be of the best. Now

[1] 'arbiter of elegance or pleasures'.

I will yield to no man in my respect for the classics; and I do not think that, at least as far as the Greeks are concerned, anyone will ever do better the things that they did. But it is absurd to suppose or maintain that the canon of literary perfections was closed when the Muses left Philemon's house.

Mr Arnold, then, as a critic seemed to me at first, and has always seemed to me, flawed with those very faults of freak and crotchet against which he was never tired of protesting, and, though a very useful alternative, stimulant, and check, not a good model, and a still worse oracle. I should say of him, and I think I have always recked my own rede from 1865 to the present day in this respect, 'Admire, enjoy, and be thankful for Mr Arnold as a critic; but be careful about imitating him, and never obey him without examination.' Of Mr Arnold as a poet there is much more to be said.

The book in which I first made acquaintance with any considerable quantity of Mr Arnold's poetry was the so-called second edition of the *Poems*, containing the first issue of the celebrated Preface: perhaps the best piece of criticism (though I do not agree with its main position) that the author ever did. The book in which one has first made full acquaintance with a poet is like no other book; it has the charm of one of the two kisses celebrated by the Spanish folk-song. Yet I venture to think—divorcing criticism as much as possible from any pathetic or egotistic fallacy—that the collection was and is an extremely favourable one for the purpose of doing full but friendly justice to Mr Arnold's poetical talent. For it was the selected collection of a good deal of separately written and published work, made by a man who was in the very prime of his intellectual strength, who was 'commencing critic' after a youth of poetry, and who was not yet tempted by any excessive public favour to spare his critical faculty on himself. A few excellent and many interesting things were written afterwards, and there is of course a certain historical attraction in *juvenilia*, such as the full form of 'Empedocles,' and other things which were only restored later. But the best things of all are there,—the best sonnets, 'Requiescat', 'The Church of Brou,' 'Tristram and Iseult,' 'Sohrab and Rustum,' 'The Forsaken Merman,' 'The Strayed Reveller,' and 'Switzerland,'—this last without its most unfortunate *coda*, 'The Terrace at Berne'. When I find myself ranking Mr Arnold higher as a poet than some do whose opinions I respect, I always endeavour to make sure that the cause is nothing illegitimate connected with this first acquaintance. And I do not think it is. For, though he himself would not have admitted it, a poet is to be judged by his best things, by his flashes, by his highest flights; and there are more of these to be found in this volume than in all the rest of Mr Arnold's verse.

It is on the whole, however, that we must correct our impressions if necessary, and a very curious and interesting study 'the whole' is in Mr Arnold's case. I still like to try first to raise and then to correct the impressions of a newcomer, taking the standard edition as it too comes. He must, I should think, be staggered and disappointed by the respectable but imitative Wordsworthianism of the first two sonnets, 'Quiet Work' and 'To a Friend.' But the Shakespeare piece is truly magnificent, and as Dryden's famous sentence has said the best and most final thing about Shakespeare in prose, so has Mr Arnold said the best and most final thing in verse. Then we relapse heavily, to be uplifted again after pages by the strains, a little Wordsworthian still but freed from Wordsworthian woodenness, of 'Mycerinus' with its splendid close. But the problem and puzzle—a problem and a puzzle which in thirty years I do not pretend to have solved—of the Arnoldian inconsistency and inequality meet us full in 'The Church of Brou.' Part I is prosaic doggerel which any smart boy of sixteen could have written at any time during the century. Part II is a little better. And then Part III is poetry,—poetry not indeed free from Wordsworthian and Miltonic echoes, but poetry indisputable, marmoreal, written for all time. 'A 'Modern Sappho' drops to Moore, and not very good Moore; and then with 'Requiescat' we are in upper air again. It is not faultless; it has lapses, flatnesses, *clichés*, but it is one of the great lyrical dirges of English.

I should have no room to go through the rest of the Poems, especially of the Early Poems, with this minuteness. It must suffice to say that everywhere we find these strange ups and downs;—now rhymes almost descending to the cockney level of Mrs Browning at her unintelligible worst, now curious little pedantries of expression, now things that show that the poet's craftsmanship altogether fails him, now affectations and imitations of every sort and kind. And hard by we shall find nobilities of thought and phrase that could only be the work of a poet, and almost a very great poet.

In considering the longer narrative poems we must remember Mr Arnold's pet theory that 'all depends on the subject,' that the epic and the drama stand high above all other forms of poetry, and so forth. I own that they do not interest me greatly, despite the magnificent close of 'Sohrab and Rustum,' or that sudden lyric burst which lightens the darkness of 'Tristram and Iseult':

What voices are these on the clear night air?
What lights in the court? What steps on the stair?

The truth is that Mr Arnold had neither the narrative nor (to take in *Merope*) the dramatic gift. For to possess either you must possess the other power of 'keeping your own head out of the memorial,' and that he could never do. Nevertheless it is something wonderful that he should be as bad as he sometimes is. And the inequality is the same in his ballads. 'St Brandan,' with a magnificent and not wholly unsuccessful strain in it, is yet not quite a success. 'The Neckan' is not much above Mrs Hemans. But 'The Forsaken Merman' is very nearly supreme. It is not popular now, I believe, and certainly it might not have been written if there had been no Tennyson; but it is good,—good all through, good in sentiment, good in music, good (which is the rarest thing in poetry) in composition, not easily surpassable in finale. The man who wrote 'The Forsaken Merman' was a poet *sans phrase*.

'Then,' says the Advocatus Diaboli, 'how did he come to write some other things, or at least to print and publish them?' And to this question I can give no answer. *Switzerland* is to me the same insoluble puzzle that it was a quarter of a century ago, and more, because of the *coda* above referred to. It contains one unsurpassed and not often matched piece of poetry, the famous 'Isolation', or 'To Marguerite continued,' which begins:

Yes! in the sea of life enisled.

It contains flashes and scraps elsewhere not far below this. And it also contains commonplace coxcombry, second and tenth hand rhetoric, cheap philosophising, indistinct description, enough to damn half a dozen minor poets.

Once more the filling of the sheets warns me that I must not proceed in this analysis. 'The Scholar Gipsy' I would fain think nearly faultless, and fain hope that it is not old Oxford prejudice that makes me think it so. 'Faded Leaves,' 'Growing Old,' and a dozen other sad descants of the later time, have a real and not only an affected strain of the true, the great Melancholia. 'Dover Beach,' though I do not in the least agree with it, and though the metaphor of the retreating tide is a singularly damaging one for the poet's meaning (for *qui dit* ebb *dit* flood), has a majestic music. And there are many others I could mention. But of mentioning there must be an end, that we may conclude somewhat more generally.

What then were the causes which made the work of a man of, as it seems to me, undoubted and real original poetic faculty, of great scholarship and apparently severe taste, a professed critic and un-doubtedly a lover of much that is best in poetry, so unreal, so trivial often, so rarely spontaneous and inevitable? I have already said that in repeated readings I have never been able quite to satisfy myself about these causes. I cannot quite make out why the critic did not say to the poet, 'It will never do to publish verse like this and this and this and this,' or why the poet did not say to the critic, 'Then we will make it worth publishing,' and proceed to do so. I cannot (for the other re-corded instances, the chief of which is Gray, are not quite to the point) understand how a poetic faculty which could yield 'The Forsaken Mer-man,' the best things of the 'Switzerland,' the Shakespeare sonnet, the finales of 'Mycerinus' and 'Sohrab and Rustum', with not a little else, should have been such a barren and intermittent spring. The only possible explanation—which is rather a statement of the facts than an interpretation of them—is that Mr Arnold's spring of poetry though fine was actually faint, that he was from the very outset a thoroughly literary writer, more sensitive to influences than fertile in original impulse, and that the considerable though somewhat late access of popu-larity after he had come to forty years turned his head a little, and in-duced him to disinter and refather things which, after the wise example of Lord Tennyson and the threat of Sir Anthony Absolute, he would have done well to unbeget, utterly refusing to rebeget them.

Be this as it may, Mr Arnold's poetical position is remarkable in our literature, and not wholly benign in its influence. He provides for those who know and love letters an interesting and admirable example of a literary poet. He provides for those who can appreciate poetry some exquisite notes nowhere else heard, and not to be resigned even if the penalty for hearing them were twenty times as great. But he provides also a most dangerous model. For he may seem to suggest, and has, I think, already suggested to some, that the acquisition by dint of labour of a certain 'marmoresque' dignity of thought and phrase will atone for the absence of that genius which cometh not with labour, neither goeth with the lack of it.

[Note by Saintsbury, 1923]

A year or two later a book in Messrs Blackwood's Series enabled me to work out these views on this subject pretty fully. The recent cen-tenary of Arnold's birth seemed to elicit from younger critics a still lower view of his criticism, an almost entire neglect of his theology, but an estimate of his poetry certainly higher than that which prevailed in 1895 though scarcely higher than mine.

40. Hugh Walker, 'Matthew Arnold', *The Greater Victorian Poets*

1895, 122–49

Walker (1855–1939), Professor of English at the University of Aberdeen and historian of Scottish literature, offers in this chapter on Arnold a careful and perceptive discussion of the poet's reputation, his characteristics—as a poet of elegy, especially—and of his relation to Browning and Tennyson. 'More than either of the others [Arnold is] the voice of his own generation.' 'And we shall find the way in which he gives expression to contemporary interests more lucid if not more profound.'

It was in the year 1849 that the name of Matthew Arnold was added to the list of poets. He had previously written prize poems both at Rugby and at Oxford; but verse of this description rarely counts in the work of a great man's life, and we may therefore regard *The Strayed Reveller, and other Poems*, as his earliest contribution to literature. From the first his work was so delicately finished and so thoughtful that it established his right to be ranked among the great poets of his time: 'established' that right, not by winning general recognition, but by virtue of those inherent qualities which we must believe will at last enforce such recognition. For recognised in any due degree Arnold is not yet. Indeed, now that death, which failed to do so in Arnold's case, has given the shock necessary to raise Browning above the danger of further neglect and depreciation, it is hardly too much to say that of all great Englishmen Arnold is the one who is farthest from the place he ought to hold in the hearts of his countrymen.

Experience proves that we must stand at the distance of several generations before we can finally and with absolute justice appraise the value of poetry. A moderate space of time is, it is true, generally sufficient to reveal the true dimensions of littleness once reputed great; but it is only from afar that we can take the angles by which to measure the mountain-peaks of thought. Some of the 'kings of thought,' like Carlyle and Browning, speak in the voice of the tempest and the earthquake. It is such men who are sure to be saluted at first with the loudest bray; but it is not they who are likely to be longest neglected or inadequately appreciated. They demand attention and at last receive it. The world is compelled to listen; and, unlike the Hebrew prophet of old, it discovers that the voice of God speaks in the storm and the convulsion. But what of the 'still small voice'? It makes no clamorous assault upon the ear, it may go on indefinitely, whispering vainly to senses too dull by nature to hear, or so deafened by the rattle and roar of the world that they cannot hear. And yet surely there is truth as well as beauty in that old conception which finds the divine rather in gentleness than in violence.

It has proved to be so in the sphere of poetry. The polished and refined and reticent literary artists of the world, its Virgils and its Miltons, wear well; their smoothness has nothing of the nature of weakness. To this class Matthew Arnold belongs; and it is well worth while to make an effort to understand him more fully than he has yet been understood by England as a whole, because, rich as are the long rolls of English poetry in rugged strength and grandeur, they are comparatively poor in that classical purity and finish of which Arnold is our best example of recent times. He was partly the cause of his own eclipse. His excellent prose has to some extent overshadowed his still more excellent poetry. And more than that, he illustrates within his own works the way in which the loud voice drowns the lower and sweeter tones. The author of *Literature and Dogma* and of *God and the Bible* arrested the attention of men because he addressed himself openly and avowedly to current controversy; the voice of 'Obermann once More' was heard by comparatively few. And yet the latter deals with essentially the same problems as the former, deals with them more profoundly and more wisely, and is free from the defect of a merely passing and temporary interest which is inherent in all controversy, and from which even the charm of Arnold's style will not permanently save his polemical writings.

And Arnold is valuable not only for what he is in himself, but for what he adds to the other two poets. He is probably the most faultless artist of the three. Browning sometimes provokes his readers to pronounce him not an artist at all, though again he redeems himself so magnificently that it becomes almost a pain to hint censure. Tennyson had very high artistic qualities, but in a tendency to excessive ornamentation, in the redundancy of *In Memoriam*, in the loose structure of the *Idylls of the King*, and in an occasional note that sounds like affectation in his metaphors and turns of expression, he showed that there were limits to those qualities. Thus, there is affectation in the metaphor, 'closing eaves of wearied eyes' (*In Memoriam*, lxvii.), and in the intolerable translation of metropolis into 'mother town' (*ibid.* xcviii.). One of the most frequently quoted passages in the *Idylls of the King* shows in its excessive antithesis a similar failure of taste:—

> His honour rooted in dishonour stood,
> And faith unfaithful kept him falsely true.

Arnold, narrower in his compass, within that compass makes fewer mistakes than either. Further, he is in some respects more than either of the others the voice of his own generation. That he is so may be due in part to his limitations; but be the reason what it may, the fact remains that if we wish to discover what men in the nineteenth century have thought on many important subjects, we shall do so more easily if not more surely in Arnold than in any of his contemporaries; and we shall find the way in which he gives expression to contemporary interests more lucid if not more profound.

Arnold was twenty-seven years of age when *The Strayed Reveller* was published. He was thus considerably older than Browning and Tennyson were when they first appeared as poets; for a difference of six years, though trifling in later life, is great between twenty and thirty. This is one reason why the chronological method is much less fruitful in the case of Arnold than it is when applied to Browning and Tennyson. At the date of his first publication he was far more mature than Tennyson, and he had far less to learn by way of experiment than Browning. Another reason for the same fact is that Arnold's whole period of poetic activity was short in comparison with the long careers of his two seniors. It began, as has been said, in 1849, and it practically ended in 1867; for the few poems published after that date cannot appreciably affect the judgment upon him.

The Strayed Reveller was withdrawn after only a few copies had been sold. So was the next work, *Empedocles on Etna, and other Poems*, published in 1852. Arnold's frequent changes of mind—or what must be interpreted as such—may be taken as indicating his extreme critical care, a care in his own case amounting almost to fastidiousness. It must be confessed that it is difficult to follow him; for poems are printed, omitted and reprinted in the most bewildering way. The puzzle is all the greater because in the end nearly everything reappears in the collected editions. Only eight published pieces, including the two prize poems, are omitted from the popular edition of 1890.

The Strayed Reveller, and other Poems proves by its contents how wonderfully complete already was Arnold's mental and moral equipment. He never changed as Tennyson did, he never even developed in the lesser degree that Browning developed. Even if we limit the view to equal spaces of time in their work, the conclusion is still similar. There is greater difference between the Tennyson of 1833 and the Tennyson of 1842 than there is through the whole literary career of Arnold. So too the Browning of *Bells and Pomegranates* changed more before he published *Dramatis Personæ* than Arnold ever did. The principal contents of this early volume, besides the piece which gave it its name, were 'Mycerinus', 'The Sick King in Bokhara,' 'To a Gipsy Child,' 'The Forsaken Merman,' 'In Utrumque Paratus,' 'Resignation,' and the beautiful sonnets on 'Shakespeare' and 'To a Friend.' There is here the circle of Arnold's interests and of his thought nearly complete. It is true there is no specimen of what afterwards he did best of all, the elegiac, but there is plenty of the elegiac spirit. It is true also that he added much afterwards which we could ill spare; but these additions are less of the nature of fresh themes than of fresh illustrations of the themes already present in his first volume. Arnold however repeats, not with the monotony of mental sterility, but with the endless variety of commanding genius; and it is of the nature of the great thoughts in the region of which he moves that they will bear illustration indefinitely.

It is evident on the most cursory examination that Arnold has neither the magnificent optimism of Browning, nor the artistic aloofness which at first marked Tennyson. All the pieces mentioned are weighted with thought, but none of them has that firm trust in ultimate success which sustains Browning, and convinces him that the worst 'apparent failure' can be no more than apparent. On the contrary, there is in them, one and all, the consciousness of a thwarting destiny. Even the sonnet on Shakespeare, alive as it is with the sense of the supreme triumph of the human intellect, has its glow darkened by reference to the 'foil'd searching of mortality,' and to the 'weakness which impairs,' and 'griefs which bow'. Far more deeply do the other pieces mentioned bear the traces of a spirit ill at ease, and with but little hope of finding in life the alleviation of his troubles. The poem entitled 'Resignation' is peculiarly instructive. It differs from the others named as being, in greater measure than they, a poem of nature. It is the

best in this early collection to which that title can be applied, and one
of the best Arnold ever wrote. We can easily gather from it Arnold's
characteristic point of view. It is Wordsworthian, without the calm
hopefulness of Wordsworth, for the younger poet was unable to 'put
by,' as his master did, 'the cloud of mortal destiny'. For Arnold, to 'put
by' that cloud would have been equivalent to putting by his own nature.
In a note to Fitzgerald's translation of Omar Khayyám there is quoted a
pretty Persian story: 'A thirsty traveller dips his hand into a spring of
water to drink from. By-and-by comes another who draws up and
drinks from an earthen bowl, and then departs, leaving his bowl behind
him. The first traveller takes it up for another draught, but is surprised to find that the same water which had tasted sweet from his own
hand, tastes bitter from the earthen bowl. But a voice—from heaven, I
think—tells him that the clay from which the bowl is made was once
man; and, into whatever shape renewed, can never lose the bitter flavour
of mortality.' So it is with Arnold. All nature has the taste of human
destiny; and in that destiny there is something akin to bitterness.

This same poem, 'Resignation,' prepares us also for Arnold's view of
human life: and indeed in it man and nature are so intertwined that it is
difficult to say on which the stress lies; only it is clear, here as always,
that the latter is interesting to Arnold for the sake of the former. Resignation, the title of the piece, is the lesson the poet draws from his study
both of nature and of the life of man:—

> Be passionate hopes not ill resign'd
> For quiet, and a fearless mind.

In all the other pieces the human element is more prominent and the
lesson from nature is less directly taught. 'The Forsaken Merman' is in
one sense an exception, for it is not humanity that speaks in it at all; but
it takes no great penetration to see that the wonderful pathos of the
Merman is essentially human. It is more important to observe that here
Arnold allowed his fancy a free play he rarely gave it; and he did so
with the best results. The pictures of the sea-caverns are painted in
beautiful verse:—

[Quotes 'The Forsaken Merman', ll. 30–47, 'Children dear', etc.]

'To a Gipsy Child' is at least as masterly in style as this. In it we find
'the soil'd glory and the trailing wing,' 'the swinging waters,' and the
picture of him

Who in mountain glens, at noon of day,
Sits rapt, and hears the battle break below.

But it is impossible without fatal loss to separate any of its wonderful felicities of expression from their context. Arnold was a man who not only wrote beautiful lines but who, beyond most poets, had the skill to make them tenfold more beautiful by their setting. The piece is even more remarkable for its richness of thought than for its melody and verbal beauty. It is the 'clouds of doom' on her brow that attract Arnold to the child. He reads into her his philosophy of life, and he prophesies that even if what the world calls success should come, she will before the end return to that mood which makes him think of her as 'some angel in an alien planet born':—

[Quotes 'To a Gipsy Child', ll. 57–64, 'And though thou glean', etc.]

There is a certain similarity between 'The Sick King in Bokhara' and 'Mycerinus.' Both show the powerlessness of the highest position to remove the limits set to human will. 'What I would, I cannot do,' says the sick king, and all his rooms of treasure are powerless to console him. Mycerinus finds that even living well cannot alter the inexorable decree of fate.

[Re-tells the story and quotes ll. 107–10, which end: 'Was calm'd, ennobled, comforted, sustain'd.']

This prepares the way for the view implied in 'In Utrumque Paratus'; for Arnold was invariably clear on the point that, whatever doubt might hang over man's ultimate destiny, it was always within his power and always his duty to live well the life he knew was his. If man has no second life, his injunction is, 'Pitch this one high'. So when the alternative is between a world made by God and a 'wild unfather'd mass,' the injunction is in the one case to remount 'the colour'd dream of life' by lonely purity to its stainless source. In the other case it is that man, under that hypothesis the chief of all things, should moderate his triumph, remembering both that his knowledge is limited and that this primacy itself has in it nothing to satisfy his nature: 'Who hath a monarch's hath no brother's part'. There is no room for boundless triumph or lawless indulgence.

Empedocles on Etna was withdrawn from circulation, as Arnold afterwards explained, because he held that a situation in which all was to be endured and nothing to be done was poetically faulty. With reference to this Mr. Hutton, who, though separated from Arnold by deep differences of view, is nevertheless one of the most sympathetic of his critics, has truly remarked that the insistence upon this principle would have condemned all that was most characteristic in Arnold's later work. It may be suggested however that the objection Arnold took to his own poem is one which applies to it principally as a long poem and as a drama. He objects to those situations 'in which a *continuous* state of mental distress is *prolonged*, unrelieved by incident, hope, or resistance'. In the lyric and the elegiac, which are Arnold's proper field, there is less reason why endurance should not be the dominant necessity. More-over, when in 1867 Arnold republished 'Empedocles on Etna,' he explained with pardonable satisfaction that he did so at the request of Browning. In the interval it had never appeared as a whole, though parts of it had been incorporated in various volumes of verse between its first publication and the issue of the *New Poems* in 1867.

Besides the title-piece, the volume thus withdrawn from circulation contained the greater part of the series afterwards entitled 'Switzerland,' and of that now called 'Faded Leaves,' and also 'Excuse,' 'Indifference' (afterwards 'Urania' and 'Euphrosyne'), 'Tristram and Iseult,' 'Memorial Verses,' 'A Summer Night,' 'Stanzas in Memory of the Author of "Obermann",' and 'Morality.'

Perhaps the most conspicuous new feature here is the attempt to deal with passion. The attempt is made lyrically in 'Switzerland' and in 'Faded Leaves;' while in 'Tristram and Iseult' there is a dramatic thread interwoven with a treatment lyrical still. These poems are highly instructive, perhaps even more for what they do not than for what they do contain. They have been called cold. They are not cold, Arnold never is so; but they certainly do exhibit a spirit which seems incapable of resting in the affection for, or in the sense of the loss of, an individual. His 'deep habitual smart' is due to a 'something that infects the world,' and thus turns the poetry of passion into a wail over destiny. The fifth poem of 'Switzerland,' beginning 'Yes! in the sea of life enisled,' laments the isolation of humanity. The poet's own loss is generalised in the feeling that in the sea of life 'we mortal millions live *alone*'. So too the third poem, 'A Farewell,' lays its stress upon that stern destiny whose doom is that

> We wear out life, alas!
> Distracted as a homeless wind,
> In beating where we must not pass,
> In seeking what we shall not find.

So too in 'On the Rhine,' the fourth poem of 'Faded Leaves,' the special passion is almost lost in the wider thoughts it awakens. Doubtless it is this that has led to the accusation of coldness; but the word is a mistaken one when applied to verse so charged with feeling:—

[Quotes ll. 11–25, 'Awhile let me with thought have done', etc.]

Equally characteristic is 'Tristram and Iseult.'

[Re-tells some of the story]

The extreme beauty of the descriptions in 'Tristram and Iseult' calls for special mention. Arnold always had an exquisite power of describing nature; but in the earlier poems he let this faculty for description play upon humanity more frequently than in later years. The picture of Iseult of Brittany's children asleep 'in shelter'd nest' is one of the finest passages in the poem; and that of Iseult of Ireland, though less varied, is hardly less admirable:—

[Quotes ll. 115–24, 'And she too, that princess fair', etc.]

'Urania' and 'Euphrosyne,' to give these pieces the titles by which they are now known, might seem to serve as a means of transition to Arnold's more habitual themes. They deal with passion or the possibilities of passion, but rather from the point of view of a spectator than of a participant. 'Urania' is an excuse for a character neither cold nor light though she seems both. What appears her fault has its root in the faults of men:—

> Eagerly once her gracious ken
> Was turn'd upon the sons of men;
> But light the serious visage grew—
> She look'd, and smiled, and saw them through.

The companion piece, 'Euphrosyne,' is a similar excuse for an opposite type of character, a character irresponsibly sunny. The boon of such characters to the world is just this sunshine, and they are misjudged because they are asked to give something for which nature never meant them:—

> They shine upon the world! Their ears
> To one demand alone are coy;
> They will not give us love and tears,
> They bring us light and warmth and joy.

It is strange that Arnold is happier in this piece than in the former, for his natural sympathy was rather with the type of character depicted in 'Urania.'

'Memorial Verses,' first printed in *Fraser's Magazine*, is in that vein of poetical criticism so distinctive of Arnold, and with the exception of two or three of the sonnets of the *Strayed Reveller, and other Poems*, was the earliest published, though not the earliest written, of its class. Arnold is rarely happier than in his criticisms in verse. Their peculiar charm is that they always penetrate to the heart of the writer criticised, and always bring into prominence his lesson to the world. Thus, in the 'Memorial Verses,' it is the Titanic force of Byron, the vast intellectual sweep and penetrating sagacity of Goethe, and the soothing calm of Wordsworth, that he insists upon; and probably nowhere within equal compass is there such illuminating criticism of these writers. It is a remarkable illustration of Arnold's fine taste that he never in these critical verses forgets the difference between prose and poetry; we never feel that this would have been better said in plain prose. The 'Stanzas in Memory of the Author of "Obermann" ' are likewise largely critical. They are dated November, 1849, and were thus written before the 'Memorial Verses,' the occasion of which was the death of Wordsworth. In portraying Senancour they reveal Arnold himself:—

[Quotes 'Obermann', ll. 21–36, 'A fever in these pages burns', etc.]

In these critical poems Arnold is quite different from Browning in his poems of art; because in the first place Browning always conceives his subject dramatically, and in the second place he tries, at least where he is dealing with poetry, to get at the principles of the art from the point of view of the poet he imagines. Arnold contents himself, both in 'Memorial Verses' and in the stanzas on 'Obermann,' with showing what, in point of fact, the writers spoken of do. It is enough for him to note the actual effect of Wordsworth's verse, he advances no theory as to how it is produced, still less does he attempt to speak in the voice of Wordsworth. In a later poem however, the 'Epilogue to Lessing's Laocoön,' he did attempt, if not a complete theory of art, at any rate an explanation of the principal differences between the arts of music, painting and poetry; and within the limits he set to himself he was completely successful.

In the stanzas on 'Obermann' the criticism of art merges so much in the criticism of life that we almost forget the presence of the former. In 'A Summer Night' and in 'Morality' the criticism of life is beyond doubt the keynote. The latter contrasts man with nature, his weary striving with her calm. So far it agrees with the earlier sonnet, 'In Harmony with Nature,' drawn from the poet by a 'restless fool' of a preacher who preaches what to him would be

> The last impossibility—
> To be like Nature strong, like Nature cool.

But in the sonnet Arnold's opposition to the preacher drives him to insist only on the contrast; in 'Morality' he sees harmony as well as difference, and he implies that the strife of humanity is a higher thing than the calm and rest of nature,—a view habitual with Browning but rare in Arnold.

'A Summer Night' gives with greater completeness, and also with greater sadness, Arnold's gloomy view of life. The alternative is that the human being must be either a 'madman' steering some false course across the ocean of life till he steers himself to ruin, or a 'slave' bending languidly over 'some unmeaning taskwork'. This, in Arnold's opinion, is the case in his own generation, because the old motives which gave dignity and meaning to life have lost their force, and those which have taken their place are mean and low. His indictment against his own time is that it either neglects altogether the necessity of nourishing the spiritual nature, and bends its whole energies to a taskwork unmeaning except as subservient to spiritual needs; or else it attempts to feed the spirit on the mere leavings of bygone ages, the husks which the swine *should* eat. Tennyson felt the same want, and he imagined that a remedy might be found in a war which should make men forget their petty interests and their absorption in their own personal comfort. He was not wholly wrong: any motive, if it will only lift above the immediate present and awaken the consciousness of union in cities and nations, will do the work in part. But Arnold saw farther and was less easily satisfied.

In 1853 Arnold published a volume of *Poems*, partly new and partly old. Of the new pieces the most noticeable were 'Sohrab and Rustum,' 'The Church of Brou,' 'The Scholar Gipsy,' and 'Requiescat,' the last of which, like Tennyson's 'Break, break, break,' compels mention by its extreme beauty. 'The Church of Brou' is uneven, but it is memorable for its close, almost the finest piece of imagery in Arnold. He pictures the dead duke and duchess waking in their tomb on an autumn night:—

[Quotes iii, ll. 33–46, 'Or let it be on autumn nights', etc.]

'The Scholar Gipsy' is permanently associated with 'Thyrsis,' first published in *Macmillan's Magazine* in 1866, and included among the *New Poems* of 1867. The early maturity of Arnold's work is illustrated by the fact that of these two poems, both among his best, most critics would probably give the preference to the one first written. One reason for this preference is that the pastoral form is better adapted to the subject of 'The Scholar Gipsy' than it is to 'Thyrsis.' That Milton chose the pastoral form has been frequently pleaded as an objection against 'Lycidas.' It is certainly still more an objection against 'Thyrsis,' two hundred years later, and dedicated to a closer friend than ever King was to Milton. But the form was in a manner determined for Arnold by his previous use of it in 'The Scholar Gipsy,' for which it was admirably fitted. The two poems are so closely related in tone and treatment that Arnold rightly considered the advantage of making them companion pieces in outward shape as well, to be more than sufficient to balance the disadvantage arising from the artificial tone of the pastoral when used for the purpose of an elegy on a friend.

'Sohrab and Rustum' has the distinction of being the first considerable specimen, not dramatic, of Arnold's blank verse, and also the longest narrative he had yet published; for though 'Tristram and Iseult,' which is about the same length, is classed as a narrative, it is in spirit much more a series of semi-dramatic lyrics. 'Balder Dead' followed it in 1855. Perhaps the thing most to be regretted in Arnold's literary history is that he wrote no more poems such as these. Not that they are his best: there is more charm in his elegiac strain. Neither can it be asserted that they are eminently successful as narratives. There is no rapidity of movement in them. But in the first place the verse is singularly beautiful, and blank verse is that which can be longest read without weariness. More important however than this is the fact that this narrative form of verse promised Arnold a wider variety of themes than he seemed otherwise able to find. As elegiac poet and as lyricist he moved within a circle of emotions refined and elevated but not wide. His inborn melancholy gave to his work, even within that circle, a certain uniformity of tint. The narrative form would to some extent have taken him outside himself, and so have introduced greater variety. It is not to be supposed that he would have chosen subjects against the bent of his genius; neither is it to be desired. His choice of subject and his treatment of it in 'Balder Dead,' show how he remains himself in his narrative poems as well as in his lyrics; and it is well that he does so, for all that is most valuable in Arnold's verse comes from the reiterated disclosure of his own feelings and his own views. But he is not, to the same degree as in the lyrics, concentrated upon his own feelings. The legends of Balder and of Sohrab take him into an external world of men and gods, and force him to follow the course of events which have happened or are supposed to have happened. The stories, moreover, are too detailed and too coherent to be treated, like the legend of the scholar gipsy, as mere pegs upon which the poet may hang his own reflections.

It may be urged that in the earlier drama, 'Empedocles on Etna,' and in the later one, *Merope*, Arnold had an equally good chance of escaping into a world external to himself. And this is true; but these very instances are sufficient to prove that the dramatic form was not suited to Arnold. There is much fine poetry in *Merope*, and still more in 'Empedocles;' but their merits are not dramatic. On the other hand, 'Sohrab and Rustum' and 'Balder Dead' not only contain fine poetry, but they are good, though not excellent, as narratives. There seemed to be no reason why he should not have written an indefinite number of equally beautiful narratives; but 'Balder Dead' was the last as 'Sohrab and Rustum' was the first of the class; and they are the only considerable specimens, written under perfectly favourable conditions, of a blank verse not surpassed since the days of Milton for refinement and charm. It is said that Arnold when asked by Browning why he did not write more poetry, replied that he could not afford it. If it was really so England has suffered and still suffers for her own want of taste and appreciation.

These poems are charged with the classical spirit and are full of phrases borrowed from or more frequently suggested by the classics. This influence is visible in the speeches, as in that of Rustum beginning 'Go to! if Iran's chiefs are old, then I am older,' and still more in the management of the similes, as for example the simile of the cranes in 'Sohrab and Rustum':—

[Quotes ll. 110–16, 'From their black tents', etc.]

This passage illustrates also Arnold's love of harmonious geographical names. Careful students of his poetry will recall many similar examples; and those who remember how he contrasted the ugliness of English with the euphony of Celtic names will readily believe that it is not by mere accident that those examples are to be found, and that the choice of names is far from being a haphazard one.

In both of these poems Arnold reveals himself in ways of thought as well as in turns of expression. He does so perhaps more in 'Balder Dead' than in 'Sohrab and Rustum'. Balder, it may almost be said, is Arnold himself; and Balder's weariness of the strife and carnage of Valhalla accurately reflects the poet's weariness of the turmoil and bustle of the world:—

[Quotes ll. 503–13, 'I am long since weary', etc.]

This was always Arnold's method. He has constantly in his mind his own age and utters his own criticism upon it. Empedocles expresses the thoughts of Arnold; and 'Tristram and Iseult' is a modern picture, with Arnold's moral drawn from it.

'Balder Dead' and 'Separation' were the only new poems in the volume of 1855; but the 'Stanzas from the Grande Chartreuse' appeared separately in *Fraser's Magazine* during the same year. Arnold seldom if ever wrote better than in these stanzas. In their range and tone of feeling they are similar to the 'Obermann' poems, and the mention in them of 'Obermann,' if that were needed, indicates the source of their inspiration. Three years later came *Merope, a Tragedy*, which will be noticed elsewhere, and in 1867 the *New Poems* almost closed Arnold's poetical career, though among his later verses 'Westminster Abbey' and the three fine pieces on dead pets, 'Geist's Grave,' 'Poor Matthias' and 'Kaiser Dead,' deserve special mention.

In that volume of 1867 Arnold returned to his early taste for the sonnet. There are none perhaps of the later sonnets quite equal to the best of the earlier ones, yet few either in Arnold or elsewhere surpass in happiness of conception 'The Good Shepherd with the Kid,' and he has seldom expressed more clearly and finely than in the third of the series on Rachel his sense of the something amiss with the world. But what most distinguished the volume was the great proportion of exquisite elegiac poetry it contained. To this class belong 'Thyrsis,' 'Stanzas from Carnac,' 'A Southern Night,' 'Rugby Chapel,' 'Heine's Grave,' 'Stanzas from the Grande Chartreuse,' and 'Obermann Once More.' The first, third and sixth of these pieces had been published separately, but they were then first gathered into the body of Arnold's poetry; and the others were new. When we consider the high quality of all these pieces, and add the other lovely elegies already mentioned, and the beautiful 'Westminster Abbey,' one of the latest of Arnold's poems, it is not too much to claim for him the first position among English elegiac poets. Others have written single elegies exquisitely; Arnold alone among our great poets has written many, nearly all of which are in his highest strain. The secret of his success is not that he dwells upon death: rather, as has been pointed out in connexion with 'Thyrsis,' he escapes from it as soon as possible. Neither is it his method to concentrate sorrow upon an individual. In the 'Obermann' poems, in 'Memorial Verses,' in 'Heine's Grave,' in the elegies on his friends Clough and Stanley, and even when in 'Rugby Chapel' his heart is filled with the memory of his father, he widens his view to human life in general. His great success is due to the fact that the mood of pensive reflection in which he is most at home is exactly right and natural in the elegy. But it is important to observe how wide is the range of this reflection; for on that depends largely the permanent interest and value of these poems. 'Obermann Once More' contains the celebrated picture of East and West in the days of Roman sway, and traces the course of Christianity from the time of its vigorous early life to its decline and death, as Arnold conceived it,—death, that is, as a faith in a supernatural revelation. The earlier 'Obermann' and the 'Stanzas from the Grande Chartreuse' give the author's view of the world in his own day. So does 'Thyrsis,' and so, sadly, yet with a ring of hope, drawn from the character of the dead man, does 'Rugby Chapel,' the elegy on the poet's father. 'A Southern Night' is the occasion for reflections, most musical if also most melancholy, on the author's countrymen, their ambition, their restlessness, their inability to 'possess their soul'; and 'Heine's Grave' contains the famous picture of overburdened England, 'the weary Titan,' staggering blindly on to her goal. This wealth of thought is never dragged in, but seems to spring spontaneously out of the subject. The exquisite style gives it that charm which in poetry nothing but style can give. Whoever glances over the list of the elegiac poems, and compares it with any other section of Arnold's poetry, will come to the conclusion that the true Arnold is there. Other things too he did beautifully; some of his sonnets and lyrics are hardly to be surpassed; but nowhere else is he so uniformly good.

One other poem in the volume of 1867 deserves special mention, not because it is superior to all the rest, but because it is the best expression of a mood of Arnold's mind rarely prominent in his verse, yet always present in it. His habitual view of the world was sad. He had no buoyant faith to help him to face the future. At times he seems almost driven to relinquish the struggle. But this is only in a momentary cry or two. He shows in 'Pis-Aller' his scorn of those who cannot find outside of creeds any firm and sure principle of life. His own permanent mood was one of resolute endurance. If faith does not remain, duty does, and its call is clear. It would be difficult to find any utterance more resolute and inspiring than 'The Last Word':—

[Quotes the entire poem, 'Creep into thy narrow bed', etc.]

There is in all this surprisingly little trace of chronological development. But if there is not much evidence of development, there is ample proof that the younger poet had an important function of his own, distinct from that of either of the two seniors.

Perhaps the first thought which strikes the student of Arnold is that in him more than in any English writer since Milton we find an incarnation of the classical spirit. In one respect even the exception of Milton need not be made; for there is nothing in Arnold so incongruous with the ideas of the Greeks as Milton's Puritan theology. There is much in him, no doubt, that was not and could not be in literature two thousand years earlier; but the sense of difference is reduced to a minimum by his way of viewing it. He is like the Greek of his own imagination, standing 'in pity and mournful awe' before a fallen Runic stone. No dogma rises like a wall between him and the ancient classical spirit. The word which he took from the Greek and expounded to the Eton boys as expressing the ideal mental attitude might be applied to himself. He is eminently εὐτράπελος, flexible, sensitive to influences, ready to see the elements of truth which may mingle even with falsehood. Milton's theological panoply sometimes mars the stately magnificence of even his style; Arnold is rather the athlete, active and supple, encumbered by no dogma extraneous to his own thought.

[Compares Arnold's 'classical spirit' with that of Goethe, contrasts it with Browning's 'Teutonic spirit']

Hence a searching self-criticism, a severe repression, an austerity of taste stopping just short of fastidiousness. But for this Arnold would probably have written more: it is almost certain that he would have written less perfectly; and English poetry could spare most things better than a single one of its not too numerous specimens of perfect finish and perfect self-restraint. How inseparable these qualities were from Arnold's very nature is nowhere more conspicuously shown than in 'Balder Dead.' The legend is Scandinavian, but the whole form and structure of the poem are classical. Valhalla is transformed into an Olympus conscious of modern needs and touched with modern feelings. The brawls and revels of the gods are as alien to Arnold as they were to Balder.

I have said that Tennyson in this respect stood between Browning and Arnold. As to the position of Browning there can hardly be a doubt, but some may dispute the judgment that Tennyson had less of the classical spirit than Arnold. In making this assertion I do not mean to imply that he was inferior, but that there were certain qualities, specially associated with the term 'classical,' in particular this power of restraint which is so important an element in it, that Arnold possessed in more liberal measure than he. Probably those who are not assured of this already will not be convinced by argument, and indeed the subject is by no means an easy one to argue about: it is rather a matter of feeling; but a few illustrations will help to explain my meaning.

Tennyson awakes to the sense of something amiss in the world around him, and gives utterance to his feelings in 'Locksley Hall.' It is a good piece and quite sincere, yet it does not ring perfectly true in the artistic sense. There is a taint of violence and almost of rant about it. Arnold is never without this sense of something amiss; it is the prevailing thought of his poetry. But he has nowhere given the rein to his feelings as Tennyson did in 'Locksley Hall.' He, like the world itself, *bears*. He contrasts the muteness of his own age in the face of seemingly irremediable evil with the passionate outcries of the preceding generation. The contrast was essentially true as regards himself. His art lay in the use of words and the stillness was not absolute; but there is always about his utterances this sense of restraint and the impression of power in reserve which restraint gives. Take again Tennyson's 'Charge of the Light Brigade.' It won and has retained immense popularity; but it is loud rather than strong. There is absolutely nothing in Arnold which can be brought into comparison with this. He never makes this mistake. Even where he may be deemed to have exaggerated, we never have the sense that he has lost self-control.

> All pains the immortal spirit must endure,
> All weakness which impairs, all griefs which bow,
> Find their sole speech in that victorious brow.

This is almost as strong as language can be, perhaps too strong even as applied to Shakespeare. But the writer has himself well in hand, he says not a word more than he means to say, he is dignified, he never for a moment foams at the mouth. The Northern taste betrays itself in Tennyson's piece, the cultured South in Arnold's. A very fanciful critic might contend that descent had something to do with it. Tennyson had in his veins the blood of the sea-rovers, Arnold, in blood as well as in spirit, was related to France.

[Discusses 'pathos' and 'pity', using *King Lear* as a standard. Tennyson's pathos is sometimes 'cheap', whereas Arnold is saved by 'restraint']

Whether or not Arnold lost anything by this restraint I am not concerned to argue here: the point is that he possessed the quality, and that by reason of it he struck perhaps fewer false notes than any of his contemporaries. He has occasionally weak lines and unpleasing expressions, but they are of the nature rather of failures in execution than of defects in taste. For example, it is to be regretted that the beautiful 'Westminster Abbey' is disfigured by the ugly word 'cecity,' introduced for the sake of the rhyme (and that a bad one); but no one supposes that Arnold's *taste* was at fault here: it is rather his command of language that on rare occasions fails. This restraint is the principal element in his style, and all the other elements are related to it; his lucidity, for he would not write until he could express his thought as clearly as, from its nature, it was possible to express it; his sureness of diction, for his habit was to pause to find not merely a good word, but the best. 'Haste, half-work, and disarray' in literature he loathed. The lesson his example taught was or might have been invaluable. The fact that it is still so much needed is one reason why Arnold has never been appreciated as he deserves to be.

In the case of Arnold it is right and necessary to think first of all of style. The lesson of a severe and chastened but most expressive style was the one with which we could least dispense. But it was far from being the only one he had to give. On the contrary, in the substance of his thought his was pre-eminently the voice of his age. This assertion may seem paradoxical in view of the facts that he never was popular, and that in many passages he speaks of his own isolation and of his opposition to the opinions of the world. But at the same time it was the problems of his own generation, as they presented themselves to it, that interested him. If his treatment of them, or his solution, so far as he offered a solution, had been a common one, he must have been a common man. His greatness is indicated by the fact that his treatment was distinctive and personal. Arnold's thoughts and Arnold's way of viewing things are to be found nowhere but in Arnold. In Browning the one absorbing interest is character, especially in its moral aspects; and with regard to character the note of time is of subordinate importance. In Tennyson the same liberation seems to be brought about by the predominance of the artist's sense of beauty; for in that too the note of time, though not absent, sinks to an undertone. But in Arnold reflection is always wedded to artistic expression. There are poems, of the highest excellence too, of which it is difficult if not impossible to say what the thought means. Coleridge's 'Christabel' and *Ancient Mariner* are examples; and perhaps Browning's 'Childe Roland' may be another; at least the attempts at an allegorical explanation are not convincing. But this is never the case with Arnold. It is always possible to detect his thought. His characteristic mode of utterance is that which we find in the elegiac poems; and in them, and in the sonnets and lyrics only less clearly, we see that he is always occupied with the doubts and difficulties and ambitions special to his own time, and its seeming triumphs which often prove to be failures. His dominant thought is the war of contending powers in modern life. He gives utterance to the thought repeatedly, he sees the war raging everywhere. Rachel is to him typical:—

[Quotes 'Rachel III' in its entirety; 'Sprung from the blood', etc.]

No one else has expressed this sense of conflict, of the unexampled complexity of modern life, as finely as he.

The fact or view upon which Arnold works is always seen with the eye of an intellect exceedingly clear and penetrating; but it is also seen as suffused with the 'moist light' of a poetic and sensitive soul. In prose Arnold tried, as he was bound to do, to keep the light dry; in poetry he well knew that emotion was essential. Not only has his thought reference always to the present time, but it is also emphatically his own. The voice which he added to poetry was his natural voice undisguised. It is possible to get at the real Browning beneath the dramatic disguise, and at the real Tennyson beneath the semi-impersonality of the artist who is first of all an observer; but in Arnold the man himself is on the surface of his work, there is no disguise to penetrate. His self-revelation is indeed very different from that of Byron; it is quite free from the defiant and boastful and occasionally vulgar tone of the latter; and it is also free from personal detail about the *facts* of life. Arnold confines himself to the *thoughts* which life suggests. Yet in this way his self-revelation is complete. He did not succeed in portraying other characters, but he left his own clearly stamped upon his verse. He is specially valuable because his poems are *his* thoughts about *his* time.

Perhaps the time of Arnold's birth helped to make him the special exponent of the thought of the middle of the century. The early attraction of Tennyson to Byron showed that he at any rate had come under the sway of earlier forces as Arnold never did. It is true, Arnold all through life admired Byron; but he was never led away to imitate him. Browning from the first showed by his vast schemes, as revealed in *Pauline* and *Paracelsus*, and by his absorption in the study of character, that he must overleap the limits of the age. Arnold stood in years just far enough away from the forces which had their birth in the Revolution, and which he saw working themselves out, to be an observer interested in but not dominated by them. It was his fortune to belong to that English University which had the greatest share in shaping the thoughts of the generation then rising, and to be connected by blood and friendship with men who played a great part in so shaping them. And he brought with him just the disposition necessary to observe and to note the working of those forces and thoughts. Critic always, Arnold is never more a critic than in his verse. I do not refer merely to verses such as the 'Epilogue to Lessing's *Laocoön*,' in which he gives utterance to literary criticism without losing the accent of exquisite poetry. There are more such pieces in Arnold than perhaps in any other poet; and he has more skilfully than any other combined the critical with the poetic spirit. But that spirit is far more widely spread through his poetry; it is indeed everywhere. Nor without reason did he define poetry as 'the criticism of life'. This, with the added proviso that it was particularly life in his own century that he criticised, was specially Arnold's work. Not unnaturally too he held that the thing which Europe in his day most desired was criticism. There was great truth in the view; and if there was also some exaggeration it was the natural exaggeration of the man who unconsciously exalts that which he has to give.

41. Frederic Harrison's assessment of Arnold, *Tennyson, Ruskin, Mill, and Other Literary Estimates*

1899, 111–23

Harrison (1831–1923), who became a professor of jurisprudence and international law, wrote many books of history, literary history, and, as a foremost spokesman for Positivism, of philosophy. Ironically, as an early butt of Arnold's satire—that is, as an enemy of culture—Harrison begins his essay by lauding Arnold's own culture, his unequalled capacity for phrase-making, his 'Attic salt', and his 'Lucianic' spirit. The classical nature of Arnold's poems, Harrison says, separates him from most English poets and sets him in the tradition of Virgil and Milton. But Arnold's 'meditative and ethical vein' also implies a characteristic of the Gnomic poets, 'who condensed in metrical aphorisms their thoughts on human destiny', and this, for Harrison, is the essence of Arnold's appeal.

The very name of Matthew Arnold calls up to memory a set of apt phrases and proverbial labels which have passed into our current literature, and are most happily redolent of his own peculiar turn of thought. How could modern criticism be carried on were it forbidden to speak of 'culture,' of 'urbanity,' of 'Philistinism,' of 'distinction,' of 'the *note* of provinciality,' of 'the great style'? What a convenient shorthand is it to refer to 'Barbarians,' to 'the young lions of the Press,' to 'Bottles,' to 'Arminius,' to 'the *Zeit-Geist*'—and all the personal and impersonal objects of our great critic's genial contempt!

It is true that our young lions (whose feeding-time appears to be our breakfast-hour) have roared themselves almost hoarse over some of these sayings and nicknames, and even the 'note of provinciality' has become a little provincial. But how many of these pregnant phrases have been added to the debates of philosophy and even of religion! 'The stream of tendency that makes for righteousness,' 'sweetness and light'—not wholly in Swift's sense, and assuredly not in Swift's temper either of spirit or of brain—'sweet reasonableness,' *das Gemeine,*[1] the *'Aberglaube,'*[2] are more than mere labels or phrases: they are ideas, gospels—at least, aphorisms. The judicious reader may recall the rest of these epigrams for himself, for to set forth any copious catalogue of them would be to indite a somewhat leonine essay oneself. Lord Beaconsfield, himself so great a master of memorable and prolific phrases, with admirable insight recognised this rare gift of our Arminius, and he very justly said that it was a 'great thing to do—a great achievement.'

Now this gift of sending forth to ring through a whole generation a phrase which immediately passes into a proverb, which stamps a movement or a set of persons with a distinctive cognomen, or condenses a mode of judging them into a portable aphorism—this is a very rare power, and one peculiarly rare amongst Englishmen. Carlyle had it, Disraeli had it, but how few others amongst our contemporaries! Arnold's current phrases still in circulation are more numerous than those of Disraeli, and are more simple and apt than Carlyle's. These ἔπεα πτερόεντα[3] fly through the speech of cultivated men, pass current in the marketplace; they are generative, efficient, and issue into act. They may be right or wrong, but at any rate they do their work: they teach, they guide, possibly may mislead, but they are alive. It was noteworthy, and most significant, how many of these familiar phrases of Arnold's were Greek. He was never tired of recommending to us the charms of 'Hellenism,' of εὐφυΐα, of *epieikeia,*[4] the supremacy of Homer, 'the classical spirit.' He loved to present himself to us as εὐφυής, as ἐπιεικής, as καλοκἀγαθός;[5] he had been sprinkled with some of the Attic salt of Lucian, he was imbued with the classical genius—and never so much as in his poems.

His poetry had the classical spirit in a very peculiar and rare degree; and we can have little doubt now, when so much of Arnold's prose work in criticism has been accepted as standard opinion, and so much of his prose work in controversy has lost its interest and savour, that it is his poetry which will be longest remembered, and there his finest vein was reached. It may be said that no poet in the roll of our literature, unless

1 'the low or vulgar'.
2 'superstition'.
3 'winged words'.
4 'nobility of nature'.
5 'beautiful and good'.

423

it be Milton, has been so essentially saturated to the very bone with the classical genius. And I say this without forgetting 'Œnone,' or the 'Ode on a Grecian Urn,' or the 'Prometheus Unbound,' or 'Atalanta in Calydon;' for I am thinking of the entire compass of all the productions of these poets, who are very often romantic and fantastic. But we can find hardly a single poem of Arnold's that is far from the classical idea.

His poetry, however, is 'classical' only in a general sense, not that all of it is imitative of ancient models or has any affectation of archaism. It is essentially modern in thought, and has all that fetishistic worship of natural objects which is the true note of our Wordsworthian school. But Arnold is 'classical' in the serene self-command, the harmony of tone, the measured fitness, the sweet reasonableness of his verse. This balance, this lucidity, this Virgilian dignity and grace, may be said to be unfailing. Whatever be its shortcomings and its limitations, Arnold's poetry maintains this unerring urbanity of form. There is no thunder, no rant, no discord, no honey, no intoxication of mysticism or crash of battle in him. Our poet's eye doth glance from heaven to earth, from earth to heaven; but it is never caught 'in a fine frenzy rolling.' It is in this sense that Arnold is classical, that he has, and has uniformly and by instinct, some touch of that 'liquid clearness of an Ionian sky' which he felt in Homer. Not but what he is, in thought and by suggestion, one of the most truly modern, the most frankly contemporary, of all our poets.

It is no doubt owing to this constant appeal of his to modern thought, and in great degree to the best and most serious modern thought, that Arnold's poetry is welcomed by a somewhat special audience. But for that very reason it is almost certain to gain a wider audience, and to grow in popularity and influence. His own prose has perhaps not a little retarded the acceptance of his verse. The prose is of far greater bulk than his verse: it deals with many burning questions, especially those of current politics and theological controversies; and it supplies whole menageries of young lions with perennial bones of contention and succulent morsels wherewith to lick their lips. How could the indolent, or even the industrious reviewer, tear himself from the delight of sucking in 'the three Lord Shaftesburys'—or it may be from spitting them forth with indignation—in order to meditate with Empedocles or Thyrsis in verses which are at once 'sober, steadfast, and demure'?

The full acceptance of Arnold's poetry has yet to come. And in order that it may come in our time, we should be careful not to over-praise him, not to credit him with qualities that he never had. His peculiar distinction is his unfailing level of thoughtfulness, of culture, and of balance. Almost alone amongst our poets since Milton, Arnold is never incoherent, spasmodic, careless, washy, or *banal*. He never flies up into a region where the sun melts his wings; he strikes no discords, and he never tries a mood for which he has no gift. He has more general insight into the intellectual world of our age, and he sees into it more deeply and more surely, than any contemporary poet. He has a trained thirst for nature; but his worship of nature never weakens his reverence of man, and his brooding over man's destiny. On the other hand, he has little passion, small measure of dramatic sense, but a moderate gift of movement or of colour, and—what is perhaps a more serious want—no sure ear for melody and music.

As poet, Arnold belongs to an order very rare with us, in which Greece was singularly rich—the order of *gnomic* poets, who condensed in metrical aphorisms their thoughts on human destiny and the moral problems of life. The type is found in the extant fragments of Solon, of Xenophanes, and above all of Theognis. The famous maxim of Solon— μηδὲν ἄγαν (nothing overdone)—might serve as a maxim for Arnold. But of all the gnomic poets of Greece, the one with whom Arnold has most affinity is Theognis. Let us compare the one hundred and eight fragments of Theognis, as they are paraphrased by J. Hookham Frere, with the *Collected Poems* of Arnold, and the analogy will strike us at once: the stoical resolution, the disdain of vulgarity, the aversion from civic brawls, the aloofness from the rudeness of the populace and the coarseness of ostentatious wealth. The seventeenth fragment of Frere might serve as a motto for Arnold's poems and for Arnold's temper—

> I walk by rule and measure, and incline
> To neither side, but take an even line;
> Fix'd in a single purpose and design.
>
> With learning's happy gifts to celebrate,
> To civilise and dignify the State;
> Not leaguing with the discontented crew,
> Nor with the proud and arbitrary few.

This is the very keynote of so many poems, of *Culture and Anarchy*, of 'sweetness and light,' of *epieikeia*;[1] it is the tone of the *euphues*, of the τετράγωνος ἄνευ ψόγου,[2] of the 'wise and good.'

[1] 'fairness, reasonableness'.
[2] Literally: 'perfect, or without blame'.

This intensely gnomic, meditative, and ethical vein in Arnold's poetry runs through the whole of his singularly equable work, from the earliest sonnets to the latest domestic elegies. His Muse, as he sings himself, is ever

> Radiant, adorn'd outside; a hidden ground
> Of thought and of austerity within.

This deep undertone of thought and of austerity gives a uniform and somewhat melancholy colour to every line of his verse, not despairing, not pessimist, not querulous, but with a resolute and pensive insight into the mystery of life and of things, reminding us of those lovely tombs in the Cerameicus at Athens, of Hegeso and the rest, who in immortal calm and grace stand ever bidding to this fair earth a long and sweet farewell. Like other gnomic poets, Arnold is ever running into the tone of elegy; and he is quite at his best in elegy. Throughout the whole series of his poems it would be difficult to find any, even the shorter sonnets, which did not turn upon this pensive philosophy of life, unless we hold the few Narrative Poems to be without it. His mental food, he tells us, was found in Homer, Sophocles, Epictetus, Marcus Aurelius; and his graver pieces sound like some echo of the imperial *Meditations*, cast into the form of a Sophoclean chorus.

Of more than one hundred pieces, short or long, that Arnold has left, only a few here and there can be classed as poems of fancy, pure description, or frank surrender of the spirit to the sense of joy and of beauty. Whether he is walking in Hyde Park or lounging in Kensington Gardens, apostrophising a gipsy child, recalling old times in Rugby Chapel, mourning over a college friend, or a dead bird, or a pet dog, he always comes back to the dominant problems of human life. As he buries poor 'Geist,' he speculates on the future life of man; as he laments 'Matthias' dying in his cage, he moralises on the limits set to our human sympathy. With all his intense enjoyment of nature, and his acute observation of nature, it never ends there. One great lesson, he says, nature is ever teaching, it is blown in every wind: the harmony of labour and of peace—*ohne Hast, ohne Rast.*[1] Every natural sight and sound has its moral warning; a yellow primrose is not a primrose to him and nothing more: it reveals the poet of the primrose. The ethical lesson of nature, which is the uniform burden of Arnold's poetry, has been definitely summed up by him in the sonnet to a preacher who talked loosely of our 'harmony with nature'—

---

[1] 'without haste, without rest'.

Know, man hath all which nature hath, but more,
And in that *more* lie all his hopes of good.

Not only is Arnold what Aristotle called ἠθικώτατος, a moralist in verse,
but his moral philosophy of life and man is at once large, wise, and deep.
He is abreast of the best modern thought, and he meets the great problems of destiny, and what is now called the 'foundations of belief,' like
a philosopher, and not like a rhetorician, a sentimentalist, or a theologian. The essential doctrine of his verse is the spirit of his own favourite
hero, Marcus Aurelius, having (at least in aspiration if not in performance) the same stoicism, dignity, patience, and gentleness, and no little
of the same pensive and ineffectual resignation under insoluble problems.
Not to institute any futile comparison of genius, it must be conceded
that Arnold in his poetry dwells in a higher philosophic æther than any
contemporary poet. He has a wider learning, a cooler brain, and a more
masculine logic. It was not in vain that Arnold was so early inspired by
echoes of Empedocles, to whom his earliest important poem was devoted,
the philosopher-poet of early Greece, whom the Greeks called Homeric,
and whose 'austere harmony' they valued so well. Arnold's sonnet on
'The Austerity of Poetry,' of which two lines have been cited above, is a
mere amplification of this type of poetry as an idealised philosophy of
nature and of life.

This concentration of poetry on ethics and even metaphysics involves
very serious limitations and much loss of charm. The gnomic poets of
Greece, though often cited for their maxims, were the least poetic of
the Greek singers, and the least endowed with imagination. Aristotle
calls Empedocles more 'the natural philosopher than the poet.' Solon
indeed, with all his wisdom, can be as tedious as Wordsworth, and
Theognis is usually prosaic. Arnold is never prosaic, and almost never
tedious; but the didactic poet cannot possibly hold the attention of the
groundlings for long. 'Empedocles on Etna,' published at the age of
thirty-one, still remains his most characteristic piece of any length, and
it is in some ways his high-water mark of achievement. It has various
moods, lyrical, didactic, dramatic—rhyme, blank verse, monologue,
and song—it has his philosophy of life, his passion for nature, his
enthusiasm for the undying memories of Greece. It is his typical poem;
but the average reader finds its twelve hundred lines too long, too
austere, too indecisive; and the poet himself withdrew it for years, from
a sense of its monotony of doubt and sadness.

The high merit of Arnold's verse is the uniform level of fine, if
austere, thought, embodied in clear, apt, graceful, measured form. He

keeps a firm hand on his Pegasus, and is always lucid, self-possessed, dignified, with a voice perfectly attuned to the feeling and thought within him. He always knew exactly what he wished to say, and he always said it exactly. He is thus one of the most correct, one of the least faulty, of all our poets: as Racine was 'correct' and 'faultless,' as in the supreme degree was the eternal type of all that is correct and faultless in form—Sophocles himself.

As a poet, Arnold was indeed our *Matteo senza errore*,[1] but to be fault-less is not to be of the highest rank. And we must confess that in exuber-ance of fancy, in imagination, in glow and rush of life, in tumultuous passion, in dramatic pathos, Arnold cannot claim any high rank at all. He has given us indeed but little of the kind, and hardly enough to judge him. His charming farewell lines to his dead pets, the dogs, the canary, and the cat, are full of tenderness, quaint playfulness, grace, wit, worthy of Cowper. The 'Forsaken Merman' and 'Tristram and Iseult' have passages of delightful fancy and of exquisite pathos. If any one doubt if Arnold had a true imagination, apart from his gnomic moralities, let him consider the conclusion of 'The Church of Brou.' The gallant Duke of Savoy, killed in a boar hunt, is buried by his young widow in a magnificent tomb in the memorial Church of Brou, and so soon as the work is completed, the brokenhearted Duchess dies and is laid beside him underneath their marble effigies. The poet stands beside the majestic and lonely monument, and he breaks forth—

[Quotes 'The Church of Brou', iii, ll. 16–46, 'So, sleep, for ever sleep', etc.]

I have cited this beautiful passage as a specimen of Arnold's poetic gift, apart from his gnomic quality of lucid thought. It is not his usual vein, but it serves to test his powers as a mere singer. It has fancy, imagi-nation, metrical grace, along with some penury of rhyme, perfection of tone. Has it the magic of the higher poetry, the ineffable music, the unforgotten phrase? No one has ever analysed the liquid diction,' 'the fluid movement' of great poetry so lucidly as Arnold himself. The fluid movement indeed he shows not seldom, especially in his blank verse. 'Sohrab and Rustum,' a fine poem all through, if just a little aca-demic, has some noble passages, some quite majestic lines and Homero-eid similes. But the magic of music, the unforgotten phrase, is not there. Arnold, who gave us in prose so many a memorable phrase, has left us in poetry hardly any such as fly upon the tongues of men, unless it be—

[1] 'Matthew without errors'.

'The weary Titan, staggering on to her goal,' or 'That sweet city with her dreaming spires,' These are fine, but it is not enough.

Undoubtedly, Arnold from the first continually broke forth into some really Miltonic lines. Of nature he cries out—

> Still do thy sleepless ministers move on,
> Their glorious tasks in silence perfecting.

Or again, he says—

> Whereo'er the chariot wheels of life are roll'd
> In cloudy circles to eternity.

In the 'Scholar-Gipsy,' he says—

> Go, shepherd, and untie the wattled cotes!
> No longer leave thy wistful flock unfed.

Arnold has at times the fluid movement, but only at moments and on occasions, and he has a pure and highly trained sense of metrical rhythm. But he has not the yet finer and rarer sense of melodious music. We must even say more. He is insensitive to cacophonies that would have made Tennyson or Shelley 'gasp and stare.' No law of Apollo is more sacred than this: that he shall not attain the topmost crag of Parnassus who crams his mouth whilst singing with a handful of gritty consonants.

It is an ungracious task to point to the ugly features of poems that have unquestionably refined modulation and an exquisite polish. But where nature has withheld the ear for music, no labour and no art can supply the want. And I would ask those who fancy that modulation and polish are equivalent to music to repeat aloud these lines amongst many—

> 'The sandy spits, the shore-lock'd lakes.'

> 'Kept on after the grave, but not begun.'

> 'Couldst thou no better keep, O Abbey old!'

> 'The strange-scrawl'd rocks, the lonely sky.'

> 'From heaths starr'd with broom,
> And high rocks throw mildly
> On the blanch'd sands a gloom.'

These last three lines are from 'The Forsaken Merman,' wherein Arnold perhaps came nearest to the echo of music and to pure fantasy. In the grand lines to Shakespeare, he writes—

> Self-school'd, self-scann'd, self-honour'd, self-secure.

Here are seven sibilants, four 'selfs,' three 'sc,' and twenty-nine consonants against twelve vowels in one verse. It was not thus that Shakespeare himself wrote sonnets, as when he said—

> Full many a glorious morning have I seen
> Flatter the mountain-tops with sovereign eye.

It must be remembered that Arnold wrote but little verse, and most
of it in early life; that he was not by profession a poet, that he was a
hardworked inspector of schools all his days; and that his prose work far
exceeds his verse. This separates him from all his contemporary rivals,
and partly explains his stiffness in rhyming, his small product, and his
lack of melody. Had he been able like Wordsworth, Tennyson, Browning, Swinburne, to regard himself from first to last as a poet, to devote
his whole life to poetry, to live the life 'of thought and of austerity
within'—which he craved as poet, but did not achieve as a man—then
he might have left us poems more varied, more fanciful, more musical,
more joyous. By temperament and by training, he, who at birth 'was
breathed on by the rural Pan,' was deprived of that fountain of delight
that is essential to the highest poetry, the dithyrambic glow—the
ἀνήριθμον γέλασμα—[1]

> The countless dimples of the laughing seas

of perennial poetry. This perhaps, more than his want of passion, of
dramatic power, of rapidity of action, limits the audience of Arnold as
a poet. But those who thirst for the pure Castalian spring, inspired by
sustained and lofty thoughts, who care for that σπουδαιότης[2]—that 'high
seriousness,' of which he spoke so much as the very essence of the best
poetry—have long known that they find it in Matthew Arnold more
than in any of his even greater contemporaries.

[1] 'boundless laughter'.
[2] 'seriousness'.

42. Other comments from the 1890s

(a) Lionel Johnson's commemorative 'Laleham', from the Century
Guild *Hobby Horse,* 1890

LALEHAM

To Arthur Galton

Only one voice could sing aright
His brother poet, lost in night:
His voice, who lies not far away,
The pure and perfect voice of Gray.
The sleep of humble men he sang,
For whom the tolling church bells rang
Over their silent fields and vales,
Whence no rude sound their calm assails.
He knew their melancholy rest,
And peaceful sleep, on earth's kind breast;
Their patient lives, their common doom,
The beauty of their simple tomb.
One thing he left unsung: how some,
To share those village slumbers, come:
Whose voices filled the world with joy,
Who made high thoughts their one employ.
Ah, loving hearts! Too great to prize
Things whereon most men set their eyes:
The applauding crowd; the golden lure
Of wealth, insatiate and unsure;
A life of noise! a restless death:
The sanctities of life's last breath
Profaned with ritual and state;
Last pageant of the little great!
But these, to whom all crowns of song,
And all immortal praise, belong,
Turn from each garish sight and sound,

To lay them down in humble ground:
Choosing that still, enchaunted sleep
To be, where kindly natures keep:
In sound of pleasant water rills,
In shadows of the solemn hills.
Earth's heart, earth's hidden way, they knew:
Now on their grave light falls her dew.
The music of her soul was theirs:
They sleep beneath her sweetest airs.
Beside the broad, gray Thames one lies,
With whom a spring of beauty dies:
Among the willows, the pure wind
Calls all his wistful song to mind;
And, as the calm, strong river flows,
With it his mightier music goes;
But those winds cool, those waters lave,
The country of his chosen grave.
Go past the cottage flowers, and see,
Where Arnold held it good to be!
Half church, half cottage, comely stands
An holy house, from Norman hands:
By rustic Time well taught to wear
Some lowly, meditative air:
Long ages of a pastoral race
Have softened sternness into grace;
And many a touch of simpler use
From Norman strength hath set it loose.
Here, under old, red-fruited yews,
And summer suns, and autumn dews,
With his lost children at his side,
Sleeps Arnold: Still those waters glide,
Those winds blow softly down their breast:
But he, who loved them, is at rest.

(b) From the *Literary World,* 21 November 1890

It is singular what an effect Matthew Arnold's death has had on the public appreciation of his poetry. For himself he had long sunk the poet in the critic, and his poems, difficult to obtain, had only a select circle of admirers. In his lifetime a popular edition was not to be thought of. He had never been broadly popular, he once wrote, and could not easily bring himself to believe that he would ever become so. In fact, as he told Browning, he could not afford to write any more poetry. But no sooner was he dead than people began to exalt the poet at the expense of the critic, and to rest his best title to fame on his poetry. Since, then the tide of his reputation has steadily risen, and his publishers have now felt themselves justified in appealing to a wider public by publishing a popular edition of his poems, ranging with their one volume editions of Tennyson and Wordsworth. Their enterprise in admitting him, so far as they are able, into this honoured company is sure to be successful. With Browning popular, no fears need be felt for Matthew Arnold.

(c) Edmund Gosse in the *English Illustrated Magazine,* July 1897

As a poet and as a prose-writer Matthew Arnold really addressed two different generations. It is not explained why Arnold waited until his thirty-eighth year before opening with a political pamphlet the extensive series of his prose works. As a matter of fact it was not until 1865 that, with his *Essays in Criticism,* he first caught the ear of the public. But by that time his career as a poet was almost finished. It is by the verses he printed between 1849 and 1855 that Matthew Arnold put his stamp upon English poetry, although he added characteristic things at intervals almost until the time of his death in 1888. But to comprehend his place in the history of literature we ought to consider Arnold twice over—firstly as a poet mature in 1850, secondly as a prose-writer whose master-pieces date from 1865 to 1873. In the former capacity, after a long struggle on the part of the critics to exclude him from Parnassus altogether, it becomes generally admitted that his is considerably the largest name between the generation of Tennyson and Browning and that of the so-called pre-Raphaelites. Besides the exquisite novelty of the voice, something was distinctly gained in the matter of Arnold's early poetry—a new atmosphere of serene thought was here, a philosophical quality less passionate and tumultuous, the music of life deepened and strengthened. Such absolute purity as his is rare in English poetry; Arnold in his gravity and distinction is like a translucent tarn among the mountains. Much of his verse is a highly finished study in the manner of Wordsworth, tempered with the love of Goethe and of the Greeks, carefully avoiding the perilous Tennysonian note. His efforts to obtain the Greek effect led Matthew Arnold into amorphous choral experiments, and, on the whole, he was an indifferent metrist. But his devotion to beauty, the composure, simplicity, and dignity of his temper, and his deep moral sincerity, gave to his poetry a singular charm which may prove as durable as any element in modern verse.

(d) W. M. Dixon, from *In the Republic of Letters,* 1898

In some sense a Greek born out of due season, Arnold was yet far separated from the Greek temper. May not a student go further and say that the scholars who have discovered the classic tone in his poetry have been misled by the classic cast, the simplicity, of its diction, into the belief that his kinship with the Greek is a close and vital one? The kinship is, I think, in reality superficial and slight. What were the motives of the poetry of the Attic stage, taking it as representative of Greek poetry in general? There is nothing more distinctly marked in Æschylus, in Sophocles, or in Euripides, than the simplicity and directness of the central motive, and the absence of secondary motives. There is nothing more characteristic of Arnold's poetry, as of all modern poetry, than the complexity of its motive—it is the battle-ground of varied and conflicting emotions, thoughts, passions. The analysis of the *Weltschmerz,* the world-pain which broods over modern life, and throws it into shadow, beside which the Greek life is bright with sunshine, this analysis is altogether foreign to classic art.

Bibliography

Part I offers a selection of various sources of information about Arnold's nineteenth-century reputation, including bibliographies, letters, and critical accounts. Some items are self-evidently central, others only of possible usefulness. I have not included bibliographies from critical studies, since these are selections pertinent to a particular approach and would be subsumed in fuller bibliographical works. Nor have I included all dissertations dealing with Arnold's reputation.

Part II is a check list of articles, notices, essays, chapters in books, and parodies and testimonial poems about Matthew Arnold from 1849 to 1900. It is based upon T. B. Smart, *Bibliography of Matthew Arnold* (1892), on Ehrsam, Deily, and Smith, *Twelve Victorian Authors* (1936), which is full but inaccurate, and on several recent dissertations. For England and the United States, it is relatively complete, except for commemorative poems and parodies, and it identifies the authors of a number of anonymous pieces. The listing here is chronological rather than alphabetical, in order to parallel the arrangement of the texts. I have indicated reprinting of items in the original entry, except for reprinting in books, for which there are separate entries. Page references are to the entire article, not simply to the pages concerned with Arnold.

PART I

ALTICK, RICHARD D., *The English Common Reader* (London and Chicago, 1957).

ARNOLD, MATTHEW, *Complete Prose Works,* ed. R. H. Super (Ann Arbor, 1960–).

——, *The Letters of Matthew Arnold, 1848–1888,* ed. George W. E. Russell (London, 1895).

——, *The Letters of Matthew Arnold to Arthur Hugh Clough,* ed. introd. Howard Foster Lowry (Oxford, 1932; reprinted 1968).

——, *The Poems of Matthew Arnold,* ed. Kenneth Allott (London and New York, 1965).

——, *Unpublished Letters,* ed. Arnold Whitridge (New Haven, 1923).

BATESON, F. W., ed. 'Matthew Arnold', *CBEL* (1940; rev. ed. 1971).

BEZANSON, WALTER E., 'Melville's Reading of Arnold's Poetry', *PMLA* (1954), lxix, 365–91.

BONNEROT, LOUIS, *Matthew Arnold: Poète* (Paris, 1947).

BROOKS, R. L., 'Arnold's Poetry 1849–55; an Account of the Contemporary Criticism and its Influence' (unpublished dissertation, University of Colorado, 1960).

BROWN, E. K., 'The French Reputation of Matthew Arnold', *Studies in English by Members of University College, Toronto* (1931).

COLERIDGE, J. D., *The Life and Correspondence of John Duke Coleridge,* ed. E. H. Coleridge (London, 1904).

COULLING, S. M. B., 'Matthew Arnold and His Critics' (unpublished dissertation, University of North Carolina, 1957).

COX, R. G., 'The Great Reviews', *Scrutiny* (1937), vi, 2–20; 155–75.

DE LAURA, DAVID J., 'What, Then, Does Matthew Arnold Mean?' *Modern Philology* (May 1969), 345–55.

DORSCH, T. S., and WALDE, E. H. S., 'A. E. Housman and Matthew Arnold', *Boston University Studies in English* (1960).

EHRSAM, T. G., DEILY, R. H., and SMITH, R. M., *Bibliographies of Twelve Victorian Authors* (New York, 1936).

ELLEGÅRD, ALLVAR, *The Readership of the Periodical Press in Mid-Victorian Britain* (Göteborg, 1957), Göteborg Universitets Årsskrifft, lxiii, no. 3.

FAVERTY, FREDERIC E., 'Matthew Arnold', *The Victorian Poets: a Guide to Research* (Cambridge, Mass., 1956; rev. ed. 1968).

FRANCIS, N. T., 'The Critical Reception of Arnold's Poetry: the Religious Issue' (unpublished dissertation, University of Texas, 1961).

GRAHAM, WALTER, *English Literary Periodicals* (New York, 1930).

HOUGHTON, WALTER, ed., *The Wellesley Index to Victorian Periodicals, 1824–1900,* vol. i (1966).

JUMP, JOHN, 'Matthew Arnold and the *Spectator*', *Review of English Studies* (1949), xxv, 61–4.

——, 'Weekly Reviewing in the Eighteen-Fifties', *RES* (1948), xxiv, 42–57.

LEFCOWITZ, A. B., 'Arnold's Other Countrymen: the Reputation of Arnold in America from 1853–1870' (unpublished dissertation, Boston University, 1964).

MAINWARING, MARION, 'Matthew Arnold's Influence and Reputation as a Literary Critic' (unpublished dissertation, Radcliffe, 1949).

POLLARD, H. G., 'Newspapers and Magazines', *CBEL*, ed. F. W. Bateson (1940).

RALEIGH, JOHN H., *Matthew Arnold and American Culture* (Berkeley and Los Angeles, 1957).

ROLL-HANSON, DIDERIK, 'Matthew Arnold and the *Academy:* a Note on English Criticism in the Eighteen-Seventies', *PMLA* (1953), lxviii, 384–96.

SEN GUPTA, SATYAPRASAD, 'The Reception of Matthew Arnold as Poet and Critic, 1849–1871' (unpublished dissertation, University of London, 1961).

SMART, THOMAS B., *The Bibliography of Matthew Arnold* (London, 1892; partly reprinted in *Works*, 1904; reprinted 1968).

SUPER, R. H., 'American Piracies of Arnold', *American Literature* (1967), xxxviii.

——, 'Matthew Arnold', *Cambridge Bibliography of English Literature, 1800–1900* (Cambridge, 1969).

TILLOTSON, GEOFFREY, 'Matthew Arnold in Our Time', *Spectator* (1954); *Mid-Victorian Studies* (London, 1965).

TINKER, C. B., and LOWRY, H. F., *The Poetry of Matthew Arnold: a Commentary* (London and New York, 1950).

TRILLING, LIONEL, *Matthew Arnold* (New York, 1939).

WARREN, ALBA H., *English Poetic Theory, 1825–1865* (Princeton, 1950).

WILKINS, C. T., 'The English Reputation of Arnold, 1840–77' (unpublished dissertation, University of Illinois, 1959)

WOLFF, MICHAEL, 'Victorian Reviewers and Cultural Responsibility', *1859: Entering an Age of Crisis* (Bloomington, Ind., 1959).

PART II

1. 'Books', *Spectator* (10 March 1849), xxii, 227–31. Review of *The Strayed Reveller.*
2. [Kingsley, Charles,] 'Recent Poetry and Recent Verse', *Fraser's Magazine* (May 1849), xxxix, 576–80.
3. 'The Strayed Reveller, and Other Poems by Arnold', *Globe and Traveller* (28 May 1849), 1.

4. 'The Strayed Reveller and Other Poems by A.', *Gentleman's Magazine* (September 1849), n.s. xxxii, 283–4.

5. [Aytoun, William E.,] *'The Strayed Reveller'*, *Blackwood's Edinburgh Magazine* (September 1849), lxvii 340–6.

6. 'Poetry of the Million', *Athenaeum*, (29 September 1849), no. 1144, 982–3.

7. [Rossetti, William Michael,] 'The Strayed Reveller and Other Poems', *Germ* (February 1850), no. 2, 84–96.

8. 'Notices of Recent Publications', *English Review* (March 1850), xiii, 211–13.

9. 'Empedocles on Etna, and Other Poems', *Spectator* (30 October 1852), xxv, 1045–6.

10. Review of *Empedocles on Etna*, *Guardian* (8 December 1852), 823.

11. [Lewes, George,] 'Recent Poets', *Leader* (8 January 1853), iv, 41–3. On *The Strayed Reveller* and *Empedocles*.

12. 'Poetry of the Million', *Athenaeum* (2 April 1853), no. 1327, 412. Brief comment on *Empedocles*.

13. [Boyle, George David,] 'Glimpses of Poetry', *North British Review* (May 1853), xix, 209–18. On *The Strayed Reveller* and *Empedocles*.

14. [Clough, Arthur H.,] 'Recent English Poetry', *North American Review* (July 1853), lxxvii, 12–24. On *The Strayed Reveller* and *Empedocles*.

15. [Smith, Goldwin,] 'Poems by A.', *The Times* (London, 4 November 1853), no. 21, 5. Reprinted *Literary World*, (N.Y., 10 December 1853), xiii, 309–12.

16. [Martineau, Harriet,] review of *Poems* (1853), *Daily News* (26 December 1853).

17. [Lewes, George,] 'Schools of Poetry. Arnold's Poems', *Leader* (26 November 1853; cont. 3 December 1853), iv, 1146–7; 1169–71.

18. [Rintoul, R. S.,] 'Arnold's Poems', *Spectator* (3 December 1853), no. 1327, 5–6.

19. [Froude, James A.,] 'Arnold's Poems', *Westminster Review* (January 1854), lxi, no. cxix, 146–59. Covers *The Strayed Reveller*, *Empedocles*, and *Poems* (1853).

20. 'A Raid Among Poets', *New Quarterly Review* (January 1854), iii, 36–44. On *Poems* (1853).

21. Review of *Poems*, *Globe* (5 January, 1854), 1.

22. [Kingsley, Charles,] 'Poems by Matthew Arnold', *Fraser's Magazine* (February 1854), xlix, no. 215, 140–9.

23. [Roscoe, William Caldwell,] 'The Poems of Matthew Arnold, etc.', *Prospective Review* (February 1854), x, no. 37, 99–118. Reprinted in *Poems and Essays* (London 1860), ii, 38–53.

24. [Aytoun, William E.,] 'The Two Arnolds' [Matthew and Edwin], *Blackwood's Edinburgh Magazine* (March 1854), lxxv, no. 456, 303–12.

25. 'Poems by Matthew Arnold', *Athenaeum* (11 March 1854), no. 1376, 304–5.

26. 'Editorial Notes', *Putnam's Monthly* (April 1854), ii, 452. Mention of *Poems* (1854).

27. [Coleridge, Sir John,] 'Poems by Matthew Arnold', *Christian Remembrancer* (April 1854), xxvii, 310–33.

28. [Forster, John,] 'The Literary Examiner: Poems by Matthew Arnold', *Examiner* (29 April 1854), no. 2413, 260–1.

29. 'Anthony Poplar' [Rev. Charles Stuart Stanford], 'Midsummer with the Muses', *Dublin University Magazine* (June 1854), xliii, no. 258, 736–9.

30. [Shairp, John Campbell, or possibly Patmore, Coventry], *North British Review* (August 1854), xxi, no. 42, 493–504.

31. 'Arthur Dudley, 'Matthew Arnold et Alexandre Smith,' *Revue des deux mondes* (15 September 1854), lxx, 1136–8.

32. Review of *Poems* (*Second Series*), *Globe* (23 January 1855), 1.

33. 'Poets and Poetasters', *Dublin University Magazine* (February 1855), xlv, 192–5. On *Poems* (1855).

34. 'Arnold's Poems', *Eclectic Review,* (March 1855), n.s., ix, 276–84.

35. [Eliot, George,] review *inter alia* of *Poems, Second Series* (1855), *Westminster Review* (July 1855), lxiv, no. 125, 297–9.

36. 'New English Poets', *Putnam's Monthly* (September 1855), vi, no. 33, 235–8.

37. Review of Poems (*Second Series*), *Examiner* (6 October 1855), 627–9.

38. Review of *Poems* (1855), *Albion* (23 August 1856), xv, 405. 'The Strayed Sightseer, by M. A.,' *Crystals from Sydenham*, ed. 'Cygnus' (London 1855). Parody.

39. [Patmore, Coventry,] 'New Poets', *Edinburgh Review* (October 1856), civ, no. 212, 355–62. On *Poems* (1855).

40. Review of *Poems* (1855), *Christian Examiner* (November 1856), xli, 477.

41. 'Editorial Notes. Literature', *Putnam's Monthly* (December 1856), viii, 658.

42. 'Matthew Arnold', in *Men of the Time* (London), 29.

43. 'Merope', *Athenaeum* (2 January 1858), no. 1575, 13.

44. 'Merope', *Saturday Review* (2 January 1858), v, no. 114, 19–20.

45. [Lewes, George,] 'Arnold's Merope', *Leader* (30 January 1858), no. 410, 112–13.

46. [Alexander, William,] 'Matthew Arnold and Mac Carthy', *Dublin University Magazine* (March 1858), li, no. 303, 331–4. Reprinted *Eclectic Magazine* (May 1858), xliv, 59–71.

47. [Roscoe, William C.,] 'Merope: A Tragedy', *National Review* (April 1858), vi, 259–79. Reprinted in *Poems and Essays* (London 1859), ii, 38–79.

48. [Roscoe, William C.,] 'The Anti-Spasmodic School of Poetry', *New Quarterly Review* (May 1858), no. 26, 123–35. On *Merope*.

49. 'J.C.' [John Conington?] 'Matthew Arnold's *Merope*', *Fraser's Magazine* (June 1858), lvii, no, 342, 691–701.

50. 'Poetic Novelties', *National Magazine* (June 1858), iii, 375. On *Merope*.

51. [Nichol, John,] 'Merope, *Undergraduate Papers* (Oxford 1858), 166–79. Reprinted in *Fragments of Criticism* (1860).

52. [Swinburne, A. C.,] 'Modern Hellenism', *Undergraduate Papers* (Oxford 1858), 38–40.

53. [Roscoe, William Caldwell,] 'The Classical School of English Poetry', *Poems and Essays* (London 1860), 38–53. Reprint of items 23 and 47.

54. [Nichol, John,] 'Merope', *Fragments of Criticism* (Edinburgh 1860), 135–48. Reprint of item 51.

55. [Alger, W. B.?] 'The Origin and Uses of Poetry', *North American Review,* (January 1863), xcvi, 126–48.

56. 'Poems. By Matthew Arnold', *Boston Review* (September 1865), v, 510–11.

57. [Collins, Mortimer,] 'Matthew Arnold, Poet and Essayist', *British Quarterly Review* (October 1865), xlii, no. 84, 243–69.

58. 'Mr. Arnold's New Poems', *London Review* (17 August 1867), xv, 190–1. Reprinted *Eclectic Magazine* (November 1867), lxix, 631–4.

59. Review of *New Poems* (1867), *Athenaeum* (31 August 1867), no. 2079, 265–6.

60. Review of *New Poems, Spectator* (7 September 1867), xl, 1003–5.

61. [Stephen, Sir Leslie?] 'Mr. Matthew Arnold's New Poems', *Saturday Review* (7 September 1867), xxiv no. 619, 319–20.

62. Review of *New Poems, Nation* (N.Y., 19 September 1867), v, 228–9.

63. Review of *New Poems, British Quarterly Review* (October 1867), xlvi, 565-7.

64. Review of *New Poems, Westminster Review* (October 1867), lxxxviii, 602-3.

65. Review of *New Poems, Manchester Guardian* (8 October 1867), 7.

66. 'The Poetry of Culture', *Chambers' Journal* (26 October 1867), xliv, 682-3. On *New Poems*.

67. 'Mr. Matthew Arnold's New Poems', *The Times* (London) (31 October 1867), 5.

68. Swinburne, A. C., 'Mr. Arnold's New Poems', *Fortnightly Review* (October 1867), n.s. ii, 414-45. Reprinted in *Essays and Studies* (London 1875), 123-83.

69. 'Books of the Month', *Hours at Home* (October 1867), v, 569. On *New Poems*.

70. Bayne, Peter, 'Mr. Arnold and Mr. Swinburne', *Contemporary Review* (November 1867), vi, 337-56.

71. Alexander, William (Bishop of Derry), 'Matthew Arnold's Poetry', *The Afternoon Lectures on Literature and Art*, fourth series (London 1867), 199-228. Reprinted *St. James's Magazine* (October; November; December, 1871), n.s. viii, 29-38; 181-4; 236-42.

72. 'The Neo Classical Drama', *Christian Remembrancer* (January 1868), n.s. lv, 39-47.

73. Ascher, Isidore G., 'New Poems by Matthew Arnold', *St. James's Magazine* (February 1868), xxi, 375-82.

74. 'Reviews of Books', *Victoria Magazine* (August 1868), xi, 374-83. On *New Poems*.

75. Review of *New Poems, Scotsman* (24 February 1868), 6.

76. [Forman, Henry B.,] 'Criticisms on Contemporaries', *Tinsley's Magazine* (September 1868), iii, 146-55. Reprinted and revised in *Our Living Poets* (London 1871).

77. Buchanan, Robert, *David Gray, and Other Essays, Chiefly on Poetry* (London 1868).

78. A.S., '*The Forsaken Merman*', *Notes and Queries* (9 January 1869), fourth series, iii, 33.

79. Barkley, C. W., '"The Forsaken Merman"', *Notes and Queries*, fourth series (30 January 1869), iii, 116.

80. 'Shirley' [Sir John Skelton], 'William Morris and Matthew Arnold', *Fraser's Magazine* (February 1869), lxxix, 230-44.

81. [Mozely, J. R.,] 'Modern English Poets', *Quarterly Review* (April 1869), cxxvi, no. 252, 353-6. Review of *Poems* (1869).

82. Review of *Poems. First Collected Edition, Globe* (12 June 1869), 1.

83. Review of *Poems. First Collected Edition, Daily Telegraph* (5 July 1869), 5.

84. 'Mr. Arnold's Poems', *Spectator* (19 June 1869), xlii, 733–5. Reprinted *Living Age* (31 July 1869).

85. 'Poems by Matthew Arnold', *Athenaeum* (28 August 1869), no. 2183, 271.

86. Austin, Alfred, 'The Poetry of the Period. Mr. Matthew Arnold, Mr. Morris', *Temple Bar* (August, September 1869), xxvii, 35–51; 170–86. Reprinted in *The Poetry of the Period* (London 1870).

87. 'Shirley' [(Sir) John Skelton], 'The Poetry of the Year', *Fraser's Magazine* (November 1869), lxxx, no. 479, 667–9.

88. Clough, A. H., *The Prose and Prose Remains of Arthur Hugh Clough* (London 1869). Partial reprint of item 14.

89. [Robinson, Henry Crabb,] *Diary, Reminiscences, and Correspondence,* ed. Thomas Sadler (1869), London, iii, 523.

90. 'Literary Notices: Poems by Matthew Arnold', *London Quarterly Review* (January 1870), xxxiii, 512–14.

91. 'The Modern Poetry of Doubt', *Spectator* (5 February 1870), xliii, 166–7. Reprinted in *New Eclectic Magazine* (April 1870), vi, 490–4.

92. Austin, Alfred, 'Mr. Matthew Arnold, Mr. Morris', *The Poetry of the Period* (London 1870). Partial reprint of item 85.

93. 'Matthew Arnold', in Frederick Martin, *Handbook of Contemporary Biography*. London, p. 13.

94. Nadal, E. S., 'Matthew Arnold's Poetry', *Dark Blue* (August 1871), i, no. 6, 711–16.

95. Alexander, William, 'Matthew Arnold and His Poetry', *St. James's Magazine* (October 1871), n.s. viii, 29–38; 181–4; 236–42. Reprint of item 71.

96. Forman, Henry B., 'Matthew Arnold', *Our Living Poets* (London 1871). Reprint of item 76.

97. LeSueur, William, D., 'The Poetry of Matthew Arnold', *Canadian Monthly and National Review* (March 1872), i, 219–29.

98. [Hutton, Richard H.,] 'The Poetry of Matthew Arnold', *British Quarterly Review* (April 1872), lv, no. 110, 313–47. Reprinted in *Living Age* (25 May 1872), cxiii, 482–99; *Literary Essays* (1877), 258–302.

99. Shairp, J. C., 'Balliol Scholars 1840–43', *Macmillan's Magazine* (March 1873), xxvii, 376–82. Reprinted in *Glen Dessaray* (1888).

100. Stedman, E. C., 'A Representative Triad. Hood-Proctor-Arnold', *Scribner's Monthly* (February 1874), vii, 463–78.

101. Hewlett, Henry G., 'The Poems of Matthew Arnold', *Contemporary Review* (September 1874), xxiv, 559–67.

102. Adams, William D., 'The Poetry of Criticism: Mr. Matthew Arnold', *Gentleman's Magazine* (April 1875), n.s. xiv, 467–80.

103. Swinburne, A. C., 'Matthew Arnold's New Poems', *Essays and Studies* (London 1875), 123–83. Reprint of item 68.

104. Benton, Joel, 'Matthew Arnold', *Appleton's Journal* (11 March 1876), xv, 341–2.

105. Stedman, E. C., 'Matthew Arnold', *Victorian Poets* (London 1876), 90–100.

106. Hutton, R. H., 'The Poetry of Matthew Arnold', *Essays in Literary Criticism* (Philadelphia 1876). Reprint of item 97.

107. Bayne, Thomas, 'Our Modern Poets—Matthew Arnold', *St. James's Magazine* (January 1877), xxxi, 59–71.

108. Review of *Poems* (1877), *Spectator* (14 July 1877), l, 889–91.

109. Review of *Poems. New and Complete Edition*, *Scotsman* (23 August 1877), 2.

110. 'Matthew Arnold's Poems', *Saturday Review* (29 September 1877), xliv, 393–4.

111. Review of *Poems. New and Complete Edition*, *Daily News* (29 October 1877), 2.

112. '*Poems*. By Matthew Arnold', *British Quarterly Review* (October 1877), lxvi, no. 132, 537–40.

113. Mallock, William H., *The New Republic* (London 1877), i, 94–7. Includes parody of Arnold.

114. Alsop, J. W., 'Mr. Matthew Arnold as Critic and Poet'. Read before the Liverpool Philomatic Society (30 January 1878).

115. 'Contemporary Literature', *Contemporary Review* (January 1878), xxxi, 443–4. Review of *Poems* (1877).

116. 'Contemporary Portraits: Matthew Arnold', *University Magazine* (January 1878), xci, 16–32.

117. [Moggridge, M. W.,] 'Idyllic Poetry', *Macmillan's Magazine* (June 1878), xxxviii, no. 223, 101–9. Brief discussion.

118. Review of *Selected Poems* (1878), *Yale Literary Magazine* (April 1878), xliii, 303–8.

119. 'The Poetry of Doubt: Arnold and Clough', *Church Quarterly Review* (April 1878), vi, no. 11, 117–29. Reprinted *Living Age* (18 May 1878), xxxvii, 410–21.

120. 'Our Library Table', *Atheneaum* (13 July 1878), no. 2646, 46. Brief notice of *Selected Poems*.

121. [Hutton, Richard Holt,] 'The Poetic Place of Matthew Arnold', *Spectator* (20 July 1878), li, 918–19. Reprinted in *Brief Literary Criticisms* (1906).

122. Towsend, Walter, 'Matthew Arnold as a Poet', *Canadian Monthly and National Review* (September 1878), i, 335–46.

123. Woodberry, G. E., 'Poems of Matthew Arnold', *Nation* (N.Y., 31 October 1878), xxvii, 274–5.

124. 'Selected Poems of Matthew Arnold', *British Quarterly Review* (October 1878), lxviii, 551. Brief notice of *Selected Poems*.

125. Griffin, Martin J., 'Another View of Matthew Arnold's Poems', *Canadian Monthly and National Review* (November 1878), i, 546–52.

126. Review of *Selected Poems* (1878), *Harper's Monthly Magazine* (December 1878), lviii, 149. Brief notice.

127. Brown, James Buchan [J. B. Selkirk], 'Modern Creeds and Modern Poetry', *Ethics and Aesthetics of Modern Poetry* (London 1878), 27–61.

128. 'Contemporary Literature', *British Quarterly Review* (January 1879), lxix, 120–53.

129. 'Poems of Matthew Arnold', *Scribner's Monthly* (January 1879), xvii, 448.

130. Review of *Selected Poems, Atlantic Monthly* (March 1879), lxiii, 410–13.

131. Merriam, George. 'Some Aspects of Matthew Arnold's Poetry', *Scribner's Monthly* (June 1879), xviii, 281–90.

132. 'Parody Prize. Four Parodies of "The Sonnet to George Cruikshank"', *World* (20 August 1879), no. 268, 26–7. Reprinted in *Parodies* (1885).

133. Swinburne, Louis J., 'The Unrest of the Age as Seen in its Literature', *New Englander* (September 1879), xxxviii, 612–36.

134. 'Parody Prize. Two Parodies of "The Forsaken Merman"', *World* (24 September 1879), no. 273, 16. Reprinted in *Parodies* (1885).

135. 'Matthew Arnold' *Men of the Time: a Dictionary of Contemporaries,* 10th ed. (London 1879), 44–5.

136. Alsop, J. W., 'Matthew Arnold as Critic and Poet', (Liverpool 1879). Reprint of item 114.

137. 'Poems by Matthew Arnold', *National Quarterly Review* (N.Y., April 1880), xl, 488–91.

138. Conway, Moncure D., 'The English Lakes and Their Genii', *Harper's New Monthly Magazine* (January 1881), 161–77.

139. 'A List of Matthew Arnold's Writings', *Literary World* (Boston, 18 June 1881), xii, 215.

140. Review of *Selected Poems, Dial* (August 1881), ii, 87.

141. 'Necklong', *Punch* (26 November 1881), lxxxi, 250 [parody].

142. Lang, Andrew 'Matthew Arnold', *Century Magazine* (April 1882), xxiii, no. 6, 849–51.

143. Nadal, E. S., 'Matthew Arnold', *Critic* (N.Y., 20 May 1882), 135–6. Reprinted in *Essays at Home* (1882).

144. Nadal, E. S., 'Matthew Arnold', *Essays at Home* (London 1882). Reprint of item 143.

145. Tyrer, C. E., 'The Poetry of Matthew Arnold', *Manchester Quarterly* (January 1883), ii, 86–99.

146. Powers, H. N., 'Matthew Arnold', *Dial* (October 1883), iv, 121–3.

147. [Whitman, Walt,] 'Our Eminent Visitors', *Critic* (N.Y., 17 November 1883), iii, 459. Not specifically on the verse.

148. Bates, K. L., 'Matthew Arnold. On hearing him read his poems', *Literary World* (Boston, December 1883), xiv, 415. Poem.

149. 'Genius and Versatility', *Macmillan's Magazine* (December 1883) xlix, 87–94.

150. Benton, Joel, 'The Poetry of Matthew Arnold', *Manhattan* (December 1883), ii, 524–30.

151. Cone, Helen Gray, 'After Reading Arnold's "Sohrab and Rustum"', *Critic* (N.Y., December, 1883), iii, 534.

152. Payne, William Morton, *Dial* (January 1884), iv, no. 45, 221–2.

153. Lazarus, Emma, 'Critic and Poet', *Critic* (N.Y., 5 January 1884), iv, 4. Poem. Reprinted 26 April.

154. James, Henry, 'Matthew Arnold', *English Illustrated Magazine* (January 1884), i, 241–6.

155. 'Matthew Arnold', *Bulletin of the Boston Public Library* (January 1884), vi, 84–7. Bibliography.

156. Preston, H. W., 'Matthew Arnold as a Poet', *Atlantic Monthly* (May 1884), 641–50.

157. Turnbull, F. L., 'The Poets and the Time-Spirit', *Critic* (N.Y., 7 June 1884), n.s. i, 265–7.

158. 'Matthew Arnold', *Chambers' Cyclopedia of English Literature*, fourth edition (1884), ii, 472–4, 734.

159. Thomson, James, 'Suggested by Matthew Arnold's "Stanzas from the Grande Chartreuse"', *Voice from the Nile and Other Poems* (London 1884), 214–27.

160. 'The Poetry of Despair', *London Quarterly Review* (April 1885), lxiv, no. 127, 129–39.

161. 'The Poet of Elegy', *Spectator* (18 July 1885), lviii, 937–8. Reprinted *Living Age* (22 August 1885), clxvi, 503–6.

162. [Henley, William Ernest,] 'Poems. By Matthew Arnold', *Athenaeum* (22 August 1885), no. 3017, 229–30. Reprinted in *Views and Reviews: Literature* (London 1890), 83–91.

163. 'On Classic Ground', *Macmillan's Magazine* (November 1885), liii, 28–36.

164. Galton, Arthur Howard, 'Mr. Matthew Arnold', *Urbana Scripta: Studies of Five Living Poets, etc.* (London 1885), 77–107.

165. 'Matthew Arnold', *Parodies of the Works of English and American Authors* (London 1885). Reprint of items 132, 134.

166. Clodd, Edward, 'Matthew Arnold's Poetry', *Gentleman's Magazine* (April 1886), cclx, 344–59.

167. Hutton, R. H., 'Newman and Arnold. II', *Contemporary Review* (April 1886), xlix, 513–34.

168. 'Matthew Arnold', Allibone's *Dictionary of English Literature and British and American Authors* (1886), i, 69.

169. Kent, Armine T., 'A Note on the Poems of Matthew Arnold', *Time* (London, January 1887), v, 1–13.

170. 'Spare Moments with the Poets: Matthew Arnold', *Wit and Wisdom* (7 May 1887), ii, 404–5.

171. Dowden, E., 'Victorian Literature', *Fortnightly Review* (June 1887), n.s. xlvii, 857–58. Reprinted in *Transcripts and Studies* (1888).

172. 'The Poetry of Matthew Arnold', *Scottish Church Quarterly* (July 1887) v, 138–47.

173. Thomas E. M., 'After Reading Arnold's "Sohrab and Rustum", ' *Lyrics and Sonnets* (Boston 1887), 114. Poem.

174. Thorne, W. H., 'The Life of Matthew Arnold', *Modern Idols* (Philadelphia 1887), 7–20.

175. Hutton, Richard H., 'The Poetry of Matthew Arnold', *Literary Essays* (London 1887), 258–302. Reprint of item 98.

176. *Celebrities of the Century* (London 1887), 62–3.

177. 'Mr. Matthew Arnold', *Pall Mall Gazette* (16 April 1888), no. 7201, 1 and 8–9. Obituary notice.

178. 'Various Estimates of Matthew Arnold', *Pall Mall Gazette* (17 April 1888), no. 7202, 2.

179. Arnold, Thomas, 'Mr. Matthew Arnold', *Manchester Guardian* (17 April 1888), 5–6.

180. 'Death of Mr. Arnold', *The Times* (17 April 1888), no. 32, 362. Reprinted *Living Age* (19 May 1888), *Biographies reprinted from The Times* (London 1893), iv, 87–96.

181. Stedman, E. C., 'Death of Matthew Arnold', *New York Herald* (17 April 1888). Reprinted in *Life and Letters of Edmund Clarence Stedman*, ii, 63–4.

182. 'The Late Mr. Matthew Arnold. Special Memoir', *Pall Mall Budget* (19 April 1888), no. 1021, 5–11.

183. Arnold, Sir Edwin, 'To Matthew Arnold; From Edwin Arnold; Poem', *Pall Mall Gazette* (15 April 1888), no. 7200, 8.

184. Le Gallienne, Richard, 'Matthew Arnold; Poem', *Academy* (21 April 1888), xxxiii, no. 833, 273. Reprinted *Living Age* (2 June 1888), clxxii, 514.

185. 'Obituary, Matthew Arnold', *Academy* (21 April 1888), xxxiii, no. 833, 273.

186. 'Mr. Matthew Arnold', *Saturday Review* (21 April 1888), lxv, 459–60.

187. [Jacobs, Joseph,] 'Matthew Arnold', *Athenaeum* (21 April 1888), no. 3156, 500–1. Reprinted revised in *George Eliot, Matthew Arnold, Browning, etc.* (London 1891), 75–94; *Literary Studies* (London 1895), 77–94.

188. Dawson, William James, 'Death of Mr. Matthew Arnold', *Spectator* (21 April 1888), lxi, 538. Reprinted *Living Age* (19 May 1888), ccxxvii, 433–41; *Critic* (N.Y., 21 April 1888), 193–4.

189. 'R. W. M.,' 'Sonnet', *Oxford Magazine* (25 April 1888), vi, 300.

190. Harding, Edward, 'Arnold's Place in Literature', *Critic* (N.Y., 28 April 1888), xii, 201–2.

191. 'Matthew Arnold', *Literary World* (Boston, 21 April 1888), xix, 136.

192. Alexander, William, 'Matthew Arnold', *Spectator* (28 April 1888), lxi, 575. Poem.

193. Gosse, Edmund, 'Mr. Matthew Arnold's Earliest Publication', *Athenaeum* (28 April 1888), no. 3157, 533–4. Reprinted *Living Age* (May 1888), clxxvii, 511–12.

194. 'Matthew Arnold', *Punch* (28 April 1888), xciv, 195. Poem.

195. Myers, F. W. H., 'Matthew Arnold', *Fortnightly Review* (May 1888), n.s. xliii, 719–28. Reprinted *Living Age* (June 1888), clvii, 545–50; *Eclectic Magazine* (July 1888), cxi, 55–61.

196. Benton, Joel, 'Matthew Arnold', *Cosmopolitan* (May 1888), v, 223. Poem.

197. Austin, Alfred, 'Matthew Arnold', *National Review* (May 1888), xi, 415–19.

198. Powers, H. N., 'Memorial Verses. Matthew Arnold', *Literary World* (Boston, 12 May 1888), xix, 152.

199. Lang, Andrew, 'At the Sign of the Ship', *Longman's Magazine* (June 1888), xii, 217–24.

200. 'Matthew Arnold's Writings', *Torch* (June 1888), i, 135–9.

201. Stoddard, Richard H., 'Matthew Arnold as a Poet', *North American Review* (June 1888), cxxxvi, 657–62.

202. Russell, G. W. E., 'Matthew Arnold', *Time* (London, June 1888), n.s. vii, 657–64. Reprinted in *Sketches and Snapshots* (1910).

203. Traill, H. D., 'Matthew Arnold', *Contemporary Review* (June 1888), liii, 868–81.

204. Field, Michael, 'The Rest of Immortals. Poem', *Contemporary Review* (June 1888), liii, 882–4.

205. [Hutton, Richard H.,] 'Poetic Charm', *Spectator* (14 July 1888), lxi, 962–3. Reprinted in *Brief Literary Criticisms* (1906).

206. 'Matthew Arnold's Poetry', *Temple Bar* (September 1888), lxxxiv, 106–11.

207. Scudder, Vida D., 'The Poetry of Matthew Arnold', *Andover Review* (September 1888), x, 232–49.

208. Randolph, Henry F., 'Pessimism and Recent Victorian Poetry', *New Princeton Review* (September 1888), vi, 221–8.

209. Lockwood, Ferris, 'Matthew Arnold's Landscapes', *North American Review* (September 1888), cxlvii, 473–4.

210. Tyrer, C. E., 'In Memoriam Matthew Arnold; sonnet', *Manchester Quarterly* (October 1888), vii, 388.

211. [Morris, Mowbray,] 'Matthew Arnold', *Quarterly Review* (October 1888), clxvii, no. 334, 398–426.

212. [Prothero, Rowland,] 'The Poetry of Matthew Arnold', *Edinburgh Review* (October 1888), clxviii, no. 334, 337–73.

213. [Birrell, Augustine,] 'Matthew Arnold', *Scribner's Magazine* (November 1888), iv, 537–45. Reprinted in *Res Judicatae* (1892).

214. Russell, E. R., 'Matthew Arnold'. Read before the Literary and Philosophical Society of Liverpool (1888).

215. Dowden, Edward, 'Victorian Literature', *Transcripts and Studies* (London 1888), 206–10; 259–60. Partial reprint of item 170.

216. Norton, Charles E., 'Matthew Arnold', *Proceedings of the American Academy of Arts and Sciences* (1888), xv, 349–53.

217. Lund, Thomas W. M., *Matthew Arnold. The Message and Meaning of a Life* (Liverpool 1888), 28p.
218. 'Matthew Arnold', *Chambers' Cyclopedia of English Literature* (Philadelphia 1888), i, 443.
219. Shairp, J. C., 'Balliol Scholars', *Glen Dessaray and Other Poems* (London 1888). Reprint of item 99.
220. Wellwood, John, 'Matthew Arnold as a Poet', *Ruskin Reading Guild Journal* (January 1889), i, 12–16.
221. Fife, M. B., 'The Late Matthew Arnold; Poet and Critic', *Sun* (March 1889), ii, 89–91.
222. Newsman, W. C., 'Matthew Arnold', *Popular Poets of the Period* (March 1889), no. 8, 225–8.
223. Galton, Arthur, 'Matthew Arnold', *Century Guild Hobby-Horse* (April 1889), iv, 70.
224. Coleridge, (Lord) Stephen, 'Matthew Arnold', *New Review* (July; August 1889), i, 111–24. Reprinted *Living Age* (28 September 1889), clxxxii, 771–83.
225. Dawson, W. J., 'Matthew Arnold', *Great Thoughts* (27 July 1889), n.s. iii, 57–60. Reprinted in *The Makers of Modern English* (1890).
226. 'What Endures in Poetry', *Spectator* (24 August 1889), lxiii, 236–7.
227. Dowden, Edward, 'Matthew Arnold as a Poet', *Atalanta* (September 1889), ii, 809–13.
228. Carmen, Bliss, 'Corydon: An Elegy in Memory of Matthew Arnold', *Universal Review* (November 1889), 425–37.
229. Russell, George William, *Matthew Arnold: a Memorial Sketch.* Printed for the Subscribers to the Arnold Memorial Fund (1889), 16p. Reprint of item 201.
230. Mallock, W. H., *Parodies of the Works of English and American Authors* (London 1889), vi, 200–02.
231. Tyrer, C. E., 'Matthew Arnold', *Manchester Quarterly* (January 1890), no. 23, 1–19.
232. Duff, (Sir) M. E. Grant, 'Matthew Arnold's Writings', *Murray's Magazine* (March 1890), vii, 289–308.
233. Johnson, Lionel P., 'Laleham: a poem', *Century Guild Hobby Horse* (April 1890), no. 18, 56–7. Reprinted in *Poetical Works* (1915).
234. Galton, Arthur, 'The Poetical Works of Matthew Arnold, etc.', *Century Guide Hobby Horse* (April 1890), no. 18, 47–55.
235. Duff, (Sir) M. E. Grant, 'The Plant Illusions in the Poems of Matthew Arnold', *Nature Notes* (June; July 1890), i, 81–4; 104–7.

236. Watson, William, 'In Laleham Churchyard', *Spectator* (30 August 1890), no. 3244, 278–9. Poem.

237. Tyrer, C. E., 'Matthew Arnold as Poet', *Manchester Quarterly* (October 1890), no. 36, 358–85.

238. 'Matthew Arnold's Poems', *Literary World* (21 November 1890), no. 1099, 426–7. Review of *Poetical Works* (1890).

239. Henley, William Ernest, 'Matthew Arnold', *Views and Reviews: Literature* (London 1890), 83–91. Reprint of item 162.

240. Dawson, W. J., 'Matthew Arnold', *The Makers of Modern English* (New York 1890), 328–40. Reprint of item 225.

241. [Johnson, Lionel,] 'Poetical Works of Matthew Arnold', *Academy* (10 January 1891), no. 975, 31–2. Reprinted in *Post Liminium* (1902).

242. Roget, F. F., 'Modern Poets: Matthew Arnold', *Ladder* (February 1891), i, 78–83.

243. Orr, A., 'Browning's Relation to Matthew Arnold', *Athenaeum* (25 July 1891), no. 3326, 129.

244. Galton, Arthur, 'The Poetical Works of Matthew Arnold. A Note Upon Literature Considered as a Fine Art, etc.', *Century Guild Hobby Horse* (July 1891), no. 23, 93–108.

245. 'Lord Coleridge on Matthew Arnold', *The Times* (2 November 1891), no. 33, 471, 7.

246. [Hutton, Richard H.,] 'Our Great Elegiac Poet', *Spectator* (7 November 1891), lxvii, 638–9. Reprinted in *Brief Literary Criticisms* (1906).

247. Jacobs, Joseph, 'Matthew Arnold', *George Eliot, Matthew Arnold, Browning, Newman, etc.* (London 1891), 75–94. Reprint of item 169; reviewed *Literary World* (15 August 1891), xxii, 269–70.

248. Sharp, Amy, 'Matthew Arnold', *Victorian Poets* (London 1891), 137–56.

249. *A Bibliographical Catalogue of Macmillan & Company Publications from 1843 to 1889* (London & New York 1891).

250. Inwright, Hulda May, 'Is Matthew Arnold's Poetry Consoling?' *Spectator* (16 July 1892), lxix, 94–5.

251. Swanwick, Anna, 'Matthew Arnold', *Poets the Interpreters of Their Age* (London 1892), 375–9.

252. Birrell, Augustine, 'Matthew Arnold', *Res Judicatae* (London 1892). Reprint of item 213.

253. Cochrane, Robert, 'Matthew Arnold', *Treasury of Modern Biography* (Edinburgh 1892), 507.

254. Cheney, John V., 'Matthew Arnold', *The Golden Guess* (Boston 1892), 75–119.

255. Oliphant, Margaret, 'Of the Younger Poets', *The Victorian Age of English Literature* (New York 1892), ii, 430–6.

256. Smart, Thomas B., *The Bibliography of Matthew Arnold* (London 1892).

257. Moore, Charles Leonard, 'The Future of Poetry', *Forum* (February 1893), xiv, 768–77.

258. [Hutton, Richard H.,] 'Matthew Arnold's Popularity', *Spectator* (25 March 1893), lxx, 382–3. Reprinted in *Brief Literary Criticisms* (1906).

259. Guthrie, William N., 'Obermann and Matthew Arnold', *Sewanee Review* (November 1893), ii, 33–55. Reprinted in *Modern Poet Prophets* (1897).

260. [Stephen, (Sir) Leslie,] 'Matthew Arnold', *National Review* (December 1893), xxii, 458–77. Reprinted *Eclectic Magazine* (March 1894), cxxii, 300–13; *Living Age* (13 January 1894), cc, 90–103; *Studies of a Biographer* (1898).

261. Innes, Arthur Donald, *Seers and Singers: A Study of Five English Poets*, (London 1893), 222p. Reviewed *Literary World* (27 October 1893) n.s. xlviii, 315; *Speaker* (21 October 1893), viii, 443.

262. Crooker, Joseph H., 'Matthew Arnold', *New England Magazine* (January 1894), n.s. ix, 632–9.

263. Waugh, Arthur, 'Reticence in Literature', *Yellow Book* (April 1894), i, 201–19. Reprinted in *Reticence in Literature* (1915).

264. Coates, F. E., 'Matthew Arnold', *Century Magazine* (April 1894), xlvii, 931–7.

265. Bradfield, Thomas, 'The Ethical Tendency of Matthew Arnold's Poetry', *Westminster Review* (December 1894), cxxxxii, 650–65. Reprinted *Eclectic Magazine* (March 1895), cxxiv, 310–19.

266. Schrag, Arnold, *Matthew Arnold, Poet and Critic* (Basel 1894).

267. Dixon, William M., 'Arnold', *English Poetry From Blake to Browning* (London 1894), 193.

268. Ward, T. H., 'Matthew Arnold', *The English Poets: Selections* (London & New York 1894), iv, 705–11.

269. Flexner, Abraham, 'Matthew Arnold's Poetry From an Ethical Stand-point', *International Journal of Aesthetics* (January 1895), v, 206–18.

270. 'The Victorian Garden of Song', *Dial* (1 November 1895), xix, 237–9.

271. [Hutton, Richard H.,] 'Matthew Arnold's Letters', *Spectator* (23 November 1895), lxxv, 719–20. Largely on Arnold's poems. Reprinted in *Brief Literary Criticisms* (1906).

272. Morley, John, 'Matthew Arnold', *Nineteenth Century* (December 1895), xxxviii, 1041–55.

273. Walker, Hugh, 'Matthew Arnold', *The Greater Victorian Poets* (London 1895), 214–19, 294–9.

274. Hudson, W. H., 'Matthew Arnold', *Studies in Interpretation* (New York 1895), 153–221.

275. Scudder, Vida, *The Life of the Spirit in the Modern English Poets* (Boston & New York 1895).

276. Saintsbury, George 'Matthew Arnold', *Corrected Impressions on Victorian Writers* (New York 1895), 138–56.

277. Coblentz, H. E., 'The Blank Verse of "Sohrab and Rustum"', *Poet Lore* (October 1895), vii, 497–505.

278. Jacobs, Joseph, 'Matthew Arnold', *Literary Studies* (London 1895), 77–94. Reprint of item 186.

279. 'Laureates and Poets', *Nation* (New York, 9 January 1896), lxii, 26–7.

280. 'Personalia: Coleridge, Arnold, and Stevenson', *Poet Lore* (February 1896), viii, 100–5.

281. Paton, Lucy Allen, 'A Bit of Art from Matthew Arnold', *Poet Lore* (March 1896), viii, 134–9.

282. Harrison, Frederic, 'Matthew Arnold', *Nineteenth Century* (March 1896), xxxix, 362–72. Reprinted *Living Age* (9 May 1896) ccix, 362–72; *Tennyson, Ruskin, Mill, etc.* (1899).

283. 'Matthew Arnold's Poetry', *Saturday Review* (14 March 1896), lxxxi, 270–2.

284. [Hutton, R. H. ?,] 'The Popularity of Matthew Arnold', *Spectator* (6 June 1896), lxxvi, 800–1.

285. Fisher, Charles 'A Triad of Elegies', *Temple Bar* (July 1896), cviii, 388–96.

286. Carr, Victor, 'On a Reading of Matthew Arnold', *In the Dorian Mode* (London & New York 1896), 81. Poem.

287. Macaulay, George C., ed. *Poems by Matthew Arnold* (London & New York 1896), intro., ix–xviii.

288. Woodberry, G. E., 'Matthew Arnold', *Library of the World's Best Literature*, ed. Warner (New York 1896), ii, 844–55.

289. Fruman, Joseph, 'Victoria's Poets', *Spectator* (3 April 1897), lxxviii, 476. Poem.

290. Gosse, (Sir) Edmund, 'The Literature of the Victorian Era', *English Illustrated Magazine*, xvii (July 1897), 490–1.
291. Fitch, (Sir) Joshua, *Thomas and Matthew Arnold and Their Influence on English Education* (New York 1897).
292. Macarthur, Henry 'Matthew Arnold', *Realism and Romance, and Other Essays* (Edinburgh 1897), 139–64.
293. Traill, Henry D., 'Matthew Arnold', *The New Fiction and Other Essays* (London 1897), 76–103.
294. Palgrave, F. T., 'The Landscape of Browning, Arnold, etc.', *Landscape in Poetry* (London 1897).
295. Nencione, Enrico, 'Matthew Arnold', *Saggi critici di letteratura inglese* (Florence 1897), 358–60.
296. Galton, Arthur Howard, *Two Essays Upon Matthew Arnold, With Some of His Letters to the Author* (London 1897), 122p. Reviewed in *Literature* (London) (12 February 1898), ii, 173. Reprint of item 244.
297. Farrar, Frederick William, 'Matthew Arnold,' *Men I Have Known* (New York 1897), 73–92.
298. Guthrie, William Norman, 'Matthew Arnold', *Modern Poet-Prophets* (Cincinnati 1897), 61–89.
299. Shorter, Clement K., *Victorian Literature* (New York 1897), 71–21.
300. 'P', 'Reputations Considered. IV-Matthew Arnold', *Academy* (15 January 1898), liii, 77–8.
301. 'A New Edition of Matthew Arnold's Poems', *Literary World* (Boston, 5 March 1898), xxix, 68–9.
302. Dixon, William M., 'The Poetry of Matthew Arnold', *The Republic of Letters* (London 1898).
303. Armstrong, Richard A., 'Matthew Arnold', *Faith and Doubt in the Century's Poets* (New York 1898), 91–113.
304. White, Greenough, 'Arnold's Character as Revealed in His Poems', *Matthew Arnold and the Spirit of the Age*, ed. G. White (New York 1898), 17–30.
305. Hodgkins, Louise M., 'Arnold', *A Guide to the Early Study of Nineteenth Century Authors* (Boston 1898), 96–101.
306. Stephen, Leslie, 'Matthew Arnold', *Studies of a Biographer* (London 1898), 76–110. Reprint of item 260.
307. Hunt, Theodore W., 'The Poetry of Matthew Arnold', *Methodist Review* (1898), xiv, 757–68.
308. Griswold, H. T., 'Matthew Arnold', *Personal Sketches of Recent Authors* (Chicago 1898), 78–95.

309. Hodgkins, L. M., 'Arnold', *A Guide to the Study of Nineteenth Century Authors* (Boston 1898), 96–101.

310. Johnson, W. H., 'The "Passing" of Matthew Arnold', *Dial* (16 November 1899), xxvii, 351–3.

311. Harrison, Frederic, 'Matthew Arnold', *Tennyson, Ruskin, Mill and Other Literary Estimates* (London 1899). Reprint of item 282.

312. Weet, H. S., 'Characteristics and Comparative Excellence of Matthew Arnold's Poetry'. Hull Prize Essay, University of Rochester (1899).

313. Saintsbury, George E. B., *Matthew Arnold* (Modern English Writers) (Edinburgh 1899), 232p. Reviewed *Academy* (30 September 1899), lvii, 329–30; Richard Garnett, *Bookman* (July 1899), xvi, 102; *Literature* (24 June 1899), iv, 648–9; *Nation* (New York, 23 November 1899), lxix, 396–7.

Index

The index is divided into three sections; I. Arnold's writings; II. Arnold: topics and characteristics; III. General.

457

II. ARNOLD: TOPICS AND CHARACTERISTICS

821.8
A757Zd

Dawson, Carl.

Matthew Arnold, the poetry: the
  critical heritage.

WITHDRAWN

82503

DAVIS MEMORIAL LIBRARY

3 7110 0002 7298 3

THE CRITICAL HERITAGE SERIES

GENERAL EDITOR: B. C. SOUTHAM

Volumes published and forthcoming

Continued